BECOMING YOU

ALSO BY JOSEPH NAFT

Non-Fiction

The Sacred Art of Soul Making

Fiction

Restoring Our Soul

Agents of Peace

BECOMING YOU

Cultivating Spiritual Presence

JOSEPH NAFT

I.F. Publishing

I.F. PUBLISHING COMPANY
Baltimore, Maryland USA
info@ifpub.com

Copyright © 2009 by Joseph Naft

All rights reserved. No part of this publication may be reproduced, stored in or introduced into a retrieval system, or transmitted in any form, or by any means, electronic, mechanical, photocopying, recording, or otherwise, without the prior written permission of the copyright owner of this book.

ISBN: 978-0-9786109-1-3

Printed in the United States of America on acid-free paper

CONTENTS

PREFACE xxi

Introduction to Presence. 1

Entering Presence 6

A Pause Before the Plunge 10

1. Stages of Body Presence 11
2. Relaxing Our Body 13
3. Body Calm 15
4. Recognizing Sensation 16
5. Sensing Parts 18
6. Sensing the Whole Body 20
7. Energy Breathing 21
8. Sensation in Movement. 23
9. Stabilizing the Inner Body 25
10. Body Presence. 27
11. World View 30
12. Curbing a Habit 33
13. Counting. 34
14. Your Word 34
15. Conscious Walking 35
16. An Act of Will 36
17. Doors 37
18. Wastefulness. 38
19. Eating with Presence 38
20. Dressing Consciously 40
21. Building the Group 41
22. Mirror, Mirror 41
23. Rating the Day 42

24. The Practice of Excellence 44
25. Awareness of Posture 44
26. Spaciousness 45
27. Courtesy. 46
28. Waiting 47
29. Touching the Stillness 48
30. Thought Awareness: I Am Not My Thoughts . . .49
31. Selfing. 50
32. Awareness of State 52
33. Inhabiting the Body 53
34. You, Being You 54
35. Lighting the Darkness 56
36. Pushing the Envelope 57
37. Understanding Our Motivation 58
38. A Shift in Perspective 59
39. Doing the Dishes 60
40. Part and Whole 62
41. Chiming In 63
42. Awareness of Talking 64
43. Developing Compassion 65
44. Duration 66
45. Intentional Walking 67
46. Well-Wishing .68
47. Frequency 69
48. Respect 70
49. Resistance 70
50. Continuity 71
51. The Roller-Coaster 72

52. Non-Identifying	73
53. First Response	74
54. Let It Be	75
55. Direct Perception	76
56. Body Image	77
57. Constancy	78
58. Non-Suffering	78
59. The Practice of Self-Acceptance	79
60. Stabilizing Attention	81
61. Wrapped in Awareness	82
62. Access to Wisdom	83
63. Hands and Feet	84
64. A Wider Context: God's View of the World	84
65. Just Breathing	85
66. Torso and Head	86
67. Body Scan	86
68. Effort and Non-effort	87
69. Aberrations of Responsibility	88
70. The Long View	88
71. Choose Again	89
72. Deep Relaxation	90
73. Daily Prayer	91
74. Success and Failure	91
75. Renewal: Deciding to Work	93
76. Consuming	94
77. Wishful Thinking	94
78. Buying Presence	95
79. Shared Joy	96

80. Review & Resolve 96
81. Potential 97
82. Back in the Body 98
83. Being Yourself. .98
84. Passivity 99
85. Persistence. 100
86. Islands: Separation and Longing 102
87. The Next Rung 102
88. small self and Great Self 103
89. Daily Goals 104
90. Shaping Your Inner Life. 104
91. Prayer in a Time of War 105
92. Inner Work in a Time of War 106
93. Moving With and From Sensitive Energy. . . . 106
94. When Is "I" Substantial? 107
95. Leaning Forward and Falling Back 107
96. The Holy Day 108
97. The Boundaries of Awareness. 108
98. Satisfaction and Dissatisfaction 109
99. In the Fog 110
100. Balance of Body, Heart, and Mind. 110
101. Hidden Treasure 111
102. Appreciation 111
103. Debilitating Daydreams 112
104. Joy and Pleasure 113
105. Push and Pull. 114
106. Pressed Buttons 114
107. Judging and Criticizing 115

108. Walking Presence 116
109. Wealth and Poverty: External and Eternal . . . 118
110. Content and Process 119
111. Perfection and Imperfection 120
112. Only This Moment 120
113. Dignity and Indignation 121
114. Earning Our Freedom 122
115. Bridging Heaven and Earth 122
116. The Eye of the Storm 123
117. Beyond Stillness 124
118. Making It Real 124
119. The Cost of Awakening 125
120. Diving into the Sacred 126
121. Scaling Up 128
122. The Petty and the Grand 129
123. Emerging from the Stream 130
124. Inhabiting Our Life 131
125. Where Does My I Come From? 132
126. Owning Our Destructive Emotions 133
127. Unification 134
128. Balance of Levels 135
129. Consciousness and Personality 137
130. Blue Collar Inner Work 138
131. Participating in Purpose 139
132. Breathing Energy 140
133. Pure Consciousness 141
134. Reaching Beyond 142
135. In the Energy Body 142

136. Managing Our Path 143
137. Exhaling the Negative 144
138. First Intention 145
139. My Universe 146
140. Increasing Our Spiritual Income 147
141. Care for This Moment 148
142. Balancing Inner and Outer 149
143. Non-Anger 150
144. The Ineffable 151
145. In Body, In Heart, and In Mind 152
146. In Contact 153
147. Non-Gossip 154
148. In Their Shoes: Intentional Empathy 155
149. Inspiring Aspiration 156
150. Grounding Our Practice 157
151. Beyond the Ordinary 158
152. Ad Hoc Tasks 158
153. Emptying Yourself 160
154. Self-Discipline 161
155. The Middle Way 162
156. Being Seen 162
157. Here I Am 163
158. Asking for Help 164
159. A Sense of the Sacred 165
160. Seeing Their Potential 166
161. Eternal Values 166
162. The Art of Climbing 167
163. Active Presence 168

164. A Person of Substance 169
165. Labor of Love 170
166. Body of Stillness. 171
167. Walking in Stillness 172
168. Hard Decisions. 173
169. Subsuming the Personal 174
170. Losing Face 176
171. Will It Matter in a Year? 177
172. Fingers of One Hand. 178
173. Sustaining Presence 179
174. Strong Will, Open Will. 180
175. Self-Image, False Image 181
176. Political Mind 182
177. Returning. 183
178. Manna from Heaven 184
179. Not Accepting the Superficial Life. 185
180. Break with the Past 186
181. Determination and Help 187
182. First Things First. 188
183. The Three Domains 190
184. A New Floor 191
185. Exercise Inside and Out 193
186. Breathing TV. 194
187. Extending Our Bodily Presence 195
188. The Peace of Being 196
189. A Steady Pace 197
190. Laboratory of the Spirit 198
191. Standing Presence 200

192. Telephone Presence	201
193. Assessment and Motivation	202
194. Personal Integrity	203
195. Barriers to Relating	205
196. Establishing Physical Presence	207
197. Entering Conscious Awareness	208
198. Turning Toward the Light	209
199. Opening to the Divine	210
200. Non-Thinking	212
201. Intentional Presence	213
202. Dynamic Presence	214
203. From Heartless to Kindness	214
204. Relaxing into Now	215
205. Wholeness in Prayer	216
206. Reading Presence	217
207. Doing This	218
208. Procrastination	219
209. Adaptive Practice	220
210. Overcoming Mediocrity	222
211. Creating the Future	223
212. Creating Ourselves	225
213. Character Matters	226
214. Integrity and Wholeness	228
215. Non-Waiting	229
216. Fervor	231
217. Our Song	232
218. Devotion	234
219. Speaking Well	235

220. Seeing with Empathy 236
221. Our Individual Program 238
222. Engagement 240
223. Staying Here 241
224. The One Who Sees 243
225. More Body, Vivid Body 244
226. Intentional Thought Awareness 245
227. Distorting Perception 247
228. The Color of Stillness 249
229. Immediate Challenges 250
230. Distracting Changes 251
231. Being in Conversation 252
232. The "I Am" Test 253
233. Finding Time 255
234. Searching for Sustenance 256
235. Filling the Down-Time 258
236. Come What May 259
237. Running Commentary 260
238. Choosing Your Emotions 261
239. Doing Your Chores 263
240. Remembering 264
241. The Sacred Chorus 265
242. Building the Inner Body 266
243. Communicating Presence 268
244. Elevating Prayer 269
245. Stabilizing Our Way 270
246. The Path of Exploration 272
247. The Web of Unity 273

248. Transition to Stillness 274
249. Starting Presence. 275
250. Lines of Time 276
251. Soft-Heartedness. 277
252. Being Useful 278
253. Identity 279
254. Inner Responsibility 281
255. Spiritual Momentum 282
256. Beyond Paradise 283
257. Dropping into the Body 285
258. Awe. 286
259. Aiming Higher 287
260. Filling and Fulfilling 288
261. Follow Through 289
262. Group Power 290
263. Ordinary Presence 291
264. The Live Wire of Will 292
265. Feet of Awareness 293
266. Casting an Energy Net 294
267. Valuing the Way 295
268. Emerging From Thought. 296
269. Spiritual Friendship 298
270. Sending Good Will. 300
271. The Unseen 301
272. This Is It 303
273. Drawing Down the Blessing 304
274. Wasteful Tensions 306
275. The Taste of Presence 307

276. Evening Presence 309
277. Swimming Upstream. 310
278. Transcending Personality 311
279. Being the Decider-Perceiver. 313
280. The Arrow of Presence. 314
281. The Field of Presence 315
282. The Ground of Presence 317
283. Demands of self 318
284. Shifting into Neutral: The Temple of Peace . . 320
285. Shifting into Reverse: Tracing the Radiance. . 321
286. Playing Our Roles 323
287. Inner Structure 324
288. One Thing at a Time 326
289. Divine Embrace 327
290. Embracing Our Life 328
291. Beyond Our Story 330
292. Within the Hour 331
293. The Sacred Dance of Emptiness 333
294. Our Inner Home 335
295. Rates of Inner Growth 336
296. Out of Our Mind, Into Our Body 338
297. Coarse and Fine 340
298. Spiritual Heroism 341
299. Soaking Up the Atmosphere. 342
300. Inner Occupations 344
301. Integrity under Duress 345
302. Listening to Sounds, Hearing the Silence . . . 347
303. Karma 348

304. Self-Acceptance 351
305. Inner Body for Inner Life 353
306. Recognizing Will. 354
307. Being Seen 356
308. Walking Meditation 358
309. Grief and Mourning 360
310. Personal Presence in Three Steps 361
311. Intentional Attention 363
312. Spiritual Breathing 365
313. Non-Panic 368
314. Showering Presence 370
315. The Continuous Choice 371
316. A Place to Stand 372
317. Meaningful Life 374
318. Total Prayer 375
319. Stillness: Warm, Intimate, and Cognizant . . . 377
320. The Challenges of Spiritual Practice. 379
321. Present Through and Through 381
322. Directed Receptivity 382
323. More Presence 384
324. The Way of Conscience 1: Discerning. 386
325. The Way of Conscience 2: Acting in Accord . 388
326. The Way of Conscience 3: Merging 391
327. The Stages of Love 393
328. Seeing the Humanity 397
329. Tolerance 398
330. Equality 400
331. Sameness 401

332. Acceptance	402
333. Empathy and Compassion	404
334. Local Unity	406
335. Global Unity in God	407
336. The Stages of Presence	409
337. The Impulse of Awakening	410
338. Receptivity to Awakening	412
339. Energies of Presence	413
340. Creating Partial Presence	414
341. Opening to Wholeness	416
342. I Am	417
343. The Peace of Presence	418
344. Stable Presence	420
345. Divine Presence	421
346. The Stages of Prayer	423
347. Petitionary Prayer	426
348. Prayer: Method and Ritual	427
349. I Pray	429
350. Commitment to Prayer	430
351. Faith and Doubt	432
352. We Serve Through Prayer	434
353. Contemplative Prayer	435
354. Ecstasy Through Prayer	437
355. Unification	439
356. Stages of Inner Unity: I	441
357. Our Fragmented Will	444
358. Awareness of Fragmentation	446
359. Learning to Integrate Our Will	448
360. Partial Practice	450

361. Responsibility, Rebellion, and Love 451
362. Inner Unity: I. 453
363. Reaching Toward God, Center of All Centers 455
364. Surrender. 457
365. The One Divine Will. 459
ABOUT THE AUTHOR 463
INDEX 465

The Seeker

After years of inner work,
A seeker found the door of the Beloved and knocked.
A voice asked:
"Who is there?"
The seeker answered:
   "It is I."
The voice said:
"There is no room for me and you."
And the door stayed shut.
The seeker engaged in ever deeper spiritual practice,
Then returned to the door of the Beloved and knocked.
The voice from within asked:
"Who is there?"
And the door opened,
And the seeker opened
And said:
   "It is You."

Adapted from Rumi

PREFACE

When a deeper reality begins to stir in our heart, we start looking for a way to open to it, to be embraced by it, to integrate it into our life, and to serve it. The inner landscape of the spirit, however, remains hidden from our perceptual capacities, untrained and undeveloped for that domain. But reason for hope lies within: we can adopt a way of life that awakens our latent soul, a way that addresses our deepest yearnings, a way that opens the sacred wellsprings of kindness and love. That is the way of intentional, intelligent, and heartfelt spiritual practice.

Without appropriate training and effective inner work, our spiritual aspirations do not approach fruition. And to develop the many facets of our soul, we need a variety of spiritual practices. In these pages you will find an extensive, detailed array of methods for cultivating spiritual presence, most of them applicable during our daily routines and each intended to be practiced intensively for a week.

One subset of these methods belongs to the wake-up bell category, in which we create triggers within our life to remind us to be present. Others prompt us to investigate and develop various spiritual qualities, deepen our perceptions, and expand our understanding. Through such week-long inner work, we gradually infuse the light of awareness and a sense of the sacred into every aspect of our lives. We further raise our possibilities for transformation when we incorporate these weekly practices into a comprehensive approach to spirituality, an approach that includes daily meditation, body awareness, presence, prayer, communal worship, and the like.

It is no easy matter to awaken. We habitually move through our days in a pre-programmed autopilot mode, in a cloud of thoughts and daydreams that obscures our contact with our surroundings and our self. In so doing, we accept to live half a life and create unnecessary difficulties for ourselves and others. To raise ourselves out of this situation, we turn to spiritual practice.

Even when attempting one of these weekly inner tasks, we often miss the intended moment. For example, say the task calls for us to eat consciously. After lunch we remember and suddenly realize that we just ate a meal without intentionally bringing awareness to the taste of the food. Depending on how strong our resolve was to engage in the week's inner work, that realization may cause us to feel something. At this point the whole process can careen off the rails. Though we may see that we neglected presence while eating, our next step is crucial.

Do we allow this moment of realization to turn against us by blaming ourselves, feeling self-pity, self-loathing, hopeless or discouraged by our forgetfulness and lack of presence? Much more profitable at that very moment of seeing our lack of awareness to redirect the energy thereby released to the immediate work of awakening and presence.

So... I see that I missed being present during the meal, as I had intended for this week. As soon as I see that, I begin to work at presence. The task did not awaken me during the meal, but it awakens me now. I have adapted the inner task to include not only eating consciously, but also to work at presence whenever I remember that I did not eat consciously.

This prevents a downward spiral into disheartenment. We do not try to hide from the fact of our lack of presence, indeed we take it to heart impartially. But we also use the resulting emotional energy and opportunity to further our practice in that moment. In this way, even our failures help us, transforming into presence and a reinvigorated sense of purpose, a strengthened resolve.

If we work seriously at one of these pursuits for a full week, it enters us, becoming part of our path, part of us, part of our repertoire of practice. Then long after the week has ended and we have moved on to other inner work, we may spontaneously rediscover opportunities for awakening that we established in prior weeks. We do not reject these simply because they come from earlier weeks. By all means, we step robustly into such moments with a renewal of our work of presence, heart, and service. Furthermore, we can quite profitably practice some of these tasks for much longer than a week, or intentionally return to them periodically over the years.

Because the multifaceted work of the soul is nonlinear, these weeklong inner endeavors are not organized by type or category. Instead they follow an arc of generally increasing subtlety as they cycle repeatedly through the many aspects of a balanced path, carrying us steadily deeper in our quest. Though we return to a method we have practiced before, our being has changed due to our efforts in the intervening time. So we come back to it with new understanding and the ability to carry it further than before. Nevertheless, you need not stick to the order presented and may find profit in skipping around within the book. Each theme stands both on its own and in relation to the all the others.

These weeklong exercises supplement our ongoing practices of regular periods of meditation, prayer, and the efforts of sensing our inner energy body and working toward presence during our daily routines. Meditation, prayer, sensing, and presence form the foundation of our path, with weekly inner tasks providing a focus, illuminating our outlook, broadening our perceptions, and leading us to discover new opportunities for practice.

As our inner work progresses, our days grow replete with spiritual practice. We train ourselves to practice in many ways and many situations. Slowly but, if we persevere, inevitably, our entire life transforms. We enter the beneficent, loving Reality that we seek.

This book serves as a companion volume to *The Sacred Art of Soul Making: Balance and Depth in Spiritual Practice*, where you can find more detailed presentations of many of the techniques and concepts underlying these week-long inner exercises. The following "Introduction to Presence" is adapted from *The Sacred Art of Soul Making*.

Joseph Naft
June, 2009

Introduction to Presence

Presence... The very word evokes a depth and potency of character, a gravitas, a charisma based on inner substantiality rather than outward flash, a simple and quiet dignity. All of that, however, only describes the outward signs of presence. Our path addresses its inner manifestation.

True living absolutely requires presence: more presence, more life. Without presence, life passes us by: we neither participate in nor fully experience our life. Presence means being at home in ourselves, being here, not only in contact with our sensory experience, but also doing what we are doing. Presence means inhabiting our bodies, inhabiting our space, inhabiting our actions and inhabiting our life, not just passively letting it all happen.

Consciousness, the basic foundation of presence, is a timeless energy of wholeness and peace. We may develop strong sensations of our body, emotions, and thoughts, even while consciousness remains weak and dispersed, submerged and mixed with the energies of sensation. Our sensory perceptual experiences, including thoughts and emotions, cover and obscure consciousness. The foreground of life, the perceptual picture on the screen of consciousness, captivates our attention and we remain unaware of the screen itself. But we cannot find consciousness by focusing on its contents, on the ever-changing play of sensations. Consciousness possesses entirely different qualities: spacious, timeless, cognizant, and unchanging. However, our contact with consciousness does change. Presence is always available, but by habit, clouded perception, and lack of choice, we are not always available to it.

Perhaps you have seen the drawing of a black vase on a white background. You shift your focus to the background and suddenly see two faces kissing, the vase having merged into the background. This foreground-background perceptual shift presages exactly what we need with respect to consciousness: to bring consciousness to the foreground, as the basic container of our experience.

We can approach presence from the front or from behind. From the front, the side of sensory perceptions, we approach through quiet relaxation and meditation, letting thoughts, emotions, and sensations settle down, until we become aware in the gaps between them, and then aware of the consciousness, the pure awareness filling those gaps. As our energies settle, consciousness may coalesce like beads of water joining to form a pool. We rest in the still pool of consciousness, not entangled with its contents, not lost in sensations. Then the foundation for presence grows strong.

Approaching presence from behind, we search deep within ourselves for that vibrant space beneath all our sensations, thoughts, and emotions. As we step behind our ordinary perceptions, the vast continuum of consciousness gradually unfolds in a new mode of perception.

Yet consciousness alone is not enough: we need the will to be present, the will to be. If we do not intentionally choose to be present, presence will be rare and fleeting. That is our role in the work of presence, to make that choice again and again, to take every moment of awakening and decide to be. If there is no one home in us, it matters little how much awareness we may have of bodily sensations or anything else. The degree of someone being there, someone (will) who actually does the seeing and moving and thinking, determines the degree of presence, the quality of our life. Thus, our will-to-be is the central component of presence.

The will-to-be can pervade our entire body, our entire being. Acting through our attention and intention, our will entrains some of the higher energy of creative light, carrying it into our body, into our inner body energy of sensation, where the higher energy blends with the lower to create more consciousness, the middle of the three energies and the primary energy of presence. The in-the-moment effort to establish and maintain full-body awareness/sensation gives our will a ready and useful target. Our will plugging into the sensitive energy in our body creates a field of presence. The key to this begins with being present in our energy of sensation, which resides in our body, not just being present in our body. The difference is subtle but significant.

This simple will-to-be supports our presence, giving us life. Our will-to-be suffuses our presence with a force, the force of will, like a wind filling our sails. When we accept to become our will-to-be, we raise ourselves out of the thrall of associative thoughts and other automatic and reactive processes, and we abide in presence. We experience this will-to-be as "I," as "I am," as "I am here." Yet this "I" is not separate from others, but rather an element of the Whole.

This will-to-be, this wind filling our sails, does not begin in us. Its source lies in the higher worlds. The challenge is to open ourselves sufficiently, so as not to block or divert that wind flowing through us from Above. God may see through our eyes and act through our hands, but only to the extent that we are present, that we engage in this moment, in being here, and in opening to the higher will.

Our will-to-be thus takes on a two-fold character. First, we are active toward the outside, toward full sensation in the body, toward full contact with sensory experience, toward activity in the world. Second, we are open to the innermost, the higher, allowing it to warm our very being with love and infuse us with proximity to the Ultimate. Between them, in consciousness, the two act in harmony as simple, relaxed presence. Thus not merely a personal matter, the effort to be present itself fulfills a sacred duty incumbent on all human beings, to serve as a bridge between heaven and earth. Presence sets the stage for love, good works, and the transformation of energies.

Presence has several measures: frequency, duration, intensity and depth.[1] Frequency connotes how often we return to ourselves, how often we remember to be within ourselves and make the effort to be present. We aim to decrease the lapsed time between falling out of presence and coming back to it. Every activity in life transforms into an opportunity for practice. Former sources of frustration, such as waiting in line, become openings into which we pour our spiritual effort. Whenever we notice that we have fallen out of presence, out of consciousness, we immediately rouse ourselves back to the moment.

Duration reveals the stability of our presence. It indicates the length of any given period of presence, how long we are able to stay within our awareness before we fall back into sensation or down into autopilot. We may effectively gauge our day by estimating the percentage of our waking hours during which we were present. Our goal is 100% unbroken presence all day, every day. But as with every other aspect of the spiritual path, we start where we are: somewhere less than 2% on a good day. Being honest with ourselves clarifies our situation. If we remain under the illusion that we are present all the time, we shall never come to the necessary effort and determination.

1   Tracol, Henri, *The Taste for Things That Are True* (Rockport: Element Books, 1994), 115

Intensity of presence depends on two factors: the quantity of energy and the strength of our will-to-be. The more energy brought together in our being, the more intensely present we can be. The more steadfast our will-to-be, the more intensely present we are. Intensity of presence should not be confused with tension of any kind. Presence comes with an inner relaxation. An intense will-to-be does not imply an experience of tension, but rather a strong, vivid, and current intention to live in presence, which enables us to actually be here at home in this body, in this place, in this very moment.

Lastly, depth results from the combination of the degree of stillness and the clarity of will in our presence: the quality of energy and will available. Is our presence underscored by the deep silence underlying everything, conferring a conscious, unifying wholeness to presence? Am I actually here in this silence? Is the whole of my attention and intention engaged in being in this moment? Our external will-to-be opens inwardly to an alignment with and devotion to the higher world. We open the very core of our being to the higher. In the center, between the open will toward the inner/higher and the active will toward the outer/lower, we stay relaxed in being conscious.

Presence builds on awareness, awareness encompassing physical sensations, emotions, and thoughts. Strong contact with sensation throughout the whole of the body serves as an excellent foundation for consciousness to arise. Contact, in turn, with the pure, underlying screen of consciousness serves as the foundation of presence, a vehicle to carry presence, an invitation to presence to reside in us. Into this basic consciousness, we, our true will, can enter. To really live, means to live in presence. Without presence, our time passes, lost like yesterday's sunset. With presence, we bring the timeless to time, transforming it, as well as ourselves and our lives.

Entering Presence

We enter presence through awakening, returning, sustaining, and deepening.[2]

Awakening: the flash of recalling our Self. This freely given moment of grace opens us to presence. Although its unpredictable arising cannot be manipulated directly, it may occur many times in a day. The flash of awakening marks a potential transition from autopilot living without presence into being our Self in presence. The realization of that potential depends on how we respond in this crucial moment of choice.

The typical and most likely response is to ignore the moment. Usually that happens because we do not even recognize the flash of awakening for what it is. With practice in presence, we grow to appreciate these moments of grace. Even so, even with knowing that the moment presents the possibility of returning to presence, we may nevertheless, through laziness or reluctance, fail to choose. However it happens, ignoring the flash of awakening leaves us in the non-presence of automatic, associative thoughts and reactive emotions.

We live under the illusion, though, that we are always awake. But the flash of awakening enables us to see our state of non-presence that preceded that moment. This seeing matters deeply because our incentive for inner work arises from breaking the illusion of constant presence, from understanding that we are not always aware here and now. Noticing that the flash of awakening ends a period of non-awareness, non-presence, can open our need to awaken. However, it also clashes with our

---

2   See for example: Safi, Mawlana Ali ibn Husain, *Beads of Dew from the Source of Life: Histories of the Khwajagan, The Masters of Wisdom*, translated by Muhtar Holland (Ft. Lauderdale: Al Baz, 2001), 22

false view of always being awake. That clash can be disturbing and we may fall into emotionally-driven self-recriminations and ruminations about our lack of presence. And that diverts us from the possibility of presence. Rightly received, the recognition that we have not been present can spur us toward presence and deepen our need to awaken. That crucial need drives our response to these moments.

The moment of awakening offers us a choice where there was none: whether to return to our Self, to presence, or not.

Returning to our Self. At this point, the flash of awakening has reminded us and we have responded by choosing to engage in presence. Now to actually return to our Self, we direct part of our attention inward, in the manner of our current spiritual practice. For this, preparation matters. We choose ahead of time how we will work when the opportunity arises. We choose for the day or for the week. We choose a method we have learned and practiced, so that we can quickly begin our engagement with the technique. Then in the moment that calls us to turn toward our inner work, we already know what to do. We avoid thinking about it or considering it, because that might quickly lead us back into automatic thoughts and non-presence.

If our current inner work is presence through the body, as discussed below in Sections 1 through 10, then perhaps we engage with the sensation of our body. We awaken and immediately turn to sensing part or all of our body, according to our capacity, situation, and state. Or we turn to breath awareness, or prayer, or noticing our thoughts as thoughts and emotions as emotions, or any of the many useful and productive techniques that lead us toward spiritual presence. But we know ahead of time which one we will practice and we turn to that.

Sustaining presence. Once established, presence tends to evaporate suddenly and soon. Too many thoughts and sensory perceptions arise and distract us from being here and now. Our presence collapses without warning and we fall back into our habitual condition of non-presence, the half-aware, autopilot life with blinders. So the challenge, at this stage of having returned to our Self, lies in sustaining our Self in presence. How can we come to "here I am and here I remain," moment-to-moment? The secret lies in being the one who has awakened, the one who has chosen to return, the one who intends to sustain presence.

We need the intention to stay present and we need to act on that intention. The most direct and effective such action is to inhabit our presence, our life. Becoming our self, we become the one who is here and aware. This inhabiting enables us to sustain presence for a time. At least temporarily, we avoid being driven along by our thoughts, although we may drive them in intentional thinking.

The ability to inhabit our life, our ableness-to-be, also depends on the availability of conscious energy, which is enhanced by whole body sensation. That fullness of sensation acts as a container, a vessel in the sea of consciousness that surrounds us. The will act of inhabiting our life, participating as its agent, not only depends on consciousness but also attracts it, bringing consciousness into our vessel, into our being.

Choosing moment-to-moment to sustain our Self, to be our Self, we sustain presence. We may even aspire to a stable equilibrium in which we stay present effortlessly. Yet that wonderful, effortless state requires inner sincerity, because it easily devolves out of presence and into an illusion of constant presence.

Deepening presence: In sustaining our Self, we begin to intuit that our Self is inextricably, intimately, and mysteriously linked to the Self of all Selves. In our better moments we go beyond even sustaining presence to deepen it. We allow our presence to reach down to the root of our being. We open our heart and soul to the sacred. We encompass the sacred immensity of life and of the higher. We love it and we serve it. This mystery unfolds beyond our awareness, beyond our thinking, beyond our mind. Yet it is not alien. It is our true home. And there we return in warmth, in peace, and with joy.

And then, at some point, it all goes and we lose our presence. Later we reawaken and start again. This is the paradigm of the kind of spiritual practice that can accompany us in our daily life. We awaken, we practice, we fall back, and we reawaken. Again and again we repeat the practice in response to awakening. But each iteration is different and new. Each time it enlivens us, vivifying and enriching our life, inwardly as well as outwardly. Our inner work is to take the opportunities of awakening as they arise, and then sustain and deepen our presence.

A Pause Before the Plunge

And so we begin our presentation of these seven years' worth of weeklong spiritual endeavors. At the end of the book, you will find four series of nine related inner work practices. These series address the Stages of Love, of Presence, of Prayer, and of Inner Unity, respectively.

We now begin with an introductory series of weeklong spiritual practices: Stages of Body Presence. This prepares our ground for all that follows in the rest of the book, in the rest of our path.

1. Stages of Body Presence

In the context of the usual spiritual notions of consciousness, presence, meditation, prayer and love, the idea of practicing awareness of our body seems at first blush mundane, uninteresting, and even unnecessary. The truth, though, proves very different than that surface assessment. Despite our many efforts, we enter the deeper realms of the spirit only briefly at best, principally because we have no anchor, no place in those realms. We may be present for a moment, but then we evaporate. We may open to the utter peace of stillness, consciousness, but we soon fall back into our busy mind. We may touch the sacred glory in silent prayer, but quickly descend to our concerns of the moment. In all these cases, we lack a place to stand and sustain ourselves.

That place can be our inner body, made primarily of the energy of sensation, if we develop it adequately. So rather than attempt to leap straight up to the second or even third rung of Jacob's Ladder, we reach for the first rung, the rung of sensation and work to establish ourselves there. Once we can stand on that first rung, the higher steps become more feasible.

We traverse the spiritual path much more sure-footedly if we are rooted in sensation, in a robust foundation of contact with our inner energy body, which mediates our perception of our physical body and supports our contact with the present moment, our presence in the here and now. A great deal of effort goes into the growth, care, and feeding of our physical body. No less effort is needed to grow, care for, and feed our inner body. The stages of that process can be outlined as:

1. Relaxing Our Body
2. Body Calm
3. Recognizing Sensation
4. Sensing Parts
5. Sensing the Whole Body
6. Energy Breathing
7. Sensation in Movement
8. Stabilizing the Inner Body
9. Body Presence

Over the course of our spiritual path, whether as a beginner or after long experience, we frequently return to these practices and will do so throughout this book, even as we also use other methods to reach further into the sacred realms. Those with extensive experience of spiritual practice may find themselves tempted to ignore sensing, the practice of contact with our body, as they move toward the deeper spirit. But sensing and the development of the inner body prove necessary, though not sufficient, for attaining greater stability in the higher. The inner body of sensation engages us in the present and offers a platform for attracting and containing the next higher energy of consciousness. Thus the importance of the practice of sensing our body cannot be overstated. Although it is the simplest way into presence, the richness and power of sensing grows enormously as it develops into our inner body. That is why sensing is so effective at all stages of the spiritual path. And it enhances our natural joy of being embodied.

This weeks' inner work is the prelude to the series of the nine stages in the work of body presence. For this week, notice how long you can be present in the here and now. Notice your relationship with your body, your frequency and degree of contact with it through direct body awareness.

2. Relaxing Our Body
(Part 1 of 9 in the series: Stages of Body Presence)

The practice of body presence begins with relaxation. We carry unnecessary tensions in many of our muscles, from the small muscles of our face to the large muscles of our arms, legs, and abdomen. Relaxing those many tensions offers at least seven benefits. First, it trains us to be aware of our body, to be in contact through attention with our body and its state. Second, it trains us in developing the receptive mode of our will by requiring us to allow the tensions to drain out of our muscles. Third, the relaxed body does not waste either physical or inner energies on unnecessary tensions. Fourth, the relaxed body allows our inner energies to move more easily within our being, by reducing or removing the blockages to those movements. Fifth, the relaxed body offers a ready and effective container for the sensitive energy. Sixth, the relaxed body allows the sensitive energy, which it naturally produces, to collect and rise into our awareness. And seventh, the relaxed body tends to be physically and emotionally healthier.

To practice relaxation, sit quietly and let your body and mind begin to settle down for a few minutes. Then with your attention start scanning your body for tensions. Begin at the top of your head and systematically work your way down through your whole body to your toes. Allow the tensions to drain away, to evaporate as you find them. For your torso, do not focus on particular internal organs so as not to interfere with their functioning. Instead just relax the surface and larger muscles. Relax the upper torso, the chest and upper back. Then relax the lower torso. As you scan and relax your way through your body, pay particular attention to those perennial zones of accumulated tensions: the face and the jaw, the muscles between your neck and shoulders, the abdomen, and the lower back.

Repeat the whole process as necessary to become thoroughly and utterly relaxed, reserving only the minimal muscular tension needed to hold your body upright in the sitting position. Sitting upright while relaxing helps prevent the process from falling over into ordinary sleep and helps keep your attention engaged.

Your breath can also help, especially the exhale, because each release of breath can carry over into releasing the tensions you find in your body. You simply expand the will act of letting go of the exhaling breath into simultaneously letting go of muscular tensions. So with each exhalation, you relax a little further. This offers the added benefit of training us to be in contact with our breath, which helps when we work at the body presence stage of energy breathing. Once you are fully relaxed, just sit quietly and be in your unfettered, open, and happier body.

Sometimes relaxation practice reveals a profound fatigue. If that happens, allow the fatigue to be there, to come fully to the fore. Do not resist it. Continue relaxing in an undemanding way, to allow your body the deep, healing, and conscious rest it needs. After a time you may find the fatigue begins to lift, leaving you refreshed and ready. Your body is thoroughly relaxed while, inside, you are thoroughly awake and alert.

For this week, practice relaxation during periods you set aside exclusively for that. Also during your daily activities, notice your physical tensions and let them go.

3. Body Calm
(Part 2 of 9 in the series: Stages of Body Presence)

After thoroughly relaxing our body, we can immerse ourselves in a deeper relaxation, a more profound calm. Tensions exist in layers, from coarser to finer. Having released the first layer of physical tension, we begin letting go of the finer tensions in the next layer. These finer tensions reside not only in our body, but also in our thoughts and emotions, and even in our will. To relax thoroughly takes patience, equanimity, and calm, non-interfering and non-doing. These are attitudes of will, attitudes we adopt in our practice of deep relaxation.

From this stance, our thoughts and emotions recede in importance and even begin to recede from view, as they naturally abate when we stop falling under their spell. We no longer resist or buy into them. We give up trying to change or direct anything. We let our thoughts be as they are. We do not follow them or think about them. We just notice them as thoughts, arising and passing by of their own accord. We do the same with emotions. We let go all our preoccupations of mind and heart.

Because our body is so entwined with our thoughts and emotions, it relaxes further when they do. When our body is calm, we can be calm. When we are calm, our body can be calm. And so we discover a new level of calm, physical and mental, a level of utter contentment, of just seeing, just being. Entering this calm opens the door of our inner world and sets the stage for further inner work. Relaxing inwardly, we allow ourselves to settle more and more fully into our body.

For this week, practice deep relaxation. Let go of all physical tensions. Let go of resisting or pursuing self-generated thoughts and emotions. Settle into your body and be there.

4. Recognizing Sensation
(Part 3 of 9 in the series: Stages of Body Presence)

The practice of relaxation prepares us for a new relationship with our body and a new relationship with our inner world. In relaxing, we may find our perception of our body growing more vivid. With energy-wasting tensions diminished, the energy that mediates our body perception naturally collects, opening a new, more direct, more visceral contact with our body. We call this the sensitive energy. And sensing is what we call the practice of being in contact with our body through the sensitive energy.

As a get-acquainted exercise in sensing, sit quietly for a few minutes with your hands resting palm-down on your knees or thighs. Then place all your attention in your right hand. Become aware of the hand directly, not by thinking of the hand or by looking at it, but by inwardly opening to the immediate perception of your hand from within the hand. Hold your attention in your right hand, in a relaxed way. If you notice your attention wandering, gently bring it back to the hand.

After some time your right hand may seem more substantial, more alive, vibrant, warm, even tingling. This marks the accumulation of the sensitive energy in the hand. To establish the "taste" of sensation, notice the difference at that moment between your perception of your right hand and of your left hand. One is full of sensitive energy brought there by your attention. The other is empty. You are sensing your right hand.

Now move all your attention into your right foot and sense it for a time. Then sense your left foot. Then your left hand. Repeat this pattern to grow accustomed to sensing: putting your attention in a part of your body, with the intention of awakening and accumulating the sensitive energy there, and then maintaining your awareness of that sensation. Give each part its due, spending enough time and attention to raise sensation there thoroughly. Once you have a clear contact with sensing hands and feet, you can widen the practice to sensing entire arms and legs, one at a time.

The process of placing and holding our attention in a part of our body actually creates the sensitive energy. Directed attention carries with it a high energy. In sensing, we bring that higher energy into contact with the lower energies already present in our body. That interaction refines and converts the lower energies to produce the sensitive energy. The inner work of transforming energies, from lower to higher, is an essential part of our true role as human beings and consequently yields an unmistakable feeling of rightness and fulfillment.

The practice of sensing offers many benefits of crucial import to our spiritual path. The sensitive energy is the principal substance of our inner body, the lower part of our soul. This inner body is as yet unformed in us. So we practice sensing to organize and concentrate the sensitive energy, to build our inner body, to create our soul, to raise our level of being, to develop an inner platform for a stable presence. Furthermore, the practice of sensing trains our attention and develops our will. So altogether, the work of sensing presents us with a very practical, effective, and immediate method of engaging our path into the sacred spirit, a method of inward service to the higher through the transformation of energies. The precious moments we spend living in the sensitive energy enrich our life and liberate us, at least temporarily, from much of the attachment and dissatisfaction we encounter in living in the lower energies.

For this week, set aside at least one quiet, undistracted period each day to practice sensing hands and feet, arms and legs, one at a time. Familiarize yourself with perceiving the sensitive energy in your body and with the practice of sensing.

5. Sensing Parts
(Part 4 of 9 in the series: Stages of Body Presence)

Our body is the hallowed ground in which our soul can grow. The energy of sensation produces awareness of our body. And this same energy also forms the raw material of our soul. By practicing body awareness through sensation, or sensing, we build our soul. Because our body always stays in the now, the practice of sensing grounds us in the present moment, the only venue for spiritual work and the only venue for a satisfying life. Sensing brings light into the semi-aware, unsatisfying, automatic moments that make up the vast majority of our day. Working with sensation offers us a foothold, an anchor in the present. To live in sensation means to live more, to be more aware, to meet each precious moment of our life.

Having familiarized ourselves with the taste of the sensitive energy in our body and having practiced sensing in quiet periods set aside solely for that, we can now begin to practice sensing during our daily life, during our ordinary activities. This offers a very practical and effective way to extend our spiritual inner work into the whole of our life. For that, we stretch our attention and intention to simultaneously include not only our life activity, or inactivity, but also the sensitive energy in our body. We walk and sense. We eat and sense. We think and sense. We listen and sense. We brush our teeth, wash dishes, get dressed — and sense. Of course this is easiest when the activity itself is not particularly complex and so does not require the whole of our attention just to carry it out. With our spare attention, we engage in sensing. Rather than separating us from our life, sensing brings us more wholly into the activity, into the fullness of living.

Choose one simple activity that you normally repeat at least several times on most days. Some examples include eating a meal, sitting down on a chair, walking through doorways, waiting in line, typing on a keyboard, reading, or watching TV. Select one during which you will practice sensing for the coming week. Then each time you begin that activity, bring your attention to the sensation in one of your limbs. The first time sense your right arm, then next time your right leg, then the left leg, then left arm, then right arm, and so on. If you forget which limb you sensed last, start over with any limb and continue the pattern from there. If the activity lasts more than a minute, then consider switching limbs during the activity. In eating a meal, for example, you might start with sensing your right arm and then cycle through your other limbs during the meal.

In this, as with all inner work practiced in daily life, we use our judgment to refrain from taking any attention away from crucial or vital complex tasks, such as driving a vehicle or performing surgery. So when we drive, we just drive, and resume our sensing practice afterwards.

This practice of sensing in life can profitably become an important staple of our inner work, throughout our spiritual journey. For this week, practice sensing your limbs as much as possible during the day. Choose one of your ordinary activities especially for this. Sense your limbs whenever you engage in that activity.

6. Sensing the Whole Body
(Part 5 of 9 in the series: Stages of Body Presence)

The inner experience of wholeness carries a sense of completeness, integrity, unity, and substantiality and relates us to a higher level of being. True wholeness comes from a high energy, the conscious energy. But we can practice basic wholeness in a more readily accessible arena, the sensitive energy. And this, in turn, prepares our nascent soul for true wholeness and imparts a foretaste of it. Acquiring the taste of wholeness gives us a measure by which to judge our state at any given moment. And not only a measure, but a direction from our current condition toward wholeness of being.

We approach true wholeness through the practice of whole-body sensing, at first in a quiet time set aside solely for that. After relaxing, we sense each limb in turn, then both arms at once, then both legs at once, and then all four at once. Finally we add the torso and head. Without trying to sense particular internal organs, so as not to interfere with their instinctive operation, we bring our attention into our torso and head, allowing the sensitive energy to arise and collect there, joining the sensitive energy in our limbs.

At this point we shift from sensing parts of our body to sensing the whole body. With our attention spread throughout our body, we open to and engage with a complete sensation, with our aliveness as a whole. We keep our attention in continuing contact with our entire body, through the sensitive energy. Whenever our attention wanders, we gently and simply bring it back to our body.

With practice we feel comfortable in and with our body, our natural place. With practice we feel off-kilter, incomplete, ungrounded when we are not in contact with our whole body. That discomfort cues us to our tenuous connection with the present and invites us to return to sensing our whole body. Contact with sensitive energy throughout our body creates for us a more substantive home in the world and we experience ourselves to be more substantial.

For this week, practice whole body sensing. You may find it easier to begin each attempt by sensing parts, like an arm or a leg, and then build up to sensing the whole. But with practice, you will eventually be able to come directly into whole body sensing and, increasingly, strengthen and maintain it.

7. Energy Breathing
(Part 6 of 9 in the series: Stages of Body Presence)
(from *The Sacred Art of Soul Making*)

A sea of precious spiritual energies surrounds us. The air, for example, contains such energies, a fact attested to by most major spiritual traditions. The Hindu notion of *prana*, which means breath in Sanskrit, refers to the energies carried by the air. The Hindu word for soul, *atman*, also means breath in Sanskrit. The Latin *spiritus* means both breath and soul, and forms the root of related English words like spirituality, respire, inspire, and expire. Numerous other languages and traditions similarly affirm the close relationship between the air and soul energies, the air acting as a reservoir of energies: Arabic *ruh*, Hebrew *nefesh*, *ruakh*, *neshamah*, Greek *pneuma*, Chinese Taoist *ch'i*, the Christian Prayer of the Heart, Gregorian chant, the Sufi zikr, and the Yoga of pranayama. In ordinary, automatic breathing, however, only a tiny amount of these spiritual energies in the air remain with us after we exhale.

Intentional energy breathing enables more of the energy to be drawn into us from the air and to stay with us, fueling our spiritual practice and strengthening our soul. In contrast with the practice of conscious breathing, in energy breathing we direct our attention to the energies in the air we breathe, rather than simply to the physical sensations associated with breathing. We intentionally draw the energy from the air into us, infusing our body with that energy. We can cast our attention as a "net" to capture the energy and carry it into us as we inhale. Alternatively, we can use attention as a "filter" placed in the nostrils to release the energy as the air enters the nose. The energy that we can breathe forms an inner atmosphere, the air of our inner world. We reach out, with our attention and intention, into this inner atmosphere and draw the energy into us with an inner breath, the inner side of our ordinary breath. As we exhale we hold our attention in our body, allowing the energy from the breath to find its own place.

This practice does not require any significant alteration to our breath, and should not make us dizzy, nor cause us to breathe at an abnormally fast or slow speed. The difference between normal breathing and energy breathing does not lie on the physical level, but rather on the level of the energy body. We breathe at a normal pace and depth. But with fine attention to the air where it enters our nose, we consciously bring the energy into our body.

As we work on becoming aware of and breathing this energy, we discover an unmistakable and wonderful flow of energy in our breath, strengthening our energy body. But this energy flow is never automatic; it requires intention and attention to separate the energy from the ordinary air. Spending time every day on this energy breathing practice proves invaluable in filling us with sensation and establishing our energy body, the first body of the soul, giving us a sturdy vessel for presence and for deepening our path.

At first your perceptions may not be refined enough to experience the energy in the air. In this case, use your imagination and practice as if shimmering particles of energy were entering you as you breathe. Allow the energy to spread throughout your body, joining the sensitive energy and strengthening your sensation. Work at this as part of your sitting meditation. If, after practicing energy breathing for some period each day for a week or two, you still find the energy flow elusive, please drop the exercise and consider returning to it again at another time. But bear in mind the many spiritual traditions affirming the presence of soul-related energies in the air. If this is possible for other people, it is also possible for you. As your other spiritual practices and perceptions deepen, your ability to contact and absorb the energies in the air will grow apace. Then this vast reservoir of energies will begin to strengthen your inner life and make it more real.

For this week, practice energy breathing to nourish your inner body.

8. Sensation in Movement
(Part 7 of 9 in the series: Stages of Body Presence)

Our bodies move all day in an amazing variety of ways, for many different reasons and purposes. From our first groggy movements on awakening from sleep to our last delighted shifting into bed at night, a vast field of movement, large and small, populates our day. From brushing our teeth and scratching our head, to driving our car, walking, jogging, typing, and talking, we move and we move and we move. We chew and we blink, we fidget, smile, and shake hands.

Our myriad movements often have an intention somewhere behind them, but usually have little presence, little sensation, and little intention in them. The typical connection between our choice or intention to move and the movement itself is an automatic one, as it must be. But it need not be solely automatic. We can bring much more awareness into our movements without interfering in their automatic operation. The opportunity calls us to spiritualize this entire inwardly-empty field of our life, the field of movement, by being present as we move. And the first step toward that consists of awakening and attending to the sensitive energy in our moving body.

To begin work on sensation in movement, sense an arm or leg while seated and not moving. Then slowly move the arm or leg while continuing to sense it, continuing to be directly, organically, and viscerally aware of the moving arm or leg through the sensitive energy.

From that rather artificial beginning we can progress to sensing ordinary but simple movements. A prime and classical example is to practice sensing while walking, a form of walking meditation. Traditionally, this kind of meditation involves awareness of the body in very slow walking. Walking slowly enough allows us time to attend to the minute sensations of pressure and touch of the floor to our feet, the detailed sensations of our legs as they move through each part of the step, and the sensations of our whole body, as its weight and posture shift.

Generalizing, we can practice sensing while walking at our ordinary pace and doing so as we go about our usual day, whether walking just a few steps from one room to another or on longer walks. Walking requires very little ongoing attention, leaving us inwardly free to sense our body as we walk. This creates for us a remarkable sense of presence and purpose.

From sensing the gross movements of our limbs, we can work toward sensing our more subtle movements. In speaking we might sense our body gesturing, our changing facial expressions, and our moving lips and tongue. In eating, we sense the lifting of the fork, we sense our jaw chewing. In seeing, we sense our head as it turns to look and our eyes as they shift to focus. Sensing these subtle movements becomes much easier if we simply sense our whole body and use that full body sensation as a platform from which to be in touch with the small movements.

The point of all this is, of course, to practice sensing as much as possible throughout our day, whether in movement or repose. Through such practice, we live more fully and we build our inner body of sensation.

For this week, sense your body in movement.

9. Stabilizing the Inner Body
(Part 8 of 9 in the series: Stages of Body Presence)

Our contact with our body through sensing comes and goes. It may come to us randomly, as unpredictable moments of grace, awakening us into sensing our body. But it does not go randomly. Rather, our contact with sensation dissipates when we stop supporting it moment-to-moment. Sensation itself can awaken us into presence. Or we may remember the practice and return to it. In whatever way we come back to ourselves, back to sensing, back to some degree of presence, all too soon we allow that state to wane. We unknowingly turn to other interests, attractions, or demands on our attention and drop our inner work entirely, without clearly understanding the possibility of doing both, of engaging fully in our life while, for example, fully present in our body.

To stabilize our presence, we work first to stabilize our sensation. And for that, we intentionally enter wholeness in our inner body. Instead of working simply to sense our whole body, we shift into being in our inner body, our body of sensation, our inner home. Our whole-body sensation becomes a new kind of body itself. No longer is sensing only a way of being aware of our physical body. Sensation becomes the substance of our developing inner body. And like an embryo, it needs our continuing care and feeding. But unlike an embryo, the care and feeding of our developing inner body requires our conscious support.

Care for our incipient inner body primarily means staying with it, residing in it, and sustaining sensation with our intention and attention. We actively and continuously sense our whole body moment-to-moment over time, not only in periods set aside for meditation, but also during our ordinary day of movement and activity. We begin where we are. If we can sense for five seconds before losing it, we aim to sense for 6 seconds. If our whole-body sensation is thin and wispy, we aim to make it a little more substantial. We develop incrementally. We strengthen our sensing with our active and continuous intention to increase the sensitive energy throughout our body. We invest and infuse our whole body with intention, with the will to establish ourselves in sensation, while staying inwardly relaxed. Our will, along with the conscious energy it carries, thereby fuses the various regions of our bodily sensation and holds them together through time.

Care for our inner body also means decreasing our energy losses. We notice those of our unnecessary activities that inherently cost us our sensation. Smoking, excessive drinking, excessive eating, needless tensions, and using marijuana or other drugs of abuse are possible examples in our physical habits. Letting anger or any other destructive emotion take us over also costs us the energy we need for our inner work, burning it wastefully and harmfully. We notice our own particular ways of squandering our inner energy and we care for our soul by decreasing those losses.

Feeding our inner body means increasing the available energy. A major method for this is energy breathing, wherein we consciously take the inner energy from the air to build our sensation. Another method of feeding our inner body is that level of prayer, of turning toward the sacred, where as a byproduct we open to higher energies. Those high energies cascade down into our developing inner body, blending with and increasing its sensitive energies.

Developing our soul is the task of a lifetime. And a stable inner body marks a major milestone on our spiritual journey. We can only start from where we are. But a vision of where we wish to go guides us along the way. So we imagine what it would be like to have a stable inner body of sensation, what it would take to come to that, and then we work toward it, drop by drop, sensing, intending, feeding, and sustaining. And at every step along the way, we enjoy the sensation and presence that we do experience. We are here and we know where we are going.

For this week, work toward stabilizing your inner body of sensation.

10. Body Presence

(Part 9 of 9 in the series: Stages of Body Presence)

Our body and our presence — how do they relate to each other? As long as we live, our body is here. But the same cannot be said for presence, which at its core means I am here. If my body is always here, but I am not, then I am not my body. But because my body is always here, it presents a prime opportunity to establish and sustain my presence. Only I need to find a way to relate my I to my body.

Over the past weeks of practicing in the inner work series on the Stages of Body Presence, we have explored and developed our perception of and facility with the sensitive energy in our body, sensation, through the practice of sensing. That practice itself already has the key elements of body presence. First is our intention, our will to sense, which supports the whole structure and emanates from our I. Second is the conscious energy through which our I operates. Third is the sensitive energy perceived and directed by our I through the conscious energy. And fourth is our body, the field in which we plant the sensitive energy. That is how the relationship from presence to body goes.

But it also moves from the bottom up. The constancy of our body offers a firm foundation and container for the sensitive energy. The sensitive energy, as whole-body sensation, serves as a vehicle for the conscious energy. The conscious energy can respond directly to our will, our I. The more conscious energy, the more our I can be in its place. Thus the sensitive and conscious energies together relate our I to our body. And this reciprocal action goes both ways: from I to body and from body to I, from inside to outside and from outside to inside.

So much for the theory — what is this next stage in practice? As consciousness serves as the core energy of presence, we look to build on our work with sensing in order to rise into consciousness. The practice for this consists of two simple aspects. First we establish, at least temporarily, whole-body sensation by sensing our entire body. Second, we relax into our whole-body sensation.

This relaxation enables us to be in our inner body of sensation. My I, my individual will naturally entrains the conscious energy. And because of the affinity between the conscious and sensitive energies, if I shift from being in my physical body to residing in my sensation body, I bring the conscious energy to a place where it can coalesce and emerge. Ordinarily consciousness is masked by and mixed with our disorganized and limited sensitive energy. Increasing and organizing our sensitive energy as a whole-body vessel, offers the conscious energy a suitable and attractive platform. We recognize the conscious energy by its quality of cognizant stillness and peace, forming a substrate beneath our thoughts and activities.

So the foundation of whole-body sensation facilitates our entry into true consciousness, which in turn allows us, our I, to be present. This I, our will, does not come to us from the outside. It is the very kernel of who we are. Our I is the most inward of our inwardness. While the conditions for presence are created by the practice of sensing, full presence begins when we, our I, take our place in consciousness and within our sensation body. We establish a place for our I, our will, to reside in our inner body and complete our presence. Here I am.

As a major benefit, the wholeness of our presence, built on our sensation body, enables unity of our will in action. Whole-body sensation supports wholeness of will. And the deeper work of prayer, in turn, depends exactly on this: the whole of our will opening toward the Divine.

For this week, be present within your whole body of sensation.

11. World View

Our world view develops as a learned set of attitudes, core beliefs, and opinions that condition our behavior. Though our world view is mostly unconscious, generally flying below our awareness, it nonetheless directly and powerfully shapes how we think, emote, perceive, act, and respond to the situations, people, and events of our life. Fortunately our world view is not fixed. Clearly it changes as we mature from childhood, through adolescence, and further stages of life. It also changes with the major events of our society and with the more significant events of our personal life.

Parts of our world view can be a benefit, while others may be a bane. Some are clearly destructive. To take extreme examples, note the criminal and terrorist world views. But for all of us, certain deeply ingrained attitudes form the foundation of destructive emotions. Where does our anger, greed, jealousy, or judgmental rejection come from? A Buddhist might rightly say that they derive from the illusion of ego. But at a more accessible level, we may see that such destructive emotions arise from a complex of attitudes embedded in our world view and ready to be activated given suitable circumstances.

Take the example of a person who has a deeply held fear of the world and of the future. From that might come reluctance to voice opinions for fear of being contradicted and shyness for fear of being embarrassed. From that basic fear might come jealousy or a conservative reluctance to change, or a debilitating risk-aversion. Take another example: greed. From basic greed might come attempts to control other people, envy, negative gossip, judgmental criticism, sarcasm, manipulation of others, lying, cheating, stealing, and generally taking more than one's rightful share. On the positive side, world view might contain deeply held love, friendliness, kindness, generosity, striving for excellence, integrity, and so on. The remarkable complexity of human beings allows the possibility that the world view of one person could have all of the above examples and more in varying degrees. The contents and relative strengths of the features of our world view define our character.

That world view forms the self-created box that we live in. As such it both limits and fortifies us. It limits in the sense of dictating how we are in the world. It limits us inwardly also, because it does not readily admit the actual existence of the higher, sacred worlds and our personal possibilities therein. This blocks our access to and perceptions of those higher realms, which lie in a direction previously unknown to us. World view forms the earth-bound walls of our mind-heart, around which our thoughts and emotions bounce and morph.

But our world view box also benefits and fortifies us by lending stability to our generally chaotic inner life. It creates a place and category for each event, thought and perception, making them all somehow familiar and tractable. By coloring our perceptions and defining our actions, our world view creates our world. It organizes our life, even when we are only half-aware and not fully present. It gives us something to know when we need or seek to know ourselves. And it enables us to present a consistent face to the people around us: they know us by knowing our patterns that derive from our world view. Like a blueprint and a foundation, it supports the whole edifice of our personality.

Our world view evolves by experience, by contemplation of experience and truth, by prayer, and by equanimity. Contemplation of experience lets us see our world view as it is. Contemplation of truth reshapes our world view. Prayer can bypass and refine our world view. And equanimity releases us from it.

The various religions and spiritual paths hold different and sometimes conflicting and irreconcilable world views. Even more than the differences in practice, the differences in world view can become a source of confusion for those who try more than one path. However, the different practices can be complementary. Buddhist meditation practice, for example, can speed one's progress along other religious paths.

But rather than attempt to reconcile the irreconcilable, we work to go deeply enough into spiritual practice that our newly evolved world view might transcend and subsume those opposing world views. In effect we discover, abstract, and evolve our world view from our deepening spiritual experience. We do this without abandoning our religion, indeed we strengthen that relationship. A view informed by the great teachings, but based in our personal experience gains the power necessary to keep us focused on our inner work.

For this week, let us see if we can understand our own world view, see how it shapes our behavior, and see whether it serves us and our society well. When you notice yourself thinking, feeling, responding, or acting in a particular pattern, recognize that pattern as ultimately arising from your world view. To know your world view is to know yourself, and to know yourself is a major step toward inner freedom.

12. Curbing a Habit

Ultimately our spiritual path leads us to freedom from all clinging, from attachments of all kinds. This does not necessarily mean giving up sweets or TV. But it does mean, in part, that no desire for a material pleasure is stronger than we are. For a better understanding of non-clinging, we can work against a habit for a limited period.

Choose one of your habits. Start with an easy one. If you begin by trying to break a strong addiction like smoking cigarettes, it may well prove too difficult. Instead, pick one of your simple, unnecessary habits like chewing gum, eating ice cream, watching TV, listening to radio, or another similar proclivity. For the coming week refrain altogether from indulging in that habit. Whenever you notice an urge to engage in the targeted activity, use that energy to work on sensing a limb or the whole of your body. Using your attention and intention, move the energy from the urge into your body, into awareness of your body. Let that energy enable you to inhabit your body more strongly.

If you should find yourself indulging in the habit, just begin abstaining from it again. If this happens often, then switch to working with a lesser habit.

Only do this for one week. After that allow yourself to return to the habit. The path toward liberation does not consist in stopping all our habits permanently, but does include strengthening, purifying, and understanding ourselves with respect to our habits. To rid ourselves of harmless habits would impoverish our life. But harmful habits are a different matter. In either case, we seek freedom.

13. Counting

A surprisingly effective and important mode of daily spiritual practice consists of resolving to repeat an inner exercise a certain number of times during the day. For example, take the exercise of sensing each of our four limbs in turn. We begin by placing our attention in the right arm. Once sensation, the direct perception of the whole arm, becomes apparent and established, we move on to the right leg. Then we sense the left leg and finally the left arm. We set ourselves to repeat this exercise a particular number of times during the day: say ten. When we remember the exercise, we turn to it, increment our count, and then leave it until the next time we remember.

The determination to work at a specific inner exercise a definite number of times provides an extra impetus to our efforts for that day. That personal and clear commitment develops our will and enables us to remember our practice more often than we might otherwise. The repetition of the exercise gradually works to open our perceptions, collect our energies, and dispose us toward the path. The efficacy of setting this numerical commitment applies to the full range of spiritual practices from how many times a day you engage in prayer to how many consecutive breaths you maintain awareness of in meditation. As you proceed along the path, your own flair will guide you in bringing this powerful method to bear.

14. Your Word

For this week, take a close look at how well you follow through when you say you are going to do something, or make a promise. What motivated you to say you would do it? Do you feel obligated to keep your word? Do you actually do what you said you would do? Do you do it with quality, or just so-so? Do you delay or put it off? Do you resent having to do it? Are you sorry you said you would do it? Are you fully engaged in doing it, or is your heart elsewhere? What do you feel when you've completed the promised action? How do your promises and follow-through, or lack thereof, affect others?

Through this week's practice we hope to increase our understanding of the value of our word, of its measure and its importance, of how it is to fulfill it — or not. If you see yourself acting in a less-than-perfect manner, be careful not to let that self-awareness devolve into self-criticism. We simply see and understand, with compassion for ourselves and others, and with the intention to act responsibly as we walk the path of the sacred.

15. Conscious Walking

To imbue our days with spiritual practice we address more of our life activities, incorporating them into the path, so that eventually our life is our spiritual path and our path is our life. We look first to activities we engage in often. Walking, a prime candidate, lends itself particularly well to the work of presence. Whether the occasion calls for a few steps or an hour's hike, we can open ourselves to practicing presence in walking, in the walking that we do in our normal daily routine.

Our base method consists of direct perceptual contact with our body, being fully in our body, aware of our physical sensations whenever we walk. We begin with the feet, extend our attention and awareness to include more of our legs, and ultimately to the sensation of the whole of our body, as we walk.

Walking with full awareness of our body offers us a new experience of wholeness and purpose: the wholeness and purpose of presence.

In walking we naturally scan the area in front of us with our eyes to avoid obstacles, adjust to the terrain, and stay directed toward our destination. All of this tends to take us ahead of our body rather than being in it. In the practice of conscious walking, we still pay attention to what's before us, but seek to balance that with direct awareness of being in our body.

This week, as often as you can remember to do so, practice conscious walking by focusing attention on your body as you walk. This does not mean changing the outer physical manifestation of how you walk, but rather the inner experience of it. No one else would notice any difference whether you are walking consciously or not. But you will know and the inner difference can be striking indeed.

16. An Act of Will

If you do not have a regular daily meditation practice, then for this week create one. For at least five minutes each day, sit in a quiet place to practice meditation or to work with bodily sensation. If you can make the time, then sit longer, say 20 to 40 minutes. The length of each sitting matters because it usually takes significant time for our minds to settle down enough and for us to collect the energy and attention to allow us to enter deeply into the meditation.

But the mere daily repetition of sitting in meditation also matters, even if it lasts only five minutes. Our intention to pursue our spiritual practice transforms into an act of will by maintaining the daily discipline of meditation. This act of will powerfully reorients us toward the spiritual. To sustain that orientation we need to reinforce it every day, without fail. If we do so, our commitment and understanding of the path will certainly grow. Sustained will leads organically to a deepening of our contact with the sacred.

17. Doors

An apparently simple but highly informative and useful practice consists of being present whenever you pass through a doorway. This applies to any and all doors in your home, your place of employment, your car, stores, and so forth. Begin your work at this by sensing a limb as you pass through a door. For the next door, switch to sensing another limb. If you can sense the whole of your body, then practice that as you walk through doors.

During the coming week, practice sensing your body as you pass through doorways. You need not stop in the doorway for this. Instead let the doorway remind you to start practicing awareness of sensation in your body, which you can continue after you have gone through the door.

As with this whole class of wakeup-trigger, inner work practices, when you realize that you have forgotten a doorway, then rather than succumb to frustration, just practice sensing then and there. That way the forgetting and later remembering becomes part of the practice. At that point you also renew your intention to sense at the next door, one door at a time, for one week

We need to create such reminders in our life, reminders to be present as fully, deeply and frequently as possible. The ubiquity of doors, coupled with the fact of our physical movement through them, makes them an excellent reminder.

18. Wastefulness

A primary catalyst for lasting transformation arises from clearly seeing and accepting unwelcome truths about ourselves, particularly our self-centeredness. One destructive manifestation of self-centeredness is wastefulness. Greed, laziness, self-indulgence and believing our own half-true justifications, all collude to create an attitude toward the material world that permits us to squander resources. The cumulative impact of billions of individual excesses on human society and on the biosphere as a whole causes profound and shameful damage.

For the coming week, let us look at the ways in which we personally waste resources, goods, and the Earth's beneficence. When we see ourselves being wasteful, we notice our state of mind and heart that turns a blind eye to our actions. If that seeing inwardly prompts us to do so, we moderate our behavior. We also notice the messages we receive through the media portraying over-consumption as desirable, conditioning us and our children to squander nature's bounty.

Meeting the true needs of a healthy body, heart, mind, and soul for ourselves and our families is not wasteful. We need not intentionally deprive ourselves of necessities or even pleasures. Rather, we seek a responsible middle path between austere asceticism and hedonistic extravagance.

19. Eating with Presence

Eating is a sacred, life-giving, necessary, and enjoyable act that enables us to fulfill our unique, personal role in the life of the Earth. But our food comes at the cost of other lives, be they plant or animal. Eating even the most benign of vegetarian foods, such as fruits or nuts, destroys their potential to grow into new plant life. Regardless of what we eat, we incur a sacred obligation to the life of the Earth.

Spiritual practices help transform food to the higher levels of inner energies needed for the growth of our being and for the spiritual economy of the Earth. One particular practice gives an immediate kick-start to the transformation of food: eating with presence. At its most basic level, this means to actually taste our food as we eat it, to be aware of its aroma and texture, aware of chewing and swallowing, aware of bringing the food from plate to mouth. Eating with presence helps us to appreciate and enjoy our food.

Because of the delight that food naturally gives us, we all too readily fall into identification with eating. The desire for food overpowers us into eating more than we need or eating the wrong kinds of food. In such cases we compound the problem by focusing attention on the next bite rather than the one we are currently chewing, ironically decreasing the taste experience and satisfaction we derive from eating. Because the whole process goes by autopilot, our food eats us. Overeating burns up energy we need for our inner life and damages our health. But we cannot give up eating altogether. And then when we do eat, as we must, the food identification takes us again.

To solve this conundrum, we not only fully taste our food, but we open to awareness of our abdominal region as we eat, for an indication of when we have eaten enough. By eating with presence we have a stronger, more satisfying experience of our food and, consequently, a diminished desire to overeat or to eat an unhealthy diet. Even if the desire remains unquenched, its power over us weakens in the face of increased consciousness.

But eating with presence is not just for overeaters. It is

profitable for all who seek to fill their lives with presence, which leads toward the sacred.

Saying a prayer of gratitude prior to eating can remind us to eat with presence. It puts us in touch with our dependence on and indebtedness for our food. It reinforces our connection with the Earth. Ultimately we may eat with respect and even reverence. So, as you say your prayer before your meal, you can use the moment to come into presence and heartfelt gratitude, to prepare yourself for the sacred and enjoyable act of eating.

For the coming week, eat with presence. Offer a prayer before your meals. Notice your food and its taste. Aim to taste every bite. See how this affects your experience of your meals. Eating with presence does not necessarily mean changing how we eat physically, but rather changing our inner attitude and state.

20. Dressing Consciously

In our quest to bring ever more light into the slumbering corners of our life, let us choose this week to be as fully aware of ourselves as possible whenever we put on or take off an article of clothing, in the most general sense of the term. We apply this to anything we wear: shoes, socks, jacket, shirt, blouse, pajamas, bathrobe, hat, glasses, jewelry, watch, backpack, purse, makeup and so forth.

At the very least we aim to be aware of the sensations in our hands as we touch the piece of clothing. And if possible at those moments, we bring ourselves into contact with the sensation of our whole body, as well as noticing our thought-stream and emotions.

For this week, work on dressing consciously, dressing with full self-awareness.

21. Building the Group

Shared inner work enlivens and quickens our path remarkably. The best approach involves meeting regularly with a group to practice meditation, prayer, or other spiritual exercises. Some of us, though, do not have contact with a suitable group.

So we try to practice on our own. Perhaps we read a book like this one and do our best to apply the suggestions. In this we are not alone. Others also read this book and try to apply it in their lives. This is a group, albeit one that may never meet face-to-face. Yet we can help each other, we can work at forming a geographically dispersed but inwardly aligned group, one that can act as a container for energies, one that can help us.

Here's how. Once a day, take a minute or two to imagine the people who read this book and practice it. Imagine them as a group, a physically separated group with a shared intention. Now send your heartfelt kindness to that group, your best wishes for the spiritual development of each person in it. Since you are also part of this group, you will find energy and good will flowing back to you as you open to the group. Gradually in this way the group of readers of this book can become a vessel of help for each other.

22. Mirror, Mirror

The eyes are said to be the windows of the soul. A mirror can be a window into our attachments. When we look into mirror, what do we see? Obviously we see our body, our primary and primal attachment. We identify quite thoroughly with our body. We see our body in the mirror and without doubt we know that it is us. "Yep, that's me." We never even suspect the truth that we are not our body. Our real Self inhabits this body, but is not identical with it. Yet the mirror mesmerizes us: "that's me."

Having cognized our body in the mirror, the reactions proliferate. Perhaps we like what we see. We start to feel proud, preening under the spell of our vanity. Perhaps we dislike what we see. We start to criticize, noting with hope what we want to change, noting with despair what we cannot change, noting with fear the changes due to aging, trying to hide what we deem needs hiding, and adorning our body to enhance the view.

Our body changes every day, as does our response to the mirror. But something in us, the kernel of who we are, transcends time and does not change. For this week, whenever you look at a mirror, let it be a reminder to awaken to self-awareness, to awareness of how you feel in response to seeing your body in the mirror, awareness of your identification with your body, and awareness of your inmost self who looks at your body but is not your body. Use the mirror as much as you normally would, neither avoiding it nor gazing longer than usual. But be aware of your inside as you view your outside.

23. Rating the Day

Time is precious. How we live today creates our future. Do we spend our time profitably in developing our soul? To answer this, we could use a daily measure.

Taking stock of our inner work helps bring clarity to the apparent fuzziness of the spiritual path. Because the path only partly belongs to our ordinary world in space and time, we do not readily see its contours. Though we may not be able to notice our progress objectively, we can gauge our efforts. By regularly assessing our practice, we see more than a vague impression of our true situation.

At the end of each day, at bedtime, look back to see the extent to which inner work, spiritual practice penetrated your life during this day. How often were you present, for how long, and how deeply? Did you make time for prayer or meditation? Did you engage in the practices you have set for yourself? To what degree did your actions accord with your conscience?

You need not make this a highly detailed review. Simply note your overall impression of the quality of your inner life during the foregoing day. To make it more concrete and to obtain a measure for day to day comparisons and goals, rate the day on a 0 to 10 scale, with 0 standing for no presence at all, and 10 representing your ideal of presence, prayer and practice. The one absolutely necessary ingredient in this review and rating process is complete honesty with yourself, the willingness to see your life as it actually is.

This important and effective ancient practice can be found in a number of wisdom traditions. It dates back at least five hundred years to the time of the Khwajagan, the masters of wisdom of Central Asia, among whom were the founders of some of today's Sufi orders. This daily evaluation helps us identify opportunities for inner work and realize our true position vis-à-vis the Great Way, thus encouraging us to redouble our efforts to practice wisely and with heart.

24. The Practice of Excellence

Excellence pays enormous dividends, both in how we affect the world around us and in our personal fulfillment. Actions of excellence shine. When we look back on an act having an appropriate mix of quality, efficiency, effectiveness, rightness, beauty and perfection, we feel an unmistakable satisfaction. The practice of excellence entails making the pursuit of excellence our normal mode of living.

To pursue excellence in more of our life, we need to awaken and forgo half-heartedness. During the day, be aware of opportunities to perform actions with more quality than you might otherwise. Set your own standards of excellence and bring them to bear on what you do and say. Let the promptings of your conscience and the effects of your actions guide you in seeking excellence. The practice of excellence can be applied at any time or situation. Ask yourself: how can I bring excellence into this? And then act to do so.

You can seek excellence in your profession and in any complex task. But you can also look for excellence in unexpected places, in the simplest of actions. What would it mean to walk excellently, to wash the dishes excellently? How about excellence in speaking, even only a few words? And so on. The practice of excellence constantly renews our interest in and perception of life.

For this week, pursue excellence.

25. Awareness of Posture

The basic bodily postures of standing, walking, sitting, and lying down display an infinite number of variations. One way to be in contact with the immediacy of the present moment involves practicing awareness of posture, awareness of how our body is spatially arrayed now.

This is not about improving or correcting our posture, though that may come as a natural byproduct of increased postural awareness. The effort to improve posture may be worthy and even necessary, but forms another subject altogether.

In this particular practice we simply bring awareness to our posture in this moment, to the arrangement of our bones, to how our arms and legs, fingers and toes, head and torso are oriented now. To support continuity of presence, we practice posture awareness by allowing part or all of our attention to rest in our posture. Since our body is always in some posture and since effective posture awareness need not occupy the whole of our attention, this practice can be useful in any situation and at any time.

For this week, enter the practice of posture awareness.

26. Spaciousness

Learning to be aware of the space around you pays subtle but important dividends. The awareness of space begins through the eyes, but can extend to a direct perception that does not depend on vision or visual cues. Bodily movement, walking for example, puts you in direct contact with the freedom of space, a reflection of the inner freedom we seek.

Space relates to consciousness: still and empty in itself, yet allowing room for everything to enter. As the core framework of our reality, space and consciousness form the timeless background of all situations, events, and experience. Their basic nature is acceptance and perfect peace. They offer a field of relationship in which we find both our sameness and difference with others. They form the receptive field for time and creative acts. Space and consciousness share all this and more.

So as we work to be aware of the space surrounding us, we thereby enhance our contact with consciousness, with spaciousness of mind. A spacious mind allows thoughts, daydreams, emotions, sensory impressions, and actions to come and go, while maintaining its own equanimity. A spacious mind is vast, not obscured when clouds pass by, and contains ample room for others in its great heart.

27. Courtesy

The simple practice of everyday courtesy serves as a mirror and antidote to self-centeredness. Acts of courtesy raise us out of our self-referential dream-world, where the people around us mean little more than cardboard cutouts or, at best, potential sources for advancing our personal agenda. Courtesy arises out of seeing the other person as being human like us. This straightforward recognition in itself strikes a blow against our egoism and self-centeredness for it indiscriminately puts others on an equal footing with us.

To be courteous also calls us to be alert in the present moment, noticing opportunities for courtesy. It requires us to inwardly slow down enough, to forgo our hurry and worry enough, to overcome our laziness, habits, and fears enough to engage in courteous behavior without regard for personal gain.

Each gesture of courtesy aligns us with the Great Heart of the World, strengthening our true will and creating an atmosphere of kindness and generosity. When someone acts with courtesy toward us, we naturally grow more willing to be courteous to others. Thus, simple courtesy creates a positive feedback loop in society, as well as in our own heart.

The more we can open to others, even in small courtesies, the more we have the clarity of conscience that enables us to open to the sacred depths within. Purity of heart is a necessary condition for entering the deeper realms of the spirit. The practice of courtesy and, more broadly, kindness supports our purification, the diminishing of self-centeredness. It helps expand our center and concern from self to the Great Self of All.

Even moments when we see our own unwillingness to be courteous, if faced squarely, can serve to awaken us to our spiritual limitations. Kindness grows through practice, but also by honestly, and without excuses, seeing our lack of it.

For this week, practice courtesy.

28. Waiting

We all wait: for our turn at the front of the line, for the traffic light to change, for the show to begin, for our appointment, for the bread to rise or the water to boil, for our boat to come in, for the bus or the plane, for the tires to be rotated, for the mail, for a phone call, for the computer to boot up or shut down, for our chance to speak, for the weather to change, for a promotion or a raise, and so on ad nauseam.

But instead of wasting our time, we notice that waiting opens a gap in the flow of life, a gap through which inner work can enter. In pursuing our path, we seek to bring the light of spiritual practice into every corner of our day. Moments of waiting, with nothing pressing to do, present a prime opportunity to practice. We need only turn to working with bodily sensation, awareness of breath, inward prayer or full presence to transform a period of waiting into a session of being-work.

Typically though, we occupy ourselves unprofitably while waiting: looking in vain for ways to shorten the wait, feeling impatient, frustrated or anxious, or just daydreaming to escape. If, instead, we occupy ourselves with an appropriate method of spiritual practice, we reclaim the waiting time. Rather than wasting time or squandering it in a reaction to waiting, we inwardly turn our attention toward the eternal, while outwardly we still appear to be just waiting. Soon we may almost look forward to waiting.

For this week, renew your inner life while you wait.

29. Touching the Stillness

A vast and welcoming ocean of peaceful stillness exists just beyond our five senses, but not beyond the reach of our finer perceptions. The stillness, the great silent ground of the world, remains ever-present just beneath our ordinary experience. We need only meet it part way by opening ourselves, by reaching past our senses through our attention and intention to touch that stillness.

The stillness is substantive, but with a fine substance, a continuum of cognizance. Touching this higher energy, we find ourselves at peace, our presence enhanced, and our perspective broadened.

The expanse of stillness is not remote from us, not deeply hidden. We need only open our being to it. Just try it, simply and directly, several times during the day. Look to the quiet background of peace beneath your thoughts and sensory perceptions. You need not stop your thoughts for this, but rather open your gaze to the cognitive context beyond the stream of thoughts, sights, and sounds. Sitting quietly for few moments, or longer, can help you acquire the taste of stillness.

The more we touch the stillness, the more it permeates, supports, and brings wholeness to our life. For this week, touch the stillness within you.

30. Thought Awareness: I Am Not My Thoughts

One of the more important obstacles to our spiritual development, and also to happiness, consists of our identification with thoughts. We believe our thoughts. We believe in our thoughts. We believe our thoughts represent or embody who we are. We spend too much of our time living in the stream of our automatic, associative thoughts, like fish living in water. When a thought passes through our mind, we assume that the thought is the voice of our true, secret self. This inner voice, hidden from the world, serves as our home, our refuge, our truth. This inner voice of thought expresses our ongoing commentary on our life, our plans, dreams, and fears.

But like TV and radio, our inner voice lulls us into a programmed, autopilot mode that paints us as a character we play unawares, not noticing the inner voice as a voice or our thoughts as thoughts. If we do notice a thought, then we tacitly assume that it is what "I" think.

However, our I goes much deeper than thought. Our thoughts nearly always arise on their own, in reaction to some stimulus or to another thought, without the participation of our I, and thus without our intention. Consequently, our thoughts hardly ever reflect what "I" think, but rather indicate our conditioned, habitual patterns and reactions to the world. We believe these familiar habits of thought are who we are, our deepest self. But they are not. Thoughts are only surface phenomena, like waves on the ocean.

Who am I when my thoughts stop, or in the gaps between thoughts?

Notice your thoughts. As you begin to see your thoughts as thoughts, you may also start to notice the you that is aware of your thoughts. That aspect of you that sees your thoughts is not just another thought.

Practice thought awareness several times each day: simply watching your thoughts, seeing them as just thoughts rather than being caught by their meaning, observing the thoughts come and go, not being lost in the story they tell, not succumbing to their seductive whispers, shifting from content-enthralled to process-aware. And when the opportunity arrives, notice the gaps between thoughts.

Practicing awareness of bodily sensation facilitates thought awareness. Grounding in our body anchors us in the present. While in contact with our body, we are less apt to be carried away by our thoughts and more able to notice and watch the thoughts. Intentional awareness of bodily sensation stabilizes consciousness and enables us to see thoughts as just thoughts, without being grabbed by them, like iron filings to a magnet.

For this week, practice thought awareness and non-identification with thoughts.

31. Selfing

Imagine a large rock falling. As it falls through the air, the rock has minimal effect. The air, being a gas, presents little resistance. If the rock falls onto water, however, the water splashes and churns. Denser than air, with a correspondingly greater resistance to the motion of the rock, the water reacts more than the air did. If the rock were to fall onto something solid, like a man-made structure or a living being, great damage might be done. The solid object puts up strong resistance to the rock's motion, which transforms into the destructive energy of the impact.

In a similar fashion, we can put up more or less resistance to the events of our lives. Take the traffic jam. If we are totally identified with getting some place quickly, traffic can send us into desperate paroxysms of fury: honking, screaming, making obscene gestures, and breaking traffic laws. If we are simply daydreaming, operating on autopilot, the traffic jam may just bring a mood of frustration. If we are in the sensitive state, aware of ourselves and our surroundings, we may only have a slight irritation with the traffic. If we are conscious, we are free within the traffic situation, courteous toward our fellow commuters, and we arrive at our destination ready to meet it with kindness and presence. And so it goes with many of life's major and minor difficulties. The more solid our walls, the more damage we take en route.

The inward walls we erect, the inner resistance we put up, temporarily forms a self in us, an illusory and ephemeral something that we protect. In fact, the self is created by the protection, by the defenses. The self is the defense. In reality, however, there is nothing to defend.

Outwardly, of course, we may need to take vigorous action to defend ourselves or our families against attack, disease, etc. But here we refer to the many moments of inner defensiveness that create our ego, our ephemeral pseudo-self. Each instance of anger, hatred, greed, fear, jealousy, envy, self-pity, arrogance, laziness, worry, lust, vanity, and the like, is a moment of resistance to what is, a moment of creating a false persona to defend, a moment of selfing.

What to do? Begin with seeing all this in action. Seeing means consciousness, even if just a brief instant of it. The light of consciousness melts away our defenses and false self, which can only thrive in the unseeing darkness.

For this week, practice seeing selfing in action, seeing your inner resistance create your pseudo-self.

32. Awareness of State

Our dominant mode of experiencing often gives way to a whole range of inner states of being. In some moments we are inwardly more alert, more alive, more awake, and more connected than in others. Usually we are passive in this, neither choosing nor developing our inner life. Our state simply reflects the condition of our body that day or the circumstances of the moment. But we have the possibility of directly and intentionally changing our state, our mode of experiencing.

Our state fluctuates up and down, but always returns to our predominant norm, our station or level of being. We can most readily differentiate among our states by the energies which characterize them. Our usual autopilot, daydreaming, associative-thinking, emotionally-reacting state operates with the automatic energy. At a step higher, the sensitive energy state puts us in contact with our body and our surroundings, able to respond appropriately. Higher still, the conscious energy frees us from time and from our self-centered egoism. In true consciousness, we operate from that silent, unchanging background of awareness that underlies all experience, in natural joy, equanimity, kindness, and presence. And higher states beyond consciousness also await us.

We need to understand our actual position directly, see our state, and discern where we are in our path. To do so, we may use the map of the levels of energies as a reference to help us recognize the state we are in, the energy that fuels our experience at any given moment. This seeing gives us a realistic appraisal of our current status, opens us to a heartfelt longing for being, and shows us how to pursue the path.

We can only begin from where we actually are in this moment. Since our states fluctuate throughout the day, we can profitably return to this practice of awareness of state frequently. Of course, as in physics, the very act of observation changes our state. Knowing where we are, we can begin to move deeper into the present. The spiritual path offers many methods to raise the level of our inner life.

33. Inhabiting the Body

The most obvious characteristic of our life is that we have a body, on which we are wholly dependent. Our body conditions our entire experience to such an extent that we consider our body to be our self. Yet despite this overwhelming bodily nature of our life, we rarely inhabit our body. We typically live at some inner distance from our body, identifying instead with our thoughts and feelings.

To inhabit our body does not merely mean feeling "at home" or comfortable in our body, which happens for most of us shortly after adolescence. Inhabiting our body means being home, being here, being present in our body, being the core experiencer and actor of bodily life.

The possibility of inhabiting our body comes through

contact with our energy body, with the energy of sensation that gives us our kinesthetic and proprioceptive bodily sense. The sensitive energy connects us, as the core experiencer, with our body. This contact can grow to include our entire body through the continuing practice of sensing, of perceiving the sensitive energy in the body. The aim of this practice is to have an ongoing in-the-body experience.

The importance of inhabiting our body, especially the whole of the energy body, consists of providing us with a solid base in the present moment, a home from which to pursue the spiritual path. Without this wholeness of bodily sensation we tend to flounder in and out of the present, we lack stability of awareness, stability of presence. Full-body sensation and attention to the entire body are mutually reinforcing. These, in turn, bring wholeness and stability to our presence, enabling us to be completely at home in our body, to truly inhabit our body, and thus to inhabit our life.

To be able to come to sensation of the whole body takes practice. If you have been working with sensing parts of your body, you may be prepared to work at whole body sensation. This ongoing practice of active and full presence in the entire energy body, if pursued diligently, proves enormously beneficial to our path.

34. You, Being You

Our usual manner of not being our self misleads us. We spend a surprisingly large fraction of our life passively being carried through the day, just like we are carried through our dreams at night. In place of the active dream images of night-sleep, during our waking sleep we let our self-generating, pre-programmed thoughts, emotions, moods, impulses, opinions, attitudes, and reactions dictate our life. Even though we may seem to be active, our activity is driven by habitual patterns to which we passively assent. Those automatic patterns usurp our true place. We just go along for the ride — or maybe not even that, with no one at home in our center.

Nevertheless, this situation, once seen for what it is, begs for our notice and action. To notice how the mask of our personality and the world view of our character create a cocoon of perceptual filters and auto-generated behaviors that causes us to sleepwalk our life away takes an unflinching self-honesty and a willingness to see. Too often my inner manifestations and my outer behaviors diverge from what I wish them to be. Why? Because of my half-aware passivity. We need more and finer energy to be more aware. We need more intention to be less passive.

Without seeing our true situation, however, the intention to transform ourselves remains weak. Fortunately, from time to time we catch a glimpse of our passivity, which is not to be confused with relaxation. A relaxed state is receptive, whereas a passive state is not. To be receptive we need a certain level of awareness. To be passive does not require awareness. Seeing truly comes from our efforts of presence, which have a byproduct of bringing more glimpses of the passivity that presence counteracts. Only as we emerge into presence can we see the passivity that enveloped us just a moment before. Together, the attraction of presence and the need to awaken from our sleepwalking invigorate our intention to practice, to pursue the spiritual path.

The action that can raise us up originates in our will, in our intention, our inner act of presencing, whereby we reclaim being the agent who chooses our acts, being the one who is aware, the one who lives and experiences and responds to our life. There is a sharp difference between being here at the center of our life on the one hand and on the other existing passively on the periphery, while the action carries itself forward, as if life were a prepackaged TV re-run. The opportunity to move into our center offers a chance for a major transformation and enhancement of our experience of living, an enlargement of the purpose and meaning of our life, a rising into real joy and even love. In some instances that move to our center just happens due to circumstances, but then quickly vanishes. For a lasting move into our center, we make the intentional and oft-repeated act of presencing, of I being I, of You being You.

We reach a major milestone when we practice presence so much that we feel when it's missing. A feeling of discomfort invades our passivity, the discomfort of missing our wholeness, and it awakens our longing to be. In our passive, semi-aware states, the memory of a better way of living jars, cajoles, and entices us back into the practice of presence, back to being our self, back to the fullness of life.

No presence means no I, no you. So for this week practice being you. Notice your passivity and transform it into presence. Inhabit the center of your experience.

35. Lighting the Darkness

Certain parts of our typical day are like the dark side of the moon, spiritually. No inner work, no light of true awareness enters there. Choose one such activity or time during which you usually do little or no spiritual practice. For the rest of the week, bring more presence into that particular period of each day. You could work with sensation, or mindfulness, or breath awareness during that time, or with whatever presence-supporting practice seems most appropriate.

Some of our normal activities take all of our attention and leave none for the work of presence. As we continue on the path, the capacity of our attention grows and even these challenging arenas open to our deepening presence. So we could choose an activity that is almost out of reach for our presence, one that flexes our spiritual muscles.

Others of our activities do not present a particular difficulty of attention, but have remained outside the field of presence simply out of neglect. So we could choose a time or activity into which the light of our awareness usually does not penetrate. Gradually but persistently, we work to shine more light into that dark corner of our life.

For this week, bring more light of awareness into a particular region of your daily life.

36. Pushing the Envelope

Unless we find ways to extend our spiritual practice, we wander and inevitably languish within a box of limiting assumptions about our lack of possibilities. That box keeps us in the same familiar, inner territory indefinitely. At times, external events break us out of our spiritual plateau and open new realms of our inner life. Though we may respond wholeheartedly to such unexpected opportunities, we also need to create our own.

Certain measures define the envelope of our spiritual life: breadth, depth, frequency, duration, intensity, and adaptability. Each of these dimensions offers ways to push our spiritual envelope. In broadening our inner work, we shine a light into areas of our lives in which we rarely practice presence. We could, for example, move from awareness of bodily sensation to also practice awareness of thought and emotion. We can plumb the depths of meditation to seek what lies just beyond our reach. We can set ourselves to practice presence more frequently. When moments of awakening grace our day, we can open to our physical sensation, to the energy body, so as to increase the time we spend in the present moment and decrease the time lost in haphazard thought and emotional reactions. Whenever our inner world is alert, we can put more emphasis on strengthening our attention, further intensifying our awareness. We can adapt the practices we learn to our own abilities and needs. We can adapt ourselves to practice in whatever circumstances we find ourselves.

In these and other ways, we can grow the envelope of our practice. It is work and requires effort. While spirituality ultimately depends on grace, honest, intelligent effort and dogged perseverance prepare the way. For this week, push the envelope of your spirituality.

37. Understanding Our Motivation

The motivations that drive our spiritual practice vary widely, just as we do. They even change from moment to moment, ranging from the wholly self-centered to the purest love.

We may want to be seen by others as a spiritual person. We may want to belong to a group. We may want solace in our suffering. We may appreciate the beauty of the world and want to touch its deepest truths. We may want an explanation for the mystery of life. We may have had an extraordinary spiritual experience that we want to understand and even repeat. We may have a heartfelt intuition of the Sacred and feel the need to serve and worship God. We may have some unknown and invisible faith or longing that carries us along the Way of love and completion. We may want a deeper meaning for our life. We may want to make a difference. Or we may have any number of other reasons.

Regardless of the particular motive, the important thing is whether it prods us to actually practice. The path will eventually transform our motives from the base to the sublime, as we ourselves are transformed. Yet if our motivation, our wish to practice, is weak or if we have little contact with it, our practice will be correspondingly weak.

So for this week's inner work, we notice our motives for following the spiritual path. We might try to recall what brought us to the path initially. We might notice whether and how that initial motivation has changed.

What is it that moves me to try to awaken, to be present, to meditate, to pray, and so on? Why do I do these things?

38. A Shift in Perspective

While walking we pass by many things: buildings, trees, people, and so on. Unconsciously we take those things, the world outside our body, as our frame of reference. In that frame, the building, the sidewalk, and the meadow remain in place as we move past or through them. We trek through space and time that way, focused on the external like a tourist. This seems, and is indeed, ordinary and natural. Yet another way is possible.

Einstein examined the relativity of motion using the example of a train passing a station. If you are on the train, the station passes you: you are at rest with respect to the train. If you are in the station, the train does the moving, while you stand still on the platform. In the first case your frame of reference is the train, while in the second the station.

In this exercise, while walking, we shift our perspective, our frame of reference from the world outside our body to the world within, the inner world we carry with us wherever we go. Centered in ourselves as we walk, we notice the buildings and trees moving toward and past us. Though our body walks, we ourselves remain still within, abiding in consciousness. The outside moves toward and around us. Calm descends. Instead of hurrying to get somewhere, we are already here and the world comes to us. Rather than dissipate our energies in an outward flow, we remain centered inside. No longer a traveler through an external world, we become the world and the world travels through us, through our awareness.

No mere trick, this exercise offers a new perception, a taste of consciousness, pure awareness not limited to space and time. This shift in perspective goes beyond spatial movement. Even when we are stationary, the world and time move through us. We remain conscious in the seeing, not dragged or pushed by the stream of time. Consciousness does not belong to space or time.

For this week, practice shifting your perspective to your own center.

39. Doing the Dishes

We inwardly sort life's activities along a scale from the dull and insignificant to the exciting and important. The commonplace chores of life, like washing the dishes, along with the unusual but unwanted ones, like fixing the flat tire, impose their necessity on us. Our attitudes toward such tasks run the gamut from boredom and resentment to hurrying and anger. We may howl at the uncompromising gate of time that allows only one event in any given moment, driving us to forgo our preferences in favor of some bothersome drudgery. We may even rush through it or indulge in daydreams for the duration, doing our very best to escape the experience. We kill the time and, along with it, a part of our life.

The fact that time is a fleeting and precious commodity exactly defines the problem. We think that if we could just avoid the chore somehow, then we could use the time more profitably or more enjoyably. But no one has such a life. Everyone has unwelcome duties pressed upon him or her. So this leaves us too often having to make the best of the undesirable.

We might ask ourselves: "Can I turn this around?" Can I make presence one of my most important and interesting activities, even in life's humdrum corners? In meditation we find deep satisfaction, even though we accomplish nothing, at least outwardly. Washing the dishes is no worse, in terms of external accomplishment. Can I use the opportunity of washing dishes to wash my mind as well, to be present fully, and even more fully? Can I not just endure the boring chore, but enter it wholeheartedly, appreciating the opportunity to do something useful, even on a small scale? If the higher can act through us, then scale no longer matters. Washing one cup, paying one bill, fixing one flat — they all matter because they all are necessary, they all restore or create order, especially if my inner life is order.

For this week, when it comes to chores, at work or at home, practice doing them with presence.

40. Part and Whole

    We have this body. We have these feelings. We have this mind. Body, feelings, and mind: each has a life of its own. They hardly know or acknowledge each other except when forced to, as in illness. We speak without feeling what we say. Our mind protests our physical appetites and recoils at our emotional excesses. Our body ignores our mind's would-be yoke of discipline. Our feelings both "love" and hate the same object.

    Yet exceptional moments of wholeness do come, with all our parts in agreement, coordinated, and effective. Such moments offer a glimpse of the possible. To increase that wholeness beyond accidental glimpses, to reintegrate our fractured nature, we practice the path of inner work and spiritual transformation.

    One way toward wholeness starts in noticing our inner divisions. For this, we seek to know our parts. We intentionally stay in contact with our body through sensation. Beginning with sensing parts, say an arm or a leg, we eventually work our way up to sensing our whole body. That gives us the stability to see our thoughts as thoughts and our emotions as emotions.

    Moving further into the path of self-integration, through more awareness and self-acceptance, we consciously embrace all our parts into our unique wholeness. Rather than live a part of our life, we seek to live the whole of it. However, attempting to force the issue deepens our inner divisions rather than bringing wholeness. Instead we work toward a more complete awareness of ourselves. Within the inclusive tent of consciousness, our parts naturally find their rightful relationships.

    For this week, focus on seeing your parts as parts, seeing them in action, loosely connected.

41. Chiming In

In our search for ways to bring spiritual practice into more of our day, the regularity of taking a few moments every hour, or most hours, to reconnect with our inner life and reestablish presence, serves as a powerful support, threading the path into our daily rounds. The idea is simple: on the hour, engage in a brief practice. Choose the hours and the practice in advance.

One excellent candidate for repeated practice involves opening to bodily sensation. For example, focus attention on each limb in turn, briefly but long enough to draw the sensitive energy there. Or you might practice conscious breathing for seven breaths, simple awareness of your breath. Or you might practice breathing in the energy from the air. Or you could work with any other practice that brings you toward presence.

We do this on the hour: say at 9 AM, 10 AM, 11 AM, and so on. Choose the hours. To work at every hour during the day may be too much: better not to overreach and crash. But to work at only one hour may be too little. We look for a balance to challenge ourselves, to push our envelope, but not break it. So you might choose three hours, or the even hours from breakfast until dinner. But choose in advance.

Then when the times come, do the exercise. If you miss the exact time, please do not indulge the self-recriminations that waste your energy. Instead, simply work at the exercise when you realize that the time for it has past. Whether 10 minutes or 4 hours late, the important thing is to come back to presence through the practice you have chosen.

If you have an alarm clock, or an alarm watch, or a watch that chimes the hours, do not be tempted to use it to remind you. One aspect of this task is to create an inner bell of awakening, an impulse within you to remember to practice. Use a watch to check the time, but not to ring the bell of mindfulness. External reminders typically lose their force all too soon.

At the beginning of the week, decide what hours you will practice each day and what method you will use to work toward presence at those times. As the week progresses, adjust those choices as necessary. Make the practice one that will not interfere with your daily activities. You can safely work at being aware of your breath or your body in the midst of many different life situations.

42. Awareness of Talking

A masterstroke of evolution, the ability to speak characterizes us both collectively and individually. To a great extent, we convey and reveal our personality by what we say. And because we conflate our persona with who we really are, we experience a strong pull to lose ourselves in talking. For these reasons, awareness of talking offers a rich, though rocky field for our spiritual work.

We adopt a concrete, physical approach to the practice of speech awareness: to actually hear the sound of our own voice as we speak, to be aware of that sound. Secondary elements of this practice include being viscerally aware of, sensing, our mouth, tongue and throat, our facial expressions and the gestures we make while speaking.

Start with simple situations that require only a minimal amount of talking. For example, as you stand in a cashier's line at a store, form the intention to be aware of yourself as you thank the cashier at the end of the transaction. Watch for the moment and then be in the sound and physical sensations of yourself speaking.

For most of us, this proves very difficult. As soon as we open our mouths to speak, we lose ourselves and talk in an autopilot or reactive manner, with little or no self-awareness. In situations where we need to be particularly careful, we may have continuing awareness of the meaning of what we are saying due to the presence of the sensitive energy of thought. But awareness of the physicality of speaking brings a new and broader dimension of presence to this most common of activities.

Shining the light of awareness onto speaking takes time, persistence, and clearly maintained intention. For this week practice hearing your own voice, while sensing your mouth, tongue, and throat. Aim to do this at least several times a day. The rigors of this practice, if faced with inner honesty, create the indirect benefit of showing us the limitations of our presence. However, the presence we develop in becoming aware of ourselves while speaking feeds our inner work in many important ways.

43. Developing Compassion

Among the fruits of a life well-lived are love and compassion. Can we develop compassion intentionally? In truth, compassion evolves as a result of all our efforts on the path. The deeper we go into our own being, the closer we come to the Great Heart of the World, and the deeper our connection with others.

But we can also work at the level of our ordinary experience to be in contact with the natural compassion in our hearts. Whenever you hear of the illness, death, loss of a job, or other misfortune among your circle of family and acquaintances, or even among strangers you come into contact with, allow yourself to feel that person's misfortune. Feel how it must be to be that person. Just for a moment, put yourself in their shoes. We do not intend this practice as a response to the continuous stream of tragedies, large and small, reported in the news media. That could easily overwhelm us. We mean this for the misfortunes we encounter during our normal daily contacts with the people we see.

If so moved, and if appropriate outward action lies within your power and means, then you might take that action in response. An inner approach involves saying a prayer for and sending our heartfelt inner light to the suffering person.

The practice of compassion lifts us out of our egoism and works against indifference, isolation and fear. To complement this active approach to developing compassion, we also work to simply see our lack of it, to see our indifference, to see the fear that intrudes onto our perceptions of others' distress. Seeing our lack of compassion prepares a place in us for compassion to arise.

For this week, practice compassion.

44. Duration

When spontaneous moments of awakening arrive, the path calls us to act on the opportunity for inner work: to sense our body, to be aware of our breathing, to enter and reside in the wholeness of presence, and so on. But all too quickly we slide back into our automatic, autopilot lifestyle. In this week's task, we set ourselves to extend those moments of practice that open to us during the day, to abide in the world of sensation a bit longer, to be in presence for an extra few seconds, to watch even just one more breath before losing ourselves again.

One of the more remarkable aspects of our work with the sensitive energy occurs when it builds up in the energy body and exhibits its own staying power. This enables us to maintain ourselves in sensitive awareness longer than otherwise possible. Persistent work with the sensitive energy in the body collects and accumulates that energy, enabling our awareness to endure and stabilize, providing a platform from which we can sustain presence.

Whatever method of inner work we choose, the dimension of duration remains important. We capitalize on the random moments of grace that awaken us and remind us of our path, expanding those moments by prolonging our inner work.

45. Intentional Walking

Will has an open, allowing side, an active side, and a harmonizing side. The open receives, the active affirms, and the harmonizing cooperates. In any given moment, our will is who we are.

For this week's task we seek to understand and develop our will through intentional action. Wholeheartedness in action, fully intending an action allows our will to work in a new way. Undivided intention completely engages us in this singular moment, in responsibility for action, and marshals all our inner resources toward the endeavor, nothing withheld, seeking utter perfection of the act.

Intentionality can enter the whole range of actions, from the simple to the complex, from the instantaneous to those spanning decades, from the fully present reaching for the saltshaker at the dinner table to raising a child in a responsible, intelligent, and loving manner.

In this task we apply our intention to a routine and frequent action: walking. We walk with intention, the intention to move, to take this step, to be in our body, to be where we are, to walk toward our destination. While walking, we intend to be present, we will to be present. We walk as perfectly as possible, with economy of motion and energy, with the appropriate balance of relaxation and exertion, relaxing those muscles, thoughts, and emotions not needed for right walking. Intention does not imply tension. Intention means, and indeed creates, purpose. We walk not only with awareness but also with a purpose, as bearers and servants of a purpose that transcends walking.

To what extent am I engaged in what I am doing? For this week, fully engage in the walking you do.

46. Well-Wishing

Perhaps you live in a shell of indifference toward most people, as if they are cardboard cutouts to be used or ignored, rather than actual persons. How can we open our hearts to the "Thou" in others, to recognizing our sameness, our shared humanity, our common personhood? How can we see that within each person lies a world of awareness, hopes, and dreams, just like in us? Though the content certainly differs, the Life, the consciousness is one and the same. How to come toward that perception of heart?

First, of course, we can look at the reality of our situation. What attitude do we actually hold toward others? Seeing the truth of this about ourselves prepares the ground for change.

Second, we can actively address our good will toward people, at least inwardly. When we see another person, even a total stranger, we can consider our common humanity. Out of this naturally arises an impulse of good will, which we inwardly direct toward him or her, silently sending our best wishes, our personal blessing to the other person. You might inwardly use words or phrases from your own heart-store that speak of health, happiness, peace, love, fulfillment, or God's blessing. Such phrases can help you form your intention of kind wishes and give it wings.

For this week, practice the heart of benevolence.

47. Frequency

As our experience with inner work grows, we notice more and more opportunities for practice. An increasing variety of life situations and events remind us of the path. This opens a fruitful line of questioning to pose to ourselves: "How often do I capitalize on chances to practice? How often do I let them slip away?"

The practice of sensation, for example, can profitably enter nearly every life situation without interfering. Indeed, sensing enhances life. Why then do I not sense more often? If spirituality matters to me, and if I am to be responsible to that, and if I am to reach the depths of transformation possible for me, then shouldn't I welcome and make full use of every opening into the present?

For this week, notice how often you engage in inner work. Set and strengthen your intention to practice more frequently during the day. Use your creativity to devise ways to respond more often to the inner call. How many chances can we afford to pass up?

48. Respect

For this week, take a careful look at your attitudes toward others and toward yourself. Is it respectful, or not? Whom do I respect? Do I treat everyone with respect? Do I consider anyone to be below me, unworthy of respect? Am I inwardly disrespectful, while outwardly feigning respect? Am I indifferent toward others, neither respectful nor disrespectful? Is indifference a form of disrespect?

Do I respect myself? Do I consider myself to be below others, unworthy of respect? Do I consider every person to be equal, in the sense that we are all children of the One God?

Respect for others begins with respect for our self, the quiet dignity that derives from self-acceptance, understanding our own destructive emotions, and keeping our word. But respect for others also reinforces respect for our self.

Seeing our own inner lack of respect shows us the path toward cultivating it, toward intentionally adopting a genuinely respectful attitude. And respect, coupled with spiritual practice, leads toward humility and love.

49. Resistance

The exercise of weight training requires weights. We do not consider the weights to be our enemy, to be harmful, avoided or ignored. The weights serve to strengthen us. Without the weights to work against, we would neither grow nor benefit from the exercise.

Similarly, in spiritual exercise our inner resistance serves as the weight to work against. Luckily, we have at our disposal a treasure trove of resistance: physical habits and appetites, mental propensities to daydream, doubt, and worry, our emotional reactivity of anger, fear, greed, and so on, our lack of higher energies, our spiritual lethargy and procrastination, and the 800-pound gorilla in the corner — our self-centered attitude. All of this, the whole catastrophe, our whole personality, provides a rich and boundless field for our spiritual practice. We have much work to do and no lack of resistance to work againstThe universal principle of resistance manifests in the material world as entropy, the tendency toward disorder. In the inner world, we experience entropy as the strong current toward lower potential, toward the more automatic, indulgent, and constrained modes of living. By swimming against this inner current, we gain strength of soul, wisdom, and compassion.

For this week, notice your inner resistance to practice. Notice your attitude toward your resistance, toward yourself. Do you add another layer of resistance by rejecting or indulging the unpleasantness you find in yourself? Or do you take this inner resistance as a challenge, as an opportunity to practice?

Any active inner effort, such as sensing the energy body, conscious movement, conscious breathing, or the practice of presence, soon reveals our inner resistance opposing the effort. Between these two rails of active effort and inner resistance, we find the path.

50. *Continuity*

Setting aside time each day for meditation conveys enormous benefits: physical, psychological, and spiritual. Yet if our inner work only occurs within the confines of formal periods of meditation, our spiritual life cannot fully flower. We also need to practice during the rest of our day, as much as possible.

In the time-dimension limit of inner work, we would practice continuously throughout the day. The process of transformation accelerates dramatically whenever we manage to enter continuity of presence. Continuous presence means in part moment-to-moment-to-moment awareness, simple and direct, unbroken and seamless. This continuity standard of practice offers us a clear and high aim by which to measure ourselves and toward which to direct our efforts.

For this week, find a block of time, perhaps one to four hours, during which you can work to be as continually present as possible. We must be realistic about this and not fall into an illusion of continuous presence. However, we also need not adopt nor believe limiting assumptions about our inner life, such as the assumption that we cannot practice continuously. The goal of continuous presence, continuous practice in our ordinary daily life, spurs us on toward a new, more appreciative mode of living, toward unexpected peace, toward kindness and generosity of heart.

So in a relaxed manner, we practice now. In the next moment, we continue to practice. And again in the next. Stringing these moments into an overlapping band, we ride the current of presence.

51. The Roller-Coaster

Like all living processes, our inner work ebbs and flows. Some days we experience an abundance of energy and strong commitment to practice. Other days find us barely connected with ourselves, much less the path.

Spiritual practice, borrowing the old phrase about politics, is the art of the possible. When we fall to the inevitable low points, the down days, the slough of despond, we practice in whatever small ways we can, just to maintain that connection with the path, however tenuous it may seem. A conscious breath, some sensation in a hand, a gesture of kindness — the efforts made despite great obstacles, great resistance, low energy and other distractions add to our being in a way not possible while cruising on a high road.

On the up days, we face the temptation of only seeking pleasure, using up the resources we have built through our inner work. We naturally and rightly enjoy the days full of energy, when events seem to conspire to serve our every whim. Yet we practice even on the up days: a prayer of gratitude, good wishes to our neighbor, a body full of sensation, returning frequently to awareness of our body or breath, taking time for meditation. This way of giving part of our best moments to the path, when our energies wax abundant, builds our will and commitment to the spirit, while serving the sacred.

For this week, notice the peaks and valleys, the highs and lows in your practice, and how you respond to these changing situations.

52. Non-Identifying

Our ego creates itself through the process of identification, also known as clinging, attachment, and selfing. You can recognize a moment of identification by the fact that your world unintentionally collapses onto one item, to which you hold tightly. Take a pleasant daydream, like winning the lottery or meeting your soul-mate. As soon as the daydream starts it grabs you, co-opting you into becoming the daydream for that moment. Similarly with fear and anxiety: the unexpected big dog barks at you, or you wake up with an unexplained lump on your head. You recoil in instant fear. You recoil into identification with your reaction to the situation. You leave the present for scenarios of impending doom.

We identify with anger. An impolite person crosses you. You wax indignant, inwardly seething, perhaps outwardly reacting. "I" am angry. This is my anger.

Our ability to identify, to create a separate self or ego, knows no bounds. We identify with the weather, with our body, with what others think of us, with a sports team, with possessions, with politicians, with the news, with our job, with anything that can grab us. Our ego mechanisms use such things to construct and define ourselves, a false and ultimately empty definition.

This week notice moments of identification and work at letting them go. This is not me. This is anger. This is anxiety. This is a daydream, a thought. This is fear. This is how anger feels. This is not *my* anger; it is anger passing through me. This daydream is just a passing thought sequence. This is not who I am. Watch these sticky items pass through your mind/heart, see that they are not who you are, and let them go their way. Remain the seer and the seeing, not the seen.

53. First Response

Whenever any inner or outer perception or event arises, our immediate response categorizes it as pleasant, unpleasant, or neutral. This occurs as a gut level, visceral reaction to the perception. Judgments, aversion, and attachment all follow close on the heels of this first response. In the Buddha's Chain of Dependent Origination, our immediate response to perception defines the point at which we can either break the chain of suffering or slide into identification, attachment, and suffering.

With the pleasant, do you immediately fall toward the grasping desire to extend it beyond its natural time? With the unpleasant, do you immediately fall into aversion, wanting to end it before its time? With the neutral, do you ignore it, become bored, and fall asleep? In all three ways, inner and outer events push the pleasant, unpleasant, or neutral buttons of our conditioning to automatically elicit our pre-programmed reactions. No consciousness required: this all runs on the lower energies.

But seeing the truth of how this operates in our own psyche and, through seeing, finding some freedom from the chain does require consciousness. It also requires the intention to seek freedom rather than habitually and unconsciously succumbing to our robotic first response of pursuing the pleasant, avoiding the unpleasant, and ignoring the neutral.

We stand alert at the inner gate of our senses, noticing our first response to each new item. That noticing is the seed of freedom, for it opens the opportunity to let the response pass without drawing us into attachment and identification. For this week, notice your direct, pre-verbal reaction to what your senses bring you and let that reaction pass.

54. Let It Be

The attitude of contentment leads to and embodies peace. Contentment allows life to be just as it is, in a stance of radical acceptance. Neither rejecting the unpleasant and painful, nor grasping for the pleasurable, we rest in open awareness in the ebb and flow of experience.

Contentment does not imply passivity. We still take medicine in times of illness, but out of caring for our sick body, not as a desperate attempt escape the unpleasantness. We take appropriate action, where we see the need or obligation. All the while, our orientation of not interfering with experience anchors us in peace. We let the weight fall from our shoulders. We live and act from the place of peace.

For this week, notice your own position with respect to contentment. To what degree do you accept experience as it arises? What do you push away? What do you run after? Can you just let it all be?

55. Direct Perception

Direct, unmediated perception revitalizes us. The simplest objects vividly express the beauty inherent in our surroundings, ordinary or not. We hear the clanking of silverware as the notes of a symphony. Every morsel of food comes alive with taste, texture, and aroma. We find once more the simple pleasures of living in our body. This may sound appealing, but how can we live like that?

Distractions prevent us from living in this natural, open perceptivity. Our attention wanders far afield from our immediate perceptions, leaving little energy behind to recognize the small miracles of daily living. Returning to our center, here in this moment, escaping the thrall of our associative trains of thought, daydreams, and emotional reactions, we can once again see and hear with the wonder of a child. Removing our attention from our mental apparatus that categorizes, comments, and reacts to perception, we enter the vivid, the true world. As the Buddha put it: "In the seen, there is just what is seen. In the heard, there is just what is heard..."

For this week, work at allowing your attention to rest in direct perception, in non-distraction.

56. Body Image

Are you satisfied with the way your body looks? Do you like what you see in the mirror? Do you want to change your body? Do you wish it were different somehow?

Entire industries exist to exacerbate and address these dilemmas. We spend enormous effort on the look of our body: clothing, grooming, makeup, shaving, all manner of potions and lotions, body-building, cosmetic surgery, and botox. For our spiritual work, perhaps the most interesting aspect of our physical appearance is the degree to which we are attached to how our body looks, the degree to which we identify with our exterior form.

For this week observe how you relate to your body's looks. What do you reject? What feeds your vanity? Can you simply accept your body in toto, just as it is? This is not to suggest that you give up makeup, or stop shaving, combing, and dressing well, but rather that you investigate where in all this your attachments lie. Where does your attitude cross the line from caring for your body and appearance according to the norms of your society, to being enslaved by vanity?

57. Constancy

We can ill afford days of no inner work, for our time is limited. Even if blessed with long life, unless we build a very firm foundation prior to growing old, we may not have the health, strength, or energy to practice well in our later years. These days, this moment offer our best opportunity for spiritual practice.

Our conditions change continuously, bouncing us among happiness, sadness, high energy, tiredness, anger, envy, elation, illness, confusion, clarity and the rest. But whatever the conditions, inner as well as outer, our compass can always point us in the same direction: toward depth of spirit and openness of heart.

We need great fortitude and constancy of purpose to continue our inner work come what may. A real blessing enters our life when we always know and act on this one thing: this is the time to practice letting go, presence, sensing our body, kindness, energy breathing and so forth. This constancy of will bears the seed of our transformation.

For this week, look at your own stance toward inner work, particularly in the face of situations that make practice seem difficult. Does your compass waver? Where can you find the constancy you need?

58. Non-Suffering

The inevitability of pain while living in a human body does not imply the inevitability of suffering. Indeed, the Buddha and others taught paths toward liberation from suffering. The root causes of suffering are attachment, aversion and identification. Difficult sensory perceptions, such as physical pain, need not cause us suffering. If we can open to the direct perception of the painful sensations without adding layers of emotional reactions, the frantic need to make it stop, or even simple aversion, then we do not suffer despite the pain.

Most of our suffering, though, has nothing to do with physical pain but rather with emotional reactions. Whenever we fall into anger, we suffer acutely. Disappointed hopes and unmet expectations bring suffering. Fear, greed, jealousy, self-pity and other destructive emotions define the spectrum of our false suffering.

However some forms of suffering, like grief or severe illness, are real and unavoidable. Those occasions prompt us to seek solace by turning toward the Highest One in prayer. But the vast majority of our suffering is an unnecessary byproduct of our egoism, of who we think we are.

If we can but step aside ever so slightly and let go of ourselves, let go of the holding on that causes our suffering, we may enter the natural joy of living, the fresh air of freedom. Even brief moments of partial freedom from ourselves, from our illusion of separateness, can reinvigorate our lives and renew our inner work.

For this week, notice instances in which you suffer, remember that nearly all your suffering is not necessary, and let go of it a little more.

59. The Practice of Self-Acceptance

Non-acceptance of ourself creates warring camps in our inner world, and vice versa. We are divided and have no unity of being or will. The casualties of this non-acceptance are our precious wasted resources of time, energy, and emotional investment, missed opportunities and half-heartedness in pursuit of our goals. And if we cannot accept ourselves as we are, then we have little possibility of fully accepting anyone else. The practice of self-acceptance gradually evaporates our inner barriers, because the one in us who accepts transcends those parts in us that either reject or are rejected. But for this we need to practice, to retrain our attitudes toward ourselves.

The practice of mindfulness meditation directly and powerfully addresses this issue of non-acceptance. We sit quietly, watching whatever crosses the stage of our mind, be it thoughts or mental images, emotions, physical urges, or sensory perceptions. Whatever their content, however "sticky" they are, we let them come and we let them go. We do not pursue or nurture, ruminate over or consider them, nor do we reject them. We let the content of our inner world be as it is and as it changes, without driving those changes. We just sit and notice all that goes on in us.

If it's a thought or emotion we don't like, we notice the thought or emotion as a thought or emotion, and we also notice the not-liking of it as another emotion. Our ordinary way of responding to this situation would be to identify with the part of us that rejects and push away what we are rejecting. In this practice of mindfulness meditation, we neither identify nor push away. We see that the part that rejects is not who we are and that the part that is rejected is not who we are. We are the one who sits and sees and allows, in a non-reactive, fully-aware, and calm state of just being. We spread the great and welcoming tent of awareness over the whole of our inner world. We embrace the whole of ourselves, the whole beauty and the whole catastrophe, with kindness and compassion.

This approach in the quiet of meditation offers an essential training for the much more complex inner and outer situations we confront in our daily life. Through this type of meditation we train ourselves to be and to see and not to identify. We become more objective and impartial toward the multitude of conflicting desires that populate our inner world. In the midst of a self-antagonistic inner conflict, we turn to just seeing both sides in us, seeing that neither is who we are, that each is a only a complex of thoughts, attitudes, and emotions, that each is a part of us to be reclaimed into the whole of us by compassion. We allow both sides to be as they are.

We realize that we need not reject our self-critical attitudes, but rather by just seeing and noticing those attitudes we further the integration of our inner world. We learn that we need not take our thoughts and attitudes as defining us. That ability comes from learning to be, to be conscious, to be more than just our thoughts, emotions, and body.

Self-acceptance enables us to move beyond our small self, beyond our fractionated, egocentric concerns to put our inner work of transformation in its rightful place of priority. Self-acceptance makes us whole. It enables us to stop wasting energy in inner conflicts and makes that energy available for our true work.

For this week, practice self-acceptance.

60. Stabilizing Attention

As our basic instrument for navigating the waters of the spirit, attention deserves more from us. The first challenge in developing attention consists of stabilizing it. Our undisciplined attention, drawn in a multitude of directions, incessantly wanders and scatters our energies in its wake. If we are our attention, then its instability is our own.

What to do? Train yourself for sustained focus. Most spiritual techniques either develop or depend upon a stable attention.

One excellent method involves counting breaths. Focus your attention on the sensations caused by the breath at the tip of your nose. Bring all your attention into this small region. Mentally count your breaths from one to ten, and then start over at one. Let the counting be light and secondary. Keep the primary focus of your attention on the sensations of the breath at the tip of your nose. Whenever you lose count, start again at one. Practice this until you can stay with the breath continuously for five or six cycles of ten.

Other opportunities for sustained attention arise throughout our day. Notice how your attention tends to wander and work on staying focused on the task at hand.

61. Wrapped in Awareness

Imagine yourself surrounded and suffused by the field of your awareness, like the space outside and in. You find yourself inside this field that serves as a stage for all your physical sensations, all your thoughts, all your emotions, all your sensory experience. But your awareness itself is more than all these, deeper than all its contents.

Sitting still, allowing body to relax and thoughts to subside, notice the silent stage upon which your thoughts arise. Be in contact with that pure consciousness underlying every moment. Intentionally open yourself to this ground of awareness that holds you, that is more profound than all your sensations.

You need not look far, for it is here in you now. If you

can recognize it once, your task becomes to recognize it again and yet again, wrapping yourself in it until living in that awareness becomes your norm.

62. Access to Wisdom

Clarity of mind and heart tends to elude us. The complexities of life confront us with an endless stream of choices, large and small. Unable to see into the future, we often find ourselves tossed about in a sea of unknown probabilities. The most important choices typically remain hidden in the realm of possibilities, unnoticed, untaken. Our thoughts and emotions offer little trustworthy guidance in the difficult decisions. So we wing it or take the easy route and leave untold treasure on the table of time.

Deep within us, beyond our minds, beyond our emotions, lies a source of wisdom. In quiet moments you can look there. Simply and directly turn your attention outside your senses, your body, your emotions, and your thoughts, even outside your awareness, toward that wisdom. Look to that inner wisdom for guidance. Because we easily fool ourselves into confusing some thought or urge with the source of wisdom, we check its promptings against our ordinary common sense, and our notions of morality and acceptability. We then test its pronouncements to see what results they bring in actual life. Little by little we learn to distinguish our inner wisdom from our inner noise.

63. Hands and Feet

Effective spiritual practice must be grounded in our body. Certainly practice extends beyond the body, for example in some types of meditation and prayer. But the persistent blue-collar inner work of actually being present in our body, while not flashy, inexorably leads toward a substantial and transformed spiritual life. So from time to time, we renew our work on the energy body by returning our primary effort to direct contact with physical sensations.

For this week, be in your hands and feet, these marvelous instruments of transportation and action. When we walk, awareness of our feet brings us into the now, into relationship with the Earth, with our body, with our life in this moment. Awareness of our hands offers immediate contact with our acts in the world, be it washing, grooming, typing, tying shoes, dialing a phone, cooking, laying brick, digging, raking, touching, or any of the other myriad functions of our hands.

Starting with awareness of the sensations in our hands and feet, we build a base for sensing the entire energy body.

64. A Wider Context: God's View of the World

Imagine an invisible but substantial body permeating everything. The Will of this body acts through all life in a very special way, the way of freedom. The Great Will endows each human with a portion of Itself, a unique gift of free will. Thus, we simultaneously enjoy our connection with each other through the Great Will, as well as the freedom bestowed upon us as unique individuals.

You can intentionally look at life, at living beings, particularly people, as manifesting the single Great Will to a greater or lesser degree, depending on how that individual chooses to exercise his or her freedom. Regardless of those choices, however, the connection of sharing in the Great Will remains intact. For that reason, evil deeds, the misuse of freedom, are a triple travesty: an affront to the victim, to the perpetrator, and to the unity of God. Acts of kindness, though, reverberate their beneficial influence throughout.

This week, catch a glimpse of this wider context of connection as you see and interact with other people.

65. Just Breathing

At every moment, as long as we live, our breath continues its in and out rhythms. The perpetual cycle of breathing invites us into the present. As presence is the basic food of our spiritual practice, the breath offers a simple inner sustenance in addition to its physical sustenance. The continual movement of the breath supports continuous attention to it.

For this week, we bring our attention to our breath, without changing the breath in any way. Allowing the physical breath to follow its natural course, we simply open our awareness to our breathing. In quiet moments, the breath may fill our entire awareness. We become the breath. Letting the breath breathe itself, our egocentric stance may vanish momentarily. The whole of us simplifies into just breathing.

66. Torso and Head

In our continuing efforts to live in presence through contact with the physical sensations of our whole body, we focus this week on the core of our body: our torso and head. Sensing and presence in the torso and head give us a powerfully stabilizing center. An important interpretation of the term "center" points directly at presence in our body, and particularly in our torso and head.

In working to sense our torso and head, we do not attempt to focus on particular organs, like lungs, liver, and so on. To do so might interfere with their instinctive and vital operations. Rather we work to establish a generalized but strong sensation spread throughout the torso and head. We inhabit this sensation; we reside in our torso and head. Moving and acting from this, our center, offers us a self-renewing and substantial presence, anchored in our real life, in our world.

67. Body Scan

One very useful method, derived from Buddhist sources, for establishing presence through contact with bodily sensations consists of scanning the body with our attention. Imagine a flat plane parallel to the ground. Starting at the top of the head, we slowly move this plane down, becoming aware of the sensations of that portion of the body through which the plane is passing, like an MRI or CT scan.

This plane of attention may reveal "dark" areas of the body where we have no physical sensations. For those regions, we take a few moments to direct our attention and draw the sensitive energy to them. Continuing throughout the body and then repeating the scan from head to feet, enlivens our inner body by smoothing and spreading the sensation. In this way we can work toward an evenly distributed sensation of the whole body. That, in turn, gives us a strong base for presence, awareness, and the ability to respond fully and effectively to life.

For this week, practice scanning your body from head to toe for sensation, taking time to build it up where it is weak.

68. Effort and Non-effort

Our spiritual practice involves a dance between effort and non-effort. On one side we engage in the heavy lifting of repeatedly bringing our attention back to the present, holding ourselves in the here and now, and sensing our body more strongly and completely. On the other, we rest in the simple joy of being fully alive and awake to this moment. On the first side we press ahead, pushing to extend the amount of time we spend in presence. On the second, we gratefully accept the moments of spontaneous awakening in sparkling clarity of mind or unmitigated warmth of heart. On the first side we avidly seek that depth just beyond our grasp, just beyond our mind and heart. On the second, we open our heart simply and directly toward ourselves and those around us. On the first side we pray. On the second we become a prayer.

For this week, notice this dance of effort and non-effort in your own practice. Bring greater vigor to the first and allow more of the second.

69. Aberrations of Responsibility

Of the most important human qualities, responsibility is second only to love. To be fully human, we must be and act responsibly toward ourselves, toward our family, toward society and toward God. One way of growing more responsible lies in seeing our many aberrations of responsibility, on small scales and large.

The worst aberration occurs when we abdicate responsibility altogether, walking away from or ignoring a situation which is rightfully ours to address. In shirking responsibility, we malinger by continually dodging actions meant for us to step up to, sliding toward the easy way out. Procrastination supports and enables shirking.

The flip side of aberrant responsibility involves inappropriately grasping responsibility not rightfully ours. One type meddles in other people's business. Another imposes their own views unnecessarily, like the parents or teachers who cannot, even when appropriate, let go of their growing children and students, to let them learn and mature through their own decisions and mistakes.

All aberrations of responsibility emanate from self-seeking, assigning priority to the wrong place. For this week, notice your own relationship to your responsibilities.

70. The Long View

As the frequency and severity of terrorist attacks increases, the world grows smaller. Events thousands of miles from our homes strike us as proximate and immediate. Yet our haven in the spiritual life, if not sterile, cannot be divorced from the world. What to do? This global complexity does not permit simple answers. Nor is the call of our own evolution compatible with naïve and unthinking adoption of others' attitudes toward the world's ills. Spiritual evolution, both individual and for the human race as a whole, requires time, a long time. Our view of right action in the present, though constrained by the scope of our own knowledge, can best be formed in the context of the long-term future.

For this week, contemplate some aspects of the world situation. Reflect upon the near and long-term possibilities for a better future, and the path toward that vision. Review and perhaps reformulate your assumptions and opinions in light of these deliberations. Reconsider your own role in the present toward building that future, toward creating a positive legacy.

71. Choose Again

The choices we make, or fail to make, determine the course of our life, externally as well as inwardly. We often face moments of choosing our inner direction: shall I continue to nurture my anger at what was said to me? Shall I continue eating even though my stomach is full? Shall I drift along in this pleasant daydream or return to working at sensing my body? Shall I continue rushing through the day in the shallows, or extend my keel into the depths of presence in my journey through time?

Our inner life, our own evolution depends entirely on the myriad of choices confronting us moment-to-moment. The choice of developing our soul, letting go of identifications, acting responsibly, inhabiting our body, embracing our presence, and opening our heart can only be made by each of us individually, by you and me, each day, each hour, each passing minute of our limited life.

Every positive choice to engage in spiritual practice creates further opportunities. For this week, choose to practice, again and again.

72. Deep Relaxation

Deep and thorough relaxation offers many benefits. It counteracts the accumulating tensions and stresses of life. It supports physical, emotional, and mental health. It refreshes and rejuvenates. It prepares us to engage fully in life, but with more enjoyment and less attachment and identification. It conserves the inner energies we need for our spiritual practice. It allows the energies we develop through inner work to find their appropriate place and settle into our being.

The first level of relaxation consists of a simple settling in, sitting here noticing the stream of inner events: thoughts, muscular tensions, labored breathing, etc. As you sit, just being with yourself, transitions come in their own time. If the breathing starts out labored, at some point it may abate into quiescence.

Next, the muscles release their excess tensions. At this stage, fatigue or other physical problems may intensify as your body/mind drops its defenses against experiencing its true state. Just sitting, watching quietly and letting go, with no agenda, offers healing and renewal. Eventually the fatigue dissipates. You feel refreshed and ready to enter meditation proper or to return to your daily activities with a new sense of calm presence.

Continuing, your thoughts and emotions relax, without you being attached or identified with their content. You enter, or rather become, the stillness between thoughts. You let go further, not trying to do or change anything. Spontaneous upwellings of energies may occur of their own accord. Still you relax into being, and not doing. You relax into complete peace.

For this week, find some time each day to practice deep relaxation.

73. Daily Prayer

Prayer can open a gap in our walls of self-centeredness. In praying, we address the Transcendent through the direct channel between the Divine and our innermost self. We may legitimately pray from our surface desires and fears. Or we may delve beneath our ordinary thoughts and emotions toward faith, harbinger of the Divine. Regardless of the level of our prayer, in the act of praying the sacred calls to us.

Daily repetition gradually deepens our relationship with the Holy One. So we pray with our heart and soul. We pray with the whole force of our being, sending the rarefied substance of our prayers up toward the Divine, even as the very act of praying purifies our heart.

For this week, pray every day.

74. Success and Failure

Egoism and self-centeredness work in the subtlest fashion, employing an endlessly adaptable variety of approaches to maintain our illusion of separateness. One important source for this lies in our perceived failures and successes. When we fail, or feel that we have failed, egoism leads us to consider ourselves to be failures, incompetent, stupid, perhaps even worthless. When we succeed, egoism leads us to inwardly preen, swell with pride, feel invincible, and consider ourselves to be better than others. And then we tell ourselves and others our story of failure or of success. In either scenario we buy into allowing our self-worth and our own reality to be defined by events external to us, by the feedback we receive from the world.

Sorrow for and learning from our mistakes, as well as natural satisfaction in our accomplishments, need not strengthen our self-centeredness. But the great temptation of the poles of success and failure consists of ascribing them to our illusory self, feeling that it is I who have succeeded or failed, praising or blaming myself, and thereby perpetuating my misguided belief in this mirage of a self.

Neither great success nor continuing failures can fundamentally alter who I am. This is a hard lesson taught by experience. And since most of us never achieve what we define as great success, it remains an unattained goal, forever enticing us to look exclusively to externals for meaning and purpose. Furthermore, the ever-present marketing machine of modern culture continually promotes unquestioning enchantment with externals.

In Sufism, the first stage of liberation occurs when the seeker ceases to hope for or expect ultimate satisfaction through externals. We need not, however, shun the marketplace altogether. On the contrary, like in the last of the Ten Oxherding pictures of Zen, we can enter life with vigor and even seek success. But all the while we know that our reality is neither diminished nor enhanced by the results we do or do not achieve. Only our spiritual inner work, our striving for integrity and excellence, and our acts of creativity and kindness can enhance who we really are.

For this week, notice your relationship to success and failure.

75. Renewal: Deciding to Work

Our inner work tends to reach a plateau, corresponding to our level of being. This comfort zone defines how much we practice, how often we enter presence, and the intensity, breadth, and depth of our inner work. Some days we wax stronger, other days we weaken, but the ups and downs fall within our typical range. After a time, we realize that this plateau has transformed into a rut, binding our efforts and inner standards of practice.

To reach a new level of practice, we must work more frequently, more intensely, and more continuously. How to come to this? No one can give it to us. There is no hidden secret in this regard. It simply requires that we decide to work at presence always, that we reach into our own depths and find the determination to practice, to give the inner life of the spirit priority over all our daydreams, fantasies, escapes, indulgences, indignation, outrage, laziness, opinions and other distractions.

Periodically, we need to renew our inner work, to become more serious about living rightly, about serving truly, about not wasting our life. Though others can help remind us, the effective impulse can only be found within. For this week, go there and decide for yourself. How will you live this precious life, this week, this day, this hour?

76. Consuming

The all-consuming fire of greed can color our whole existence. When we conflate what we want with what we truly need, the ravenous flames render satisfaction transitory at best. Looking toward that next bite of chocolate cake, we fail to taste the one in our mouth. The siren song of advertising breeds discontent. That perfectly functional five-year old car starts to look long in the tooth. Our comfortable home pales next to images of lavishly appointed mini-mansions. Suddenly our paycheck seems too small. We question the wisdom of settling for less than we might otherwise get.

For this week, explore the difference between what you need and what you want. How much of your life do you devote to getting what you do not need?

77. Wishful Thinking

We all need realistic goals and the hope of attaining them. But our ego tends to turn this upside down, creating unachievable goals toward which we make no real effort. So in the place of steady efforts toward real goals, we indulge in wishful thinking, daydreaming about how one day our boat will come in, how the big stroke of luck will transform our life in a blazing moment of glory. In the meantime, we plod our way through our daily rounds, secretly nurturing unrealistic dreams, and waiting for it all to just happen. Such wishful thinking paralyzes us, substituting an imaginary life for our actual life, and preventing us from achieving what we could.

For this week, observe the role of wishful thinking in your life.

78. Buying Presence

A wide range of purchases enters our lives, from necessities to luxuries, from the essential to the frivolous, from morning until night. Each transaction calls forth a process that may include research, comparisons, visualization, calculation, projection, choice and decision-making. We may consider the degree of necessity, how much to spend, what to buy, how to pay for it, what brand, color, style, and size. The modern market economy produces such a cornucopia of goods and bombards us with such an onslaught of advertising that, except for routine buys, purchasing decisions consume a good deal of our energy and attention. With some of this attention we can work to become aware of ourselves in the process leading up to each purchase.

The whole of this culminates in the moment of the transaction. We write the check, swipe the card, count out the cash, or click on "Buy." We can turn this event to account for our inner work. Whenever we buy something, we can make that act a reminder to be present, to work at sensation in that very moment of transaction. We experience the actual touch of the pen, or the plastic, or the cash, or the mouse click. We notice our emotional state, be it harried, excited, anxious, relieved, satisfied, generous, or neutral. We maintain presence as we take possession of our purchase and move on.

Presence in buying can open a new window into our inner world and a new impetus for spiritual practice.

79. Shared Joy

You meet someone who seems on top of the world with everything going for them. Luck, health, happiness, fortune, talent and romance all meeting at once in him or her. How do you feel in response? Or an acquaintance has some wonderful event happen in their life and informs you of the good news. How do you feel? Do you start to pick it all apart, looking for the holes and gaps? Do you tell yourself that it's all temporary and that they will surely be brought back down eventually? Are your congratulatory comments hollow? Do you secretly begrudge them their happiness, while inwardly criticizing them?

Seeing such attitudes at work in ourselves reminds us of our pettiness and self-centeredness. But seeing those inner reactions also loosens their grip on us and opens the door to freedom from them, toward allowing ourselves to share another person's joy. Cultivating a benevolent emotional response sympathetic to others' happiness pierces the shell of our egoism and works against our envy and jealousy.

For this week, notice your thoughts and emotions in responding to another's happiness. Allow yourself to feel that person's good fortune, to share their joy, even if just for a moment.

80. Review & Resolve

From time to time, it behooves us to take stock of our situation, to see where we are and where we're going. At the New Year or our birthday, for example, we can look back on the past year, or even the past several years, and reassess. What have I accomplished in the past year? What have I avoided that I should have addressed? What are my goals and what actions have I taken toward achieving them?

How is my inner work? Am I in a rut or a plateau? Do I need a new approach? Do I still blindly react in kind to anger, rudeness, or criticism? Is my spiritual practice static or does it have an inner dynamism? Has my being grown this year? Have I worked as much as I could or have inner laziness and lassitude dominated me? What are my possibilities?

Spend some time, at least an hour, contemplating such questions, contemplating your recent life, inner and outer. Make a realistic assessment and look toward how you can best create the future you wish for. Make a resolution for the coming year, a resolution not so easy as to be of little value and not so difficult as to be beyond your reach, a resolution that will exercise your will and stretch your being in a meaningful way.

81. Potential

We define ourselves by our patterns, by how we act and think, by the routines of our daily environment. We get up, brush our teeth, read the paper, eat breakfast, go to work, come home, eat dinner, and so on, day after day. The pattern extends also to our inner life, to the level of our inner work. Beneath these patterns of our life, our potential remains hidden.

What is possible for me? What is my highest potential? How can I work toward achieving it? Can I do more, inwardly or outwardly? Have my patterns become ruts, entrapping me in my personal mediocrity? How can I step into a new day? How can I make more of the patterns I live in?

82. Back in the Body

Without regular work at presence in our body, our spirituality tends to lose its steadiness, maturity, and reality. Can you imagine trying to develop your soul without having a body? But the life of our body is limited, defining the length of our opportunity to practice while in this world of space and time. Of course, our growing soul transcends our physical presence. However, the development of soul arises out of our body, step by step.

And the first, basic, and continuing step consists of sensing and inhabiting our body as deeply, as often, and as long as possible. Sensing this body grounds us in the present. That matters because the whole spiritual reality can only be accessed through this present moment. So regardless of how long we have practiced and how far we have come, the work on continuing contact with the energy of the body remains important. The energy body offers the first threshold toward the spiritual heights. The work of sensing lies within our possibilities and is a necessity for us if we wish to deepen our soul.

So from time to time, even as we seek to enter the spiritual, we come back to the body, to review, assess, and renew our work on sensing, on the energy body.

83. Being Yourself

Who am I? This small question leads to layer after layer of mystery and revelation. It subsumes all the important questions framing and defining life. Its answer would reveal all. Yet without knowing the whole answer, without knowing who I am, we can still be more or less ourselves.

In the spiritual pursuit, we move toward being more ourselves. The most basic approach to being ourselves requires that we actually inhabit our own body. Who is here? Who lives in my body? Who is reading these words? We sometimes materialize as this indefinable and elusive "I" that lives here. But more often we do not appear, we do not inhabit this body. Rather, a haphazard, habitual and motley collection of impulses, thoughts, reactions, and desires lives as if they were who we really are.

Some modern psychologists hold that conscious will is an illusion. This correctly assesses our usual in-the-moment incarnation as an unrelated bag of impulses and the rest. But when we feel ourselves to be wholly present, when we feel ourselves to be the tangible agent behind our actions, the source of presence, choice, and decision, we stand closer to the answer to "Who am I?"

For this week, notice where you stand in relation to who you are.

84. Passivity

The Sufi Master asked, "What is meditation?"
The student replied, "Waiting for God."
The Master said, "Can you meditate on God when you have not seen Him? You may wait for God to show Himself to you for 1000 years — with no result."

Passivity of heart and soul shackles us. If we bide our time while life passes, we will grow old in years but not in wisdom. Spiritual practice demands even more of us than does the practice of a musical instrument or an art: a wholehearted commitment expressed in active, continual and intensive efforts of presence, of reaching beyond ourselves, of service and kindness. Despite the fact that we rarely achieve the gold standard of continuity and intensity in practice, we do not shrink from it, we keep it before us as our goal, we see ourselves in relation to it, and we work to approach it. We assess and adjust our inner work every day.

Notwithstanding the need for an active approach, the path also encompasses acceptance. We distinguish between passive and accepting, between laziness and openness, between apathy and the passion of hope and faith. Some times call us to receive and submit, while others call for passionate inner and outer activity. But the slothful passivity of putting off our inner work leads to more of the same.

For this week, notice the degree to which passivity dominates your inner life.

85. Persistence

Persistence underpins our most significant endeavors. This holds as true in the spiritual path as it does in other pursuits. Indeed, in spiritual practice persistence is the key, secret ingredient, the will that enables the whole process to move forward.

We can view persistence in two ways. First, persistence means continuing to practice despite obstacles, difficulties, and failures. We encounter an enormous range of difficulties along the path, such as destructive physical habits and emotional patterns that drain our energies and spend our precious time wastefully. Persisting, we learn to forgo dissipation and maintain our practice. Doubts can sidetrack us. Persisting, we accept the presence of our recurring doubts and we practice nevertheless. The normal ups and downs of living can leave us less able to practice in the down cycles and less interested during the high times. Persistence means remembering that all things pass, that the ups become downs and vice versa, and practicing through it all.

The second type of persistence involves continuing to practice in all relevant time scales. On the shortest scale of human time, we practice moment-to-moment. We stay present for this step, for this breath, and then stay for the next. In praying we maintain our intended attitude, our prayerful emotional and mental posture, our attention to the prayer, moment-to-moment. When we lose our presence, we just start again.

On the scale of minutes, we form our intention for a period of meditation or prayer and carry it through the allotted time, reinvigorating our effort of heart, mind, and attention as necessary.

On the scale of hours, we practice during all parts of the day, not just at formal times set aside for spirituality. Presence and the service of inner work always await us.

On the scale of days, we renew our practice daily. We engage a weekly cycle of practice, perhaps with prolonged periods of formal practice on weekends.

On the scale of weeks, we observe special extended periods of practice such as Lent, Ramadan, the Omer, or spiritual retreats.

On the scale of months, we notice how the seasons each afford a particular tone for our inner work. Perhaps we see a renewal in the Fall, a movement inward in Winter, a reassessment in the Spring, and a constancy in Summer.

On the scale of years, we engage in spiritual practice as our open-ended, gradually evolving, lifelong pursuit.

On the scale of our lifetime, we leave a legacy of our work, inner and outer, to benefit future generations.

For this week, persist in your spiritual practice.

86. Islands: Separation and Longing

Experiences, perhaps "accidental," of a deeper state, and intimations that the spiritual realm actually exists, draw us forward. We see our usual mode of living and recognize its greatest shortcoming: our chronic separation from what matters most, from each other and from the Divine. We live as islands in a sea of roiling waters. At the surface our isolation appears insurmountable. Yet we need only learn to look toward the depths to realize that our own little island actually connects with all the other islands. Our separation is an illusion, since we actually arise from the same source.

An important aspect of the path consists in not closing our eyes to the fact of separation, to see full-sober how we remain cut off from what matters most. To feel this separation, in its full impact, naturally arouses our longing, even our determination to find our way to the Real, to do what's possible toward that in this and every moment.

For this week, notice the island-like qualities of your personal world.

87. The Next Rung

If I believe that time alone will deepen my being, bring love and wisdom to my heart and mind, and liberate my soul, I will either be disappointed or deluded. Freedom comes at a price, whether the outer blessings of a free society or the inner blessings of the spirit. On the path to the sacred that price includes the ever-deepening effort to practice continuously and wisely. On this count we dwell on plateaus, levels of comfort with our inner work. Ask yourself what it will take for you climb out of your current plateau to reach the next rung on Jacob's ladder. Do you need to practice for longer periods or more often or in a different way? Inner evolution will not come from inner stasis and complacence. I cannot just wait for grace; I must prepare a place for it to enter. What will it take to change my level of being?

88. small self and Great Self

How can God act through me, how can I serve truly, if "I" am busy serving myself, concerned exclusively with my own well-being? God's Will does not operate by overpowering our individual will, but only in cooperation with our surrendered will. When I am angry at something done to me, or when I am worried about what might happen to me, or when I am taken by a desire for more, my will focuses on self-referential obsessions. My self-engaged will usurps the place where I could be engaged with the Great Self of God, Which includes us all in our uniqueness. The arrow of engagement can point either to self or to Self, but not both at the same time.

Notice how your interest and passion habitually and continually flow toward yourself and perhaps against others. See this at work, in particular moments, and make the effort, the instantaneous decision to let go of your concern with your self, to make way for the Great Self.

89. Daily Goals

We need clarity in our practice, clarity about our practice. For example, if we sit in meditation for a certain period each day, this is definite and clear. At the end of the sitting we know we have engaged in an unambiguous piece of inner work. But what about the rest of the day? Does our inner work melt into the fog of the daily routine, losing itself in the murky confusion of our associative thinking, reactive emotions, and our habitual, unmindful activities and distractions? At the end of the day, can we assess with confidence how much we have practiced that day?

One way to cut through this morass consists of setting ourselves a particular goal of practice for the day. These daily goals can and should vary. Examples include doing some inner work like sensing or practicing presence a specific number of times in the day, which we actually count, or attempting to notice and let go of anger today, or to be aware of the tone of our voice today, or to actually taste our food today, and so on.

The important thing is to be very clear at the beginning of the day, what your inner work will be. Then in the evening review and evaluate your practice for that day.

90. Shaping Your Inner Life

Unless we bring some intention to the matter, our inner life goes almost entirely in a haphazard and automatic fashion, often with unpleasant results. Rudderless, our mind and heart falls prey to each passing whim, buffeted by the winds of impinging events, at the mercy of habitual emotional reactions and thought patterns. This is no way to live, yet we accept it as our norm. To shape our inner life, to give it a direction takes work, persistent, subtle, and intelligent work. If we abdicate our responsibility for this work, then we stay in our automatic, reactive jungle of thoughts, emotions, and impulses.

To climb out of this morass, we set our feet on the spiritual path, in a day-to-day, moment-to-moment, year-after-year engagement with the practices of our chosen way, such as presence, sensation, prayer, kindness, meditation, and letting go. And we take it seriously, for example by working at sensation throughout the day. Pliant, yet steady, we persevere. Over time, we find more meaning, joy, creativity, and love seeping into our inner world, as we allow ourselves to be shaped by the path.

For this week, renew your practical efforts to shape your inner life, rather than being shaped by its erratic impulses and its chronic repetitiveness.

91. Prayer in a Time of War

In wartime, some people die while others suffer terribly without dying. Regardless of our own view of the rightness or wrongness of a particular war, we face the question of what can I do to help, as a person who aspires to follow a spiritual path. One way we can help is by directing our prayers toward the benefit of those who are dying and/or suffering. The inner world offers a venue in which we can provide effective help by the quality and direction of our prayers.

During war, take some time each day to direct your prayers to the aid of combatants and non-combatants suffering the effects of the war.

92. Inner Work in a Time of War

Regardless of their views of the justifiability or necessity of any particular war, everyone agrees that war causes great suffering. Even those not directly affected by the war feel its anger, hatred, fear, anxiety, outrage, hysteria, or an irresistible fascination with it. All of this pollutes the emotional atmosphere. If in the midst of this raging storm, some people continue or even redouble their spiritual practice, they help create an antidote to the destructive tone of the times. By relinquishing our own anger and fear, our anxiety and blame, we become the bearers of inner peace and compassion, helping clear the poisoned atmosphere that we all share. Transforming the raging emotional energies released by war, we turn them, through our inner work, into a force for presence and kindness.

93. Moving With and From Sensitive Energy

Contact with our body serves as the most basic and valuable of spiritual practices, providing us with a platform to live in the present moment. Bodily contact comes through sensation, awareness of the sensitive energy in the body. Sitting still, we may find it relatively easy to sense our body. A more difficult but invaluable practice involves sensing our body in movement, moving with and from sensation. This extends our presence into more of our daily activities.

One way to start is to move deliberately and slowly with full awareness of bodily sensation, for example by slow walking. We can practice this during times we set aside for meditation. After establishing that taste of moving with and from sensation, we can extend it to normal-speed activities throughout the day.

For this week, practice moving with and from sensation.

94. When Is "I" Substantial?

We say and think "I" numerous times every day. Usually it simply, and somewhat vaguely, denotes either our body or our personality. As such, the word "I" has no more weight than words like "car," "bread," or "tree." In fact, if we examine closely what we mean by "I," we find no definite meaning at all. On some occasions, though, when we say or think "I," it has real substance, the force of our will, behind it.

For this week, notice how you use the word "I." See what it would mean to have the weight of your full presence engaged in saying "I."

95. Leaning Forward and Falling Back

Any given moment of presence passes all too quickly as we fall out of the now. Too much of the time, we anticipate the future or dwell on the past in such a way that we abandon the present. When we walk or jog, for example, we typically lean forward, inwardly, toward the next step or toward our destination. But we could foresee and plan for the future or consider the past while remaining fully rooted in our body, in this one moment.

For this week, notice how you slide into the past or future, unknowingly and unintentionally. Work to create a new equilibrium centered in the present.

96. The Holy Day

Every major religion designates special days for worship and observance. Several religions have such a Sabbath each week. Choose one of the days of the week as the day for you to reinvigorate and deepen your inner work, as the day for more concerted and continuous efforts of presence and prayer. Such a day can light up your whole week. Perhaps you will choose the day corresponding to your religion: Friday for Muslims, Saturday for Jews, or Sunday for Christians. Make this your sacred day on which to seek a more profound relationship with the spirit. You might incorporate extra periods of meditation or prayer, reading texts of the spirit, a renewed attention to being kind, some creative work, and other inner or outer actions that open your heart and nurture your soul. As the sacred text tells us: we remember the day and keep it holy.

97. The Boundaries of Awareness

The source of the spiritual lies hidden beyond our consciousness. In meditation we can become explorers of the inner world, seeking to discover the limits of our awareness and the realms outside those limits. Beneath our sensory perceptions, beneath our thoughts and emotions, we find the pure awareness of consciousness. Delving beneath the stillness of consciousness itself, through a combined emptying of ourselves and reaching beyond, we can open to a deeper source, to a potent energy, to the Heart of hearts. And our exploration need not end there, but can lead us toward Ultimate.

The key to all this rests in our attitude. Can we bring our commitment, interest, investigation, and explorer's mind to bear in seeking a more profound understanding and experience, through plumbing the depths within the silence?

98. Satisfaction and Dissatisfaction

To what degree are you satisfied with your life, or even with your day? What brings you satisfaction? Are you ever completely satisfied, utterly content? How long does that last?

From our ordinary perspective, this world we inhabit never reaches perfection. Even the most satisfying event, person, or object always has feet of clay. Nothing in time lasts forever, everything decays eventually, and everyone has shortcomings.

These facts, however, do not in themselves explain our dissatisfaction, which derives from our rejection of what is and our desire for something other than what is. Dissatisfaction emanates from our attitude of not being satisfied with our life as is, wanting more or less of something or someone. That non-acceptance in turn arises from non-presence. Experiencing the fullness of this moment opens us to acceptance and deep satisfaction. Non-acceptance, on the contrary, pushes aside any possibility of inner peace or of love.

From a deeper perspective, this world embodies perfection, even in its imperfections. The essence of this moment reaches beyond time and decay. The spiritual path leads us toward a sense of appreciation and love that rises above the imperfections, a sense bestowed on us by the Unconditioned Source of Perfection.

For this week, look at the role of satisfaction and dissatisfaction in your life. How do these factors and attitudes drive your actions and responses? Does your work at presence make a difference in this regard?

99. In the Fog

We live in a fog of thoughts and emotions, walking through life mesmerized by the continuous stream of mental chatter, the ongoing inner commentary and reactions. Instead of being inside this fog, can we find a way to live so that the fog is inside of us? Can we live in the contextual consciousness where we see the fog calling to us, without succumbing to its siren sound?

For this week notice the inner fog. Notice times when you have been lost in it. Bring yourself strongly into presence, so that you can see the mental fog without being the mental fog.

100. Balance of Body, Heart, and Mind

To be fully human means, in part, developing and harmonizing our body, heart, and mind. Most of us live unbalanced lives, operating primarily through only one of these, with one or both of the others playing a minor role. Perhaps our feelings lie dormant except in occasional reaction. Or we neglect our body and its true needs, say by merely feeding its appetites while shunning physical activity. Maybe we abandon our minds to random associations and daydreams, while avoiding study and directed thinking. Our body, heart, and mind live separate lives, pulling us in at least three different directions.

Through the practice of presence we can awaken, balance, and unify our body, heart, and mind, making us whole in our individual, unique spirit.

For this week, notice where you live, whether in body, heart, or mind. Notice the relationships, or lack thereof, among your three major parts.

101. Hidden Treasure

Treasure hunters use every clue they can find to guide them toward their goal. Maps, the last known whereabouts of the treasure-laden vessel, and the testimony of witnesses together form a puzzle that the treasure seeker attempts to decipher. Some maps and testimonies may be reliable, while others offer only partial truths or even whole-cloth fabrications.

Our spiritual pursuit also has it maps and witnesses. The great religions and paths each include maps, simple and elaborate, of the spiritual realms. Saints and seers throughout the ages leave behind descriptions, direct and allegorical, of the sacred landscape. Nevertheless, we experience great difficulty attempting to decipher all this guidance, because it speaks in terms so alien to our everyday reality. One fact shines through clearly, though: the spiritual treasure exists and can be found by human beings.

Like the seeker of buried treasure, the spiritual seeker must work with diligence and perseverance, with intelligence and determination, through all kinds of inner and outer weather. Yet the goal of liberation and love, the sacred and Divine, draws us forward, to the extent that we can keep our sights fixed on it.

For this week, remember the spiritual treasure more often. Let the reality of it, though unseen, touch your heart and enliven your practice.

102. Appreciation

Indifference drains all the color from life. We tend to walk through our days with only a minimal contact with the life around us, our hearts encrusted by a ho-hum attitude: been there, done that, seen it all before. But an inescapable truth tells us that our days on this Earth are all too limited; each day we live means one less day left to live. This timeless truth can pierce our crust and soften our heart. We can live differently, relishing each day, each person, each living thing, each experience, and each opportunity. Appreciating our life, appreciating others, we live more fully, more responsibly, and more kindly. The ephemeral in our personal system of values evaporates, leaving behind the eternal values at the core of life.

For this week, notice the extent to which you appreciate your life and the life around you.

103. Debilitating Daydreams

Pleasant daydreams, images playing our mind about winning the lottery or meeting our perfect soul mate or some other personal predilection of the moment, substitute for real life. Such daydreams keep us from taking the actions necessary to reach our goals. Why work for some result when we can simply imagine already having it?

Unpleasant daydreams, dwelling on imagined but unlikely personal calamities, recalling past insults and affronts, watching some imaginary inner drama unfold, also keep us mired in a half-lived life.

Daydreams seem innocent enough, yet they waste our energies and take us away from this moment, diminishing our presence. They keep us tuned to the story in time rather than the timeless present. With our attention drawn into the daydream, we lose contact with the depths that constantly call to us, if we could but listen.

For this week, notice your daydreams and their effect on you.

104. Joy and Pleasure

What is the difference between joy and pleasure? We can best discover their difference with respect to time. Pleasures exist in time, fleeting moments in which one of our appetites or desires temporarily finds satisfaction. With pleasures, the satisfaction does not last. It even turns into its opposite of dissatisfaction or pain as we grasp for more of the pleasure or suffer the consequences of overindulging in it.

Those consequences usually prove costly to both body and soul. Overindulgence in pleasures can harm health of our body. It also weakens our soul by wasting inner energies and channeling our interests and intentions down unprofitable paths.

Joy comes from beyond time. Externally, beauty or kindness can open us to contact with the timeless strata underlying all. Inwardly, deep meditation, prayer and creative acts bring us face to face with the timeless. Either way, joy touches us with a lasting imprint. Later, after the initial burst passes, joy continues to buoy our appreciation of life. That first moment remains with us. Further moments of joy gradually infuse our life with a satisfaction that surpasses any fleeting pleasure, a sense of the rightness of this remarkable universe, a sense of participation in its richness.

Rightfully conducted inner work inevitably leads toward joy.

For this week, notice the difference between pleasure and joy.

105. Push and Pull

We must be active in our inner work: exploring, setting inner goals, staying here in this moment as deeply and frequently as we can manage, making every effort to push our way along the path. This active side of the path is the side that we can do, the side that is up to us and within our purview.

Moments come, though, when we find ourselves pulled along the way, attracted by the Unfathomable, Loving Source of the world. Though we may not see that Source, our push eventually brings us to be open and receptive to Its pull. The Source acts on us, heart and soul, palpably but invisibly, behind the scenes. Certain, often small, events remind us, awakening our hearts to long for reconnection with and service to our Source.

Our primary job is to make the efforts, to push. And in moments of opportunity, to stand ready to open to the pull of the Sacred. But the subtleties of inner work go beyond the polarity of push and pull, active and receptive, toward effortless balance and harmony. At times our practice is actively receptive, as in listening or in certain forms of prayer. At other times we are receptively active as in creative work or in presence. So we learn to navigate the various modes of will in how we approach our inner life.

For this week, push your way along the path and notice how the Source draws you effortlessly on.

106. Pressed Buttons

With the right attitude, life becomes our teacher. Daily living presses our emotional buttons as situation after situation induces us to react with anger, jealousy, fear, indignation, outrage, greed, etc. While emotions can be our strength, more often they drain the precious energies we need for our inner work. When we react without choice, we lose ourselves, our presence, our energy, and our natural joy of living.

Our reactive emotions should alert us to the fact that we are stuck, identified with something. If we see ourselves drawn toward some emotional reaction, can we turn it into an occasion to see more clearly into ourselves and our motivation in that moment? Rather than trying to escape, can we just stand without judgment in the presence of the inner difficulty, allowing it to reveal itself fully to our consciousness? This approach of conscious kindness toward and acceptance of ourselves gradually heals us and conserves our energies for more profitable uses.

For this week, when your emotional buttons are pressed, let them ring an inner bell that reminds you to look deeply and kindly at yourself — just looking, without commentary or judgment.

107. Judging and Criticizing

When others fail to live up to our expectations or cross us in some way, we tend to inwardly judge and outwardly criticize, scold, or insult them. Even if fully justified in our opinions and responses, our lack of compassion nevertheless reinforces the wall separating us from the other person.

Criticism of others may be a habit of our mind. Mental habits of all kinds remain harmless as long as we do not identify with them. But as soon as we claim the critical thoughts as our own, or allow them to claim us, we fall into the world of separation, pushing the other away. Rather than being objectively matter-of-fact in our criticism, we layer on an emotional reaction against the person, as if their faults make them less human.

If instead we simply notice critical, judgmental thoughts as they arise, seeing them as just thoughts, and letting them dissipate, then we find greater opportunity to live in an open acceptance of others as they are and of ourselves as we are.

For this week, notice your critical mind at work and see how it seduces you into emotionally reacting against the other person.

108. Walking Presence

Though the most ordinary and common of activities, walking nevertheless offers a particularly potent opportunity for the work of presence, for several reasons. Often when we walk, we are not engaged in anything else. For example, we are not talking or listening, unless we have a cell phone or iPod at our ear. Furthermore, once set in motion and given direction, our body continues walking with little further input from our intention. This inherent simplicity of walking leaves us enough spare attention to devote to our inner work. We can even utilize the extra energy generated by walking to support our presence. All this applies to short walks of a few dozen steps, and even more to longer walks.

As always, we begin by grounding our awareness in our body. We put our attention on the sensations of our legs, arms, torso, head, and ultimately the whole body, while we walk. We inhabit our inner body of sensation as we walk, staying in contact with our physical body through the sensitive energy. With practice, we can quickly enter whole-body awareness. Keeping our attention in the body channels the excess energy produced by walking into our inner body sensation. We become fully alive, walking.

The key element is to stay engaged. We do not allow the walking to become solely automatic and we do not give ourselves over to the stream of thoughts. We stay fully here, in this body, in this place, taking this step. We allow our body to walk, utilizing its habitual, automatic patterns of movement. But we stay with it. We maintain the experience: "I am walking." The inner action of staying here, in our body as it walks, takes us beneath the continuing flow of thoughts into the stillness of consciousness. Thereby we become walking presence, engaged at multiple levels: our body, our sensation, the pure consciousness, and "I" the walker. We unify these levels; we unify ourselves in the simple act of walking. We walk in wholeness and joy comes naturally.

Although you have a destination, walk as if you had already arrived. As indeed you have arrived, in presence, in this moment, our only moment.

Walking presence provides excellent exercise for body and soul. The same methods work for running/jogging and for other sports and physical activities. But walking may be the easiest because it presents a workable balance between the physical activity and the inner effort of presence, a balance wherein the two sides complement and join each other.

For this week, practice walking presence whenever you walk more than a few dozen steps.

109. Wealth and Poverty: External and Eternal

"It is easier for a camel to go through the eye of a needle, than for a rich man to enter into the kingdom of God."[3]

I have long felt that the privilege of having time for meditation and other spiritual practice is true wealth. Such wealth is available to nearly everyone, but requires the sacrifice of not spending the meditation time on other pursuits. Yes, we can and should multi-task our spiritual practice with our other activities through inner work in the midst of life. But setting aside some time each day exclusively for meditation or prayer remains an indispensable aspect of our path.

Carving out that time, however, from a busy life presents us with a continuing challenge. Life repeatedly questions our priorities, our values. We cannot simply ignore the necessity of providing for the material and emotional needs of ourselves and our families. And that takes time. But with a creative, intelligent, and values-based approach to living, we can remind ourselves to provide not just for our external needs, but also for our eternal needs, for feeding our soul and serving the Divine.

This continuing sacrifice of our time, this spiritual investment, inexorably leads to spiritual wealth, to joy, meaning, satisfaction, generosity, and love. Paradoxically, spiritual wealth actually arises through spiritual poverty, the relinquishing of self-centeredness, of egoism, the inner emptying and opening.

All this clearly does not mean that the materially wealthy person cannot also find spiritual wealth. Examples can be found both in history and among those we have met. The real issue regards what a person holds most dear: God and fam-

3   Matthew 19:24

ily or the number of zeros in his or her net worth. With respect to the path, these values need to translate to actual time spent in spiritual practice. The regular investment of time in meditation and prayer creates our soul, transforms spiritual energies for the Earth, and builds our account in the higher worlds.

For this week, notice how you invest your time.

110. Content and Process

A true leader of society must be a person of vision who sees the big picture and large scale possibilities. Within our own personal domain, within our individual inner world, the responsibility of leadership can only rest with us. But we abdicate our role, remaining stuck in the quagmire of all the petty, banal thoughts and emotions continually coursing through us. As long as we concern ourselves exclusively with the content of our experience, we have no chance of ordering the course of our inner life.

Spiritual practice, while rooted in the content of experience, brings us toward a perspective on the whole, toward seeing our various processes of reaction and identification, toward stabilizing our sensitive energy and standing in consciousness. We work to see thoughts as just thoughts and emotions as just emotions, instead of allowing ourselves to be driven by their content. Letting the stream of sensory and inner experience pass through us, we learn to live on a larger scale, in the energetic and intentional processes. While attending to the details, we also widen our perspective to the whole.

For this week, notice where you stand in regard to the balance between content and process.

111. Perfection and Imperfection

When you look objectively at yourself, you inevitably see numerous shortcomings and imperfections, some minor, some significant. The same holds true as you look at others, friend or foe, family or stranger. Nor does any particular animal or plant reach absolute perfection. The uncertainties and hazards of life reveal the inherent, structural imperfections of the world.

Despite all this, hope remains in us that somehow, somewhere, an uncompromised perfection exists, something we can count on absolutely. But if I cannot look to myself for this, or to the best people I know, or to anything in this world, what then?

There is a source within and beyond our ordinary world, a place of no half-measures. On our side, something always lacks. On the other side, fullness prevails. We discover a degree of freedom when we stop demanding perfection on this side: striving for perfection, yes, but expecting or demanding it, no. Instead, we seek perfection in the only place it can truly exist, in the Divine realm. Here we strive for perfection, emulating the Divine, while there we find it.

For this week, look at your attitudes toward perfection and imperfection.

112. Only This Moment

Although our body can only inhabit this present moment, our mind, heart, and attention continually lean toward the future or fall into the past. Anticipating the future and reliving the past create a ghostly, dreamlike pseudo-existence that draws us away from our only reality: this one moment. At times we even intentionally escape from some unavoidable unpleasantness or boredom by inwardly drifting away. If instead we bring the full force of our intention to being, experiencing, and acting in this one moment, in all its sensory dimensions, we immediately live more deeply and fully. In place of the thinness of the not-now, we discover the richness of this one moment, we discover our real life.

For this week, practice enriching your life by coming back to this one moment, wholeheartedly, whole-bodily, and whole-mindedly.

113. Dignity and Indignation

True dignity flows from presence, warmth of heart, openness, self-acceptance and service to a higher purpose. False dignity flows from egoistic self-centeredness, and presents a demand to the world, an insistence on deference. True dignity naturally elicits the respect of others, while false dignity imposes a requirement of respect from others. True dignity acts with grace and kindness, while false dignity grasps to fill the egoism at its core, egoism of attachment to a virtual, non-existent self.

True dignity remains untouched by insults, while the flag of indignation alerts us to an affront to our false dignity. For this week, notice your indignation and the glimpse of your own egoism it affords.

114. Earning Our Freedom

Inner freedom means liberation from egoism, both the individual ego and the group ego. This freedom, this relinquishing of the burden of self-centered views, this fresh air cannot be given to us. If we are to come to inner freedom, we must earn it. To be able to step outside our myriad attachments and identifications requires a long-term commitment to the spiritual path. Like frequent flyer miles, every effort of presence, kindness, and letting go accrues to our account. As our soul grows more coherent and stable, we move toward that ultimate liberation, toward a direct, "conscious" relationship with the Divine. But these personal efforts cannot be avoided. Even the grace of God cannot liberate us before our soul is properly prepared.

For this week, notice the extent of your spiritual efforts. Half-heartedness will not achieve the goal.

115. Bridging Heaven and Earth

We humans occupy a crucial link in the spiritual ecosystem: our animal nature arising from the Earth and our spark of Divinity descending from Heaven. The role of bridging Heaven and Earth represents our destiny, if we choose to fulfill it. A good bridge carries two-way traffic. And so the spiritually developed person can transform energies from the Earth and offer them upward, while also serving as a bearer of the higher sacred on the Earth.

But what does this mean in practical terms? Outwardly it means right and moral action as embodied in the contemporary Christian phrase: What Would Jesus Do? Our goal of always doing the right thing imposes a demanding self-discipline on us. Yet this is only the beginning of fulfilling our role of bridging

Heaven and Earth. Spiritual practices lead us to create the inner bridge, the true bridge. Prayer and meditation, for example, directly address those inner possibilities.

For this week, see how you can better fulfill your role as a bridge between Heaven and Earth. What does your conscience tell you in this regard?

116. The Eye of the Storm

Life rages all around us: the demands of performing our duties to our body, family, and society; the emotional reactions to untoward events large and small; the thoughts and opinions, debates and arguments; the unexpected episodes, both welcome and unwelcome. Yet it remains possible for us, through our spiritual practice, to step into the eye at the center of the storm of life, while remaining fully engaged.

The step is an inward step, outside of thoughts, outside of emotions, outside of sensory experience, into a place of utter peace and natural joy. This step into pure awareness, pure consciousness releases us, at least temporarily, from all that drags us down. Conversely, by relinquishing attachments and identification, we step toward the freedom to live in the peace at the center of life, at the center of our being.

For this week, look within your awareness and take the step toward peace. First, explore to find the direction. *Where is inner peace?* Then, step into it. Then learn to abide in the eye of the storm.

This is not the end of the road for our spiritual work. In fact, this place of peace, this eye of the storm, is the place where God may draw us close. We return from peace, in peace, to serve.

117. Beyond Stillness

One great and worthy goal of spiritual practice consists of achieving entry into and abiding in stillness. Indeed, liberation, joy, and kindness emanate from the realms of stillness. The peace of stillness removes us from our multifarious attachments to thoughts and emotions and weakens the self-identification and self-reification of egoism. Ready access to stillness marks an important milestone on the path.

But what then? Often, people who reach this stage consider it the ultimate enlightenment and remain on this comfortable and warm plateau of peace. At best, teachers rightly exhort the seeker to bring the fruits of stillness into compassionate action in the world. But even this falls short.

Beyond stillness, the Ultimate Source awaits us, awaits our purification, with the simultaneous promise of Unity and Individuality. So if by looking beyond thoughts, you find yourself in the realm of stillness, look again. Reach beyond the stillness itself toward the utmost Fundamental that constantly creates and sustains and loves this universe.

118. Making It Real

On the spiritual path, actual practice makes the difference. Thoughts, dreams, hopes, plans, intentions, strong feelings, and beautiful ideas do not change our being. Learning to be in touch with our feelings, to feel good about ourselves, or to communicate better does not move us a step closer to transformation. Even the inspiration we draw from a great spiritual teacher does not in itself advance us along the path.

Wholehearted prayer, presence, contact with our body,

meditation, letting go of attachments, acts of kindness: these are the types of actions that deepen our being, form our soul, and open us to the power of grace. Perseverance in such practices actually profits our soul. The rest — dreams, intentions, and so forth — is fluff.

For this week, make your spiritual work real.

119. The Cost of Awakening

Those who recognize the necessity of pursuing spiritual practices such as presence and mindfulness, throughout the day, every day, and who make a serious effort at it, realize how difficult it is to achieve even a small degree of awakening from the continuing thrall of associative thoughts, emotional reactions, and sensory seductions. In the face of this, we all too readily give up or lapse into half-hearted efforts. We think that we cannot awaken. We believe that the ordinary demands of living preclude and overwhelm our chances to be relatively awake, in the spiritual sense, for a substantial portion of our typical day.

Yet this is our life, each precious day of it. Are we condemned to live lost in our inner fog of automatically flowing thoughts and reactions? It would seem to be so.

But if we look again we may see our assumptions and beliefs that this automated, half-lived life is the best we can hope for. It is not. We can live fully present to this moment, and this moment, and this moment. Only we must be willing to pay the price. Unlike the air we breathe, awakening is not free.

Some spiritual teachers say we are all already awake: we only need to realize it. But if you look honestly at your own experience, you cannot escape the fact that such teachings mislead, that you live on the automatic level, hardly in contact with the real world, rarely in substantial presence. We all do have another level within us, a depth in which we could live consciously. However, the intervening layers of fog rarely part, and then only briefly.

But we can cut through and awaken, if we truly decide to do so. It is really that simple and that hard. Given some knowledge of how to work at presence, all it takes is a real and constantly renewed decision to practice. That is the price of awakening. We give up all our notions that we cannot be present, that there are too many distractions and demands, that we have too little energy. We give up our attachment to the flow of associative thoughts and emotional reactions that we falsely take to be who we are. We give up the comforts of being half-alive, not responsible to anything greater than ourselves or perhaps our families. We pay the price by letting go of all the inner baggage that keeps us asleep. And we decide to awaken, to stay in contact with the present, to abide in conscious presence, in every situation.

Do you really want to awaken? If so, what's stopping you? Your inner world is your domain. You can awaken, if you genuinely decide to do so.

120. Diving into the Sacred

An inquisitive attitude of experiment and exploration accelerates our spiritual journey. Our inner world is an unknown territory, but not entirely unknowable. It contains layer upon layer of depth and richness, sources of energy, healing, and renewal, oceans of understanding and compassion, and the ultimate Source of all. Though teachers, teachings, and scripture offer clues, only our own wit, faith, and determination can see us through. To navigate these inner waters, whose surface turbulence masks the underlying peace, we each set sail, like the great explorers of the spirit before us.

Our periods of meditation and contemplative prayer tend to consist of repeatedly practicing the same approach, the same method. This is as it should be, because by continued practice of a method, we gradually master it and allow it to take us into new inner territory. At the same time, actively exploring the spiritual depths, beyond the limits of method, serves a purpose complementary to regular, repeated practice of a technique.

For that active exploration, we dive into the spiritual unknown. Through and past our own center, we search.

Here are sights and sounds and physical sensations. What lies beneath them?

Here are thoughts and images and feelings. What lies beneath them?

Here is the cognizant stillness of pure consciousness. What lies beyond that?

Here am I. What lies through and beyond my I?

Can I somehow invert my I, so that instead of facing outward and instead of occupying the center, I look back through myself, tracing back through my very core, toward the Source from which my I emanates, from which we all emanate? Perhaps along the way I touch the world of sacred light and high energies. Wonderful indeed! But after a time, I continue to dive deeper, to touch or be touched by that One Who is there, to see how I can intentionally become a particle of that Sacred Source, how I can allow, invite, beg that Sacred Source to be who I am, how I can utterly let go of every aspect of myself to become that Sacred Source. I dive and dive deeper. And it is no longer I who dive. There is just the diving and the hope and the search.

Toward the end of our sitting practice of meditation or prayer, we can find great benefit in spending five or ten minutes diving into the sacred, plumbing the spiritual depths. This is not simply another spiritual technique, for it has no boundaries and no particular form — just a direction of depth, which at present for us remains only vaguely defined and understood. But that's the purpose of spiritual exploration: to seek beyond the limits of what we know, to seek out the Ultimate.

For this week, dive into the Sacred.

121. Scaling Up

Life forces us to focus on the immediate, the short-term. Our present moment stays circumscribed with nearly all our attention narrowed to the scale of minutes or hours or days. Even if we fill in our calendars with events planned weeks or months ahead, we take little or no thought or attention for the long-term. On rare occasions we might consider time scales as long as our own lifetime or even the lifetime of our children. But that's as far as it goes in time.

Our spatial neighborhood has a similarly circumscribed extent. We consider our house, our place of work, perhaps our block and the city we live in. Except in extreme cases, we rarely take into our heart our state or nation; only looking at how they affect us.

To enhance our life and our spirit, we can change perspective, enlarge our here and now. If this change is only an intellectual exercise, then it has little effect. But we can work toward enlarging our vision and our concern, both spatially to encompass the Earth and temporally to encompass the vast sweep of the past and future of life on the Earth. This grand scale can open us to an entirely new attitude toward life, toward asking what role we might play as a small, but unique and intelligent, particle in the majestic stream of life's evolution. As a byproduct, our identification with the hurry and worry of life may weaken and allow us to live at ease with our neighbors and ourselves.

For this week, work at scaling up the context in which you live.

122. The Petty and the Grand

We spend far too much time and energy concerned with small-minded, self-centered pettiness. Every little thing takes us, from the hurried and discourteous driver to the distracted retail clerk, from the coworker who forgets to consider us to the spouse who doubts our infallibility. Any little thing said or done in our presence may at any time set us off into inner turmoil. We give ourselves up far too easily to the unimportant, losing our opportunities for presence, purpose, and kindness.

Our spiritual practices can help lift us out of petty concerns by giving us a larger perspective, a stronger presence, and a surer hold on what does matter. Conversely, lifting our concern out of the petty must be one of our spiritual practices. Time spent in meditation or prayer quickly evaporates if we descend into quaking over trivialities. Our grand purpose in life vanishes when we heed our egoistic impulses. Our heart of kindness shrivels when we elevate our reactive emotions beyond their true place.

For this week, work to distinguish the truly significant from the insignificant. Notice your moments of pettiness and by contrast allow yourself the peace and space to open to the grandeur.

123. Emerging from the Stream

If we wake up in the midst of our life, we see that we have been carried along with our inner stream of thoughts and emotions, hopes and fears, daydreams and opinions, reactions and disconnection. This swiftly flowing stream enthralls us and provides us with a false identity: "This is who I am. This is what I think. This is what I feel. This is what I want."

But it is all a sham nevertheless, a hoax perpetrated on us by a culture that knows no better. Our real self does not lie in the swirling, foaming surface of life. To approach who we really are, we need to open to consciousness, to the depth of the stream, to the silent, contextual awareness that we share with all.

This may sound far away from our daily life, but it is not. It is right here, now, surrounding us and penetrating our every cell, supporting our every perception. We may glimpse consciousness in the gap between our thoughts, in our quiet moments. Through meditation we can steep ourselves in the stillness, so that we may recognize consciousness and live in its peace throughout our days. In consciousness, our narrow, false sense of self dissolves and we open our hearts to the great world of which we form both part and whole.

For this week, work to extricate yourself, at least momentarily, from identification with the stream of thoughts and emotions continually flowing through your awareness.

124. Inhabiting Our Life

If we were to honestly assess our life, we would see that our days pass largely without our real participation. How much of your day do you feel yourself to be present? How often can you honestly say, "I am here." Not that just my thoughts and daydreams are here, along with my aches and pleasures, my emotions weak and strong, and my habits, but me being here in the midst of all these inner and outer events.

As you sit reading these words, bring yourself here, come into contact with your body, your eyes, your mind and ask, "Who is reading this?" "Is it just my body and mind doing the reading, or am I reading this? For this one moment, I can inhabit my body, my life! I can feel myself being here, present, alive."

Inhabiting our body through sensation helps us come toward presence. Being in our consciousness, the context of all experience, brings us into the realm of presence. But to actually be present means that "I am" here. This "I am here" is not some far off, high spiritual experience reserved only for monks and nuns and other special people. Through your attention and your own choice, you can, at any time, at this time, cut through all the wheels turning within you, and be here, really be here. When you are here, you know it, in a simple and direct way. Then by contrast you can recognize that in the immediately preceding moments you were not, you were only half-alive. There was only a haphazard collection of automated processes of thought, emotion, movement, and perception occupying your organism, owning you.

For this week, work at coming fully into presence.

125. Where Does My I Come From?

Once we begin to be able to work at presence, to be present, to understand and know the taste of presence, new questions naturally arise. Notably, we may wonder who we really are. Am I out here, an independent unit of consciousness, related to the rest of the world only through my body, through its needs and its genetic makeup? Certainly that's how it usually feels: that I am inwardly isolated but able to reach out and connect. I am myself. No one else is me and I am not anyone else. And up to a certain level, this holds true.

But delve deeper into yourself and a different picture begins to emerge. First, you start to see your own boundaries as artificial, that you are not so utterly separate from others. We share something in the very core of who we are. We can, for example, have an intuition, a perception of what it is like to be each other. We see our common essence of being human, being aware, being ourselves.

Looking deeper still, we ask what is that core that we share? What is that core of who I am? By surrendering through and beyond our own most basic sense of ourselves, into and behind our own I, we discover a hint of what truly unites us all, an intimation of the Source, of the great Will that sustains the universe.

If we look toward where our attention comes from, we are led toward our I. And if we look toward where our I comes from, we are led toward the ineffable, silent, active spirit.

For this week, look as deeply as you can into and beyond yourself.

126. Owning Our Destructive Emotions

The progress of our inner life depends in part on creating a vessel in ourselves to contain energies. The first task in this regard is to discover the ways we waste energy. Then we work to plug those leaks, to conserve energy. The most obvious drain, and the easiest to work on, comes from unnecessary tension in our body.

But another and more potent energy drain lurks within all the destructive emotions that prey on us. These emotional reactions not only waste energy, but also twist our will down unwholesome paths. Psychologists, spiritual teachers, and others develop ways to help us deal with our destructive emotions, usually based on increasing our awareness of these emotional processes in us. As awareness increases, self-acceptance, understanding of root causes, and letting go become possible.

However, the crux of our problem with emotional reactions lies in the way we ascribe their cause to people or other factors outside of us. We shirk responsibility for our reactions, blaming them on others or on our "situation." If instead, we realize that someone else, or even we ourselves on a different day, might respond quite differently to the same event, then we can begin to own our unwholesome emotions, to see that they arise from our own conditioned patterns. If we see that the cause of some destructive emotion lies within ourselves, we then have a greater possibility of choosing to let it go. As long as I think that he or she made me angry, I will nurture that grudge and resentment. But as soon as I see that the anger in me is mine, not his, not due to him, but due to my own habitual emotional pathways, it becomes palatable for me to choose not to perpetuate this uncomfortable and wasteful state in myself.

For this week, work at owning your emotions.

127. Unification

A fragmented and contentious collection of parts pervades our life. Competing desires pummel us. We want more money, but not a second job. We want more cake, but not more weight. We want to practice piano, but not lose TV time. We want time with our family, but also time to earn money.

Conflicting emotions confuse us. We get angry at someone we love. We fear heights but enjoy the views. We envy another's good fortune, but admire them nevertheless. We want love and friendship, but fear rejection.

Our thoughts and opinions lack consistency. We agree with the latest Op-Ed column, even though it directly contradicts what we believed yesterday. Two well-reasoned but opposing arguments leave us befuddled. We believe, and yet are skeptical.

A deeper layer of conflict emerges in our opinions about ourselves. We hate certain aspects of ourselves: our shortcomings and weaknesses, our lacks and fears, our bodily imperfections, our naiveté, ignorance, and slowness, our distractedness, selfishness, and more.

Can we heal these inner divisions? Self-unification requires first that we work to extend the range and subtlety of our awareness to see the mass of inner contradictions that populates our psyche. This includes work at sensing our body, awareness of emotions as emotions, and seeing our thoughts as thoughts. It includes becoming aware of both our negative and our inflated views of ourselves.

Self-unification also requires self-acceptance. We gradually let go of all those dislikes we have about ourselves. We come to love ourselves as we are. We drop our reservations about accepting every aspect of our makeup.

Extending the range of our awareness and accepting ourselves prepare the ground for self-unification, for extending the domain of our will, our I, to our whole body and being. We learn to own our body, our mind, our heart, and everything within us. But this ownership, this integrated wholeness of who we are, comes not through domination but through love. This is not, as sometimes depicted in spiritual teachings, a matter of our will mastering our body, mind, and heart. Rather, our will, our I becomes the glue which holds it all together, which unifies us. Our I becomes the core which touches everything within us. Absent this core, we have no center, our disparate and unruly parts vying for dominance. But inhabiting our center, through our unified will, we inspire and relate all our parts.

Further unification comes in how we relate to ourselves, to others, to all life, and ultimately to God. At each stage, who we are, the domain of our will expands, joins with, and serves a higher will.

For this week, work at unifying your own nature.

128. Balance of Levels

We need balance in our spiritual practice: balance of heart, mind, and body, balance of inner and outer, balance of active and receptive, or effort and effortlessness, and balance of individual and group practice. But another necessary and perhaps more subtle type of balance is of levels of inner work, which we may summarize as sensing, presence, and prayer.

On the first level, sensing, we practice body awareness from within the body, grounding ourselves in our body, building up the sensitive energy of our inner body. At the same time we practice sensitive awareness of thoughts and emotions. On the second level, presence, we become ourselves; we enter the experience of "I am conscious, here and now." On the third level, prayer, we address the higher, exploring and developing our relationship with the sacred, and ultimately becoming one with the One. Here we take prayer in its broadest sense of any human action, inner or outer, intended to relate us to, or raise us into contact with, the Divine.

These three levels depend on each other. Building up sensation in our inner body gives consciousness a more stable platform. Otherwise consciousness would be momentary at best. Standing in conscious presence brings us closer to the sacred, setting the stage for us to reach beyond consciousness toward that higher level through prayer. Opening to the sacred can release a downpour of higher energies that profoundly enhance our inner body sensation and our conscious presence. This closes the loop of interdependence of the three levels of practice. Will acts as the central factor in that loop, first our will and then the higher will.

What if we feel distant from the sacred? Should we only focus on inner body sensation and presence? Should we postpone prayer until a later stage of our path, when we might deem ourselves worthy and prepared? That approach ignores the nonlinear character of the journey, the nonlinearity of spiritual realities not limited to time, but rather residing in the timeless. So any prayer work we do today directly affects our ability to relate to the Divine and thus prepares that relationship for our future path. If I pray today, in the deepest way I can, then that exploratory action reverberates through my life, enabling me to pray deeper still at other times.

Alternatively, what if we feel drawn only to prayer and neglect the other levels of inner work. Without the work of inner body sensation we tend to flounder. If we touch higher levels, such as conscious presence or the sacred world of light, we cannot maintain ourselves in those rarefied districts and our contact quickly evaporates. Without the work of conscious and intentional presence, we cannot maintain the wholeness of inner body sensation and we have no springboard into the sacred.

For this week, adjust the balance of levels of your inner work through sensing your inner body, through intentional, conscious presence, and through deepening your approach to the sacred in prayer.

129. Consciousness and Personality

A major milestone in the spiritual path emerges when we begin to have contact with and understanding of real consciousness, not just the content of our ordinary thoughts, emotions, and sensory impressions. Consciousness embraces all our experience through the dimension of context, the cognizing stillness underlying all that goes on.

A corollary development weakens the grip of our personality, our conditioned patterns of thought, emotion, and action. Personality responds to the content of life, but does so in a programmed way, with no real freedom of choice. Do we choose to get angry at rude behavior? Not likely. The anger comes as a powerful and automatic conditioned response, to which we passively acquiesce. The same holds in every other department of our lives. In many ways we are effectively little more than what robots will be some decades from now.

Consciousness, though, carries a greater degree of freedom. Instead of being in our personality, our personality is in us. When we open to consciousness, we become the context, the silent basic awareness underneath all the content of life. We relax into our inner stillness, which is our pure awareness itself. By living in contact with our contextual awareness, we become able to see our personality patterns in action without being totally caught up in them, able freely to choose our responses to the events of life. Abiding in consciousness we live fully, experiencing the joy and love of living in wholeness.

For this week, notice how you are always caught up in your personality. Work to open to the pure seeing of consciousness, to be able to say "here I am, fully present."

130. Blue Collar Inner Work

To move toward the heights of liberation and love, our spiritual practice must be grounded in the every day reality of blue collar inner work: time for meditation, time for prayer, direct work on being in contact with our body through sensation, transforming our destructive emotions, loosening the grip of self-centered attitudes, and the frequent practice of presence. The more we work in such ways, the stronger and purer our soul grows.

There is no spiritual substitute for real inner work. If we wait for the lightning bolt of grace to whisk us into heaven, or if we think that embracing some system of belief will do the job, we shall be disappointed. Grace finds receptive soil and belief flowers into faith only if we till the ground through persistent, balanced, and practical inner work.

For this week, renew yet again your actual practices on the path of soul building and purification.

131. Participating in Purpose

Life presents us with so many competing demands that any thought, much less action, toward a larger purpose gets lost in the noise. Our days are consumed by chores: taking care of our body, our family, our job, and our possessions. Remaining spare time often dissipates into our favored distractions. We talk to people without really connecting. With the notable exception of the love we give our family, too much of what we do has little or no meaning.

The meaning of any act, no matter how small or routine, derives from its purpose. But we tend to lose touch with the purpose of what we do. In our job, we fall into the routine of details, not relating to how the job serves society, as all jobs do. For the rest, we respond to the needs of the moment or the day, letting slip the opportunities of our lifetime and beyond.

The spiritual path aligns us with the Great Purpose of the universe. Although we remain only dimly aware of that Purpose, our faith tells us that when we practice presence, prayer, and kindness, and when we actively seek wisdom, we simultaneously serve both our own purpose and the Great Purpose. Though building a soul takes place in our hidden interior, it is not a private matter, but serves the Greatness.

The real truth of purpose goes even further. One could say that God is Purpose, the profound mountain of Purpose behind the universe, the Purpose that creates and sustains the universe and us. By our spiritual practice, by our creative work, by our acts of love, kindness, peace, and responsibility, we participate directly in that Great Purpose, in the Divine.

Standing in line at the grocery checkout stand, am I connected with my purposes: to feed myself and my family, to be kind to the people around me, to be present? To live in intention connects us with the Great Intention from which all true meaning derives, including the meaning of each moment of our life. Participating in purpose brings you the confidence that what you do matters, that your inner work matters beyond yourself. Participating in purpose brings you the real happiness of a meaningful life.

For this week, live in intention, participate in Purpose.

132. Breathing Energy

Consciously drawing energy from the air through attention to our breath can provide an enormous boost to our ability to inhabit our body, to strengthen our energy body, to build the sensitive energy in our body. In the beginning, to have some contact with this practice, sit quietly until you are thoroughly relaxed. Then focus your attention on your breathing with simple and direct awareness of the physical sensations associated with breathing, particularly at the nose and upper lip. Then, with your attention, begin drawing the energy from the air into yourself, allowing it to spread and settle throughout your body.

This practice does not require any significant alteration to your breath, and should not make you dizzy, nor cause you to breathe at an abnormally fast or slow speed. The difference between normal breathing and energy breathing does not lie on the physical level, but rather on the level of the energy body. Breathe at a normal pace and depth. But with fine attention to the air where it enters your body, consciously bring the energy into your body. Let it build up the sensation throughout your body, so as to enhance your presence by supporting your contact with your body after the period of conscious breathing. In the beginning, practice this energy breathing for short periods only, perhaps 10 minutes per day.

133. Pure Consciousness

Our lives consist of an endless stream of sights, sounds, smells, tastes, physical sensations, thoughts, images, emotions, intentions, decisions, non-decisions, actions and non-actions. All this absolutely captivates us and totally commands the foreground of our awareness, obscuring any possible view of its context: pure consciousness. Yet consciousness precedes and supports all of our perceptions. It is the blank screen on which we perceive the movie of our lives.

Just as the space of a room allows the furniture to be there, consciousness allows all our perceptions. We rarely notice space itself because of its inherent emptiness and container-like quality, and so it is with consciousness. Space is endless and without boundaries, but with illusory boundaries created by objects within it. And so it is with consciousness. But unlike space, consciousness not only defines our inner framework but also imparts a living wholeness to our experience. Furthermore, consciousness has more dimensions than space-time, indeed it contains all of space and all of time. Thus, consciousness does not begin or end.

The problem is that we overlook and ignore consciousness. We leave it in the background of life while we fly headlong into the foreground. Yet consciousness forms the medium of the enlightened and the saintly. The practices of presence, stillness, and non-dual awareness all aim toward opening our experience to include consciousness.

134. Reaching Beyond

Behind and hidden by our ordinary five senses, behind our thoughts and emotions, behind our mental images, lies the domain of consciousness: still, empty, and peaceful. Behind consciousness we begin to approach the foothills of the Divine. For this we need to reach beyond the space-like inner realm of consciousness. The question is how. We have enough difficulty simply recognizing the conscious context of experience. Beyond that, we cannot conceive.

Yet we make the attempt, repeatedly. What attempt? The classical, yet timeless, way of prayer beckons. We find many forms of prayer in the world's religions, yet its essence continues to elude us, unless we experiment to find an effective inner attitude, an appropriate inner posture toward the Divine. The heartfelt words of prayer serve as links in a chain reaching toward Heaven. With our will, we reach beyond ourselves in search of and in submission to the Great Will. Turning toward our innermost inwardness, we seek the Divine beyond inner and outer.

Gradually something begins to flow back toward us: an energy, certainty, love, and light. These out flowing markers hint at the rightness of our endeavors and point the way. And then we continue our search, hoping to be found.

135. In the Energy Body

As we work to increase our contact with the sensitive energy in our body and with energy breathing, our energy body steadily grows more robust. We may feel that our whole body is filled with the sensitive energy, which begins to create a new life within us, a vehicle of stability and freedom. At this point, we can work to shift our place, our residence from our physical body to our energy body. Instead of feeling that we are in our physical body and it is filled with sensation, we can move into the sensation (or energy) body, inhabit our energy body as our body, which also resides within the physical body. We shift from being in our physical body to being in our energy body.

This movement is not in space, but within our inner world, a movement from distraction to presence, from a lower energy to a higher energy, from a lower world to a higher world. Doing this, at first during sitting meditation periods, provides us with a new and suitable platform for our inner work. Our path becomes more palpable, more continuous, freer of self-centeredness and filled with heart.

136. Managing Our Path

As our spiritual practice continues, we notice all too many tendencies that impede our way, such as overeating, substance abuse, too little sleep, laziness, limiting assumptions, emotional reactions, self-centeredness, fear, anger, greed, jealousy, busyness, distractions, defeatist attitudes, and so on ad nauseam.

On the flip side, we also can see what helps us along the path such as meditation, eating well, sleeping enough, physical exercise, calm and equanimity, body-mind-emotional awareness, kindness and generosity, prayer, determination, fasting, energy breathing, sacred music, spiritual reading and contemplation, spiritual companionships or community, work at presence moment-to-moment during the day, letting go of the identifications revealed by self-awareness, acting in accord with the promptings of conscience, and so forth.

We need to be intelligent in managing our inner life. This requires a clear understanding of the particulars of our situation with regard to what helps and what hinders our path, which of course changes over time. To acquire and maintain such understanding demands continuing cognizance of our inner state coupled with experimentation to fill in the gaps, balance and harmonize our inner world, recognize unexpected openings, and discover and capitalize on new opportunities to deepen our inner work.

Having discovered which practices are most effective for us individually, we persevere with those, letting them act on our soul until the creative promptings once again show us what to change. In this way our practices evolve as we do, leading our way toward ever-deepening presence in every moment, kindheartedness, and intelligent action toward our goals.

For this week, look at what helps you along your path.

137. Exhaling the Negative

Destructive emotions drag us down into an unreal world, a world far removed from the possibility of spiritual work. To work with these emotional downdrafts requires presence and an appropriate attitude. First, we need to be aware of our inner state, to see these emotions as they begin, to see the initial whisperings in our mind/heart that kick off the process of a destructive emotion. If we try to cut them off, we end up adding a layer of self-recrimination and even self-loathing to the already problematic situation. So we accept that this is how we are in this moment. From that state of acceptance, out of respect and kindness for ourselves, out of our wish to end our personal cycles of succumbing to anger, fear, greed, and the rest, out of dedication to moving along the path of transformation toward our highest destiny, we decide to let go of the emotional trauma, be it large or small. We choose to sacrifice the deluded pleasure of being overcome, even briefly, by the destructive emotional attachment.

Yet it persists, or disappears temporarily only to catch us unawares later. And so we work with an ancient but simple technique: exhaling the negative. Instead of dwelling on and reacting to the cause of the emotion, we bring awareness to its physical manifestation, particularly to our chest, seeing the constriction, tightness, and holding. As we exhale normally, we relax our chest and imagine the emotion flowing out of us with our breath. Repeating this several times, we release ourselves from the danger of the gathering emotional storm. To the extent that we are ready and willing to let it go, exhaling the negative can cleanse us of the destructive emotion before it costs us too much precious time and energy.

138. First Intention

When you first wake up in the morning, even before you get out of bed, take the opportunity to set the tone for the day. Practice awareness of the sensation in your body, or awareness of your breathing, or overall presence for a few moments. Notice the residue of your dreams and preoccupations in your thoughts and emotions. Then create your intention to pursue your inner work throughout the day. Be specific.

When you do get out of bed, do so with full awareness of the sensations in your body, of your movements as you get up, of your first steps as you walk away from the bed. Keep up this work of sensing as long as possible: while you brush your teeth, etc., while you get dressed, while you eat breakfast.

Beginning this way will transform the tenor and possibilities of the whole day.

139. My Universe

Our ego, or who we think we are, is not a thing but rather a process, a malleable set of self-centered attitudes which typically guide the software of our mind and heart. These attitudes focus on and purport to emanate from our "self." Looking deeply, though, we may see that no such self exists and that the ego attitudes themselves create the illusion of this self. However, we implicitly trust our concept of our self as a person separate from others. We believe in our self more than we believe in God or anything else. Our ego is our god. This is the core illusion of our life and the process of dispelling it forms the axis of any true spiritual path.

We fear that losing our ego would mean losing ourselves, that we would wander the streets babbling gibberish. But on the contrary, the great teachers have shown us that true sanity and real maturity derive from freeing oneself from oneself, from the ego process, from our illusory, self-referential "I." Like a set of Russian dolls, the deeper we look into ourselves, the more emptiness we find. Our seeing reveals our ego as empty of substance and that very emptiness opens our way into the spiritual world, into love. In this opening we discover the heart of compassion for ourselves, our body, our family, our neighbor, and our society. But as long as the ego process continues to seduce our faith, we remain enclosed in our own little shell, seeing our "self" and its desires as paramount.

The process of liberation begins with clear seeing and proceeds by progressively letting go of our illusory self. To see ego in action means to see all our contractive, self-centered impulses: the anger, grasping, fear, conceit, indignation, vanity, over-indulgence, self-pity, the self-focused daydreams, the firmly upheld opinions, the backstabbing, the insulting humor and gossip, the desire to take more, and the whole universe that revolves around "me." To see any of this within the stream of moments that make up our day requires a willingness to see our truth, an accepting and unflinching approach, and a grounding in presence. What we do not see controls us and binds us to a world of unreality, dependence, and dissatisfaction. Each increment of freedom unburdens us of some of the weight of our "self," allowing us to breathe easier and discover less ephemeral satisfactions.

For this week, look to see the self-centered reflections of egoism in your thoughts, emotions, attitudes, and actions.

140. Increasing Our Spiritual Income

"...Give us this day our daily bread..."[4]

This phrase from the Lord's Prayer can be understood on multiple levels. On the most obvious material level, we ask for food for our physical body. Given the widespread malnourishment and hunger in the world, this is no small matter. We can ask not only for ourselves but also for the hungry around the globe.

We take the prayer further in asking for nourishment for our soul. Given that our soul remains unformed, incomplete and insubstantial, this modality of the prayer addresses our

---

4   Matthew 6:11

spiritual needs, the growth of our soul, and our possibilities for service. Just as we must work for our material sustenance, we also must work to feed our soul. The prayer asks for help in both endeavors. If we ask sincerely, with a heart of need and determination to do our part, we may well receive an answer.

Perhaps the most important example of working to feed our soul can be found in the practice of energy breathing. Through that practice we gradually accumulate the substance, the flesh of our nascent soul. Coupling energy breathing with the practice of sensing our body, gradually transforms our inner being, building our platform for presence, for joy, for new freedom, and for new possibilities.

For this week, ask for your daily bread and work to feed your soul by practicing energy breathing coupled with sensing your body.

141. Care for This Moment

Our life is made of moments, large and small. Our approach this particular moment, when repeated, defines how we approach our whole life. If we care for and respect this moment, then we care for and respect ourselves and our life. How do we treat the material objects and the living beings around us in this moment? Do we offer them our presence and sensitivity in our interaction with them? Or do we sleepwalk through this moment, clanking and jabbering unawares.

Caring for this moment means interacting through awareness, both of ourselves and our surroundings. But not just any awareness, we need a sensitive awareness with a heart that feels and a mind that understands the effects of our every action, or lack of action.

We can begin with man-made material objects. We practice by handling objects with appropriate care, placing rather than dropping, cleaning and putting away, appreciating their design and the knowledge embodied therein, appreciating the efforts required to create and bring them to us. If we can stop taking material objects for granted, ignoring their sources, we may stop taking life for granted and respect our Source.

142. Balancing Inner and Outer

Our lives lack balance in several dimensions. For this week, we look particularly at the imbalance between inner and outer, in the sense that nearly all our attention goes to our outward circumstances. We woefully neglect our inner world. Consider the time and effort you spend on your outer world: working at your job, shopping, organizing your home, maintaining your possessions, serving your family, taking care of your body, watching movies and all the rest. Now contrast this with the concern and effort you give your inner world, a domain no less rich, complex, and important than your outer world.

The inner landscape, almost totally unknown to us, invites our exploration to understand and develop it. Furthermore, our inner world determines our measure of happiness and fulfillment, as well as our response to the circumstances and events of our life. Yet we remain almost completely focused on the outer, neglecting our ultimate welfare and possibilities for service   Balancing inner and outer need not detract from the outer. Indeed, it enhances our interaction with the outer. Except for periods of formal meditation and prayer, our inner work proceeds in tandem with our outward engagements. We work at sensation, kindness, and presence while we traverse the marketplace of life. We can live in both worlds simultaneously. But to realize that possibility, we must give the inner its fair share.

For this week, during your ordinary daily rounds, compare your concern for your inner world with your concern for your outer world. Rebalance through your work on sensation and presence.

143. Non-Anger

Depending on our type, we experience more or less anger every day. We say "I got angry" when the real truth is that "anger got me." Indeed, in any given episode, anger can have us for hours, days, years, or even a lifetime. So what's the problem, you might ask. The more obvious problems with anger are that it makes us unhappy, clouds our attitudes towards people, ruins relationships, wastes our energy, and leads us to say or do things we later regret. The less obvious problem with anger is that the identification and attachment that give rise to, feed, and are fed by anger also block our path to liberation, service, and the Divine.

To practice non-anger we first need to recognize our anger as anger while it's actually happening. We look to see the whole package: rapid heartbeat, labored breathing, tightness in the chest, flushed and contorted face; the supporting, urgent and repetitious thoughts; the fleet of subsidiary emotions like indignation, outrage, hatred, malice or frustration.

Seeing our own anger in action opens the key issue: the question of our willingness to let it go, not to add a sense of identification on top of the body-heart-mind details of the anger, not to claim it as "my anger" or think "I am angry," not to buy into and fuel the justifying thoughts. To help establish this willingness to let go of anger, we note that we ourselves suffer the results of our own anger: the constellation of unpleasantness in our body, heart, and mind. Then out of kindness toward ourselves, we may be willing to allow the entire process of anger to subside and relax.

For this week, practice non-anger.

144. The Ineffable

Looking at the world, we believe, and believe in, what we see. This obvious, tangible world of material objects, energies, and events in space-time completely occupies our senses and our concern. But right behind it, just over the horizon of our senses, lie incomparably vaster realms, not subject to the conditions of space and time. As the highest of these realms surrounding, subsuming, sustaining and thoroughly permeating our world of space-time, the Divine invites us to recognize and serve the ineffable Whole.

Imagine that the fact that the Divine permeates our world is literally and precisely true. This truth has real consequences. If the Divine is present here and now, then at the very least it behooves us to work assiduously and intently to open our hearts and minds toward a direct perception of That.

For this week look in depth. Look beyond your ordinary vision, beyond the ordinary contents of your heart and mind. While we honor, respect, love, and care for this world, we reach out, open to the ineffable, surrendering our small self to our true Source and Purpose, in this very here and now. Utterly emptying yourself, use your creative imagination to see that the Divine is right here before you, even within you: the One in

Whom "we live, and move, and have our being."[5] Work at this opening in the quiet of your inwardness.

145. In Body, In Heart, and In Mind

A tremendous possibility of a vibrant and deep inner life awaits us. But to approach that, we must first see where we are. In particular, we can see that our attention, which defines us, typically remains passive and weak. With our presence so ephemeral, we collapse into associative thoughts and daydreams, emotional reactions, or our physical and sensory experience. The possibility of becoming more fully human and forming our soul depends, in part, on strengthening our attention and broadening our awareness to live in body, heart, and mind simultaneously.

We begin with sensing our body, opening to the sensitive energy in the body, gradually building up to sense the whole body, strongly, as often as we can. This work of sensing the energy body forms the foundation of the path, for it always brings us into the present.

In such moments, the bodily platform of sensation stabilizes our awareness and enables us to open our attention to encompass our emotions and thoughts without collapsing into them. Seeing our emotions gradually purifies them, which in turn opens us to the deeper emotions such as love, in relationship and in prayer. We also join our thoughts to this dance of our full humanity, using our thoughts to remember to practice, to drive our prayer, to consider how best to pursue the path.

The power of this practice of living in and through all three, body, heart, and mind, cannot be overstated. Ultimately,

---

5   Acts 17:28

the three parts unify into one whole human being. For this week, work toward simultaneous presence in body, in heart, and in mind.

146. In Contact

Do you ever misplace a material object: cannot find your keys or your glasses? Do you ever forget the name of someone to whom you were just introduced? What did you have for dinner a week ago? These and other memory lapses do not necessarily indicate a problem with our brain, but rather a lack of awareness. The more alert, aware, and attentive we are during an experience, the better we remember it. But since we spend the vast majority of our time on autopilot, we remember very little. So interrogating your memory, or lack thereof, can show you your level of awareness. Life on autopilot remains very thin.

The true way to enrich our life consists of being in full contact with each moment. The more we notice, the more we live. This contact can extend to our whole presence, all our thoughts, emotions, and all our ordinary sensory experience. Our whole life grows vivid in the light of awareness.

For this week, practice being in contact with your life, inner and outer, moment to moment. Choose a block of time each day, during which you will practice contact with your ordinary activities.

147. Non-Gossip

So much of what we say concerns people who are not there to participate in the conversation. And so much of that, perhaps subtly, judges, criticizes, maligns or generally puts down the person spoken about. We know this as harmful gossip or talking behind someone's back. Sounds ugly, and it is. Yet we engage in this behavior all too often.

If we could see how much harm this does us by feeding our egoism and by feeding our destructive self-criticism, we would stop immediately. When we speak, or even think, in a personally judgmental, faultfinding, disapproving, blaming or disparaging manner, it strengthens the side of us that seeks to diminish other people and, by comparison, build our own ego. The unfortunate result is a wall of isolation around us. Furthermore, the judging mind readily turns to self-judgment: we love and accept neither other people nor ourselves. Compassion weakens as we harden our hearts in such negative gossip.

Fortunately, the converse also holds true: refraining from harmful gossip helps free our heart and mind to be more accepting and kind toward ourselves and others.

For this week, notice your intention when you talk about someone. Are your words critical or harmful? Do your comments distance you from the person commented upon? Whenever possible, extend this noticing to your judgmental thoughts about others.

148. In Their Shoes: Intentional Empathy

The true ability to put oneself into the position of another person belongs to the level of being of the saint. The rest of us, however, can profit heart and soul by the intentional practice of empathy, by attempting to understand the feelings, thoughts, and experience of another person through seeing ourselves in their place, with their background, propensities, and life situation. Such inner work transforms our attitude, changing the whole tenor of our interactions.

Intentional empathy can be particularly valuable when we practice it for people with whom we have some difficulty or toward whom we are indifferent. Putting yourself in the other person's shoes opens doors to compassion, forgiveness, kindness, and love. Understanding the other person's position from inside their situation brings us toward seeing the humanity of the other while weakening the grip of our own self-centered egoism.

Intentional empathy does not rest on intellectual consideration of the other person's life, but rather on a direct seeing, an unmediated perception of the within of the person. Through practice this new mode of perception opens to us, as we open to others.

For this week, practice intentional empathy toward at least two people each day.

149. Inspiring Aspiration

What we value shapes our life. In the long run, the quality and depth of our aspiration determine the quality and level of our being. Three great realms offer the possible fields of aspiration. First, we can and should have goals and ambitions within the material world. However, the quality of these material goals is determined by what they serve. Second, in the moral sphere we can aspire to always do the right thing, to be unfailingly trustworthy and kind.

Our spiritual aspirations form the third great field of endeavor. The worlds of depth offer many possibilities. We can strive to be present in body, heart, and mind, even to the point of continuity. We can aim for a deeper presence that opens to the vast stillness of consciousness. We can wish to enter the creative realm of light and sacred beings. And finally, we can aspire to Love and the Divine.

Each of these worlds presents attractive stopping places, which may appear to be the ultimate goal. Yet while working diligently and of necessity toward presence, consciousness, and the creative, we can set our ultimate aspiration, our deepest, heartfelt yearning upon the world of Love and the Divine. In proportion to the degree of our longing, we discover a flow of inspiration drawing us inevitably onward in presence, service, and love.

To find inspiration, deepen your aspiration.

150. Grounding Our Practice

To make our spiritual practice real and effective, we need to continually return to the present moment. And our body serves as the primary vehicle for that. Although we seek the ineffable, that search and aspiration always begin in the present, in our body. Presence in our body provides a stable, tangible platform for our entire path. Unlike our thoughts and emotions, the body always remains here and now. In any given moment outside of deep meditation, one good measure of our inner work can be found in whether and to what degree we are aware of our body.

Through the sensitive energy, we can stay in contact with our body and with our energy body. By sensing our body and then also staying aware of our thoughts and emotions, we ground our practice in the present moment. Intentional contact with our bodily sensation opens the door to awareness of the endless stream of thoughts and reactions without being swept away in it. Sensing gives us a place to stand in non-identification with the content of our mind. This body of practice anchors us in the here and now, the only gateway to reality.

For this week, practice sensing your body more frequently and more completely. Begin with hands and feet. Then entire limbs. Then the whole body. As always with sensing, the best time to start is now.

151. Beyond the Ordinary

In the ordinary way of living, we believe we are our thoughts, emotions, and body. We take for granted that the thoughts and emotions passing through us are what "I think and feel." But there is no substantive "I" in this, just conditioned, habitual patterns of thinking and feeling that form our personality. We are not this programmed, automated set of inner and outer responses to the world. However, as long as we believe unquestioningly and wholeheartedly in our personality, we relegate ourselves to be less than we could.

How then can we move beyond the personality? First we need to see the current state of our inner life as it is. We look at our thoughts arising on their own, bubbling up out of prior experience, memory, and conditioning, bubbling up without any intention on our part. Noticing this repeatedly leads us toward recognizing that nearly all our thoughts and emotions belong to this conditioned part of us. That realization loosens our attachment to our make-believe self.

At the same time, we look beyond thoughts and emotions, beyond personality toward our inner depth of spirit. In prayer, meditation, stillness, and presence, we can discover our own Truth, we can become who we really are.

For this week, notice how enthralled you are with your own thoughts and emotions, with your personality.

152. Ad Hoc Tasks

We can create opportunities for inner work during our ordinary activities by choosing to practice in particular situations and events as we enter them. For example, I am about to go into the grocery and suddenly remember that this offers me a chance to work. So I decide, on the spur of the moment, just before entering the store, that I will attempt to practice full awareness of my body through sensation during the entire period I am in the grocery. Then as I shop, I keep returning to my intention to practice and keep strengthening my contact with the sensitive energy in my body.

Similar possibilities abound in which we can choose discrete events, on an ad hoc, opportunistic, non-premeditated basis, to be venues for inner work: going to a party, a concert, a commute, a walk, a meeting, a meal, doing a household project, pumping gas, watching a TV program, performing minor tasks like taking out the garbage or washing dishes, and so on. The power of this method lies in the fact that the inner task is limited to one time interval, which becomes a field for our will, for our intention. Because we can envision the entire event ahead of time and because it has a clearly defined duration, we can fill the event with our intention to practice and bring stronger, more frequent effort to bear on our inner work than might otherwise be possible.

For this week, be prepared to respond to the unexpected impulse to pursue your inner work during a situation or event you are about to begin. When you recognize the opportunity, set yourself a particular form of inner work to practice during the event. As you go through it, stay in touch with your intention and actually practice for the duration of the event. If you lose your intention, then as soon as you remember return to working at sensation, conscious breathing, kindness, listening, opening to stillness, presence or whatever your chosen practice is.

153. Emptying Yourself

Emptying, surrendering, and letting go. All three are facets of a unique act of will, an act essential to our path. If God's will penetrates every corner of the universe, every point of space-time, and if humans are endowed at birth as a particle of God's free and independent will, and if we insist on our personal independence, fearing a loss of identity in rejoining the Great Whole, then we remain divorced from God.

But we have nothing to fear. Our independence is both true and an illusion: it depends on the level. In our ordinary world we are indeed individual, independent actors. In the higher worlds we paradoxically become both more individual and more united with each other and with the Whole. In emptying ourselves, we give up the illusion of complete independence and we open to the reality of having deep roots that connect us with the Whole.

Meditation and prayer present excellent opportunities for the practice of emptying. We empty ourselves of believing that all the thoughts and self-centered emotions coursing through us are who we are, or even represent who we are. We let go of our personality and all that drives it. We leave aside our impatient ambitions, our insistent demands, our stories and dramas. We let go of all our doing and acting, and enter into the peace of non-doing. At least temporarily, we give up our small self to taste the Great Self that unites us. And then we return, not as our fears would have it a spineless blob, but rather in renewed contact with the source of clarity and wisdom that informs our actions in this world of space and time.

For this week, practice emptying yourself, utterly and completely.

154. Self-Discipline

Substance abuse, watching too much TV, overeating, gossip, and other forms of self-indulgence rob us of the energy and will we need for our inner work. Self-discipline involves imposing moderation on our immoderate behaviors and serves our spiritual aspirations in at least three ways. First, instead of unnecessarily wasting the energy, we conserve it, making it available for our practice. Second, self-discipline builds a steadiness and strength of will, which directly translates into enhancing our presence. The will to persist in limiting our actions becomes the will to persist in being present. Third, the sacrifice of giving up a personal indulgence in order to better serve the higher can prepare us to empty ourselves of egoism.

After surveying all the ways we waste our inner energies, we may be tempted to change everything at once. The result of overreaching, of trying to change too many things or even one deeply ingrained behavior, is nearly always failure. We might give up and become even more self-indulgent or we might enter the useless cycle exemplified by yo-yo dieting. Instead, we start with one small behavior. After mastering that, we move on to tackle other indulgences, one at a time, without reverting to our old immoderate habits.

Watch out for becoming obsessed with self-discipline to the point of forgetting that self-discipline is a means toward purification and presence, and not an end in itself. Obsession with self-discipline and its difficulties occurs when our ego takes over the discipline project. We need to be moderate even in our efforts at self-discipline.

For this week, look at the ways you overindulge to the detriment of your inner work. Choose one immoderate behavior and temper it.

155. The Middle Way

Extremism nearly always results from identification and grasping, from a desperate desire to have things our way, the "right" way. When such a desire periodically consumes us, we disappear, our potential for presence and kindness squandered. We may fall into extreme positions in many ways from sharp political views to uncontrolled appetites, from road rage to laziness, from paralyzing fear to preening braggadocio, from giving more than we can afford to taking all we can get. In our spiritual practice also we tend to move in a rut on one side of the balance scale, forgetting the value of both effort and non-effort, kindness and self-discipline, focusing and letting go, solitude and community, prayer and meditation.

Freedom awaits us in the middle way, in moving away from the extremes toward a sane and stable synthesis. For example, we strive diligently for excellence without demanding perfection. We see truth in opposing opinions and discover a new center. We find satisfaction in the first slice of cake and forgo the second. We fast one day, but not two.

For this week, notice areas of extremism in your own life and see your way toward a middle path.

156. Being Seen

Even in our quietest moments of calm, non-clinging, and peace, a residue of egoism remains. We feel ourselves. We feel ourselves not quite totally clean. What to do? We cannot cleanse ourselves of ourselves. That purification can only come from something deeper. So we allow ourselves to be seen by that depth. We present ourselves, offer ourselves, in whatever bold humility we can muster, to be seen. We lay bare our soul before the Ineffable. There is our hope. In being seen by the truly Pure, our stains exposed to that bleaching clarity, the center of our motivation begins to shift from our separateness.

So we raise ourselves up, in our deepest meditation or prayer, and we ask that living light to see us, to accept us, to purify us, to prepare us to pass through the gate to the halls of love. What could matter more? To do our duty to our family and our society. And toward that ultimate Purity, we allow ourselves to be seen in truth.

157. Here I Am

In Genesis, God calls Abraham, who replies "Behold, here I am." Clearly, this was not about letting God know *where* Abraham was, but rather to let God know *that* Abraham was.

The words "here I am" can be just as thin and empty as any other words. But try this. From the whole of your being, say to yourself "here I am." And as you say it, really be here, present, as strongly as you can muster for that moment. Do this not with tension, but rather with intention, with your will-to-be, with the whole of yourself. Simple and direct, you say the words and you mean them, you experience their truth in the very instant you say them.

We all have the capacity to be present for a moment. Make this your moment, five times a day. Inwardly say "here I am" and as you say this, come out of your preoccupations and distractions, come into this moment, into your life, and be the one, the only one who can say those words in truth.

158. Asking for Help

The very idea of spiritual independence and separateness is an illusion: unique, yes, but separate, no. And because we are not spiritually independent, we have both the opportunity and the need for help in our inner work. The lowest level of help comes from texts. The written word can be an enormous support in instructing us, developing our understanding, and even enlivening our heart. But we need to ask for this help by staying alert for books that appeal to our current, personal spiritual situation and by actually taking the time to read and digest the concepts.

The next level of help comes from other people, from our family, our fellow seekers and our teachers. Sometimes such help comes unbidden: by example or by unsolicited advice. Sometimes we find this help in communal spiritual practice, wherein the shared intention, energy, and openness bring all involved higher than each could go by their own efforts. If we are fortunate enough to come into contact with a genuine spiritual teacher, a selfless person of heart and understanding, the benefits can be incalculable. In all these cases we need to ask for help from others, whether by being open to the unbidden help, by participating in communal practice, or by presenting ourselves to be taught.

Another level of help flows to us from deep within. When our mind and heart settle down and stillness pervades our being, we may touch the ocean of peace and wisdom that forms and informs our very consciousness. For this we must ask by doing the lengthy, difficult, and subtle work of letting go of all that binds us, most notably our self-centeredness.

Our path cannot extend very far without help from the

Higher Power. For this we ask through our heartfelt prayers and through our continuing efforts with spiritual practices. This level of help comes in unexpected and sometimes unrecognized ways, but is nevertheless crucial. Indeed, our real possibilities wax and wane in direct proportion to our need for connection with the Source of All.

Perhaps this week, we can genuinely ask for help.

159. A Sense of the Sacred

If the blinders suddenly dropped from our eyes, no doubt we would see ourselves surrounded by the sacred. An external approach to the sacred entails putting ourselves into places that remind us of what lies behind appearances. Nature, in all her wondrous manifestations, settles our mind and opens our heart to a sense of the sacred. Great art, certain paintings, sculptures, music, and literature, can communicate the sacred. Houses of worship, in their design and in their essential purpose, serve as repositories for the energy of countless prayers. Entering such a place subdues our ordinary concerns and invites our heart to allow the sacred in. Communal worship ceremonies, by intention, work to open us to the sacred.

But if we depend solely on external reminders, our sense of the sacred will remain all too limited. We already bear a seed of the sacred as our innermost core. The path of purification gradually clears the way for that sacred to emerge into consciousness. This does not simply mean seeing the world in all its vivid energy. Rather to see the world as holy ground upon which we are privileged to walk. Like Moses at the burning bush, we are commanded to remove our shoes, to set aside the defenses of egoism, and listen. We look to reconnect the external sacred with our internal sacred, closing the loop in our quintessentially human role.

For this week, be ready to open to the sacred, whether outwardly, inwardly, both, or beyond the distinction between outer and inner.

160. Seeing Their Potential

Around the dimension of actual and potential, we have this strange double-standard in our attitude toward people. We give ourselves the benefit of the doubt in assessing our own actual behavior because we rightly credit ourselves with having such amazing potential for the future. We define ourselves more by our potential future than by our actual present. But with other people, we often feel critical of their actual manifestations and discount their potential to change or improve. We look at the surface of a person and define them thereby. This attitude of ours arises from and perpetuates our inner isolation from people.

For this week, look past the surface of other people and see their potential.

161. Eternal Values

Our personal system of values determines how we live. From the vast array of possibilities in our life, we choose those that we value. However, our value system lacks coherence, holding contradictory and conflicting values. We also suffer the shifting nature of our hierarchy of values: today we place great value on one thing, tomorrow another.

Broadly speaking, though, we can sort our values into two great categories. The first consists of all time-based values: those concerned with things and events in space and time. The second category encompasses eternal values that transcend time.

In some instances these categories overlap. Take the case of someone you love. That person's body resides in space and time. Most likely, though, what you really love is not that body, but the person who inhabits that body. The person transcends time and your love is an eternal value. Another case is that of earning a living. We work to put food on the table, a roof over our heads, and clothing on our bodies. All these things are in space and time. But responsibility stands behind the act of performing our duties toward our body, our family, our employer, and our society. That responsibility is an eternal value.

Our dedication to spiritual practice is also an eternal value, directed toward the timeless, the deathless.

For this week, notice your personal value system, what actually drives you, in terms of time-based and eternal values.

162. The Art of Climbing

To climb, be it a mountain or a ladder, we reach for what lies above and let go of what lies below. Both the reaching and the letting go play their necessary roles. The same holds true in climbing the spiritual path. Step by step we reach up and let go.

We let go of physical tensions and reach for awareness of sensation in the present. We let go of attachment to thoughts and emotions and reach for presence in the vast stillness of consciousness. We let go of our personality, of being who we typically are, we let go of consciousness itself, and reach for the realm of the sacred. Finally we let go of ourselves, we let go of all our agendas other than finding God for the sole purpose of union with God. Through prayer or a sacred name, in an attitude of love and surrender, we reach into the deep unknown toward the Source of All. The qualities and energies of these higher realms create our being. Standing in their presence, we know we have found the road toward transformation.

For this week, practice the art of climbing.

163. Active Presence

Every day, moments of awakening descend upon us unbidden and unexpected, but are they unwelcome? When they happen to show us one of our own unbecoming manifestations, then we well may wish to fall back into oblivion. At other times we may simply not recognize or not care about our moments of awakening and allow them to slip away as we slip back into autopilot. To properly welcome a moment of awakening means to take the opportunity to enter into presence, to extend our presence in time, and to deepen our presence in the realm of being.

Not all inner work arrives through openness. The path also requires an active approach. For example, we can actively work to be present, whenever the moments of opportunity arise. We extend our awareness of sensation to our whole body, so that we "own" our body. Whatever its posture or movement, we fully occupy that. We embrace our wider awareness that includes our thoughts, emotions, and sensory perceptions. We occupy our deeper consciousness, the context of all experience. And we become the active agent in ourselves, the source of our actions, the decision-maker, the director of attention. To reach the sacred, we must first come into our own, into "I am."

Only our "I am" can truly surrender to the Ineffable Source, the Always-Everywhere. Without this "I am" there is nothing in us capable of making the step toward the sacred, no vehicle for the spirit.

For this week, actively work to be, to be more, more often, more deeply, and more vividly.

164. A Person of Substance

How substantial is your presence? To what extent do you feel yourself to be here? Do your words ever carry weight? When you walk, are you aware of your own weight, both physical and inner? Do you reside within your own body and space, or are you constantly drawn outside yourself, flitting or hurrying here and there? Do you fidget? Do you blow your energy in unnecessary tensions, overeating, or substance abuse? Do you think for yourself, or do you blithely accept others' views as truth? Do you finish what you start, or do you follow the latest whim crossing your mind, or make excuses and give in to laziness? Are you responsible? Are you kind?

All these questions offer indications of what it means to be a person of substance, and how we can work toward that. For this week, please ponder one or more of these questions and apply the results to your inner work.

165. Labor of Love

Make no mistake: spiritual practice is work, hard work, both physically and psychologically demanding, sometimes requiring the difficult sacrifice of our desires, although not of our love. The obvious difference between labor of the spirit and earthly labor is that by the one we earn and pay for spiritual sustenance, and by the other our material sustenance. While the necessity of latter imposes itself on everyone, the need for the former eludes most. Even in those who recognize it, the need for spiritual labor waxes and wanes. Only in the recesses of our being does the spiritual need always reign supreme. The more we engage in the spiritual work, however, the more the need for it emerges into our ordinary daily life. Eventually we see that life is meaningless without love, and that the labor of the spirit is a labor of, by, and for love.

We pay our dues to care for body, family, and society, while at the same time we give our love, heart and soul, in responding to the great call of the spirit. The two need not be separate, as in the love and care for family. But to neglect our inner work leaves our soul emaciated and grasping at externals for the satisfaction that can only come through the spirit. Pursuing the labor of the spirit, sooner or later, saturates us down to our very bones with joy, fulfillment, and connection to the sacred, surpassing our wildest imagination.

For this week, give your own labor of love its rightful place.

166. Body of Stillness

When we sit still, our possibilities increase for contact with the sensitive energy in our body, for creating the energy body. In bodily repose, we can intensify and stabilize our attention to our whole body. The energy in the body can grow richly dense, solidifying our position in the inner world of presence. Ultimately, the concentrated, energetic stillness of the body can connect us to the pristine, timeless, and infinite stillness of the pure consciousness. The traditional approach has us practicing this in the quiet of a formal meditation, in time we set aside to devote exclusively to inner work. But this unnecessarily and severely limits our work to a relatively brief block of time, a small percentage of the day.

We need more. So we look to any situation in which we sit still for a prolonged period. Riding as a passenger in a vehicle, be it a car, subway, plane, bus, boat, or train, leaves us with time and attention to bring to bear on our bodily presence. Similarly, we can sense the whole body while reading. Sitting in an audience for a performance, be it a play, symphony, opera, movie, TV program, or a lecture, also presents an excellent opportunity for building our energy body. We can give our mental attention to the event and reserve our physical attention for sensing our whole body, strongly and continuously. Rather than detracting from our experience of the event, sensing keeps us more totally present to take it in more vividly.

For this week, practice whole body sensation, as thoroughly and robustly as possible, for the duration of situations where you need not move and can safely and appropriately be present in the whole body.

167. Walking in Stillness

A sacred ocean of stillness surrounds us constantly. And the way toward the Divine leads through that. Yet we remain unaware of it. Even if we have had a taste of that sacred stillness, say in meditation, we lead our life as if the stillness, the sacredness were reserved for and only accessible on special occasions. To bring that sacred stillness to our ordinary, daily life would constitute a profound transformation of our being. We can embark on that transformation, simply and directly.

Perhaps we have practiced opening to the silence, the stillness beyond thoughts, during meditation. Now we practice opening to the stillness during activity. Take the example of walking. Our body well knows how to walk and requires very little attentiveness on our part to maintain the walking. That leaves us with excess attention available as we walk. We open our attention to the stillness underlying experience. Behind all we see, hear and touch, a warm, loving and boundless ocean of silence intimately embraces and supports everything, including us. As we walk, we relax into the utter peace of that stillness. When we notice that our attention has collapsed into some feature of our ordinary physical or mental world, we reopen ourselves to the sacred ocean of stillness.

This opening is easier to catch than we might expect, at least for brief moments. It takes practice and persistence to begin to recognize the all-pervasive expanse of stillness. But that practice pays enormous dividends in lightening our load, warming our heart, and offering fulfillment. The stillness brings us to the fullness of our being and to contact with the sacred.

The practice of opening to stillness need not be limited to walking, or to meditation, but can be brought into any activity, except for safety-critical ones, like driving, that require our full attention.

For this week, practice opening to the sacred ocean of stillness while walking.

168. Hard Decisions

Navigating the waters of life sometimes confronts us with difficult choices, which are not black and white but make their appearance in tangles of gray. Worse still, the pros and cons of such choices seem to change from day to day in response to our changing view of the considerations and ramifications. In the face of such situations, large or small, we may be paralyzed into inaction and just live by habit and momentum, which will sometimes be exactly the wrong choice. Or we may be pressured into acquiescence by forces around us, which we later regret. Or we dive in head first without enough understanding of what's below the surface. We may even luck into appropriately responding to what turns out to be a golden opportunity, or we may miss that window.

The decisions we make in the face of uncertainty and conflicting motivations can determine the course of our life. We can and usually should seek counsel from friends and others with experience; good advice certainly can help inform our deliberations. But if we let others make our decisions for us, we lose a precious piece of our freedom. No one knows our total situation as well as we do. We can search our own heart for guidance, but typically only find what we put there. So we are left with making a hard choice, one that may seem to be a loser whichever way we go.

Yet such decisions define us and form us. They express

our uniqueness and, by reflection, the uniqueness of the One. This is precisely why we should not abdicate our personal life decisions to someone else, not to a friend, a therapist, a professional advisor, nor to a spiritual mentor. While we may ask for advice, to fully develop our soul, we need to make our own life decisions and, yes, our own mistakes. Then we take full responsibility for the consequences and sometimes reap the benefits.

An important part of our inner work is to squarely face those situations which require a decision. Choice and decision are aspects of will, and our will, at its core, arises from the Divine Will. So choosing with wisdom and compassion strengthens our true channel to what really matters.

For this week, look at the hard choices in your own life, particularly ones you may be avoiding. The buck stops with each of us.

169. Subsuming the Personal

When a significant bodily ailment enters our life, we fall under its sway, not only physically — we have no choice in that — but also psychologically, emotionally. The state of our body then dominates our whole inner world. Perhaps this is necessary, as we need to bring our compromised and limited forces to bear on treating the problem and on healing. When we interact with someone who is ailing to that extent, we immediately recognize how totally wrapped up they are in their physical problem. Of course, the same happens to us when it's our own body's turn to suffer.

Such illness, though, only illumines the shadow of how consumed we normally are by our personal world, by our opinions, desires, needs, failures, successes, habits, plans, grudges, reactions, fears, jealousies, indulgences, and so on ad nauseum. We hardly see beyond our own skin, except for what we want to take from our surroundings. Ultimately, though, our whole self-centered program proves unsatisfying. Yet we hold onto it for fear of losing the only reality we know, for the inability to imagine subsuming our personal agenda into a greater purpose.

But the larger world keeps knocking at our door. First is family, toward whom we properly relate in kindness, concern, and love. Next is society, toward which we must make our constructive contribution, be it through our job or otherwise. But here things can go sour, if we trade our personal egoism for the egoism of a group, be it a nation, a race, a religion, a political party, or a cultural stance. Through exclusivity, xenophobia, exploitation, or group animosity, we extend and multiply our problem from self-centeredness to group-centeredness. Group egoism can enmesh us and block our path to spiritual liberation and love, just as surely as personal egoism.

Can we vote our views and act on our convictions, but the leave the rancor behind? If so, we may turn toward the truly Great Purpose, into Whom we can whole-heartedly subsume our personal purposes, thereby undermining the walls of egoism. This gives us the release from inner divisions, contradictions, and attachments that opens to freedom, to the ability to appreciate and to serve ourselves, our family, our society, our planet, and the one God worshipped by all religionsIn our deepest meditation, in the stillness of the inner silence, we orient ourselves, mind and heart, toward the Greatness beyond that stillness, and surrender the personal for the Divine. Like everything else on the path, this is a practice. We do not expect to get it right the first time, but we continue to work at it, fumbling in the dark, and by doing so our understanding grows. We may even learn to walk, not merely as our own individual self, but in and as the sacred emanation that suffuses the world and everyone in it.

For this week, notice what subsumes your personal agenda, your inner convictions and drives. Explore subsuming the personal into the Divine.

170. Losing Face

The chairman of a large corporation recently noted that we only need to make one or two good decisions in our life. Whether true or not, the idea certainly points to the fact that many of our choices, large and small, miss the mark. We make mistakes or fail, and experience a kind of remorse.

Furthermore, we all have limitations. To the extent we either do not recognize or do not fully accept those limitations, we repeatedly enter situations that impose a rude awakening upon us. Unpleasant situations and events whose roots lie in our own shortcomings cause us to lose face. What is this painful experience? What face do we lose?

The sum total of our conditioning, experience, habits, and patterns form a psychological face, our personality, that we mistakenly believe in as our authentic self, as who we are. This personality face looks toward externals for fulfillment. When something in life goes badly, especially due to our own inadequacy, it can happen that our personality face, our mask, loses part of its overarching and unchallenged grip on us.

In its place, through that hole in the mask, we may glimpse what in Zen is known as our Original Face Before We Were Born. Instead of solely looking out through the eyes of our externally-oriented personality face, we begin to face the rich, vibrant, living depth beyond thoughts and reactions, a depth that encompasses both inner and outer.

The shock and discomfort of the inevitable failures, disappointments, and humiliations of life, present us with a choice. We can wallow in self-pity, self-loathing, despondency and anger, or we can use the occasion to turn toward Something incomparably greater than any passing situation, Something that will never fail. We use the shock and energy of mistakes and failures to reinvigorate our spiritual quest.

We never seek out failure, for life readily provides us our share. Externally, when we fail, we forthrightly pick ourselves up, assess what we can learn from the debacle, and then work to succeed. Inwardly though, when we fail or suffer humiliation, we turn from our personality face. Then comes the opportunity to return to our Original Face, looking toward and from the Real.

For this week, notice how you respond to mistakes, failures, and disappointments in life, be they large or small. See if you can extricate the released energy from its downward spiral and turn to face what will always matter.

171. Will It Matter in a Year?

To gain some perspective on any situation, ask yourself whether what is confronting you today will matter a year from now. This question can help us separate the wheat from the chaff. We often make the mistake of being too concerned with situations and issues that lack real importance, while neglecting those that do matter.

Perhaps another driver's rudeness upsets me terribly, even though his actions lose their significance almost immediately. On the other hand, maybe I forgo the small, but regular, daily work of practicing a musical instrument that I want to learn, or a daily period of studying a subject to advance my career, or practicing presence or meditation to complete my soul. These little efforts may seem insignificant taken separately, but they can add up to a major impact on the course of our life.

To value the important and devalue the unimportant in any situation, ask yourself whether it will matter in a year. Spiritually this helps us be less identified and more focused.

172. Fingers of One Hand

When you look at other people, what do you see? Perhaps you see them in the ordinary way, from the outside, as animated, physical bodies, each with their own personality, talents, and limitations. But our most basic assumption about others goes unnoticed: that we are separate from them. You have your body and I have mine. You have your opinions, concerns, and interests and I have mine. Unless we are family or friends, we matter little to each other. We see others through the filter of our self-centered egoism.

But the reality remains that the closer contact we have with the depth of our own true spirit, the closer we come to other people, all of whom share in that same spirit. First we might notice our shared humanity: other people are like I am inside, with their own hopes, fears, and dreams. Deeper still, we may notice that our very awareness, our consciousness is not really ours alone, is not individual, but is a sea of energy in which we all partake. This can lead to a revolution in how we see others, in recognizing our essential sameness within our individual diversity.

But finally, most subtly, we may realize that our core

individuality and drive, our most basic free will itself emanates from the Great Universal Will, in Whom we humans are like the fingers of one hand. This is the source of the magic of cooperation, in which individuals give a part of their free will to coalesce into the greater will of a family, a team, an organization, a nation, or a community of worship.

So when we see others, we can look beyond the surface, beyond our differences of body and mind, to open to that base-level conscious awareness shared by us all. And beyond even that pan-human consciousness, we may glimpse the one Root of free will in all people, that Source in Whom we are the fingers of one hand.

For this week, notice how you see others and work to deepen that perception toward the true reality.

173. Sustaining Presence

Choose to be here, in the whole of yourself, inhabiting your entire body, heart, and mind. And now that you are here, choose to be here more powerfully, more fully, more robustly. Keep yourself here in the whole of yourself. Do not fall away. Do not shirk the effort. When you notice that your intention to be present has faded, then come back to this moment and reinvigorate that intention. But stay relaxed in body, heart, and mind, while your intention to maintain your presence in this moment stays firm and effective. Let your intention to be present arise from your depth, not from your surface. From the surface it brings tension; from the depth it brings relaxed openness, rooted in the moment.

Choose an hour each day this week to practice this. At first choose times when the external demands on you are minimal: perhaps while sitting quietly in meditation or in a meeting or in the audience at a performance. Eventually, you will be able to work this way in any situation.

The essence is to maintain your presence, strongly, intentionally, and continuously. It is a difficult practice, requiring the whole of your attention and intention. Do not demand perfection of yourself in this, but do strive toward the reality of sustained, wholehearted presence. Even brief efforts in this direction can yield profound results.

174. Strong Will, Open Will

To have any hope of opening to the Divine, we first need to be. In strength of presence we find our opportunity to become more than just our personal self, to be touched by the spiritual Reality. Even if we only attain that for a moment, the event shows us the way toward the Ultimate. For this week, try working at the following meditation.

After thoroughly relaxing in body, heart, and mind, turn toward full awareness of your body. Keep your attention in your body, the whole of your body. Gradually the sensitive energy builds up and your awareness and connection with your body strengthens. Whenever you notice that your attention has weakened or slipped away in thoughts or daydreams, gently and without self-recrimination bring your full attention back to the whole of your body. While staying thoroughly relaxed, let your attention grow stronger and stronger, filling your entire body. Inhabit your whole body in increasing immediacy and intimacy. Keep at it. If you can stay relaxed while you work at this, your attention will not tire. Bright and steady, you are here in full presence in your body.

Once you feel well established in your attention, anchored in your body, move toward being your attention itself. Your attention is your will. Be that.

Now the subtlety. Notice that your attention does not really begin in you. While maintaining yourself in that strong attention, open toward the Source of your attention. You will find It shrouded in a cloud beyond perception. No matter. At this point, we are not aiming to enter that Divine Source of all free will. Rather, we are now working to open a channel toward It. Your attention itself is that channel. Let the back-stop fall away from your mind, heart, and attention, and open to the Source of who we all are.

175. Self-Image, False Image

We labor through life under the weight of a complex, loosely-integrated set of assumptions, attitudes, self-stories, material goals, dreams, fantasies, habits and obsessions that form our image of who we are. We take this pockmarked image to be our truest reality and we vigorously defend it, nurture it, and act on its impulses. We are enslaved by this self-image, this pseudo-image that does us such a great injustice by hiding our authentic Self. This personality image, whose fundamentals we acquire in childhood through the exigencies of family situation and haphazard conditioning, becomes such a comfortable mask that we forget it's only a mask and adopt it as our true face.

Inner freedom begins in seeing. But like water for fish or air for land animals, our personality is too all-encompassing for us to readily become aware of it. One approach is to notice how it colors our perceptions. If I am overly concerned with thinking

I am too fat, or too short, or too poor, or too dumb, or too something, then my inner world revolves around that issue, boxing me into a small, partial, filtered view of myself and the world. What I see when I look at other people then is whether they are fat or thin, short or tall, poor or rich, etc. My inner response to others too often consists solely of comparing myself to them along the dimensions of primary concern to my personality. If I can see no further than my self-image, my pseudo-identity, if all my perceptions are tainted in that way, then I miss the real splendor both of others and myself.

For this week, notice how you see other people and what this says about your own self-image.

176. Political Mind

Whether or not political action forms part of our repertoire of service, as long we intend to devote ourselves to the spiritual path we need to beware of growing too identified with any of our views, including our political convictions and opinions. Identification in this sense means that instead of holding a position, the position holds us. We live in reaction to all we see as wrong. We may even fall into demonizing people in the other camp. But our true reality far surpasses events in time. Maintaining that timeless perspective helps us keep our center as we navigate the turmoil of this world.

This is not to say that we should not hold or even passionately promote our political views. Nor does it imply a moral relativity. Objectively evil deeds do occur, perpetrated by misguided people lacking real contact with conscience. But political or any other action in this world can be much more effective if we live in inner freedom while embodying our convictions.

It is one thing to act in compassionate ways. But it is an entirely different matter to give oneself over to righteous or indignant passion. The former validates and strengthens our connection with conscience, whereas the latter usurps and betrays conscience, mixing its truth with egoism. The passion that arises in freedom and conscience is a force for good, a force that neither harms others nor wastes our energies.

For this week, notice when political mind takes over your inner world, drawing you into reaction, anger, disgust, indignation, or obsession. The seeds of freedom are sown by seeing.

177. Returning

The theme of return appears in many aspects of spiritual work: returning to God, returning to our spiritual home, returning from waywardness, and so on. For this week we practice returning to ourselves, returning to awareness of our body, returning to presence, returning to this moment in its fullness. In a real sense, this returning is the most basic and most important of all spiritual practices, for it brings us into this moment, into ourselves, into the only place from which our spirit can unfold.

In the practice of presence, the most apparent characteristic is that we fall away from it. The crux of the practice then is to return to presence whenever we notice that we are not. Our attitude shapes the possibility of return. Perhaps we do not wish to return just at this moment, because to return to presence means to see. If we are reacting or indulging, griping or sniping, or behaving in some other unbecoming fashion, be it inwardly or outwardly, we may not want to see. To face ourselves at that moment exposes us to an intimate and difficult kind of suffering. But the suffering that comes in the self-exposure of seeing, if not reacted to, leads to healing and freedom. Can we accept to see and to live in that seeing?

Or, more typically, we put off returning to presence because we are passive and lazy in our inner work. We lose contact with its importance. We would rather not be bothered with it just now. Can we muster the will to be active in returning to presence, again and again?

For this week, practice the art of coming back to presence whenever you notice that you are not. Return to presence without self-recriminations at having fallen out of it, without shrinking from what you might see, and without postponing it. Whether in happiness or in sorrow, in pleasure or in pain, in boredom or in exuberance, we respect every part of our life by returning to be present in it, to live it fully. Step by step, this carries us closer to our true center of peace, our refuge and our hope, the source of our possibilities for good.

178. Manna from Heaven

The bulk of our inner work must of necessity be active: actively sensing our body, actively extending our continuing contact with our body from part to whole, actively raising ourselves out of entanglement with associative thoughts and reactive emotions, actively experimenting with our inner approach to practice, actively managing our destructive habits, actively seeking out spiritual community to support our inner work, and actively becoming and sustaining presence. Yet all this activity amounts to very little without some crucial help from above.

The missing ingredients that we cannot produce

through our own efforts consist of the higher energies, which belong to the deeper spiritual realms. These energies enable the growth and transformation of our soul. And their status of necessity extends beyond the personal to whole of human society. Humanity depends on those who work inwardly to be the means of its redeeming connection with the higher energies. All our active inner work serves to prepare our vessel to receive the higher energies, the manna from heaven. Through letting go of all self-centeredness in deep meditation, in heartfelt prayer, or even in a simple gesture of receiving, we open ourselves, we reach toward the Divine, and accept the gift of the sacred substances.

Two levels can be distinguished in these energies beyond consciousness. The first, an active energy, cascades through us in waves of light. The other, deeper one comes in utter emptiness, formlessness, and awe as the substance of a higher will, which we can allow to enter our own will.

For this week, renew your work at heartfelt prayer and meditation in stillness, to empty yourself, to reach toward the Divine, to gather that most crucial nourishment for your soul and for your neighbor.

179. Not Accepting the Superficial Life

Our interior life consists almost entirely of a cacophony of mutually-reinforcing trivia: associative thoughts, reactive emotions, and petty desires, all bouncing off our sensory impressions of the external world. This is a most uncomfortable and ultimately meaningless way of living. Yet we are so accustomed to it that we passively accept it as the only life possible for us, forgetting the tastes we have had of another way of living.

Or if we don't accept it, we merely look to change our external circumstances instead of changing our inner world.

There is another way of living, a way not mired under thoughts, under emotional reactions, under desires for this and that. Those who pursue the path of spiritual inner work, seek this other way of living, perhaps because they see they are still immersed in the superficial. If my attention is constantly drawn into a self-perpetuating, alluring whisper of thoughts, or if I always lose myself in hot or cold reactive emotions or trivial desires and entertainments, then I am only half alive. The days of that life pass all too quickly, yielding nothing of real value.

But the more clearly I see this situation, the less likely I am to continue accepting it. And the degree to which I do not accept to live this life of inward banality is one measure of my commitment to spiritual inner work. The other measure is the quality of my openness to the higher worlds.

For this week, notice whether you accept to live in automatic mental associations, reactive emotions, and superficial desires. Notice this in actual practice, perhaps as you "come to" after a long train of thoughts or as you return to yourself after a bout of anger or fear. Notice whether you accept your inner thralldom, while discounting the possibility of inner freedom.

180. Break with the Past

We live under the tyranny of our past, safely presuming that the way we were yesterday is how we will be tomorrow. Our conditioning, our habits of body, feeling, and mind, possess a momentum that we grant to them by our passivity. In the matter of our inner work, we may wish for transformation, for enlightenment and a loving heart, but we do not really believe it is possible for us, for me. We feel stuck in our current level of being and assume that our spiritual practice can only lead to temporary states, not permanent change.

One quality that can help us through this conundrum of our past is faith, the spiritual attraction that draws us forward and imbues us with the confidence and trust to practice beyond our presumed limits. The higher can reach down to us, but we have our essential role to play. A major part of that role is to be active in our pursuit of the spiritual path, and not passive toward the limiting patterns we inherit and accept from our past.

We may fear inner change, in the false belief that it means leaving our familiar self. In truth, our ordinary personality stays with us throughout the path, but gradually assumes a less dominant role in our inner life.

How strongly can I be present? How deeply can I be present? How long can I be present? What lies beyond my ordinary awareness? Yesterday I remained within my self-imposed boundaries, short of what I might hope for. But today is a new day, a time to begin afresh.

For this week, notice your passivity to the shackling weight of your own past. At least for some moments, break with all that, into new levels of inner work, into stronger sensation, into more continuous presence, into deeper, more heartfelt prayer, into active inner exploration of your spiritual dimensions. Can your inner life be vibrant, alive, and fresh?

181. Determination and Help

Determination and commitment to the spiritual path, to daily work on meditation, sensing, presence, kindness, and prayer, lie within our purview, within what is required on our part. Without determination and commitment we will not make the efforts required to move along the way. Built from our oft-renewed decision to do the sacred work of the soul, that determination is what we bring to the path.

On the other hand, determination is not enough. We need help. In the earlier stages we need help from other people to learn the how-to of the path. In later stages, we need help from above. For example, regardless of how determined we are to be continuously present, we are most unlikely to attain to that without the help of higher energies and without opening our will beyond ego toward the Divine. Both these kinds of help come through turning our innermost core toward the higher, utterly emptying ourselves in the heartfelt depths of worship or meditation. The higher stands ready to help us, if we stand ready to receive it.

But any help we do receive dissipates rapidly and wastefully, if not put to work in the practical way of sensing, presence, and so on. Here determination plays its role. We need to create an inner vehicle, a mode of spiritual readiness both to receive the blessings from above and to engage them in the work of perfecting our soul. The regular cultivation of both our ability to worship and our ability to be present gradually builds the necessary inner environment.

For this week, examine your situation in regard to these crucial and complementary aspects of the path: determination and receiving help.

182. First Things First

Details are the stuff of life. The particulars of our many moments, when taken together, form a whole, which is our life.

And to each moment we bring our priorities, or lack thereof. To the details of how we live, what we perceive, and what we do, we can put the question of what those details serve. Sometimes they serve nothing, just wasted or worse. Sometimes they serve the necessities or the pleasures of living. And sometimes they can serve our greater goals.

One aspect of conscious living involves knowing and acting on our priorities. From time to time we can profit from meditating on our priorities and goals. After sitting quietly for some time and bringing ourselves to a state of presence, we consider where our life is going and what matters to us. This is not the place for should's and ought's, which are conditioned responses, external to our true nature. Instead, we examine what we truly wish for, from the bottom of our heart. These more essential passions hold the key to our own uniqueness. Perhaps we see priorities of developing and applying our own talents and gifts, of how to give more to our family or society. From a spiritual standpoint, the way of becoming ourselves serves our true destiny, our role in the great world.

Within those priorities we include our inner work, which need not detract from our external priorities and can even support them. As we meet each moment, can we stay focused on the work of presence, of contact with our body to keep us centered? Moment by moment: that is the way to build our soul, to create our inner wholeness. Recognizing an inwardly empty moment, we begin again straight away: relaxing our tensions, sensing our body and awakening to conscious presence. This moment, and this moment, and this moment, throughout the day, until presence becomes our norm.

For this week, examine your priorities and bring them to life.

183. The Three Domains

In our usual, ordinary state we are neither active nor open. Instead we are passive, swept along in the stream of thoughts, emotions, physical impulses, and sensory perceptions. But when we rise out of that stream and turn toward spiritual inner work, we have a choice. What approach shall we adopt: inwardly active, inwardly open, or some harmony of the two? Our answer depends on the domain in which we choose to work at that moment.

The outer domain of body, thought, emotion, and surroundings, a region on which we can have some influence, calls for an active approach to inner work. This includes focusing our attention, sensing our body, energy breathing, acts of kindness, working against destructive habits, not clinging to thoughts and reactive emotions as me or mine, doing the right thing, and so forth.

The inner domain, the higher worlds, calls us to receive, simply and directly. In moments of prayer and deep meditation we open ourselves, heart and soul, utterly and completely, toward the higher. Perhaps we are allowed entry, or better still, we allow the higher to enter us. Either way, in approaching the spiritual worlds, inner openness is the path upward.

Of course, it's not always so absolute: openness plays a role in the active, and vice versa. In the outer domain we open to physical sensation and we listen to our neighbor. On the inner side, we actively turn toward the higher, inwardly calling out to the Divine.

But between all of these, between the higher and the lower, the outer and the inner, the active and the open, we stand in harmony in the center of our being, in the place of presence, in "I Am," in the stillness of consciousness. Inhabiting this center, we work actively toward the outer, toward our surroundings, our body, and the habitual patterns of our personality. Inhabiting this center, we open toward the higher, toward the realms of ecstasy and love.

Sometimes we work actively toward the outer. At other times openly toward the higher. And when possible, we rise to all three simultaneously, active toward the outer, open toward the higher, and fully present as our own true conscious nature in the center. At those times, the higher flows through us and into this world. And in the process, we begin to emerge as a whole human being.

For this week, find the balance in your inner work.

184. A New Floor

Both life and the spiritual path put us on a roller coaster of inner states, limited to a range that characterizes our level of being. Sometimes we rise to our personal heights, our ceiling, consisting of, for example, certain degrees of presence in joy, love, kindness, generosity, responsibility, excellence, and so on. At other times we fall to our personal lows, our floor, consisting of, for example, certain degrees of reactive emotions like anger, greed, jealousy, fear, and self-pity, our own menagerie of destructive habits, inappropriate or unethical acts, and our favorite flavors of self-centeredness. Usually, though, we live in a kind of muddle in the region between our two extremes, between our individual floor and ceiling.

A change in our level of being, a permanent transformation, promises to raise both our floor and our ceiling. If our being were to change, we would no longer fall into the same old problematic patterns and we would occasionally rise to new, unexpected heights. These great milestones in our personal journey result from the whole array of inner work and outer actions we bring to bear on our life. We work to raise our ceiling through the quality of our meditation and prayer. In the middle region, we work to increase the frequency, duration, and quality of our presence, as well as the quality of our interaction with the world.

But working to raise our floor is crucial to transforming being. This is where our energy and our will drain away, wasted. This is where we disappear, having surrendered to the impulses of an upside-down existence. We need to learn to not identify with all those things and events that drag us down into our lower states, to not follow the siren song of anger, greed, jealousy, fear, self-pity, gluttony, pride, lust, destructive habits and the rest. If we can raise ourselves out of this muck, so that we no longer fall into it so completely, then we will have raised the floor of the inner states we live in, and our being will have changed. This is not the end of the spiritual path, but it is a major step toward that end. Without the baggage of identification, we can travel much more lightly and quickly.

Through the steady work of non-clinging, letting go, plank by plank we build a new floor under ourselves, so that we live with greater ease and no longer drop as low as we once did. This enables us to conserve our energy for raising our ceiling.

For this week, look at your own floor and see what you can do, specifically, to begin to raise it.

185. Exercise Inside and Out

To enliven our spiritual practice, we need to be alert for every opportunity to build our inner life. One way to spiritualize more of our life is to look for those particular situations that do not require all of our attention. When we find ourselves in such a circumstance, we can choose to turn part of our attention toward our inner work. Example situations include waiting, watching some form of entertainment, and routine or repetitive activities. For this week, we focus on physical exercise.

Exercise creates significant amounts of extra energy. We typically let this energy drain away by passively daydreaming while we work out. But instead, we can exercise body and soul at the same time. We base this inner action in contact with our body through sensing, keeping our attention in the actual physical sensations of our body as it moves.

The energy generated during exercise may enable us to take our inner work one or two stages further. After establishing and maintaining full-body sensation, we gradually open to being in the whole of our presence: in body, heart, mind, and consciousness. We work to be fully and deeply present in the midst of the exercise session, at peace in the center of the action.

Beyond that, if we are quite centered, we can even turn toward the higher energies, directing our innermost core toward the prayer of the open heart-mind. Then we begin to taste what it might be like to be a complete human being: engaged in the body and the material world, present in consciousness, and connected with the higher.

For this week, exercise inside and out, body and soul. If you do not regularly exercise, find one of your typical daily physical activities which leave you enough extra attention to turn toward inner work.

186. Breathing TV

A commonplace activity that can be particularly numbing to our inner life is watching television. The programs and advertisements seem designed to manipulate our emotions while keeping us passively mesmerized, sometimes in excitement, sometimes in a stupor. Yet so much of our entertainment and information come from TV, that it is difficult, and perhaps unnecessary, to break away from it. Because TV watching is not in itself a destructive habit like smoking, excessive alcohol, or drug abuse, we can work our spiritual practice into it.

An immediate difficulty reveals itself in seeing that because we are so passive when we watch TV, our energy falls to a low ebb, both in quality and quantity. The apathy engendered in TV watching naturally keeps us in autopilot mode of functioning. Flowing along with the images, sounds, and words puts us into a state not so very different than dreaming. We tend to lose whatever self-awareness we had prior to watching.

So ... we look to raise our energy level while sitting in front of the TV. To do this we practice energy breathing, which is a special form of conscious breathing, while we watch TV. Because of its physical movement, the breath offers a prominent object toward which to direct our attention. Adding the further step of refining our attention enough to intentionally draw energy from the air gives us a strong base in a non-automatized present moment, helping keep us inwardly alive. The energy extracted from the air fuels our inner life, dramatically increasing our awareness and the level of our presence. Whether we practice breath awareness or energy breathing, we make our time count toward our lasting welfare.

For this week, work at conscious breathing, and if possible energy breathing, while you watch TV. This practice is not intended to encourage us to watch more TV, but rather to make our existing TV time more profitable, more soulful. If you are among those who watch little or no TV, find another of your activities for the breath practice, like web browsing or reading newspapers, magazines, or novels.

187. Extending Our Bodily Presence

Through prayer and deep meditation, we sometimes find ourselves in contact with a very high energy, one that changes our entire perspective and state. And we may naturally want to come back to that again and again, feeling it to be the leading edge of our inner work. However, if we focus solely on coming to high states, we tend to lose our moorings. To be an effective bridge between heaven and earth requires keeping our feet on the ground. Furthermore, the true leading edge of our inner work is wherever we happen to be and whatever state we happen to experience in this and every other moment.

Work at sensation is indeed work on our soul, on the absolutely necessary foundation soul that can serve as our vehicle for access to the higher worlds. We can work at sensation almost anywhere and any time, with the exception of safety critical situations like driving. Although it may seem relatively mundane compared to what happens in deep meditation, sensation is the basis on which all our inner work stands. And so we continually return to sensing our body.

For this week, work toward extending your practice of sensing. You might consider increasing your sensing work along one of more of the following dimensions, which also apply more generally to our work at presence:

- Frequency: how often you come to sensation
- Duration: how long you work at it each time
- Intensity: how strong it is
- Breadth: how much of your body has sensation

In addition, if you are able to come to full-body sensation, then you can work at shifting your perspective from being in your body and sensing it, to being in your sensation body.

188. The Peace of Being

Life is a river of time, with events, actions, reactions, thoughts, sensations, and emotions, like anxiety and impatience, passing through us at every moment. And our awareness, our being is the riverbed through which all this flows. We can just be, standing on the still bank of the river, peacefully watching it all happen. Whatever comes down that stream, however tempted we are to jump in to grab a piece of it or to prevent that piece from passing through us, we calmly abide in being, rooted in awareness, letting everything come and go, as it will anyhow. In the process we enter the natural peace of simply being.

This is not to say that we become spectators rather than participants in life. On the contrary, by stepping back from time to time, into the peace of just being, we refresh our energies and clear our vision. We become more able to act effectively, productively, and in accord with the highest potential of the situations life presents.

If we practice just being during a sitting meditation session, then the practice is to do nothing. This is more subtle than it sounds, because we always want to do something, to change something, to follow what attracts us, escape what repels us, or even to do not doing. To do nothing is just to sit and see.

For this week, practice just being, at least three times each day, during your normal life activities. Relaxing into being here in this moment, in this awareness, not holding onto or pushing away whatever we see, we begin to live in peace. Our heart and mind settle into the present, as we learn to savor its delicious and palpable simplicity. And the taste of that simplicity is unmistakable peace.

189. A Steady Pace

Step by step, we walk our path toward the Divine. But if we take frequent and extensive detours or stop for lengthy vacations from our inner work, we lose our momentum and tend to regress. Even our understanding seems to evaporate as we forget the tastes of presence and warm-hearted devotion. If we rely on crises, extraordinary experiences, or temporary peaks to set us running toward the spirit, the energy soon dissipates and our progress is fitful at best. But by putting one foot in front of the other, by keeping to a steady pace of daily spiritual practice, the accumulating weight of our dedication and effort slowly and surely builds our soul, transforming us with a reliable anchor in presence and heart.

But while we do seek a steady day-to-day pace, we also strive to accelerate that pace gradually. Each year our inner world should be more vibrant than the previous year. The more we enter the spirit, the more our devotion and obligation to that spirit grows. As our engagement in the process of spiritual evolution advances, we begin to entrust our aspirations, our very life to the Sacred One. And the steady pace of practice becomes our home and our refuge, our breath and our most immediate nourishment. Without it we stumble about, flat and empty. With it our horizons merge with the Boundless.

For this week, assess your practice in terms of its peaks and valleys, and work to create a steadfast orientation toward the path of the spirit.

190. Laboratory of the Spirit

Each of us is unique, not only in the DNA of our body and the particulars of our life experience, but also in the very core of our individual will, of who we are. To reveal its ultimate spiritual fulfillment this uniqueness must first find its own distinctive path. In Kabbalah for example, it is said that every Tzaddik, the equivalent of a great saint or fully enlightened master, follows his or her own characteristic path to attain that destiny. So while a teaching can provide a set of important, effective practices, no standard recipe suffices to bring the seeker to the Sought.

Even from its earliest stages, the path depends on our own uniqueness, our own insight, intuition and creativity, our own conscience. Through these powers we see how to engage humanity's remarkable collection of spiritual practices in a way that serves our evolution. Exploration and testing develop our discrimination and individuality, thereby answering the call of the spirit to become our Self. We soon discover those practices most effective for us at the current stage of our path.

A fixed recipe also cannot work because we lack the perceptions to see into the spiritual realms. Thus we could not in any case understand or receive a true recipe, even if one did exist. Again the answer is to explore our spiritual practices and variations on those practices, to find our way.

Intuition and conscience will tell us what is right for us today, what works and what does not. That intuition can be based in part on our own judgment of how our practices affect us in terms of presence, kindness, clarity, joy, peace, energy, depth, and so on. Like any scientist, we seek empirical confirmation of our understanding of the spiritual path and how to proceed along it. The attempt at objectivity helps us navigate between self-delusion and self-doubt. The experience of others certainly can help, but we bear in mind that what works for them may not for us, and vice versa.

A major difficulty with the empirical approach to spirituality is that the results of our inner work may be completely hidden, even from us. Our practice may be building something in us that will only manifest much later, making our intuitive sense of what's true our best and only guide. Furthermore, we do not work for results, like a day laborer before the Ineffable, expecting immediate payment or gratification. We work because it is right to do so and because we are drawn by love. Nevertheless, the path does have its immediate effects on us. Those effects can help us follow our own unique route toward the realms of the spirit.

For this week, reevaluate your inner work. See what is effective and what is not. If necessary, adjust your practices, extending some, decreasing others, trying variations, or adding new ones.

191. Standing Presence

Most of us spend a good deal of time each day standing: cooking, engaging in a brief conversation, washing dishes, looking in a mirror, waiting in line, waiting for the elevator, waiting for the train or bus, viewing a work of art, and so on. To bring our spiritual practice into more of our day, we seek to extend it into every posture we take. For this week we work on standing in presence, one good way to make our spiritual aspirations real.

Whenever we find ourselves standing, we take the opportunity to sense our body. We can begin with sensing our feet as they do they work of supporting our body. We can then move the sensation up until the whole body is filled with the sensitive energy. At that point we can work to become aware of ourselves, here, standing, in this body full of sensation. We become our will-to-be and enter the wholeness of presence. We can work toward this whenever we stand, whether we are standing still or engaged in some activity while standing.

If we need to stand still for long enough, we can turn it into a standing meditation, standing in presence and peace. If thoughts come, we just let them go on their own without grappling or engaging with them. We stay rooted in our sensation, in our intention to be here, in the simplicity of presence.

192. Telephone Presence

We know the scenario. The telephone rings, or we dial the call, and we immediately lose ourselves in the conversation, lose contact with our surroundings and our body. If driving under the influence of a cell phone, we find it difficult to stay wholly in touch with the road situation. This action of the phone, to collapse our entire awareness into hearing and speaking, presents an excellent challenge for expanding our awareness and broadening our attention.

Just before we touch the phone, whether it's ringing or we are about to dial, we come back to ourselves, to our presence. As we reach for the phone we bring attention to our hand, to the physical sensations in the hand, to the sensations of holding the phone. If dialing, we stay aware of the touch of the keypad on our fingertips. If using a headset or earbud, we stay aware of their touch on our head or ear. In speaking, we open our attention not just to the meaning of the words we say, but also to the actual sound of our own voice, hearing ourselves speak. In listening to the other person, we notice the sound, tone, and feeling quality of their voice, the meaning of their words, and our own inner responses in thought and emotion.

Conversations draw us willy-nilly into the conditioned patterns of our personality. What presence we may have had soon evaporates. That makes conversations a prime arena for extending the domain of our inner work. The telephone can help because it gives a clear signal of an impending interaction and a reminder to be. If we practice telephone presence seriously, we can gradually train ourselves to awaken into presence whenever the phone rings or whenever we dial a call, and to stay present throughout the conversation.

For this week, practice telephone presence.

193. Assessment and Motivation

Unless we live in a monastery, surrounded by constant reminders of the sacred work of transformation, one of the biggest difficulties we face in our spiritual path is simply remembering to practice, remembering to work at presence and the rest as we go about our daily business. We become so engrossed in our life situations, that we continually lose ourselves. And what enables us blithely to carry on living in this half-aware, pre-programmed, personality-pattern-driven style is that we remain generally unaware of it. Perhaps in our minds we intend to practice presence and awareness of sensation throughout the day. But when it comes down to actually doing it, we forget about it. And we largely ignore that fact, letting it slide out of awareness. We accept and expect to live without presence. We even adopt the unstated assumption that we ourselves have no real possibility of awakening, that our inner life will always be pretty much as it is now.

To find a way out of this conundrum, we consciously face our true situation by directly seeing the level of our inner work, or the lack thereof. And in facing up to it, we discover the possibility of doing something about it; we find our motivation once again.

The practice is simple and direct. Three times a day, late morning, late afternoon, and before going to bed, we stop to look back at our inner work during the preceding part of the day. We recall the quantity and quality of our presence, of whatever spiritual practice we may have engaged in during the previous hours.

In the effort to create our spiritual inner life, we take our motivation wherever we can find it. Self-assessment works.

Knowing that soon we will face our own self-imposed reckoning, we find ourselves deciding to practice now so that we will have something positive to look back on when the time arrives to assess our inner work. Seeing our lack of inner work motivates us to fill that vacuum. We do not wallow in negative self-criticism, blame, or hopelessness. Instead, our growing discomfort with our half-aware life spurs us to pick ourselves up and practice more. Facing our own truth helps us act to shape that truth. Seeing the gaps in our inner work shows us how to improve and extend our practice. Seeing our moments of presence encourages us and moves us toward more. And the one who sees all this is our own conscience, our deepest self.

For this week, three times each day, at the end of the morning, at the end of the afternoon, and at the end of the evening, review the level of your inner work during the preceding part of the day.

194. Personal Integrity

Why does every religion embrace a code of morality? On the face of it we can see that society as a whole benefits enormously from the morality of individuals. We can live in relative peace instead of constantly watching our backs. Though the significance of this societal benefit of morality cannot be overestimated, another reason stands at least equal to it.

Religions are first and foremost about our relationship with the Divine. Through right action in our dealings with the world we place ourselves in a position to embody Divine action. This alignment of our own acts with the Divine Purpose can only come through our inner perception of that Purpose. That inner perception of the high Purpose comes through conscience. And the voice of conscience, for example in those inner twinges of discomfort with wrong action, falls mute unless we heed it. This chain brings us back to the reason we need to practice and protect our personal integrity. With a clear conscience we can walk the path of the spirit forthrightly and in peace. With a troubled and disappearing conscience, we lose our bearings and stumble.

Yet only the rarest of people make their way through life without lapses of judgment and damage to their integrity. For the rest of us, when we realize we have done the wrong thing, we pick ourselves up, make amends if possible, and renew our resolve to live in accordance with our own conscience.

The morality of religion and the laws of our governments are just the starting point, however, for integrity. With those as a foundation, we pursue a style of living that holds the mirror of conscience before all our actions, large and small. Through the channel of our personal integrity, we approach our true purpose and destiny in this life.

Often the question of right and wrong seems clear. Yet we find ourselves sorely tempted to take the unethical path. In speech we might stretch the truth, fail to say some true thing we should have said, or say more than we should. In the ongoing action of life, morally dubious situations abound and beckon. At other times, the ethics of a choice are murky and we descend into confusion. In both the obvious and the murky situations, only the force of our personal integrity, our self-respect, and the value we place on a clear conscience can steer us through the thickets of life.

If the voice of conscience is vague, we come back to our baseline of public morality and the laws we share. Indeed, to protect ourselves from fanaticism and believing we know God's will, we test the promptings of conscience against ordinary morality, legality, and common sense. Conscience will not violate those. But conscience can guide us through regions not addressed by public morality. Conscience can guide us into becoming ourselves, into living our lives well, into fulfilling our unique destiny. A person of conscience is a person of integrity.

For this week, examine the state of your personal integrity. Notice the temptations to ignore what you know is right. Notice how you respond in those situations. And above all, notice the promptings of your conscience, your personal sense of right and wrong, propriety and impropriety.

195. Barriers to Relating

Perhaps you can recall an experience with another person in which the boundaries between you vanished, in which your consideration for the other person equaled your consideration for yourself, in which the question "Who am I?" seemed irrelevant.

Our relationships with people matter on many levels. Physically we need others for the care and feeding of our body. Our highly elaborated society provides all our necessary and desired material goods and services, which we could not possibly produce on our own. Emotionally we need others to care for and be cared for by, to relax with and share with, to enjoy, to respect, to have compassion for, and to love. Intellectually we need others to learn from, to debate with, and to collaborate with.

Spiritually we need others to help us see beyond our egoism, to teach us the practices of the path, and to share our sacred work. Each of these brings crucial help on the way.

Yet despite our great need for others, we remain far from the true possibilities of relationship. To understand how and why this happens, we can look to see our own inner barriers that separate us from other people. These barriers come in a wide variety of forms, with each of us sporting a unique subset of them. A partial list includes inner criticism and negative attitudes, arrogance and aloofness, anger and animosity, jealousy and envy, fear and timidity, disgust, lust, neediness, hurry, worry, self-centeredness, indifference, talking too much, and not talking enough. More generally, we consider our own life, our own needs, and our own desires to be so much more important than those of other people. We fill our inner world with ourselves and leave little or even no room for anyone else.

All these walls of non-relating can dissipate if we do not identify with them and if we let them go. For that we need first to see them in action in ourselves and then not believe in our thoughts, emotions, and attitudes as speaking for or defining who we really are. Rather, we see this whole inner menagerie of our personality as a set of habitual patterns which need not direct or control us and need not separate us from others. By relaxing these barriers our connections with people naturally widen and deepen.

Distance from others is distance from ourselves. The self-centered life of separateness and isolation focuses on our egoism and neglects the truth of who we are. At a very basic level, we are not really separate from others. We can catch a glimpse of that by looking beyond our personal thoughts and emotions, to enter the pure consciousness we all share. So how we treat others, both outwardly and inwardly, is how we treat ourselves.

For this week, look at your relationships or lack thereof. Look at the quality and openness of how you relate to others, both the casual stranger and your loved ones. See and begin to let go of the barriers that keep you so separate from people.

196. Establishing Physical Presence

The lower part of our soul develops from the energy of sensation, the energy that puts us in touch with our body and our senses. Through our inner work, sensation gradually forms a place for us to stand and be present, a place which we can inhabit. This foundation soul provides a robustness and concreteness to our experience of our body, emotions, and thoughts. It is an inner house which we can occupy.

Too often we only half-experience our body, a complex of flesh and bone that carries us along. In that state, although we believe that our body defines who we are, we rarely come fully into our body, into the wholeness of being in our energy body. The persistent practice of sensation leads to exactly that: being in our body, wholly, fully, and now. Through that practice we establish a physical presence, a foundation for our soul, and a strong place in the present moment, the first doorway toward the sacred.

To further augment the foundation soul, we intermittently practice energy breathing, consciously drawing energy from the air and allowing it to accumulate as sensitive energy within our body. The sea of energies that surrounds us provides an open and ready source of soul nourishment. It only requires a focus of attention and intention to tap into it.

For this week, renew your work to establish physical presence through the steady practice of sensation, supported by energy breathing.

197. Entering Conscious Awareness

To enter the spacious stillness of consciousness that always awaits us, that underlies thought and emotion, sight and sound, that forms the timeless context of our life, is not so easy. Consciousness is so fundamental that we habitually overlook it, leaving it in the background while we remain distracted with the surface phenomena of our life. We can, however, take steps to enter consciousness.

But why bother? Why does it matter? Simply put: consciousness is the gateway to the higher worlds. To establish the capacity to open to the higher in anything more than a rare and haphazard fashion, one key factor lies in first recognizing true consciousness and developing an ability to enter it. Furthermore, because the vastness of consciousness so obviously supersedes any person and any personality, it mitigates the egoistic feeling of being special, another key factor on the way to the higher.

We begin with establishing a strong base of sensation in our whole body. This full body awareness provides a stable platform for our awareness in the here and now. Even this is not easy though. It requires persistent work on sensing the energy in our body, on relaxing our physical and emotional tensions so as not to waste the energy, and on methods like energy breathing and fasting to raise the level of our sensation and to consolidate it.

As an adjunct to this process of increasing and condensing the energy of sensation in our body, we practice non-clinging toward all the thoughts, emotions, and sensory perceptions streaming and cavorting through our awareness. Repeatedly letting go of all these inner events that seduce us into losing ourselves, we create the possibility of looking beyond them.

Then through a deeper act of relaxation, we open to the great silence of consciousness, the medium in which we can and do live, the stillness underneath thought and sensory perception. Entering consciousness is like entering an immense cathedral with high, arching, domed ceilings, vanishing in the distance. Sounds merge with the silence of the great space, just as our thoughts and perceptions fall off into the unboundedness of consciousness. Yet it wraps us in its comforting presence.

Consciousness is not beyond our reach. You can open to it at any time, at least briefly, by looking beyond your thoughts and relaxing into the clear awareness in which you are.

For this week work to gain a better taste of true consciousness. Find your way to enter here.

198. Turning Toward the Light

Beyond consciousness, beyond stillness and peace, lies a sacred world of creative activity and Divine light. One approach toward that begins with relaxing inwardly and outwardly, letting thoughts and emotions lose their charge and subside, and entering the spacious context of life, the peace of consciousness. One more step and the light begins to open to us.

How to take that step? We gather ourselves inwardly, totally focused. With the whole of our being, we reach beyond our very awareness and open ourselves heart and soul. We call out to the Divine in words we hold sacred, empty-handed and spiritually impoverished, pleading for succor. And we continue reaching, opening, and begging at this doorway to the sacred, keeping the faith that eventually it will open. The very attempt brings a measure of fulfillment, for in our devotion to it we find the satisfaction of giving our all toward this most sacred task.

With persistent practice, that light does open and stays accessible. At any time, without any preparation, it requires only that we turn toward it with the whole of ourselves. That purifying, transformative, ecstatic energy begins to rain down upon us, filling our whole being with its joyous largesse and love.

For this week, practice turning toward the light.

199. Opening to the Divine

Beyond and behind the world of the Divine light, lies its beneficent Source, the Source of all, the One in Whom we live, the One Whom all life and all religions serve, the One Who lives in us all. To our minds, that Greatness seems so far beyond our daily experience that we dismiss any notion of actually opening to or having contact with the Divine Immanence. We live with the assumption that, while certain great people of the past had such contact, we cannot. Against that assumption we pin our hope, our faith, our love, and the realization that what is possible for some must be possible for all.

One avenue of contact with the Divine begins with standing in simple prayer, asking for fulfillment of true needs, both our own and our neighbor's. If we make prayer a regular practice, be it ritual, communal worship or individualized and free-form, the very repetition of the attitude of praying gradually does its subtle work on our soul. We begin to have a sense of the sacred, of standing before the Ineffable, in awe, in humility and in love, during our time of prayer.

This dim but growing awareness of the truly sacred draws us to reach beyond ourselves, beyond everything, toward the Divine. In such moments, our soul looks for ways to breach the familiar and behold the Immeasurable. Our deepening faith spurs us on. Again and yet again, we search for release from our ordinary self to arrive in the Sacred Presence. In these times, we engage our entire being and every last ounce of our will in seeking and opening to the Divine.

And then one day, seemingly by accident, the veils drop away, and there beyond all things, beyond space, time, and consciousness, even beyond the ecstasy of the Divine light, we find ourselves before the Greatness. We stand transparent and empty-handed in awe, wonder, and love.

The event ends. We return with renewed fervor to the prayer of stillness, peace, and reaching beyond. Slowly, in an attitude of selflessness, we find the means of returning to the Sacred Presence.

But even that stops short of complete transformation, for we need to surrender. Instead of seeking to live in the Divine, we allow the Divine to live in us. With the core of our will, we repeatedly and joyfully engage in opening and humility, surrender and love.

Because that Sacred lies beyond time, the amount of time devoted to deepest prayer does not matter as much as the strength and purity of our intention. Even a few minutes a day completely dedicated to entering the sacred place works a profound and beneficent influence on our soul.

An open and inviting road stretches before us. For this week, take your next steps.

200. Non-Thinking

Our deeply ingrained propensity to identify with our thoughts may well be the single greatest hurdle to progress on the spiritual path, preventing us from fully entering the present moment. We passively allow our focus to bounce along with our thought stream, which is sometimes dull and ordinary, sometimes chaotic and bizarre, but always pretending to be the real me. In truth our thoughts only form a small and relatively insignificant fraction of who we really are.

We do not attempt to stop thoughts. We cannot ban them from our minds. Rather, we follow two approaches that offer us a way to shift beyond thought: laterally beside or vertically above the meandering thought stream. The lateral approach entails moving our attention, our center of gravity into another part of ourselves on the same level as thought: emotion or physical sensation. Since emotions do not readily offer a stable platform for presence, we work to center ourselves in our bodily experience, in the sensitive energy in the body. We relax into our body, resting in the direct and ongoing awareness of arms and legs, torso and head, and in the sensitive energy that powers that direct awareness, that forms its substance.

The second approach to releasing the grip of our thoughts is to shift vertically into the context of our life: pure awareness, consciousness. All thoughts, as well as emotions and physical sensations, take place within the context of consciousness. Opening our being into the spaciousness between and beneath thoughts, the subtle energy of consciousness carries us into a world of peace and stillness, a world not buffeted by the whims of our self-propelled, associative thought processes. For this we need to relax thoroughly, base our presence in physical sensation, and then let go into the silent realm of consciousness.

For this week work to shift your center out of the continuing stream of automatically generated, associative thinking.

201. Intentional Presence

To be present, to live fully in our immediate experience of this moment, is most natural for us. To our misfortune, however, we have fallen from the grace of natural presence. Instead we live a disjointed, distracted life, taken by every passing thought, feeling, and sensory impression. To re-enter the natural state of presence requires great intention and diligent practice. Permanent entry to that state marks the first great transformation of a person's being.

What is the intention, the inner act called for in presence? It means to be, to embrace the will to be, and to be able to say with the whole of our being, "Here I am." This results from a slight and simple shift within us, an inner movement into being our own source, the author of our script, the one who decides our decisions and acts our actions, the agent of our life.

Awareness is not enough. We need to become the will to be, continually deciding to be here, to be our self. Deeper than thought, emotion, and sensory impressions, we can be. For this week, explore your own willingness to be.

202. Dynamic Presence

Life brings endless change. Each day, each moment differs from the one before. Even if we have fixed routines, the experience always varies: the external situation changes, as do our inner state and the state of our body. Time and entropy constantly conspire in a kaleidoscopic dynamism that is our life.

Into this unfolding reality we bring our spiritual practice, uniquely tailoring our presence to every situation. Sometimes we can work more deeply, entering into the peace beyond time, and even into the sacred beyond that. At other times, we repeatedly work to bring part of our attention to our body, to the physical sensation of being in our body, to anchor us in this moment, amidst the whole complex of engagements, problems, and distractions currently calling us to lose ourselves in them. Or we practice kindness even when everything in us rebels against it. And some days we experience such mental, emotional, or physical malaise, that the most we can do is dimly and intermittently to remember the reality of the sacred spirit.

Spiritual practice, to be in any degree sustained, must be dynamic. With that ever-ready ability to enter wholly into each moment of our life without completely losing ourselves, we live with kindness, joy, and openness to the sacred.

For this week, bring more dynamism to your inner work, to match your ever-changing life.

203. From Heartless to Kindness

All too often we notice ourselves falling into a heartless attitude toward others: some ill-will, criticism, anger, hatred, or an impulse toward emotional cruelty or even physical violence.

If we aspire to the spiritual path, we need a way to deal with such unbecoming processes in our psyche.

The noticing itself forms the first essential step. If we do not see how we are inwardly, we have no chance of changing. The practice of clearly seeing our own inner and outer manifestations supports us in noticing our occasional heartlessness.

But only if the seeing is strong and objective, can it enable us not to identify with the thoughts and emotions, and not react against them. Then our situation can begin to change. For that we can take an inner action to replace our nastiness with kindness. If we try to stop the callous impulse directly, it will nearly always find a way around our effort. However, if at the very moment we see the heartlessness, we deliberately evoke a feeling of friendship or warmth, kindness or compassion, appreciation or well-wishing, we may well succeed in overwhelming our unkindness with love. With persistence, the deeper and truer feeling of connection supplants the more superficial, though possibly powerful, feelings of antagonism.

For this week, when you notice a heartless thought or feeling in yourself, make an effort to shift into kindness.

204. Relaxing into Now

So many forces conspire to pull us out of this moment, out of ourselves: thoughts and emotions, hurry and worry, pains and pleasures, fascination and aversion, people with their needs and demands, their beauty and their quirks. To leave be all that impinges on us, to just relax into this moment without collapsing into the kaleidoscope of life, brings a real and welcome liberation, even if only temporarily. This does not imply a lack of engagement, enjoyment, or concern with all that enters our life. On the contrary, being able to relax leaves us free to participate in life wholeheartedly.

Although this ability to relax does reduce stress, like an instant vacation, the implications and possibilities run much deeper than the necessary help it provides our body and emotions. To be relaxed means not to be inwardly held captive by the chains of life. This prerequisite puts us into a position to reach beyond ourselves through presence, meditation, and prayer. The first freedom of inwardly releasing all those constraints enables us to begin approaching the ultimate freedom found in the Divine. Emotional and physical tensions prevent the preoccupied parts of us from entering the deeper spiritual work. Relaxing through and through brings us naturally into a state of presence, into our body, heart, and mind, into the now, the springboard toward the spiritual depths.

For this week, allow yourself to relax into the ever-present now. Let go of all that grabs you, until you are free to be here.

205. Wholeness in Prayer

The quality of prayer and its efficacy in opening us to the Divine depends primarily on how much of our heart and soul enters the act of prayer. The greater our wholeness in that moment, the deeper is our prayer. To pray fervently means to leave aside our other, perhaps conflicting, agendas and gather the whole of our intention to the act. We ignore all other thoughts and images, feelings and sensations, as we plunge into reverential prayer. In the immediacy of worship, we empty our heart and soul to make room for the Divine.

Intensity cannot readily be grafted on from the outside,

but must come from within. Communal worship appears to bring such help from without, but actually it is the collective within that provides the help. The quality of the prayer of each individual in the church, synagogue, mosque, or temple contributes to the quality of the help that flows to his or her fellow worshippers. So whether we pray alone or in community, we make the effort to offer the whole of our being in prayer. That is the key to growth in our prayer life, to an ever-deepening ability to approach the Divine in purity of heart and strength of will.

There comes a point in prayer where the effort of wholeness falls away, as contact with the Higher opens and draws us near. The effort transforms into intense and total surrender, humility, joy, awe and love.

The centrality of prayer in our spiritual life calls us to give it our best, to approach our times of prayer with utmost respect. For this week, seek a deeper quality in your prayer.

206. Reading Presence

In our continuing work toward living in presence, we look for the underutilized areas of our life. Time spent reading affords one such opportunity. When we read we tend to collapse into our thinking brain, with little or no awareness of the rest of our being. By grounding ourselves in our body, in physical sensations, we can expand our presence while we read, without interfering with the reading process. Indeed, extending our awareness to include both our thoughts and our body actually enhances our experience of reading by raising our awareness of our thoughts. No longer do the words read us, moving our passive thought processes. Instead, we become inwardly more active in reading, aware of the words and thoughts, ideas and images, better able to analyze, critique, and understand nonfiction, better able to enter and enjoy a fictional world, and better able to find inspiration in words of the spirit.

At the same time, we do not leave aside our spiritual practice while we read. By sensing our body and becoming aware of our thoughts as we read, we step into the world of presence. Another step and we enter the act as the one who is reading, as the one who is choosing to read, the one moving our eyes across the words, seeing our thoughts echo the words on the page or screen, thinking or feeling in response, and sensing our body. We become the one who lives our life, instead of being passively carried along by the river of time.

Whenever you read anything, let that very act remind you to come into presence, to sense your body, to be aware of your thoughts and feelings, to be the one who is reading. If you enter an extended session of reading, your inner effort of presence will almost inevitably wane. When you notice that or remember your intended inner work, simply and gently renew your effort of presence, beginning with being in your body while you read.

For this week, practice reading in a state of presence.

207. Doing This

All day long, every day, we are always doing something, even if it is just relaxing. Sometimes we do what we enjoy or find meaningful, sometimes we do things we would rather not be doing, and at other times we have a neutral attitude. From the point of view of the spiritual path, one significant problem with what we do occurs when we just go through the motions of an action without really engaging ourselves in it, without really being there for it. We let too much of our life happen without our participation, without being the one who is doing it. We allow ourselves to do things by habit, by momentum, and by autopilot. Such a passive, disengaged way of living only yields half a life.

This is not only a matter of being, of awareness. The doing matters. Acting as the agent behind our actions brings a new and unsuspected dimension to our ordinary situations. We enter whatever action is taking place in this moment as the one who is doing it. It is a matter of will: attention and intention, choice and responsibility. The act emanates from us. You become the immediate source of your actions. You are the one who is doing "this," whatever "this" happens to be.

Of course, there is a higher, sacred Source, with Whom we can seek to align our actions. But to that Source we bring the offering of our own individual will. The practice of "doing this," as described above, is one important way to develop our will. In becoming the source of our own actions, we create the possibility of opening our will to the Divine Will.

For this week, practice "doing this."

208. Procrastination

Because a part of our nature touches the eternal, we mistakenly transfer that sense of timelessness to our attitude toward time itself. We live with an unarticulated and unexamined assumption that our days will never end. But clearly they shall. Meanwhile, by ascribing the nature of eternity to time, we all too readily fall into the trap of procrastination.

We put off the difficult and distasteful but necessary in favor of the easy and frivolous. We neglect the more important and long term in favor of the less important but more immediate. In that way the big goals, the larger accomplishments that require unlimited commitment, elude us. We kill time by frittering it away and, in so doing, we kill a part of our life. The voice of laziness, shirking, and procrastination is the voice of time, triviality and death. The voice that speaks of depth, love, and action is the voice of life, eternity and will.

When it comes to the inner action of the spiritual path, the problem of procrastination multiplies. Any minor entertainment or irritation and we dive off our base in presence, figuring we can work at presence later. But that later future is imaginary because it lacks the force of our will to create it. When we slip out of presence, we never look back. Our attention and interest flow toward the distraction. We put off our inner work and impoverish our life in the process.

The only time we can practice presence is now. Procrastination eviscerates our inner life. But by seeing this clearly and by keeping our true priorities close to the surface of our mind and heart, we can ignore the subtle, seductive call of inner laziness, and work to be and to do.

For this week, notice how procrastination operates in your life and act despite it.

209. Adaptive Practice

Everything changes. Buddhism even teaches that a deep, visceral understanding of the fact of change leads to enlightenment. In particular, our individual situation with respect to our possibilities for inner work keeps changing. We may have more energy or less energy, more time to meditate or less time, more or fewer urgent matters to attend to, good health or illness, pain or the absence of pain, the ability to focus or the lack thereof, inner peace or emotional storms, reminders of the sacred or distractions from it — in short, the whole kaleidoscope of life. An unavoidable question is how to maintain our spiritual practice in the face of all this continual change, both outer and inner.

We need to be flexible and adaptable, like a surfer on the waves of life. The adaptability of human beings provided a major evolutionary advantage over other species. Adaptability also offers spiritual advantages.

No two moments of our life are exactly alike. So our inner work also must adapt. While keeping ourselves firmly grounded in the realm of time and change, we seek through our practice to establish our place in the eternal and to serve the Divine Purpose. Those latter efforts, though, depend on continually adapting our spiritual work to our conditions in time and space.

So in any and every situation, we reach into our toolkit of practices: relaxing and sensing our body, energy breathing, deepening presence, heartfelt prayer, levels of meditation, inner peace, acts of kindness and responsibility, and so on. Creatively, we adapt our practice to this moment. In that way we prepare a brighter future, come what may.

For this week, look for ways to adapt your inner work to your current situation.

210. Overcoming Mediocrity

At times we may labor under a self-limiting feeling of being mediocre, of being not quite a failure but far from a success, of not being as good or as accomplished as others, of being resigned to a non-achieving life. Although this debilitating attitude can block us from moving forward, we can work instead to make it spur us on.

One aspect of that work is to examine the sources of our feeling of mediocrity. Is it deeply ingrained in us by a difficult childhood? Does it arise from failure to achieve our goals? Who defines success? Does our consumer-oriented culture define it for us, or do we define our life in our own terms? How do our tendencies toward laziness and procrastination interact with our feelings of mediocrity? What triggers our feelings of mediocrity? What role does comparing ourselves to others play?

Looking carefully at such questions can shed important light on our inner world and help prepare the way for the clouds of mediocrity to disperse.

Feelings of mediocrity can apply to our inner life, our spiritual work, as well as to our outer abilities and activities. With inner or spiritual mediocrity we feel that we are not able to practice or that our spiritual work is weak and ineffective. And this may have more than a grain of truth about it. With outwardly-oriented mediocrity we may see ourselves and our life in a negative light, feeling that we are weak and ineffective. In either case, we run the danger of capitulating, of giving up and giving in to suffer a life beneath our possibilities.

The prescription for overcoming mediocrity consists of finding one area to get right, one area to strive for excellence in, and to work diligently at that. Everyone has gifts and possibilities. We owe it to ourselves, and to the One who gave us those gifts, to develop and realize them. Outwardly we look to the productive pursuits that we enjoy or could be good at. Inwardly we look for a simple spiritual practice that we relate to, or a wasteful or destructive habit that is within our reach to stop. We choose one thing, one thing to which we bring the whole of ourselves, body, heart, and mind. We study it, we practice it, and we give it the time it requires. And in doing that one thing very well, we crack the monolith of mediocrity. And after we have fully settled in with that one thing, we follow up with our next step.

For this week, choose one thing to improve in yourself and act on that.

211. Creating the Future

Our primary responsibility as human beings is to create a better future, for ourselves, for our children, and for the generations of coming millennia. The future that will take care of itself would be immeasurably impoverished compared to the future we might intentionally create. An immediate difficulty, though, lies in how to define a "better future." Because of the wide disparity among people's views of this and because our personal situation is best known to ourselves, we can only look to our own conscience for decisive guidance on the choices we make and the approaches we adopt. Furthermore, conscience is our one innate tool for connecting with the future, for conscience enables us to foresee our actions and their consequences.

Changing the present is difficult because so much is fixed, subject to constraints and momentum from the past. But the nano-scale uncertainties of the present evolve into the large scale uncertainties of the future, making the future the natural field for our creative action, whether in creating our own soul or in creating a "better" world. Of course, the creative action aimed at the future, can only be taken in the present and is best taken in presence.

But besides the different possibilities for any given moment of the future, we also face the wildly different scales of future time, from days and weeks to centuries and millennia. The longer the time scale we expand our perception into, the more responsibility we naturally feel.

Choice, decision, practice, repetition, commitment, adaptability, intelligence, and passion are the means for creating the future. We make choices and decisions affecting the future. We carry these into the future through practice, repetition, and commitment, all tempered by the unexpected developments we encounter. Toward the latter we adapt intelligently to maintain our commitment for the future and to take new opportunities as they arise. But if through passivity, inertia, and momentum, we allow ourselves to be carried along the stream of time, then we rob our future of its higher possibilities. Inner peace and the consciousness of being are intended as our platform for truly human action, not as ends in themselves.

The issue is not whether we fear the future or look forward to it. If we love, then we care. And if we care, we play our individual role in contributing to a better future, for ourselves, for our children, and for the societies of the long future. And for that we consider the various levels of the material, the social, the natural, and the spiritual, on smaller and larger time scales. For the material, the social, and the natural levels we envision the possible scenarios unfolding over time and we take the appropriate steps. If we wish for spiritual freedom, a loving heart and a meaningful life, we follow the path of practice on all these levels.

For this week, examine your own relationship to the future. Are there decisions you are neglecting to make or to carry out?

212. Creating Ourselves

We live with the advantages and the limitations of our genetic heredity, our experiences, and the interaction of those factors. But, crucially, we also bring our own inherent spark of freedom to the mix. That freedom allows us to rise above the limitations of heredity and experience, to lay claim to greater possibilities and modes of acting in the world. That same freedom, however, also allows us to drift rudderless within the boundaries of our history and genes. Either way, we continually create our place in our body and in this world, in relationship and in action. Who we are depends on who we create ourselves to be. This last is not intended as a new-age slogan, but rather as a prescription for inner work, for a path to becoming and fulfilling our highest potential.

Self-creation constitutes our own primal act, recapitulating on our personal scale the original Divine act of creating the universe. Our act of becoming, of entering the fullness of presence and right action, holds unlimited significance because it makes possible the entry of the Divine into this world through each of us, even with our imperfections and limitations.

Given our circumstances, what we make of ourselves depends solely on us. Certainly we can and do ask for help. But even that asking is our own creation. And we cannot wait for that great hand from the sky or for the right lottery ticket to take responsibility for our life going forward. In our inner world, this can take the form of spiritual practice, of the work of self-discipline, presence, and prayer. Externally, it can take the form of responsibility and kindness to others and to our own creative flair, toward making real what is possible, toward our own small contribution to this evolving world.

For this week, please examine what kind of person you are creating yourself to be and whether you need a new direction or perhaps a renewal of an old direction.

213. Character Matters

We usually think of good character in terms of honesty, responsibility, kindness, productivity, sobriety, and so on. These standard criteria certainly hold true and provide us with a beacon to guide our actions. But from a spiritual standpoint we also need to look more deeply into our own character defects. In particular, we pay attention to those aspects of our character that limit our inner work and impede our progress toward the sacred.

As we each have a unique pattern of character, our problems and their remedies must also be unique. Widely applicable spiritual practices such as body awareness, presence, and prayer, though fundamental to the path, generally do not address the subtleties of individual character issues. Perhaps non-clinging comes closest to being a general prescription for character-based limitations.

Consider the following partial list of character traits: passive, aggressive, stubborn, timid, shy, lazy, sad, fearful, selfish, inconsiderate, flippant, rude, mean, quarrelsome, self-pitying, withdrawn, vain, reticent, and loquacious. For each of us, no doubt, some of these do apply. The task is to come to know ourselves well enough to recognize our own character. Even more importantly, we need to understand which of our traits impede our spiritual development and keep our soul impoverished, compared to our spiritual possibilities.

Character traits stay with us as the ongoing shape of our interactions with the world. Some manifest daily, others rarely. More important than frequency, though, is the severity of the problems caused by our various traits. This offers us clues to which ones we need to address.

For purposes of our spiritual work, we take care not to select traits to try to change simply because we do not like them or to create a more attractive version of ourselves, because then we make our character work into an ego-centered project. In working on our character, we do so from a position of self-acceptance, not of rejecting parts of our makeup.

Changing one's character is even more difficult than breaking a habit. The all-at-once approach may yield dramatic results, but tends to cause unproductive dislocations in other parts of us. You push the balloon in one spot and it bulges in others. Instead, we gradually and steadily take notice when the chosen trait manifests, inwardly or outwardly. Then we develop the ability to notice when it is about to manifest. Then we pull ourselves back from it, or step beyond it, a bit at a time, gently nudging ourselves toward freedom.

For this week, assess your own character to see what particular trait you might need to change to further your spiritual practice.

214. Integrity and Wholeness

To say that both the world and human beings are complex grossly understates the situation. From the remarkably intricate structure and pathways of DNA, RNA, proteins and the rest to the 100 trillion connections among the neurons in our brain, the complexity of just one ordinary human being far surpasses our ability to comprehend. Our civilization embraces both the six and a half billion of us now living and the remarkable legacy of discovery, creativity, and industriousness of humans past. Our planet hosts millions of species besides our own. Our universe incorporates countless stars in a prodigious cosmic dance. And in the midst of it all, here we are, trying to make sense of this vast diversity and our own life. But if we focus solely on the innumerable parts at any given scale, we lose the integrity of wholeness.

The levels of wholeness include:
- our individual presence
- our family
- our community
- our state or province
- our nation
- our civilization
- the biosphere
- the planet
- the solar system
- the galaxy
- the universe
- the Divine

Integrity comes from wholeness. When we act from a part of ourselves, from a thought or an emotion or a physical appetite, we lack integrity. When we act from a part of society, placing our personal desires above the needs of other people, we lack integrity. When we act from a part of the biosphere, placing our current human desires above the good of other species and of future humans, we lack integrity. When we act without a sense of the sacred whole, we lack integrity.

Consideration for the whole also brings integrity to our spiritual practice. At a basic level, recognition of other valid ways to the sacred imbues us with tolerance and largeheartedness. More deeply, awareness of the spiritual needs of society gives us a reason to practice that is more than personal, as we see that our manner of being and acting can contribute to a more peaceful and joyous world. Finally, we realize that our prayers and meditations, our transformation of energies, our work of presence and non-clinging, support the Sacred directly. All these connections with wholeness take our path beyond the realm of self-centered motivations.

For this week, enhance your integrity by widening your field of vision toward a perspective of the whole. Inwardly or outwardly, how does what I do or fail to do now affect the whole? Let this movement toward wholeness and integrity inform, enliven, and enhance your inner work.

215. Non-Waiting

In our outer life, we often must wait for something. Circumstances constrain us: a traffic jam, the slow grinding of a bureaucracy, an overabundance of people, or a schedule that cannot be accelerated like baking a loaf of bread. So we accept the wait and perhaps make the best of it by doing something useful or entertaining in the interim. Otherwise we wallow in boredom or frustration.

In our inner life, we also frequently wait, but not because we must. We wait for the right moment to practice presence, a free moment not taken by some busyness. Or, if something is off-kilter in our body, we wait until we feel better. Or, if we deem our immediate circumstances not to be conducive or propitious, we wait for a better time or place.

During the day, when we remember about our spiritual practice, we might think: "After I get off work, I'll sense my body." And during the commute we think: "After I get home, I'll attend to my inner work." Then instead of practicing kindness and acceptance toward our fellow commuters, we practice anger and frustration at those who get in our way. And during dinner we think: "After I finish eating and cleaning up, I can practice being here." And after the cleanup we think: "I'm really tired, I'll practice presence in the morning and right now I'll just relax with TV and cookies." Then in the morning we think: "I'm running late, I better hurry," and we forget to be in contact with our tense body and give little or no time to prayer or meditation. And so it goes with us, as we wait for that perfect moment for our spiritual work.

Now perhaps all that is an exaggeration. I hope it is. But you can look at your own inner life and judge for yourself how much unnecessary waiting you place between you and your path.

Because it is now, every moment is the perfect and only moment for awakening our spirit, for creating our soul, for serving the higher. For this week, stop waiting.

216. Fervor

Our spiritual work, be it the practice of presence, prayer, kindness, sensing, meditation, or other inner work, needs fuel. A crucial element of that fuel, one that enlivens our inner life and provides the emotional drive toward purification, love, perfection and service, is fervor. Wonderful in theory and wonderful when we have it, yet how do we find the fervor that ends any given wandering in the spiritual desert? All spiritual seekers wrestle with this basic question of how to move toward the sacred when our heart is just not in it.

To approach an answer, we first recognize that the source of fervor, the spark that ignites our passion for the spirit, enters us in those moments when we touch the higher or when the higher touches us. We hear certain music or read graceful words, we see the beauty of nature or the smile of an infant, and our inner veils momentarily lift, flooding our heart with love and our being with a hint of Divine ecstasy. That sacred flame suddenly awakens our fervor, reminding us yet again of the One Whom we all serve.

While our inner work can bring us to a state of greater openness to those moments of grace, we dare not depend solely on such unpredictable events to earn our spiritual livelihood. In our deepest meditation or prayer, we approach the realms of ecstasy. While our control over our emotions may be rudimentary, it is not non-existent. So each time we enter those deeper states, we allow our heart to take wing a bit more, to fly toward the sacred and return with renewed ardor for the path.

Communal prayer or meditation also can lift us across the threshold of fervor. Indeed some types of prayer ceremonies directly seek to induce a state of ecstasy, often through some physical movement, dance, song or chant. The crucial point is whether, as worshippers, meditators, or recipients of unexpected moments of grace, we allow that outer fervor to enter us deeply and transform into an inner fervor, awakening our heart in a way that reverberates through time.

We cannot all the time participate in communal practices of the spirit, but we can work toward an undying and unquenchable sacred fire, an everlasting light in our heart. Whether in communal practice or in solitary inner work, we cultivate that flame, that inner fervor, which guides us toward our true home. Indeed, fervor for contact with the sacred is itself an opening to, reflection of, and emanation from the Divine.

For this week, notice, welcome, and perhaps create moments when you can rekindle your fervor for the spiritual journey.

217. Our Song

We each have our own characteristic set of patterns of thought and emotion that use our mind and heart to replay themselves again and again. These repetitive, mental processes sometimes retell a particular story of a trauma or triumph in our life. Often they look for triggering events to start them up. Examples you might experience include worrying about money or your job, about your health, your weight, or a habitual indulgence, about a difficult relationship or a non-existent one. Angry patterns may ruminate about past wrongs committed against you, look for new ones, or daydream about future wrongs. Grasping patterns may plot and scheme to get more of your current object of desire. Self-doubting patterns may dwell on what they hold to be your weaknesses and failures. Critical patterns jump on the shortcomings of other people.

Our major patterns are relatively few in number, but endless in application. Their siren song convinces us of their importance and seduces us into following blindly along as their unwitting host. They are so ingrained that we believe them to be who we are: "I am my patterns of thought and emotion. That's my personality. That's who I am." But it is not really that way.

Some of our patterns are benign, simply serving to give us our style and flair for living. Others, however, sap our inner strength, distract us from presence, and kill our natural joy. We need to address these insidious robbers, first by becoming aware of them as they play on our thoughts and emotions. We do this by noticing our mind processes of thought and emotion, seeing the familiar, recurrent ones, and perhaps seeing what triggers them. These habitual thoughts and emotions often represent larger repeating patterns and provide a window onto them.

The seeing itself weakens the hold of our patterns. We see these frequent visitors with clarity as well-established pathways in our brain and psyche, but not as definitive of who we are. A further step toward freedom comes through gradual deconditioning: not clinging, not identifying with our patterns of thought and emotion, not reinforcing them with the emotional charge they typically elicit from us, and reclaiming our energy and initiative. We see the pattern arise and we simply watch as it goes by.

We cannot easily eradicate a pattern, nor do we need to. But if we can temper our response and limit our acquiescence to it, the song of our conditioned self grows stale. The behavior it once prompted grows rare. We begin to see that we do not need it, that it was only a limitation on who we really are.

For this week, look to see your own songs, your patterns

of thought and emotion, particularly the ones that rob your freedom. Work to stop reacting to them so readily, to stop singing their lyrics and playing the role they write for you.

218. Devotion

All forms of devotion share the flavor of dedicated service combined with love. In the material world, the paradigm of devotion is that of parents to children. We also find the devotion of a scientist to science, an athlete to a sport, an artist to an art, a healer to healing, a lover to the loved one, and sometimes a worker to a job. Because its aim is service, devotion does not primarily seek profit, though profits may come. Instead, devotion bears its own success, its own inherent payoff in terms of fulfillment, in the satisfaction of doing what one is meant to do.

You may find it illuminating to ask yourself certain questions. To what, if anything, am I devoted? To what degree? Is there anything I wish I could devote myself to? Can I take steps toward that?

These questions relate directly to spiritual growth. Being devoted to other pursuits need not interfere with our spiritual work. Indeed, an important piece of our inner work involves becoming ourselves fully and uniquely, through devotion to our chosen pursuits. Your individuation renders unto God and society what only you can offer.

The spiritual paradigm of devotion is prayer, where devotion describes the inner attitude one adopts in a sincere act of worship. Though it waxes and wanes, in praying we seek moments of utter devotion to the sacred. That is a major part of the work of prayer: to unite the whole of ourselves, body, mind, heart, attention and intention, in complete devotion to the Divine.

With our body we adopt a posture appropriate to the prayer. Our thoughts are the words, if any, of the prayer. Our mind stays in contact with the meaning of the prayer. Our heart fills with reverence, awe, supplication, joy, and love. Our attention encompasses and supports all these aspects. And our intention becomes the core act of devotion, of opening to the spirit beyond our heart and mind, in love and in service, in fulfilling our sacred duty to the Divine.

Doubts, fears, unwillingness, self-centeredness, distractions, and preoccupations block devotion. We grow by allowing ourselves to become more devoted. A life of devotion is a life well-lived. For this week, reinvigorate your devotion.

219. Speaking Well

A core aspect of conscious speech concerns awareness of our intention behind what we say and, further, to do the right thing in speaking. We contain a whole hierarchy of impulses and intentions, some of which have harmful aspects and find their way into our speech. Negative gossip, for example, attracts us to hear and to spread the latest, juicy tidbits that shed a disapproving or embarrassing light on someone. Everyone has moments of weakness. Negative gossip broadcasts someone's weak moment, damaging their reputation unnecessarily and perhaps unjustly. This type of gossip also harms us when we engage in it, by involving our will in an unwholesome act and thereby driving our conscience away. Our path is to notice when the opportunity for negative gossip calls to us and to refuse that impulse.

We also tend to succumb to another type of wrong

speech in moments of pressure or emotional distress. Lashing out with abusive words usually leads to regret. Our work is to restrain ourselves in the heat of that moment, to temper our words appropriately.

We can sometimes judge speech by its quantity. Often, right speech simply means to chat with someone. Such exchanges bring contact and relationship. But we can err by going on and on about ourselves or some topic that fascinates us, without a real, two-way exchange. Or we can err by not engaging, by not saying enough, by appearing, or actually being, distant.

In some cases we speak to defend or establish our position, to attack, to argue or to debate. Whether such speech injures us by strengthening our egoism or harms another person depends mainly on the intention behind what we say.

Speaking well includes speech based in kindness, friendship, caring, love, gratitude, humor, or just an exchange of information.

In every one of the foregoing cases, intention is the key. To complicate matters, though, our intention in speaking can change from moment to moment with the flow of a conversation. So we need to stay cognizant of our intention.

For this week, notice your intention in what you say and, if necessary, raise it to a higher level.

220. Seeing with Empathy

We frequently pass by strangers as we go about our day, strangers who mean little to us, to whom we have less connection than to the computerized voice that greets us when we phone most any large organization. We know in our minds that these strangers are flesh and blood, thinking and feeling people like ourselves. But in our heart and even in our perceptions, none of that registers. They may as well be cardboard cutouts. Until we have a direct interaction with someone — and possibly even after that — their personhood stays hidden from us.

In the ordinary way of life, this does not matter. Indeed it simplifies and saves time not to consider as people those unknown strangers whose paths intersect our own. This non-perception of strangers as persons like ourselves offers an efficient mode of living, as we automatically relegate them to some stereotype. But those of us who aspire to the spiritual way also need to develop our capacity for a very different mode of perceiving others, even people we do not know. That capacity is to see with empathy.

The first step is to actually look at the people passing us by, to look at their faces, at their posture, their gate, their gestures. We take the other person in detail and as a whole into our perception. But we do this quickly, without staring or making the other feel uncomfortable. A slightly extended glance can suffice.

Yet in this brief glance, we see the person, we see what it is like to be them. We see them as they are in themselves, not as they are in our judgments, reactions, or indifference. Each detail tells us something, providing a clue to who and how they are. We do not think about or consider the meaning of these details; we just notice how they make a whole picture and let them shape our perception intuitively.

And we put ourselves in the other person's place. Extrapolating from our own life, we feel how they feel and experience as they experience. We enter their world for a moment.

This is a practice, a practice toward true empathy. We may not do it perfectly and would not even know if we had. Yet the effort of seeing with empathy gradually opens our heart, our being toward our true, primal, and intimate connection with all people. And that naturally leads beyond perception to empathic action, be it inner or outer.

For this week, practice seeing with empathy.

221. Our Individual Program

We can approach inner work opportunistically by responding spontaneously to those moments of grace that awaken us. Such spiritual work might include letting go, relaxation, following the promptings of conscience, kindness, excellence, and full engagement in our actions, gratitude, and the work of presence. A complementary and even more necessary approach erects the scaffolding to support our path by creating a program of practice. Without regular, repeated, balanced practice, we tend to lose ourselves in the movement of life and make little progress in our spiritual development. Such a program of inner work creates the essential foundation for growth of being and purification of will. Within that context of regularity, our spontaneous inner work can flower.

But blanket prescriptions for practice miss the mark. We need to adapt our inner work to our own current propensities and imbalances, understanding and abilities. We work from where we are toward where we wish to be. All that blocks us from simple, stable presence, all that limits our vision to a small, self-centered world, all that keeps us from absorbing and responding to the grace that continually flows from the sacred, all this forms the field of our inner work.

To that we bring the wonderful tools of transformative spirituality developed by those who have gone before us. Primary among these are meditation, prayer, awareness of our body of sensation, conscious breathing, and presence. Given these tools, we fashion a regular program of practice that fits us and that we return to again and again, day after day, week after week, year after year. The importance of that regularity cannot be overstated. Each instance is a step along our path. While we may not notice the changes day to day, the long term impact of repeated practice is profound. New perceptions, understanding, openness, and inner freedom develop gradually as our level of being changes.

To discover the forms of meditation and prayer most effective for us now requires experimentation and adaptation, seeing what works and what does not, what needs to be added, subtracted, or changed. Repetition does not mean stagnation: rather, it creates an opportunity to grow. We offer our best at each instance of practice, seeking new depth in our meditation, an ever-closer approach to the sacred in our prayer, a more constant and robust presence in our daily routines, a more loving involvement in our relationships, and greater creativity, engagement and efficacy in what we do. In the earlier stages of our spiritual path, we turn to others for guidance in these matters. But as our work deepens, we need to rely on our own intuition of how to practice and how to contribute to the spiritual economy of the Earth.

For this week examine your path, your own program of spiritual practice. What are its elements? Is it alive with the vibrant potential for transformation? Does it need adjustment? To what degree do you carry it out?

222. Engagement

When walking, just walk.
When sitting, just sit.
Above all, don't wobble.
                    Zen Master Lin Chi (Rinzai)

To bring the whole of ourselves into everything we do would, for most of us, constitute a radical remake of our life. Many fissures undermine our would-be wholeness. We do one thing while wishing we were doing something else, while planning or worrying about tomorrow, while hurrying toward the next thing, or perhaps stewing over the last insult we received. If we move slightly closer to what we are doing, we may fall into criticism or fear of what's happening, of the people around us, of the situation. We may have one foot in this moment, but the rest of us flees elsewhere.

To engage fully in what we do means not only to be the one doing it, through our attention and intention, but also to bring our body, heart, and mind into it. It means to jump into this moment with both feet.

Let's take a common example. We find ourselves in a conversation that does not interest us. Rather than fall into boredom or inattentiveness, we switch gears by choosing to engage. We listen carefully and without being distracted by our inner criticism, our disinterest, our concern with what the others may think of us, or our pressing urge to state our opinion right now. Bringing our inherent curiosity to bear, we ask questions. We speak on the topic at hand or, at the right moment, we segue into another. We adopt an attitude appropriate to the situation. For the moment, our entire world consists of this conversation.

In the end we may find ourselves a notch closer to other people and our energies conserved or even enhanced.

More mundane examples abound in all the necessary "chores" of life, activities we would prefer not to engage in. That lack of engagement while doing the "chore" makes us wobble off our center, out of the present moment. Full engagement rights us, brings us wholly into presence. It does not necessarily imply an intense, furrowed brow approach. Rather, full engagement can be very relaxed, but always with its hallmark of wholeness.

With inner work, such as prayer or meditation, our level of engagement largely determines the depth we attain. Distractions eviscerate such moments of practice. Without our whole mind and heart turned toward the sacred, we pray a perfunctory, half-hearted prayer.

For this week, notice situations in which less than the whole of you participates. Choose to engage fully at those times.

223. Staying Here

Stray moments of awakening enliven our days; we remember our inner work and rise into a more complete awareness of ourselves and our immediate situation. Nearly always, though, we evaporate within a matter of seconds, dissolving back into the stream of experience, living with little or no self-awareness. Why is that? Why is our real time so brief, when our path calls us to remain awake?

Energies matter. By not wasting ourselves on hurry, anxiety, overindulgences, anger, fear, distractions, and all the other myriad ways of misusing energies, we conserve our resources for inner work. The sensitive energy builds up naturally. We can also accelerate its accumulation by attending to being in our body and by the occasional practice of energy breathing. Paying attention to the silent background awareness, to the stillness beneath our thoughts, we open to the conscious energy. These two energies, the sensitive and the conscious, form the basis of presence, our inner home.

But the single most important factor in extending presence beyond a few seconds is will. If we have decided ahead of time that when moments of opportunity come to us we will make the effort to stay present, then we may stay here, in this body, in this place, in this time. Intention is the key. The continuously reiterated intention to be draws the necessary energies to us. This is the path toward stabilized presence, the doorway to love.

How to stay here? Given the requisite decision to stay present, we simply watch the flow of experience. We become the one who sees, the one who lives our life. Moment to moment, breath to breath, we stay. We stay with ourselves. We stay with our awareness. In walking, step to step. In eating, bite to bite. In speaking or listening, phrase to phrase. We stay in this immediate, elemental chunk of experience, and then in the next piece, and so on as the pieces naturally and seamlessly blend together within our growing presence.

The practice of staying here, established in presence, is akin to learning to ride a bicycle. We easily fall off to one side or the other, unless we pay continuous attention to staying in the center of balance. We pick ourselves up and begin again, and again. Gradually our stability grows and what seemed impossible becomes feasible.

For this week, work to stay here and now, a little more each day.

224. The One Who Sees

In self-agency we find the true meaning of "to be centered." In becoming the one who occupies our central core, we become our "I," the hub from which all our intentional actions emanate, the witness of all our actually-perceived sensory impressions, the one who is present in presence, and the one who is part of the Source of all.

One of the easier ways to understand and experience this "I" is to be the one who sees with our eyes. When you see, is there someone in you who is the seer? Or is the seeing just happening on its own, like a video camera connected to a television, with no one watching.

When you see a scene or an object, ask yourself who is seeing it. Are you taking in the sight, or is it just passing you by? Enter the seeing so that you can answer with confidence "I am seeing this." Be the one who sees, the one who watches.

That seer, that watcher is you, the agent of your life. Though the watcher often remains absent, rousing yourself to see brings your will, the inner you into the situation. You live your life, rather than passively being lived. The one who sees is the same one who perceives all that your various senses bring you, that is if they are perceived.

For this week, practice seeing what you see, being the one who sees the images your eyes and brain offer.

225. More Body, Vivid Body

Sensing your body means intentionally placing your attention in part or all of your body and opening to the sensitive energy there, which brings you into vivid, direct contact with your body. Gradually the energy accumulates and grows more vibrant. This ancient spiritual practice can be traced back at least as far as the Buddha, for example in the Satipathana Sutta where he discusses mindfulness of the body in the body.

The impact of sensing on our spiritual path manifests in obvious and subtle ways. It trains our perceptions to enter an arena beyond the thrall of self-generated, automatic thinking and reactive emotions. It gives us a place in the here and now of our life and forms the basis of our presence. It lifts us closer to freedom from attachment, destructive emotions, and self-centeredness. It brings us the natural joy of having a body and being alive. And it provides an inner platform for deepening our practice beyond sensation into the higher worlds.

So, although our spiritual work may include more profound practices like prayer, meditation on pure consciousness, or opening beyond the silence, we nevertheless maintain our work on sensation as the enabling foundation for all the rest. To build a better inner future, we sense more now.

For this week, please work to increase your contact with bodily sensation:

- If you can sense a finger, work on sensing two.
- If you can sense a hand, work on sensing the whole arm
- If you can sense an arm, work on sensing both arms.
- If you can sense both arms, work on sensing all four limbs.

- If you can sense all four limbs, work on sensing the whole body.
- If you can sense your whole body, work on sensing it more evenly, more strongly, more frequently, and for longer.

We aim to live in our body of sensation.

226. Intentional Thought Awareness

Whenever we actively consider an issue or a problem, we think intentionally, an important life skill cultivated in school. If we add a further element of awareness to intentional thinking, it can be a liberating spiritual practice.

To increase awareness of the process of thinking, we can collapse our thought stream into a short phrase, repeated intentionally. For this, at least once a day use a repetitive phrase or prayer as the focus of your thinking. When extraneous thoughts intrude, leave them alone while you return to your intentional thought. While keeping attention on your intentional thought, on the inner repetition of a brief phrase or prayer or a sacred word, see that you are not your thoughts. The fact that you can control your thoughts, even if only briefly, shows that you and your thoughts are not identical. This trains you to understand that thoughts are just thoughts.

As you work with thought awareness, notice the quiet space between thoughts. Relax into that wider stillness of pure consciousness underneath thought, into that silent context and transparent container of all thought, emotion, and sensory perception. And with that relaxation into consciousness, temporarily put down the burden of believing in your thoughts and stand free in that clarity.

Of course we could direct our entire being and will into the prayer of repeating a sacred word or phrase and seek thereby to transcend even the stillness of consciousness. Though this exercise of intentional thought awareness has a different purpose, it does help pave our way toward deeper prayer. Here we work instead to extricate ourselves from identification with our thoughts.

Practicing awareness of intentional thoughts helps us enter the conscious space surrounding all thought. From that wider perspective we can see the unintentional, self-perpetuating, associative, reactive, and ego-generated thoughts that usually occupy our minds and masquerade as who we are. Ordinarily our thoughts mesmerize us with their endless stories, the opinions they spin, the outrage and criticism, the daydreams and worries, the sad and self-critical thoughts, the arrogant and self-aggrandizing, the patterns of regret and the memories — oh, the memories — of mistakes, failures, triumphs, victimization, abusive acts, loss and gain. Thoughts collude with emotions in a mutually-reinforcing feedback loop. All this funnels into our thought stream and paints a false but convincing picture of who we are.

When we catch a clear glimpse of our ordinary thoughts in action, we naturally start to emerge from our thought stream. The more we see, the freer we are. We become ourselves rather than being our thoughts, being identified with our thoughts as who we are. Opening to the pure consciousness beyond thought shows us that our inner world is much more than just thoughts, emotions, attitudes and desires.

We need not attempt to practice this type of intentional thought awareness throughout the day. But we do need enough of it to thoroughly accustom ourselves to not identify with our thoughts. Releasing the grip of identification, we stop being so concerned with and driven by our thoughts. We enter a peaceful coexistence with our thought stream.

For this week, work to disengage yourself from identification with the whole range of your thoughts. Practice intentional thinking coupled with full awareness of your intentional thoughts. See that you are not your thoughts.

227. Distorting Perception

Our ego distorts our perceptions according to its desires and concerns, its fears and its attitudes. Egocentric filters prevent some things from getting through at all, while others acquire new colors. If, for example, we worry about being overweight, then when we see other people, we first notice their weight. If they are less overweight than us, we may feel antipathy, jealousy, or self-critical. If they are more overweight than us, we may feel successful or superior. We compare ourselves to others on the basis of weight. We even focus our own body awareness on our overweight bits and feel disgusted or burdened. All this forms an undercurrent of attitudes around weight issues, an undercurrent that influences our perceptions, usually without our realizing it. We no longer see people as people, but rather as fat or not fat. We no longer see ourselves as a person, but rather as fat or not fat. Much of our experience passes through that distorting lens of fatness.

If we feel financially unsuccessful and worry about it, then we see others and ourselves through the filter of money. If we feel unattractive, we measure others and ourselves in terms of physical appearance. If we think we're too short or too tall, we see people in terms of their height. To the extent that our sex hormones drive us, we see people in terms of whether they are sexually attractive or not, usually ignoring the latter. If we feel lonely, we see people as having a mate or not. If we feel sad or depressed, we may see in terms of happiness and unhappiness.

All this originates prior to thought, in self-centered attitudes that shape our perceptions, thoughts, emotions, and actions. Our ego unconsciously defines us as someone who lacks a certain something and then builds our life around acquiring or wishing for that something. These unexamined but powerful attitudes take our freedom and enslave us to egoism. Instead of being fully here, open, present, alert to the wonder of life and actively contributing to it, we waste so much in these distorted, limited views of the world.

Unfortunately, our perceptual filters do not announce themselves; they just do their work without us even noticing the damage they inflict. Whenever we encounter one of the triggers of our ego-based filters, we automatically fall right into its power. Our emotions and thoughts collapse into the corresponding reactions without us even realizing that there are other ways to see, think, and feel.

We can, however, work to shine the healing light of direct awareness onto these inner processes. We set the intention to notice how our ego distorts our perceptions. We remind ourselves several times a day to look for such inner events. When we feel emotional reactions, strong or weak, we suspect our ego filters have been active. Perhaps the easiest situation to notice these ego-filters occurs when we see other people and our comparing mind takes hold. See what kinds of comparisons your mind makes and how those comparisons make you feel. Seeing these automatic, ego attitudes in action shaping our perceptions, thoughts, and emotions, helps diminish their power and free us.

For this week, notice your perceptual distortions.

228. The Color of Stillness

The best kind of interior decorating consists of dyeing our inwardness with the clear color of stillness during meditation. After utterly relaxing into the gap between thoughts, into the inner space around thoughts and emotions, we enter the stillness, pure consciousness. There we savor its taste, soak our being in it, and adopt its color of peace. We let that color of stillness become our color, our mode of being underneath all our inner and outer activity.

We can carry stillness into our life in two ways. First, when we find ourselves lost on the surface of life or confronted with its difficulties, we inwardly relax to reconnect with the stillness that informs our periods of meditation. This intentional act of opening to stillness in the midst of life soon becomes a source of confidence and peace in itself. Just knowing that inner peace is always available helps us through the inevitable peaks and valleys of experience. It offers the taste of real freedom.

The second way keeps that peaceful layer of our being with us. As we repeatedly soak in stillness when we meditate and as we repeatedly reconnect with stillness in the midst of life, we begin to recognize its growing presence in our ordinary awareness. Indeed stillness becomes the basis of our presence in this world, the behind-the-scenes foundation of an increasing share of our experience.

That expansive inner spaciousness widens the sphere of our awareness, even as we actively engage with life. Part of us remains inwardly at rest, coloring our life with peace. We spend less of our time in frenzy or fear, identification or greed, anger or regret. Our inner peace tames our emotional reactions, thus translating into easier relationships with people and with life. It leaves us the energy to contribute effectively in our own unique way. And it keeps us a little closer to the sacred Source of all. By embracing peace we can learn to love.

For this week, color your inner life with the peace of stillness.

229. Immediate Challenges

Because life seems to have so many moments, an apparently endless stream of them, we find it difficult to muster the intensity to work at presence in this moment. We feel that we can wait until later, until a more propitious moment. But in truth there is only one moment — now. Events flow into this moment from the future and leave transformed into the past. But it is always now. So putting aside our inner work for a moment eliminates our practice from its only possible venue: here and now.

One way to counteract this tendency to wait until some indefinite later is to pose immediate challenges to ourselves, challenges of presence. We choose to be present from now until a certain near-term event. Then we repeat that in a contiguous series of efforts of presence. Instead of waiting until later, we engage in spiritual practice until later. Some examples:

- Until reaching the next lamppost or corner on your walk
- For the duration of one commercial on TV
- Until you reach the end of the paragraph you are reading
- Until finishing washing this one dish
- Until finishing brushing your teeth
- Until reaching the cashier in the grocery line

The possibilities abound for such immediate challenges. In every department of our life, in every kind of circumstance, we can create an immediate goal for our inner work. Because of the short-term, clearly circumscribed nature of such challenges, because of their concreteness, and because we can foresee the end point, the effort seems manageable and possible. We feel ready to take it on, to rouse ourselves to meet the challenge by staying present for its duration.

For this week, bring more inner work into your daily life by creating and using opportunities for immediate challenges of presence.

230. Distracting Changes

Changes, large and small, inhere in the very structure of the universe and especially of life. Our body lives in time, which is nearly synonymous with change. But our hearts and minds can live in the changeless, the eternal. Usually though, the changes in time distract us from the eternal.

Major life changes, like a new or lost job, moving, a sudden illness, a birth or death in the family, or the start or end of a significant relationship, capture our minds and hearts. Lesser changes, like acquiring some new thing, dramatic weather, some outrage in the news, a threat to our status quo, an insult, a failure or a success, also take us. Our minds go into the high gear of autopilot, perseverating around and around the new situation, repeatedly mulling it over from every angle. In these roiling waters of time, our inner peace evaporates and along with it the quality of our inner work.

Presence derives from the timeless. Everything that happens passes through this gate, this one, always-present moment. Presence can be the container, the context of our life and all that goes on in our time. When changes pin us to the surface of life, to the events in time, we lose our anchor in the timeless.

Toward the events of life, we respond and adapt, feel their impact, and consider the past, the present, and how to create a better future. All of that is our sacred responsibility. But we also have another responsibility, a deeper opportunity, to hold the events and things of time within the timeless vessel of conscious presence.

In practical terms: when we notice our thoughts and feelings attaching around some situation, we find time to rebalance and reconnect with the timeless through our inner work. Perhaps this requires more or longer meditation than usual, a redoubling of our efforts to sense our body, a more intense use of counting our inner work through the day, a greater focus on setting immediate challenges of presence, or a return to heartfelt prayer.

For this week, when you notice your mind and heart captured by changes in time, thrashing on the surface of life, work to return to your roots in the timeless, while continuing to respond appropriately in time.

231. Being in Conversation

So many conversations each day, some brief, some lengthy, but all afford an opportunity for presence. A basic issue to address is awareness of what's going on in ourselves as we engage in a conversation. Any verbal exchange has great power to draw us to the shallow layers of our being, into a state of identification. That action moves quickly. Before we know it, we completely lose ourselves in the event.

When the other person speaks, do I listen attentively or am I distracted in formulating what I will say next, in anxiously looking for my chance to say something, or in nurturing my own inner commentary? Are my emotions reacting to the other person or persons? For example, does an emotional wall of anger, fear, grasping, or indifference, inferiority or superiority arise within me, separating me from the other? Can I let it go and be clear and openhearted toward this person before me? If I have an agenda, can I still be there? Can I relax and just be?

To be in conversation means first of all to be. We let the presence of the other person remind us to settle into our own presence, out of respect for us both. Being in our own presence affords an opportunity to open further, into the shared presence of the conversation, of being together. The real exchange then takes place not in the words, but within that shared presence. Beneath the words and the appearances, beneath the agendas and reactions, we enter a stillness that embraces us both. We connect by letting go of the inner separation. Being able to converse well with people, paves the way toward conversing with God.

When in conversation this week, practice being there with the other person.

232. The "I Am" Test

A simple yet profound test of your inner state and the quality of your presence consists of whether and to what degree you can say "I am." Can you say to yourself "I am" and have it be truly meaningful, have it come from the whole yourself, from the very core of who you are? To be able to say "I am" means to be your intention, to be at the inner center of the stream of experience, to be the one who lives your life. While presence does have other dimensions, such as the breadth and strength of your bodily sensation and your openness to consciousness, the crucial aspect reveals itself in this "I am," in someone being home in our body and in our being.

To be in ourselves is simple and always available. Just by saying "I" to our self with meaning, we come to in that moment. But that very simplicity and availability mislead us into the illusion of permanence. Our "I" proves all too fleeting. "I" quickly disappear, to be replaced by the programmed habits and ingrained patterns of personality. My body and mind "normally" function in this programmed and reactive mode, without any direction from my "I."

But to climb toward my own and the higher reality, I can apply the "I am" test. It awakens my "I." I say to myself "I am" and mean what I say by being the one who is saying it. That vivid moment serves to open me to the reality of my self, my surroundings, and other people. Then I stay. I persevere in being that one who I am.

The importance of this goes even further than becoming real. It brings a sense of power, a power derived from the true Source of power. "I am" also brings humility and love. If "I am," then I realize that you are, or can be, also and equally. In that deeper sense, we all share an essential core. At that level of shared sameness and uniqueness, we approach the unifying, sacred Source. The only way that love and the Divine Will can enter this world lies through our I.

For this week, say to yourself "I am," mean what you say, and be the one saying it. Notice that immaterial central will in you, the one who directs your attention, the one whom the word "I" points toward. See the degree to which you can feel yourself to be the one who is here, the one saying "I am." Practice this repeatedly during each day.

233. Finding Time

In today's world, because we experience so many competing demands on our time and new opportunities for spending it, we must continually triage our possible engagements. Since our spiritual work does not obviously and unequivocally contribute to our material well-being, we tend to let it slide, allowing other musts and wants to take precedence over our time for meditation and prayer. Even if we were to live a hundred years, our life would be all-too-brief compared to our possibilities. How can we manage this precious, limited resource of time to give our inner work its due?

First and foremost we examine our priorities. Do I spend my time in ways that matter? Does my lifestyle support and express my inner work? Do I allow the spiritual attraction of the sacred to shape my commitments and drives?

We might seek to understand how much time we really need for meditation and prayer. How much is useful at our current stage of inner evolution? Toward that, we can experiment with longer and shorter periods of formal practice and see how they affect our level of presence during the day.

Once we have a clearer picture of what would be useful, we can look to adjust our life accordingly. Perhaps we need to go to sleep earlier so as to have more time for morning meditation and prayer. Maybe we take a half hour out of our evening to practice, or extra time on the weekends, or a brief meditation in the midst of our busy day.

But a whole other realm of time also awaits us. By distinguishing between inner and outer time, we can more than double our time. The quality of our presence determines the quality of our time. To the extent we live in presence, we add a vivid inner experience to our outer experience, vastly enhancing the value and perceived length of any interval of time. With presence we live in two parallel times: one belonging to our body and the outer world, and another belonging to our inner life.

Some of our outer activities require our full inner resources, while many others do not. But as our attention grows wide and deep, and as our practice fills our reservoir of energies, more of life falls into the latter category, leaving us free to discover an inner space-time that parallels the outer. We then live two lives: an inner life and an outer, each enriching the other. Further along the way, these two merge back together in the fullness of a unified spirit.

Within that spirit, our practice touches what is beyond time altogether. A brief moment lived in depth can hold as much life as an entire day lived on the surface. As we enter deeply into the present moment, time disappears as our "now" becomes timeless, eternal. The events of life pass through our contextual consciousness, which fashions them into a seamless whole. By way of that timeless dimension, the sacred enters, offering substance and meaning to all our moments.

For this week, see if you need more outer time for your inner work. If so, look at how to find it. See, also, how the work of presence creates more life and more time.

234. Searching for Sustenance

For those who yearn for the sacred, spiritual sustenance proves just as necessary as physical sustenance. Physically we work to earn our food, while the air we need comes free.

Similarly with spiritual sustenance: for some we must work, while for other kinds we need only open our soul.

In the first category we find the inner energies carried by the air. To extract and absorb them requires the intentional, conscious effort of energy breathing, placing our full attention on the air as we breathe in, noticing the vibrant energies contained in it, and welcoming those energies into our inner body. Also in this category is the energy we can intentionally and directly draw from the Earth, if our attention and perceptions are sufficiently focused and refined.

Beyond those lies the realm of the sacred energies. First we find the true presence of consciousness, which opens as quiet stillness ushering us into the halls of inner peace and freedom. Next we seek the sacred light by opening our hearts and directing our attention beyond, or orthogonal to, everything, even our own consciousness. A Divine name can help with this, as a pointer toward where our attention needs to go. Beyond that sacred light we may discover the Love that emanates from the beneficent Intelligence that sustains all worlds. We can only enter there in Love and in letting Love enter us. Again, a Divine name can help focus our attention, humble us, and open our hearts, our innermost self to that Love.

These are the layers of sustenance that can feed our soul. Only we need to take it as real, not as a theory. Even if we cannot presently find our way through all, or even any, of these levels, we work persistently and patiently, practicing inwardly, as we search for our own personal connection. Slowly the levels open to us, gradually but joyously transforming our very soul.

For this week, several times a day, search for the spiritual sustenance that is always available and present. This need not take long, perhaps a minute each time, but the impact can be enormous.

235. Filling the Down-Time

Interludes of passivity punctuate our day. More often than not, our passive states do not arise from fatigue, but rather from the need to balance and not always be active, or from a situation like waiting that does not demand our full attention. This non-fatigue type of down-time presents a prime opportunity for certain kinds of inner work.

The physical ease of down-time naturally allows the sensitive energy to arise, especially if we give our attention to it by relaxing into the experience of being in our body, opening to its basic aliveness, to sensation. This kind of sensing practice blends well with down-time, co-opting it into our spiritual path. Through inhabiting our body, resting in sensation, we remain in the present, less prone to identification with the various wasteful, frustrating, and destructive habits of thought and emotion. On the contrary, simple presence in our body renders us open to natural joy and offers a foothold in a higher, freer mode of living.

Although our inner work may include practices aimed toward the spiritual heights, the simple practice of sensation always remains a fundamental gateway into the now. A foundation of robust sensation creates the platform from which all deeper spiritual work can be effective. Because the practice of sensing integrates easily with daily life, we can return to it again and again, until it becomes our second nature. The stronger our sensation, the stronger, clearer, and more joyful our inner life can be. The peace and stillness of consciousness rests on the ground of sensation.

For this week, notice situations that do not demand all your attention and fill those down-times with sensation, with presence in your body. Turn your attention to your body, to its aliveness, and be in it.

236. Come What May

If we abandon our spiritual work in moments of difficulty, we abandon ourselves. Whether in the face of minor annoyances, moderate problems, or major troubles, we can always find a way to return our inner life to its sacred orientation. Not only do we then reclaim part of the energy being wasted in the difficult situation, but our inner work of that moment also helps us see the problem more objectively, not identify with it, and thereby remove an unnecessary layer of it.

If I am mildly ill or caught in a traffic jam, stuck in a long line or discovering a flat tire, arguing with someone or overloaded with work or errands, rejected in my proposal or failing in some other way, my mind will start spinning a story. That story creates a personality and identity built of thoughts and emotions about the problem "I" have. The more intensely I feel the "problem" and my inner rejection of it, the more energy goes into feeding the story and aggravating the situation.

The work of body awareness, of conscious breathing, of presence, or of touching the stillness can interrupt that story, reclaiming its energy to feed my soul. If I come back to myself, to my simple presence here, the belief in the situation as "my problem" also weakens, making it less of an issue. I am freer to be fully in this moment, to experience it, and to respond appropriately and even creatively to the "problem." The dimension of depth returns.

The keys to spiritual work in the face of difficulties consist of remembering the path and choosing to return to it in this moment. That requires us to let go of our complete immersion in our "plight" and to accept what is. In acceptance we stop pushing or pulling on the situation; we stop wallowing in negative thoughts about it. However, acceptance is not acquiescence, but rather an openness that allows us to act from unbiased clarity. The choice to let go of being caught in the time-bound and to open to the timeless restores our balance.

For this week, notice your life difficulties when they arise. Notice your identification with them, your thinking of yourself as someone who has this problem. Notice the associated story your mind spins to cause and feed your identification. Choose to turn part of your attention back to your inner work, to presence.

Stick to the path, come what may, and it will be a good friend in need.

237. Running Commentary

Our minds produce a nearly continuous stream of commentary on anything and everything in our life. It sounds as if we have a miniature news reporter in our head, continually speaking as us, about us, about our situation, about other people, and about everything around us. Every event and every plan, big or small, loom large to this commentator, this inner voice that seems convinced that it actually exists in some real way beyond the comments themselves.

This running commentary profoundly affects our life. It distracts us from direct and open perception of the world, diminishing our alertness and clouding awareness. The attitudes and opinions exhibited in our play-by-play and color commentary take on a self-reinforcing life of their own, driving our emotional reactions and enmeshing us in futile inner rejections of situations we cannot change. Life shrinks to a circle revolving around our running commentary, effectively blocking us from reality, from simple being, and from peace, joy, and love.

Our inner commentary cannot be stopped. Though it may subside for a time, it always reemerges. Thus our practice is not to try to stop it, but rather to not identify with it, not to take it as who we are, or even as representative of who we are. That intention to be free of identifying with our running commentary confronts the difficulty that our thoughts seem so close to who we are. The commentary is so intimate, so secret, that it seems to be the real me.

For this week, work persistently to notice your running commentary and to see it as just thoughts, not as defining or embodying who you are.

238. Choosing Your Emotions

We usually choose, but sometimes fail to choose, how we express our emotions. We may modulate them, adapting to our immediate circumstances. Or we might let loose an emotional outburst or implosion. Or we might try to push them down and away, repressing our emotions. But actually choosing how you will feel is a different matter entirely, a matter of changing the character of your emotions. Instead of your emotions controlling themselves, reacting in their conditioned and predictable patterns to the events of your life, you start to influence the very nature of your emotions, intentionally and directly.

Why do this? Our difficult, discordant, destructive and reactive emotions make life unpleasant and painful for us, and sometimes also for the people around us. Those emotions usually make us less effective, although in certain fairly rare situations they can be properly channeled toward positive results. But inwardly our reactive emotions spell disaster, enslaving us in attachment and burning up precious inner energies that could otherwise go toward our spiritual work. Repressing emotions exacerbates the damage by planting a bad seed in our heart. The bottom line: destructive emotions embody our suffering.

Choosing our emotions begins with noticing our thoughts, which so often serve as precursors to emotion. When our thoughts turn negative about a situation or a person, our emotions soon follow. We may become very upset. By that time it is too late to choose to feel differently. The storm must pass first. But if you catch your reaction at its earliest stages, you can channel your thoughts toward a more benign, even positive, joyous, or compassionate pattern. And again your emotions will follow.

The Buddha discussed this in relation to what he called the chain of dependent origination. The essence of the chain can be summarized as perception, reaction, and attachment. If we can be present at the moment of perception, we may choose not to react and thereby break the chain. If our presence is strong and clear enough, it does not even require a choice: the conditioned reaction simply does not materialize. More typically, though, we might notice the chain at a slightly later stage, when the reaction has already started and begins to drive our thoughts toward negative patterns. By watching our thoughts and their results, we acquire a taste for where they are leading us.

At this point we may be able to choose an alternative direction. We might begin to think differently about the situation, or we might distract our thoughts onto another subject entirely, or we exert a mitigating influence on the developing negative thought pattern. Of course, some difficult situations do require thought and consideration. And we give that, but with clarity, not negativity.

Notice that this is not a matter of repressing our emotions. Once a destructive emotion involves us, we face it and feel it as we normally would. But before the reactive emotion gets started, we can choose to direct our thoughts so that it never does start. Out of compassion for ourselves, we choose not to go down that path of suffering.

For this week, work at choosing your emotions.

239. Doing Your Chores

Our life in time presents a series of events and tasks, many repetitive. Thankfully, we can use that outer structure to support and develop our inner life.

For this week, choose one or two physical activities or chores that you typically engage in daily. Set yourself to work at body awareness, sensing your body while you do the chore. For that period, intend to do what you are doing. Inwardly be the one doing the activity: don't just let it happen without your full participation, both inward and outward. At the same time be sure to bring the appropriate level of quality to what you do. Each day, as the moment for the chosen activity approaches, prepare your inner work by recalling and renewing your intention to practice for its duration.

Pick clearly delineated activities such as preparing or eating a meal, cleaning up after a meal, exercising, brushing your teeth, bathing, or getting dressed. Let your chosen built-in activities become occasions to build your inner work into your day. In this way, you can extend your spiritual practice into previously untouched regions of your life. By setting yourself to practice for the duration of the activity, you also extend your inner work in time and stability.

A boring, uninteresting, or distasteful task acquires vividness in the light of your focused attention and full presence. To enliven, strengthen, and broaden your inner life, enter the mundane and inspire it with your practice.

240. Remembering

Our limited ability to remember the path constitutes one of its major hurdles. The extent to which we remember its value, remember to practice as we go about our day, remember the sacred — all these measure our progress. The value we place on approaching the sacred determines our possibilities for remembering. The more we value the sacred, the more we remember it. But the converse also holds: in remembering to practice, we deepen our connection with sacred values.

In the great domain of our life, the spiritual path seems to compete with the multitude of our interests and needs. Everything we do or experience takes us. We continually lose ourselves in life. Yet the path to the sacred always remains available, if only we remember it and turn to its practice. Inner work need not compete with our life interests and activities. The practice of presence, for example, can embrace and even enhance any situation. Our spiritual path creates a parallel life in us, a rich inner life, wedded to and embedded within our outer, material life, which it does not diminish.

But the apparent competition for attention results in forgetting the sacred. With our ordinary, limited attention, we typically have nothing left for presence while we engage in our life activities. We may counter this with regular periods of meditation and focused prayer to increase our inner energy and strengthen our intention. In that way, we find it more possible to practice presence in the midst of life. We attend both to life and to our practice simultaneously.

We need to remember the path and act on it. That remembering itself is an act of will: the sacred remembers us. Our own higher nature breaks through the thrall of life and reminds us of the path. And in that moment we turn our inner life to the practice.

For this week, examine your own remembering and forgetting of the path. What helps you remember? Can you increase that? What circumstances cause you to forget? Can you bring the remembering into the situations of forgetting?

241. The Sacred Chorus

Although a great part of spiritual practice must be an inward, solitary affair, we are not alone in our inner work. Beyond whatever spiritual communities you participate in face-to-face, consider all the people on this Earth who practice prayer, meditation, or presence in all their multifold varieties. These millions, perhaps billions of "voices" form a chorus singing the spiritual song of the Earth in service to the sacred. To the extent that we ourselves participate in that sacred chorus, it reciprocates in supporting us, making our path more possible, making more energy available to us, and strengthening our intention to practice. To be a part of that is a blessing and a privilege.

It is also an obligation we all share: to add our own "voice" to that sacred chorus. What if you knew that human violence on this Earth waxes and wanes in response to the amount and quality of your own personal inner work, whether solitary or with others? What if you knew that the Earth actually has an inner ecosystem of the spirit, to which your practice contributes? Would you then feel the need to make your spiritual "voice" strong and pure in supporting this sacred human chorus? Even if we cannot know these things directly in the ordinary way of knowing, we can see their truth in our vision and understanding.

We each can contribute our own unique "voice" to the spiritual ecosystem, in which it blends to create a wholeness far surpassing our individuality. Just as a group meditation brings strength beyond the sum of the individuals in the group, so does our practice create a synergy with others around our planet. At any given moment, untold millions of people across the Earth engage in prayer, meditation, or conscious presence. Whether conscious of it or not, the inner energies we produce thereby spread their beneficial influence far and wide. But by looking at the state of our global civilization, it becomes painfully obvious that the need for these energies outstrips the current production.

For this week, take it as a working hypothesis that the sacred chorus exists and that its efficacy depends on you personally. Let that vision inspire your determination to sense your inner body more and more, to raise the quality of your prayers, to deepen your meditation, and to open your heart in kindness.

242. Building the Inner Body

The inner body, or lower part of the soul, does not come to us ready-made, nor does it grow naturally, like our physical body, through the ordinary process of living. The inner body forms through conscious and intentional efforts directed expressly for this purpose. Our physical body gives us a place to live on this Earth. A stable and robust inner body would give us a place to live in a deeper, more spiritual world, one that also encompasses the physical. Thus, a major part of our inner work must address the care, feeding, and creation of the inner body.

What is the inner body made of? Primarily sensation: the sensitive energy. Through the practice of sensing our physical body, we come into contact with this substance from which our inner body can form. We discover its value in connecting us with our physical body, with establishing our place in the present moment.

The more we practice sensing, the more we notice it arising unbidden, calling us into presence. Further practice increases the duration, depth, and frequency of our episodes of living in sensation, in our nascent inner body. We can find other sources of help by learning to open our perceptions to intentional energy breathing, drawing raw material for the inner body from the air around us. We can even learn to draw it directly from the Earth, our mother. And deep meditation or prayer can put us into contact with very high energies that cascade down to blend with the sensitive energy and nourish our inner body. Those high energies play a crucial role in transforming our sensitive energy into the substance of our inner body.

Awareness of the state of our inner body teaches us what helps build it, what weakens it and what wastes its substance. You may find, for example, that certain disruptive emotions, overeating, rushing, tobacco, and lack of sleep deplete your inner body, diminishing your contact with sensation. On the constructive side you may find proper care of your physical body, positive emotions, a relaxed presence, and full but easy attention to whatever you are doing. A well-conducted lifestyle, repeated and sustained practice of sensing, and drawing on various sources of energy gradually builds our inner body, thereby establishing and deepening our presence, and creating new possibilities of contact with the sacred.

For this week, work on building your inner body through the sustained and repeated practice of sensing. Notice the times when sensation spontaneously reappears and follow up on those moments by relaxing into the sensation, into your developing inner body.

243. Communicating Presence

A great part of our life involves communication. Many professions consist primarily of communicating: law, medicine, education, journalism, the arts, politics, management, marketing, sales, and knowledge work of all kinds. Family, social, and religious life all revolve around communication. Whether by speaking or listening, by writing or reading, by facial expression, tone of voice, gesture, posture or touch, every mode and venue of communication presents an opportunity for inner work, for presence, for kindness, quality and effectiveness, for aligning communication with intention.

Can we bring our inner work to the field of communication? Can we be fully present in the very act of communicating? Can we bring our intention into it, to say what we mean to say, and to mean what we do say? Can we see and repair our lack of appropriate consideration in our interactions, whether by commission or omission? Can we be firm or gentle as befits the circumstances? As we communicate, can our situational awareness be comprehensive, including both other people and our own inwardness?

The flip side of communicating presence reveals that by being present when we are with other people, we communicate the living fact of our presence itself. This form of inner communication happens directly and without external signs: the deeper the presence, the stronger the effect. Another person's presence helps us come into our own, and vice versa.

For this week choose one of the four primary modes of communication, during which to work at presence: speaking, listening, writing, or reading. These modes cut across many applications, e.g., writing can be with pen or with keyboard, emails or memos. Listening can be with iPod, cell phone, TV, radio, or in person. Whenever you engage in the chosen mode of communicating, also pay attention to your inner work. Begin with sensing your body as you communicate. As you are able, extend your practice in those moments to more complete presence, to awareness of the meaning and quality of the communication and how it is affecting all those involved.

244. Elevating Prayer

From time to time, we experiment with stretching beyond our familiar inner spaces toward the Ultimate, in an active receptivity. We move, in our will and intention, in a direction other than our usual categories of outer and inner. We ask what would be a different direction altogether and we step toward that. We look beyond this world of space and time, beyond our body and mind, even beyond consciousness itself. We find that direction by moving, by reaching toward it, and by responding to its call, however faint that may be. We trust our innermost self to know where to turn. In bold humility we approach the

One we have always longed for.

And in that place, or toward that place, or toward the best orientation we can come to, we pray. We pray from our heart, from our wholeness, with words and without words, with awe and with love, with tears of gratitude and with unimaginable joy. That prayer embodies and gives wings to the most basic intention of our life: to enter direct relationship with the Divine. That prayer itself connects us with the Sacred Source.

This connection knows no limitation. It is not reserved for special people, but stands ready with the warmest of welcomes for each of us, for you and for me, just as we are. As if to a loving parent, we return in simple truth and peaceful joy to embrace and be embraced by the Great Heart of the World.

For this week, try to elevate your prayer. Try to make your relationship with the Divine more direct and immediate. Like a scientific explorer and a poet lover, find your way toward your truest Friend, Who lives in you and in all your friends.

245. Stabilizing Our Way

The natural ups and downs of living turn even more markedly in the inner life. At times we rise to unexpected heights, touched by the sacred and full of energy. At other periods we fall flat, our inner work vanishing altogether. The causes of the latter prove varied and complex, from emotional upheavals to physical imbalances to situational impediments. We may avoid these spiritual deserts, if we arrange our path with the reliability of balance.

Competing priorities often destabilize our desire and determination to live a soul-fulfilling life. But we can counteract such episodic waning of our spiritual orientation by establishing several disparate legs for our practice. When one leg weakens, the others can carry us forward. Two bases for such stability of practice can be created. The first is wholly within ourselves and the second orients us within greater wholes.

In our personal domain we can work in several interacting streams of practice. For example, we can install ourselves in a regular time and mode of prayer, in a regular period of meditation, and in continuing efforts of presence during our day. When one or even two of the three slips, as will happen, the remaining ones keep us linked to the sacred. The joyful effort of working in all three ways not only feeds our soul a balanced diet, but helps us stabilize our path, thereby transforming our being into a home for the sacred.

In a larger context, our personal inner work interacts with our practice in community and with our service to people, life, and the sacred. Participating regularly in communal practice, be it worship or meditation or some other form of sharing in spirit, offers many important benefits. And translating our spirituality into some concrete form of service to the greater whole puts the entire enterprise of our individual path onto a surer footing by taking our motivation beyond the purely personal. These three domains of inner work, communal practice, and service all support each other. Each stands ready to pick us up if one or two of the others slacken, helping stabilize our way.

For this week, create a more stable path for your spiritual life by renewing your efforts, where necessary, along several streams of inner work, in communal practice and in service.

246. The Path of Exploration

Routines and rituals can help or hinder our path. If the routine brings us to regular periods of inner work, like a daily meditation session or morning prayer, then it usually works wonders for our spiritual development, while offering a venue for inner service to the Ineffable. But even such beneficial routines can stifle our progress in subtle ways. Perhaps a different form or length of meditation, a new mode of prayer, a more constant presence, a more penetrating and continuous attention, or a more refined and reinvigorated intention could transform the routine into an ever deepening appointment with the sacred.

The path of exploration keeps the necessary and valuable routines of the spirit from growing stale. Like an investor who seeks to maximize return or a scientist testing a theory, we try various approaches and evaluate and adjust our inner work. This ongoing examination of our way of practice enlivens it. At times we inject whole new elements, while at others we explore within the boundaries of our current modes of spiritual work. Bringing our intelligence and creativity to bear on the path helps ensure that the steps we take actually carry us toward our highest destiny.

Reading or seeking advice about our inner life can prove invaluable. But the most effective help comes from our connection to the higher, from intuition, from direct and active perception, and from objective appraisal of our true situation. Recognizing our spiritual work as an ongoing way of life, without a definite end, we look within for a lifetime of guidance. And to make the most of this one life, we constantly explore how to extend our inner life further toward the sacred, how best to serve.

For this week, renew your attitude of spiritual exploration.

247. The Web of Unity

The practice of equanimity, an abiding attitude of acceptance, both leads toward and derives from seeing the sameness in all things, in all people. Acceptance dissolves the walls we consciously and unconsciously erect to separate everything: what we want from what we do not want, us from them, me from you, beauty from its perceived lack, what we fear from what we do not fear. To enter the web of unity, the continuum of sameness, we need to empty ourselves of all our inner separateness.

That everything shares this sameness does not mean that nothing matters, but rather that everything matters. In our daily life we need to discriminate and separate one thing from another, one person from another, one value from another. But connection with the sacred, with the deeper level of sameness, can inform our values and shape our actions in the ordinary world of separateness.

To see our underlying sameness is to behold our unity. Moments come when you look into another person's eyes, perhaps even a total stranger, and you sense your unity with that person. At other moments you may drop all your inner machinations and just be. In seeing the other's humanness or in letting go, you connect that with your own essential humanity, with your heart of unity.

For this week, approach the web of unity by presence, acceptance, equanimity, and allowing yourself to be in that web. Such great things of the spirit must be and are approachable, even participation in the love that shines on us all.

248. Transition to Stillness

During quiet meditation or in particularly favorable situations we may taste stillness, the vast, empty, and peaceful spaciousness of pure consciousness. We also can practice intentionally making the transition to stillness during our ordinary activities. To do so, we need familiarity with stillness, born of that stage of meditation where we enter the space behind and beyond thoughts and sensory perceptions. By entering that true consciousness again and again, we come to recognize it and learn how to open to it in meditation. We see that thinking does not help. Instead it involves an act of perceptual broadening, of entering an already existing region of ourselves that forms part of the great silent ocean of awareness.

Our task now consists in discovering how to transition into stillness during more of our life: to begin living in the great world that envelops our ordinary world. You may well find that starting with a foundation in awareness of physical sensation, whole body sensing, makes the transition to stillness more possible during your ordinary activities. Established, even if briefly, in sensation, we widen our inner horizon past the shores of our ordinary sense experience. We shift our attention from the emotional, thought, and sensory content of awareness to the context, to our awareness itself, to that ever-present stillness underlying all that moves in time, both inwardly and outwardly.

Thoughts, sights, sounds, and actions may continue, but we stand in the stillness that accompanies us wherever we go. We participate in life from the context of the peace of consciousness, from the settledness within.

For this week, study how to make the transition to stillness, both in sitting meditation and in the run of life.

249. Starting Presence

Beginnings pervade our life. We awaken from slumber to start each day anew. We begin each meal. We start journeys: some lengthy, some shorter, like our commute to work. Every activity has its beginning, be it brushing our teeth or getting dressed, sitting down to meditate or preparing food, entering a store to shop or each phase of our daily work. Every breath has its own beginning.

All beginnings present opportunities for inner work. The religiously inclined might ask for or offer a blessing when beginning something. Muslims, for example, traditionally begin any undertaking with "In the name of God, the compassionate, the merciful." Invoking the higher at beginnings can suffuse life with a sense of the sacred.

To further explore the deep wisdom behind this focus, we can use beginnings as reminders to be present. If we can muster conscious and intentional presence when we start an activity, several important elements can enter. First, we can resolve to work at presence for the duration of the activity. This opens a door to extending our inner work into more of life. Second, because real presence includes intention, we can set our intention for the activity, for example, the intention to bring a certain level of quality or kindness to what we do. Third, awareness of beginning inspires a vision of the whole, infusing greater reality to that time and potentially transforming the activity into a real event.

For this week, be present when you start.

250. Lines of Time

Innumerable possibilities open before us at every moment, offering paths along different lines of time. Our choices, or lack thereof, determine the trajectory of our life. With the many roads not taken, our possibilities continually bifurcate, propelling us along the particular, zigzagging line of time that we actually live. All this is obvious — from an external viewpoint. What is not so obvious is that (1) our inner, spiritual state defines our experience and our time, and (2) there exist different possible levels of time for us, corresponding to the possible levels of our inner states.

The higher our state, the more sacred is our time. In conscious presence, for example, we live more than we do in our typical, half-conscious states. Each moment arrives in vivid fullness and depth, embraced in our being. Our time is enriched and seems longer, in a positive sense. Instead of being completely taken by and identified with the details and our reactions to them, we live in openness both to the details and to the larger perspective simultaneously. We see and feel and experience more.

Even when we cannot change difficult circumstances, we still have the possibility of changing our inner world by adopting a different attitude. And this act selects our line of time, the line of our life.

This moment is our life. How we live this moment is how we live our life. If we reject or ignore this moment, we reject or ignore our life. The quality of our presence in the mundane details of life, the depth of our prayer and meditation, the selflessness of our kindness, and the joy of our creative engagements — all these can raise the level of our time, the line of our life.

For this week, notice the line of time you are living in any given moment. Can you raise it to a higher level?

251. Soft-Heartedness

All the anger, fear, and hatred in the world today teach the way of hard-heartedness. "Enemies" demonize and dehumanize each other. Disagreements result in anger, not compromise. Rushing to get ahead pushes others aside. In general, hardness of heart shows egoism in control and all sacredness blocked.

The way toward the sacred is the way of soft-heartedness. The compassionate waters of the spirit flow around the dams of hardness, softening and dissolving them. Soft-heartedness means kindness, openness, and a non-harming attitude toward all people, all life.

For some of us, hardness of heart is our normal mode of being. If that describes you, look for opportunities to soften your attitude. Perhaps with children or your family, practice dropping the walls that keep others at a distance.

For others of us, indifference characterizes our approach to people. If that describes you, find more moments and situations in which you can allow your heart a feeling of warmth toward someone.

Even those for whom soft-heartedness comes easily have their non-moments. When others get in your way, block you from having what you want, or impose what you do not want, can you stay inwardly soft toward them?

Soft-heartedness should not be confused with soft-headedness or spinelessness. We meet situations where outer toughness is absolutely required. But even then, in the midst of standing your ground, can you allow an inner softness, a non-rejection? Can you be as tough as necessary externally without peremptorily banishing the other from the warm shelter of your heart? By practicing soft-heartedness, we hasten the day prophesied by Isaiah when *"... they shall beat their swords into plowshares...,neither shall they learn war any more."*

For this week, find the softness in your heart for people and for life. Live in that.

252. Being Useful

A primary source of true satisfaction in life consists of being useful. Though innumerable opportunities to be useful present themselves to us, many questions arise. Do we recognize the opportunities? Which do we choose? How do we maximize our usefulness?

The basic principle of being useful involves the creation of order rather than disorder. In the material world, this can range from cleaning, cooking, building, repairing, and putting things in their place to un-polluting, conserving, and creating. In the inner world, order means presence, seeing clearly, and not basing our identity in things, thoughts, or emotions. In the spiritual world, the work of order means the work of prayer and of love, of non-separation from others. In all of this, quantity counts but so does the quality of one's usefulness: the higher the quality, the higher the order.

The question of how to be useful depends on many factors. Foremost among these is our own possibilities, our talents, style, propensities, knowledge, skills, and level of being. We may need to hone our skills, learn new knowledge, and develop our talents. We all need to cultivate our being.

Consider the possible domains of usefulness: to family, to others with whom we have contact, to society, to the earth, to the spirit, and to oneself. Through their interrelatedness, usefulness to one inevitably helps the other domains as well. Nevertheless, this breakdown into domains does provide a basis for assessing our usefulness.

How do we apply ourselves in the various domains? With other people, for example, simple acts of courtesy and kindness, concern and support, wit, patience, and compassion are all ways of being useful. With society, our skills and their application, our integrity and creativity prove useful. With the earth and its life, appreciation and responsibility are needed. For the spirit, our inner work of meditation, presence, and/or prayer feed the necessary energies up the chain of being. These also serve to enhance our own being, as do self-discipline, care, and exercise for our body, mind, and heart.

The importance of being useful goes well beyond bringing satisfaction to our life. Any act of being beneficially useful is an act of will that aligns us with and serves the Divine Will.

For this week, examine and assess your own usefulness. Can you be more useful? Do you need to change what you do in any of the domains of usefulness?

253. Identity

All too often we borrow our identity from things, thoughts, emotions, processes, or events. The thing may be our body, our car, our house, our clothes, or other valued possessions. Thoughts and emotions combine in patterns of opinions and reactions, views and beliefs, style and memory to form our personality, which we unquestioningly assume is who we are.

Many of us take our identity from our position in life or our job, our hopes and dreams, or our lack of money or relationship. Or we may define ourselves in terms of some traumatic event or some great and glorious success. Or all of the above as our identity shifts in reaction to this moment.

But this inherent instability shows that we do not really "know" who we are and that who we are is not a thing, thought, emotion, process, event, nor any combination thereof. Indeed it shows that who we are cannot be "known" in the ordinary way with our minds. Our true identity belongs to a higher order than anything in time and space. From the perspective of time and things, that true identity appears as, in, and through emptiness and stillness. Though even there we can go a step too far.

Those who, even momentarily, come into the utter peace and stillness of consciousness face the temptation to take that as their identity. Consciousness does indeed enable witnessing, but it is not the witness. Our true identity uses the high energy of consciousness analogously to the way we use our body.

That one who we are is our will. We find our self in acts of responsible, compassionate individuality at the one end and in surrender to oneness with the Divine at the other. Attention, intention, and the act of choosing offer the most accessible paths toward understanding ourselves as will. Being is not who we are, but the will-to-be is. The difference is both subtle and great.

For this week, notice what you take as your identity. Notice how this changes and its recurring themes. See that you are no thing, thought, emotion, memory, process, event, energy, or being. It does matter, because those who are truly themselves can serve the sacred directly. Act yourself.

254. Inner Responsibility

With increasing self-awareness comes increasing responsibility, even for our secret thoughts and emotions. Though we do not have full control of our thoughts and emotions, we can be responsible for what we agree to, for what we accept as proper, and for what we inwardly own as an expression of our truest self. How we relate to our thoughts profoundly influences and shapes our life.

Happiness begins with accepting the whole of ourselves as we are, but we need not and should not accept all within us as being appropriate and right. We accept ourselves as we are and we work to improve. Part of that means adopting a discriminating attitude toward our inner life, toward this ever-changing and repetitive jungle of thoughts and emotions.

While we do not fight or reject our destructive and unbecoming thoughts and emotions, neither do we feed them, agree with them, take them as who we are, nor act on them. What then? We give them space. We expose our wasteful, distracting, and unwholesome thoughts to the great, purifying spaciousness of consciousness. Within that boundless inner space of awareness, all thoughts and emotions gradually dissipate, leaving us in peace. If we refrain from bothering the thoughts that bother us, they cease their problematic manifestations, healing the wounds that drive them.

But our thoughts and attitudes are subtle and ingenious, selling themselves to us. Inner responsibility means not buying into the wasteful, distracting, and unwholesome ones. Although our true reality lies well beyond thought, who we are in the external world is a function of what we think, of the thoughts we adopt as our own.

Nearly all our thoughts consist of randomly patterned associations reacting to inner and outer perceptions. Where are we in this? Surely not everything in the stream of thoughts represents who we are. The mere fact that some thought runs through my brain does not mean that is what *I* think or what *I* intend. When do we think intentionally?

A similar situation exists with our emotions.

Inner responsibility means to stand our ground in the midst of this endless stream of thoughts and emotions: to be ourselves, not our thoughts. For this week, work to be more responsible for your inner world.

255. Spiritual Momentum

As in sports, politics, and so much else, momentum makes a difference in the spiritual path, helping carry our practice and search. Newton's first law of motion teaches that everything maintains its own direction and pace unless other forces act. Likewise, our inner life would continue at its current level, were it not for the frictions attendant on daily life or for our dedication to the path.

Most of what goes on in life distracts us from our inner work, slowing its pace and deflecting us into unproductive channels. If we do not work to move up, we steadily fall down. Unless we rededicate ourselves to spiritual practice on a daily basis, life eventually brings our inner work to a halt. At that point, we lose all our spiritual momentum, grow accustomed to that state, consider it the norm, and waste our days floundering rudderless.

However, a certain level of ongoing effort can enable our inner work to withstand the disorganizing friction of life and maintain a steady pace toward the spirit. Our inner life thereby attains a plateau.

Depending on its particular level, a spiritual plateau can be very pleasant or not. If pleasant, inertia draws us to stay as is. A momentum-changing level of effort, though, can hasten our movement toward new heights.

When we feel frustration or dissatisfaction with life, it is often due to our lack of spiritual momentum. By returning to the basic roots of inner work such as body awareness, presence, meditation, and prayer, and by practicing diligently we soon find the dissatisfaction evaporates, as we attain a positive momentum.

For this week, assess your own spiritual momentum. Consider what a momentum-changing effort could be in your situation. Choose and apply specific practices to engage in, to maintain or even increase your momentum.

256. Beyond Paradise

O God,
Although Heaven is bright and beautiful beyond compare,
Without the vision of You it is painful and searing ...
A beautiful and pleasant station is Paradise,
But it has not the splendor of Your lane.[6]

The ability to abide in consciousness, to live in pure awareness, having dropped ego-centered subjectivity, feels like

---

6   Khwaja Abdullah Ansari quoted in Danner, V. and Thackston, W., *Ibn 'Ata Illah-Kwaja Abdullah Ansari: The Book of Wisdom-Intimate Conversations* (New York: Paulist Press, 1979), 187

paradise and often passes as enlightenment, as the ultimate enlightenment. Nevertheless, the bliss of consciousness does not mark the end of the spiritual path. The capacity to cruise through life, even intermittently, in the broad halls of perfect awareness, allowing and not identifying with thoughts and destructive emotions, certainly brings true and lasting happiness. That high level of development signifies a real achievement of soul. But the sacred emanates from well beyond that paradise.

This misunderstanding goes even deeper in making the mistake of considering our true essence to be consciousness, the mistake of identifying with and reifying the conscious energy. But consciousness is not who or what we are. Our reality is more subtle than that.

At each level, the corresponding energy functions as a body, as what we live in, but not as who we are, not as who lives there. This holds on the material level where we live in our physical body, on the sensation level where we live in the sensitive energy, on the conscious level where we live in pure awareness, in the conscious energy, and finally in the world of sacred light, the creative energy, an even higher paradise than the conscious energy. Like our physical body, these energies are what we use. The conscious energy, as the formless substrate of all perception, enables us to perceive, to cognize, to "see." We are the non-subjective one who sees, who cognizes, who perceives. We are the one who sits peacefully in consciousness, just being there.

That peace results from non-identifying, from letting go of self-centered grasping and rejecting, pushing and pulling. Letting go is an act of will, or rather a non-act of will. Will is action and non-action. In its simplest manifestations, will is attention, intention, and choosing. Will comes from beyond consciousness, beyond the energies. Will is who we are. Will is most real when open to, connected with, and serving the Sacred Source of All, the Divine Will, the unfathomable, loving and intelligent Purpose behind the universe.

This dialectic between East and West, between the bliss of consciousness and the service of will, forms and informs our path. Paradise, even for a moment, is bliss, but not the end of the one, true, unfolding story.

For this week, re-examine your spiritual aims. Do you seek paradise for yourself? Do you seek meaning in service? Are these mutually exclusive?

257. Dropping into the Body

Our body gives us not only our physical life but also a venue for our inner life, such as it is. So often we collapse into our heads, following some chain of thoughts, daydreaming, scheming, rehearsing, complaining, whining, worrying, mulling over, remembering, or ruminating. Just as often we fall into destructive emotions, into anger, fear, greed, jealousy, envy, lust, grasping, disgust, disdain, contempt, superiority, inferiority, indifference and the rest of the emotional spectrum. When we abandon ourselves to such thoughts and emotions, we lose our center and let chaos rule our inner life.

The simplest remedy consists of dropping into our body, enabling our center to reemerge by locating ourselves in our physical presence. We "come to" in our body, awakening from the thrall of the thoughts and emotions that had so thoroughly mesmerized us.

By what mechanism can this radical, in-the-moment change come about? First an impulse arises from a deep place in us, a part of us uncomfortable with being lost, with having vanished into thoughts or emotions. That impulse reminds us of a better way to live, a way accessible now. If the impulse comes strongly enough and if our commitment to living in presence has taken root, we respond. From the wilderness of self-propagating thoughts and emotions we collect our self and enter our physical home. Dropping our center of attention into our body, into the sensory experience of being in our body, if well-practiced, is a natural, immediate, and effective first response in our transition from dispersion to presence in this moment.

For this week, practice dropping into your body whenever you notice yourself lost in thoughts or emotions, whenever you feel discomfort with your dispersed state. Drop out of the world of distraction and into the world of collected cognizance.

258. Awe

A rare element of our emotional portfolio, the feeling of awe, when it does emerge, connects us viscerally with the sacred. We travel though a life in which everything and everyone occupies about the same level, a life in the material world. Nearly the whole of it comes to us familiar, expected, and perhaps a little flat. This situation, however, does not arise from life itself, but rather from our own attitude, perceptual limitations, and state of being.

Sometimes we confront a situation that shakes us out of the flatness: the sacred space of a house of worship, the majesty of a mountain, the vastness of the ocean, the power of a storm, or the birth of a child. We stand in awe, reminded of our forgotten relationship with the truly Awesome. This unique feeling, awe, has elements of fear, veneration, humility, and wonder.

And it functions when our perceptions open to some aspect of the true nature of the Divine. Thus awe indicates nearness.

Now rather than wait for the unusual and propitious circumstance, can we bring ourselves near the Divine by way of awe? Can we penetrate our expectation of the ordinary and gather an intimation of that Infinite and Loving Intelligence? Can we direct our attention beyond this material world and beyond our own awareness, even for a moment? Exploring, invoking the rightful feeling of awe carries us closer and makes the ordinary extraordinary.

For this week, explore your own feeling of awe and what it relates you to.

259. Aiming Higher

Even in meditation, we get distracted, following stray thought streams or images, remembering the past, anticipating the future, comparing, and rehearsing. The distractions pile up, clamoring for our attention. And we certainly let them take us.

Time-tested approaches toward non-distraction include focusing on some object like the breath, the body, or a particular thought or image to push the distractions aside. Alternatively, one can open to a spaciousness that allows the distractions to exhaust themselves.

But for this week we examine another approach: wholehearted, immediate attention directed toward the Divine. By turning our heart-mind and attention beyond our ordinary reality, even beyond consciousness, toward what is truly higher, we find our attention more riveted, more focused than otherwise possible, because at that level there is nothing else to distract us and because the wonder of the sacred attracts us irresistibly.

The higher one aims, the greater the unity found. Lower levels might distract us, but staying wholly oriented toward the higher brings total focus and immersion.

Prayers, chants, rhythmic movement, and other methods exist to collect and aim our totality toward the higher. But no method can carry us near or through that doorway. Only by reaching toward and into the Sacred does the whole of our nature converge. Only then do we enter the nearness that surpasses all. And in that nearness, all distractions pale.

For this week, work at reaching toward and into the Sacred with your will, with your immediate attention and intention, with the whole of yourself. Notice whether distractions fall away at such times.

260. Filling and Fulfilling

Many of us occasionally suffer a seductive malaise of dull emptiness, questioning the value of our life, bemoaning our lack of better fortune, wishing for something new and exciting but not quite knowing what, trudging through the repetitive weight of our job, our commute, and our chores. Fortunately, however, hope awaits us in the realm of spiritual inner work.

Those who have practiced meditation seriously know that a good long sitting in the morning can brighten and change your whole day. And changing enough days, changes your life. But what if you have not yet entered deeply enough into the peace and energy of meditation practice? Or what if your commitments today do not leave time for enough meditation? Are you doomed to dullness?

No! The opportunity to fill this moment with presence always stays with you. Working at presence transforms you into a sun, lighting your life from within. Seeing the dullness, emptiness, or whatever color disquiet inhabits your heart, you let it be, as part of your presence. Presence embraces and eventually heals your emptiness, filling you with peace, and even joy. As the bearer of a positive spiritual force, you create meaning. That force can brighten each moment no matter how mundane, each activity no matter how many repetitions this makes. Consciousness sees everything anew. The physical presence of sensation tastes every perception fully. The increased clarity may also show the way toward necessary outward changes.

The work of presence opens us to the art of living. For this week, when some malaise overtakes your feelings and thoughts, rather than acquiesce and succumb to it, let it be a reminder to work at presence now.

261. Follow Through

When you make a promise to yourself or to someone else, or when you set an intention by inwardly agreeing to it, what happens next? Do you always follow through? And if not, how does that affect you?

Looking carefully at such situations, we may see the damage we sometimes cause ourselves. If I make a promise or form an intention and then fail to carry it out, I may rationalize about it, blame the situation, and refuse to acknowledge my responsibility. Or I may block the event from my awareness, relegating it to some unwanted backwater of memory, unsuccessfully attempting to keep it from discoloring my self-image. Or I may see my failure to follow through, blame myself, lower my inner standards, wallow in guilt and shame, and become resigned to my weak-willed ways. And if it involves a broken promise to another, that person may be hurt as well. All of these explode my integrity, sap my strength, undermine my self-credibility and self-esteem, debase the value of my word, insulate me from the sacred, and seriously erode the clarity and purity of my inner life.

If, on the contrary, I carry through on an intention or a promise, one that is not based in self-centeredness and is not harmful, then I strengthen the bond between my own will and the One Sacred Will. Otherwise, that spiritually-crucial bond weakens.

For this week, look at your own promises and intentions, be they large or small. See what you do or fail to do. Evaluate the consequences.

262. Group Power

The spiritual power of a group seems to grow exponentially with the number of participants. Even with the smallest group, when two people practice together they multiply their possibilities and deepen their experience. When we meditate, chant, or pray with others, we enter a sacred space, a vessel created by our shared intention. The choice to participate fully in the event merges our individual will into the joint spiritual action of the group, forming a far greater will. This group will temporarily and mysteriously becomes our own will, empowering our practice in those moments. In addition, the act of opening to participate in the group will trains us toward opening to participate in the Divine Will.

Of course, many things can go wrong and impair the effectiveness of the group action: any ego-driven orientation, inappropriate attempts to dominate, doubts or fears about the group or the practice, inadequate understanding of the practice, or less than wholehearted willingness to engage in the shared effort. The limiting factors are the intention of each person involved and the inherent qualities of the chosen practice.

The surface experience of well-conducted group practice appears as our taking the practice more seriously than when alone and having an enhanced ability to enter it. This is priceless, matched on an individual basis only by certain exceptional practices, like fasting.

For this week, if you have a group with which you meditate or pray, notice and embrace the difference between that and your lone spiritual work. If you do not have a group, consider joining or creating one, even a group of two.

263. Ordinary Presence

Although it has its highs and lows, most of life is ordinary. We live in the usual and the typical, in the routine and the repetitive. This mass of ordinary moments, toward which we feel neutral or even bored, offers a gateway toward peace and equanimity through presence. Even the most ordinary of moments contains the miraculous secret of life. Here we are: breathing and aware, inhabiting this fabulously complex body, earth and universe. That is, if we are aware.

A bizarre blindness descends on us as we half-close our heart and mind to this ordinary moment. We want special. We want different. We want new. But it is special, always different, and ever new. If we can enter this ordinary moment, accept it as is, our wanting subsides and our awareness grows. The less we want, the more we see. The more we see, the less we want. And in that way we find peace, equanimity, and the extraordinary richness of ordinary life.

In our more extreme moments, the ups and downs of emotion, we identify with inner and outer events, naturally wanting to have the good and be rid of the bad. Even more than our ordinary moments, the extremes bind us, robbing our inner freedom. But deeper presence in the ordinary carries over to pacify the extremes.

For this week, practice ordinary presence. In your usual and routine moments, be there. Be present inwardly and outwardly, to yourself and your surroundings.

264. The Live Wire of Will

If you attempt to sit in silence, in deep silence, doing nothing, you may notice that instead you continually look for something to do. You would be happy to think or to purposely not think, to plan, daydream, or ruminate, to fidget or to sit rigidly, to react to an ache or to scratch an itch, to try to deepen the meditation or to get up. But if we do nothing, we see this live wire of will in us, eager to do something, anything to complete its circuit. When we actually can meditate on stillness, we let our will turn to its receptive side, just being open to what is, and complete itself in that openness.

The live wire of our will always finds ways to complete itself, to connect with something. Usually our will does this without intention, reacting by rote to every haphazard thought, emotion and sensory perception. Or this non-intentional will, operating on automatic, spins out a stream of thoughts and emotions, substituting that for a real life in presence.

Like electricity, our will has endless applications. Consciousness can create a channel for our will to follow, allowing us to act with intention. When the circuit completes itself in intentional presence, we are whole. Will flows through us in presence. In worship, we direct our will back toward its Source, completing the circuit in a different way. In sensing, the circuit of will completes itself by finding a ground in our body. In anything we do intentionally, whether inwardly or through our body, our will, our choosing is the central animating factor.

For this week, become aware of the live wire of your will and how you use it intentionally or let it use you unintentionally.

265. Feet of Awareness

As the farthest extremities from our head, the feet can lay claim to not interfering with our cherished daydreams and ruminations, nor even with that rare bird of intentional thought. But as our point of contact with the Earth, our feet are uniquely positioned to keep us grounded, both physically and spiritually. By basing part of our attention in our feet we stay rooted in the present moment. In so doing, we enter the only venue for true spiritual presence and practice, the boundless Now.

Awareness of our feet need not intrude, but rather enhances our life, our presence, and our freedom. Installed in that contact with the Earth, we keep more readily to what matters, to the practical and the real. And then when we turn to broader presence, to conversation, to kindness, and to prayer, we do so with a sense of our humanity that guides us truly.

For this week, as much as possible, whether sitting, walking, or standing, practice sensing your feet, that direct perception of having feet, of being in your feet. If you are standing, walking, or running, become aware of the contact at the bottom of your feet. Become aware of your weight pressing down and the Earth pressing up through your feet. If you are sitting, become aware of your shoes touching your feet. In all cases, become aware of the sensation within your feet.

266. Casting an Energy Net

The air around us not only contains nitrogen, oxygen, carbon dioxide and other gases, but carries spiritual energies as well. This fact and the opportunity for inner nourishment it presents have for many centuries attracted corresponding practices of energy breathing in Sufism, Yoga, and Taoism, among others. Beyond simple awareness of the breath, energy breathing enables us, consciously and intentionally, to gather energies from the air and retain them in our body to feed our soul. The experience is direct, palpable, and unmistakable. For those who are able to come to it, energy breathing serves an invaluable role in their inner work, serving their progress on the sacred path.

The yogic "breath of fire" notwithstanding, energy breathing does not require any significant alteration of our physical breath. In fact any substantial, intentional change to our normal physical breathing can have serious, negative ramifications on our health. Instead, the essence of energy breathing lies in the "inner" breath.

Using your powers of attention and visualization, imagine that the air around you is filled with shimmering particles of energy. Visualize a net that you cast out from yourself and draw back in as you inhale. The net consists of attention and intention. Casting is almost instantaneous as it moves with the speed of attention. As you draw the net back in, you capture particles of airborne energy and bring them into your body. You can sense the energy entering you with the air. As you exhale, allow the energy particles to stay in your body and spread throughout it.

Repeat this cycle in a relaxed manner. Let your physical breathing remain more or less normal and unchanged. The "less" here refers to the possibility that you may slightly emphasize the inhalation. If you grow dizzy or experience any other ill effects, stop. It means that you need a more relaxed approach.

As you practice energy breathing, the energy accumulates in your body. After a few minutes you begin to notice that your bodily sensation grows more vivid and stronger. After the energy breathing session, the energy stays in you, available to support your practice of presence.

For this week, spend some time each day practicing energy breathing.

267. Valuing the Way

At the hidden core of all spiritual practice lies our valuation of the way. The priority in our heart and mind that we give to our inner work determines the role it plays in our life. The more we value the spiritual, the more it can operate in us.

But this valuation fluctuates, waxing and waning with our moods, our preoccupations, and the events of our life. And the quality of our inner work fluctuates correspondingly.

So a central question confronting us on our path is how to raise and stabilize our spiritual priorities. In addressing this we might look to teachers and friends, to sacred texts and spiritual writings. All these can help. However, the most direct route toward valuing the way consists of increasing our contact with the Divine Source of all value. Whenever a sacred value touches us, it is that Source at work.

For this week, several times each day, turn your heart and mind toward the Sacred Source. Let the sacred imprint its value on you. Let it touch your core. Put that value into action, the action of spiritual practice: presence, prayer, kindness, meditation, service, and the rest.

When we live by sacred values, the sacred lives in us.

268. Emerging From Thought

Most of us live in our own subjective world of thoughts, in the endless bazaar of concepts, images, commentary and inner chatter that is our mind. We recognize the more objective reality outside our brain only insofar as it impinges on our habitually patterned thought-stream. Our thinking takes on any convenient subject. Whatever makes it through our perceptual filters becomes food for thought. So accustomed to this unquiet morass, we take the world of thought as our normal mode of being.

If a thing does not enter our thoughts, then it holds little or no reality for us. Thus we mistakenly conflate our thoughts with reality. It may be the reality that we experience, or rather half-experience, but it pales before even the ordinary reality of the physical world. Purposeful, intentional thinking makes up only a tiny portion of our day. The rest of the time our self-activating thought-stream encircles and captivates us, limiting our horizons to its narrow confines. Often one thought decides to do something, while the next forgets completely about it. Even when we think "big" thoughts, we still remain in the orbit of thought.

But a deeper world and a more satisfying way of life await us. For all these reasons and more, one major thrust of any true spiritual path consists of learning to see that we are not our thoughts and of increasing our contact with, our place in, non-conceptual reality, the locus of joy, peace, and the sacred. For this, many techniques exist, but all share the characteristic of bringing our perceptual focus out of our ordinary modes of thinking. In practicing such methods, whenever we notice that our attention has fallen back into ordinary thinking, we return to the exercise.

Examples include:
1. Counting breaths: attention to the physical sensations associated with breathing while mentally counting each exhalation up to 10, then beginning again at 1. We also start over at 1 whenever we lose the count or return from being lost in thought.
2. Repetitious prayer: mentally repeating or vocally chanting sacred words, especially in contact with their meaning and their feeling.
3. Attention to the body: sensing in turn the right hand, right foot, left foot, left hand, right arm, right leg, left leg, left arm, all four limbs, and finally the whole body.
4. Sitting patiently, relaxing, noticing thoughts until they dissipate.
5. Opening to and entering the formless, empty stillness, the consciousness beneath thought. This depends on the experience, taste, and attention acquired through exercises like those listed above.

For this week, practice emerging from thought.

269. Spiritual Friendship

Among the valuable, central relationships we can have, spiritual friendship occupies a special position. Such friendships normally have two essential features: recognition of equality and shared commitment to spiritual practice. Spiritual equality does not concern itself with outer or inner equality, with who holds greater wealth, fame, knowledge, or spiritual development. Rather, spiritual equality derives from the core truth that we are all equally children of our common Father God, as taught in the Jewish, Christian, and Hindu scriptures.

Those with a taste for effective spiritual practice sooner or later arrive at this understanding of other people as their equal. No one, regardless of his or her position in life or personal qualities, is above or below any another person. All are equal in their intrinsic nature. Democracies are founded on this bedrock principle and so is spirituality. Spiritual friendship can only flow with acceptance of this implicit equality.

God the Father gives the freedom of His will to us. We all possess a spark of the Divine Will and we instinctively honor people who pursue the path of embodying that sacredness. To use that freedom to act in friendship aligns us with another aspect of the sacred: God as Friend. This we also find in scripture, in the both the Old and New Testaments, in the Koran, and in the Bhagavad Gita.

Beyond equality, the specific character of spiritual friendship depends on a common pursuit of the spiritual path. Those with whom you share the search for the sacred naturally earn your interest, your care, your trust, and your joy in their presence. You also find that you need each other, because you support each others' inner evolution. If you practice together, that practice exceeds the sum of its parts. If you exchange views and experiences, you both grow in wisdom. You realize that with regard to your spiritual friends, both you and the world as a whole need their inner work. People who undertake spiritual practice contribute directly to the spiritual ecosystem of the world, a contribution necessary to any hope of peace on this planet or of environmental responsibility.

In a deeper sense, acts of friendship connect us separate human beings to each other in a greater whole. Friendship embodies the way of shared will, a way toward the emergent symbiotic wholeness of humanity. Like particles interacting to form atoms, atoms to molecules, molecules to cells, cells to organs, and organs to complex living beings, we may one day form a great human unity, a new and sacred wholeness. Friendship, and especially spiritual friendship, steps us toward that wholeness.

But many factors militate against true friendship: the busyness of our life, our shy or overly judgmental nature, not taking opportunities to meet people or to follow up after meeting them, fear of closeness or rejection, unwillingness to consider ourselves no more and no less than equal with others, unwillingness to share our spiritual aspirations, lack of interest in other people, an erroneous attitude that we do not need others, worrying about what others think of us, not wanting to give time to cultivate friendship, focusing on the features we dislike in people, and substituting acquaintanceship for friendship.

For this week, look at your friendships, your attitudes, your words and actions toward others. Is there something you need to change in this department of your life? Something you are neglecting?

270. Sending Good Will

One purpose, perhaps the primary purpose, of the spiritual path is to enable us to give more. Development of soul creates in us the inner capacity, sensitivity, and willingness to offer our good will to others, especially those in need. We all know of individuals and whole nations, near and far, who suffer from illness or debility, poverty or war, natural disasters and other misfortunes. In addition to personal, outward acts of compassion, inner actions can help. On this, all the major religions agree.

You can make such inner acts of compassion part of your normal daily meditation or prayer. Visualize the person or group of people toward whom you will direct your good will. You might, as in one Buddhist practice, begin with yourself and those closest to you and then move out to others. Simply and inwardly send your good will, your concern and prayers, your bright energy of heartfelt blessing to them. If it helps, use words of prayer or good wishes specific to their situation.

The essential thing is to send your very best, from the innermost recesses of your heart and soul, without holding back. It will be replenished, even immediately, as the energy passes from the spiritual depths, through you, to your intended recipients. Your willingness to give your best opens the gates of light from Above. Receiving the light of the sacred and giving it in turn, becomes one continuous action flowing through your soul. If God is benevolent will, then the practice of sending good will must align us with the Divine.

Such inner giving also has the happy side effect of fostering our personal transformation. We need not concern ourselves with whether it actually helps the people toward whom it is directed. Those results will take care of themselves. But we can see its effect on us. Sending good will softens our heart and loosens the grip of self-centered egoism on our soul. It trains us to understand that the world does not revolve solely around me. It prepares us to respond appropriately, compassionately, and wisely to people in need who come into our life. It teaches us how to open to a deeper level of energy and spirit.

While the barriers of our partially malformed personality, such as ill will, anger, schadenfreude, and self-centeredness do stand in the way, this intentional practice of good will strengthens a deeper part of us. Gradually it helps us connect with the sacred in ourselves and in other people, diminishing the importance of those inner barriers. It overflows our period of meditation or prayer and enters our ordinary life, enabling us at times spontaneously to adopt an attitude of greater acceptance and even warmth toward others, both those in need and those apparently not in need.

For this week, practice sending good will.

271. The Unseen

"The kingdom of heaven is like treasure hidden in a field."[7]

"The inability to perceive is perception"[8]

We should not expect to see God with our physical eyes or touch God with our hand. Indeed, the reality is just the reverse: God may see with our eyes or touch with our hand. But to

---

7   Matthew 13:44
8   Abu Bakr as-Siddiq, close companion of the Prophet Mohammed

come toward this realization, we first understand that we do not see God and that our not-seeing does not rule out God's reality. How else could it be? The Creator cannot be confined to space and time. That may be obvious, but …

Taking the realization of not-seeing as our guide, we catch a hint of the Unseen sacred. The Unseen hides beyond our senses, beneath the surface of this physical universe and our mental world. If we cannot perceive God with our senses, then perhaps we have another, dormant perceptual capability appropriate to the spiritual depths.

By remembering the Unseen and embracing the understanding that we cannot see God, we can seek a different mode of perception, of recognizing and touching the silent inwardness of the world, of perceiving the sacred Light invisible to eyes and instruments, and even of reconnecting with the Transcendent beyond the Light. Nothing in this physical universe can approach there.

Only our innate spiritual capacity, the very core of who we are, belongs to that sacred inwardness. Only that "I am" volition can slip through the veils of the senses and consciousness to discern the True. We learn where and how not to look by looking everywhere until we exhaust all conceivable directions. Then one day, without knowing how, exploring, we look beyond the conceivable, beyond thought and consciousness. We delve into the quintessential marrow of who we are and into the hidden Foundation of this world. And there discover the trail to the Treasure.

For this week, remember the Unseen as unseen. Let your non-seeing open the gates of wonder and search for the Real.

272. This Is It

Though we well know the truisms that the present is all there is and that we should "be here now," we nevertheless live "This is it?" or "Now is not enough." The present moment nearly vanishes under the weight of our hopes, fears, dreams and plans for the future, our regrets, resentments, anger and sadness for the past, and our aversion, distaste, procrastination and boredom with the present. By all these we justify our heedlessness for this moment, our view that the real action lies elsewhere, that what we want is not available right now, and our tendency to drift in a haze of haphazard thoughts. We ignore and sweep aside our better nature that prompts us toward presence. And thus, through inaction, we impoverish our life.

The cure is both sudden and long-term. Suddenly we find the timeless, not in the past or future, but in the heart of the present. We let go our non-acceptance of this moment and live. We breathe the fresh air of this one eternal now and realize that our joy lives here.

But we tend to relapse. So we undertake a course of spiritual practice, a disciplined path that does not require self-imposed forcing but rather draws and attracts us into the natural wonder of simple presence and into the comfort, warmth, and connection of prayer. We take care not to allow the long-term commitment to spiritual practice to detract from living in the now, which after all is where every instance of spirituality occurs.

Expanding our time scale, we see that what we do today and this week is our life. Despite our hopes, fears, plans, and dissatisfactions, this life that we lead now is our life, our only life. Yes, we work for a better future, but all the while we only live today.

How? Our practice serves both the present and the future. Meditation, prayer, presence, and kindness — these bring us to a deeper appreciation for this moment, while also serving and shaping our future. If we take time to meditate in the morning, our experience and response to the rest of the day is markedly different than if we had not meditated. Over the weeks, months and years, that effect builds, gradually transforming the very marrow of who we are. New and unexpected sources of joy, contentment, satisfaction and meaning open to us. But these are also now, not just in some hoped-for future at the end of a long path of practice. Unmitigated acceptance of our self and our life ushers us into the heart of the present, into the heart of presence.

For this week, remember that *"This Is It."*[9] Whether we consider the moment, the day, or the week, this is our life, our only time. Out of self-respect, we savor and honor this, our one and only, present moment.

273. Drawing Down the Blessing

The core purpose of prayer, and all spiritual practice, may well be to open a channel through which the blessing of Divine potential can flow into this world. Spiritual practice, if continued beyond presence and beyond the level of pure consciousness, gives us access to the world of Divine potential, the sacred luminosity. That creative light carries the seeds of all healing, goodness, beauty, wisdom and kindness, qualities so sorely needed on the global scale of this Earth.

No single person, group, lineage, or religion has a mo-

---

9   Title of a classic book on Zen by Alan Watts

nopoly on that Divine potential, whose overflowing love offers a means toward resolving the difficult issues confronting us all. No sensitive person ignores the terrible poverty, violence, and environmental damage on our little planet. And in facing that, we face our apparent powerlessness. But we can each play our personal, constructive role in the drama of this planet. That role can include both outward service and inward action.

Through our spiritual development, as our being grows and our will purifies, the world of Divine potential opens to us. When we turn toward the sacred, that potential pours vividly through us, as a high spiritual energy, into the life of this Earth. We can even direct it to where the need is greatest. Herein lies our secret hope, both for ourselves and the whole community of life.

The inner act is simple and direct. Bring yourself into your best state, perhaps through meditation. Adopt an attitude of devotion to the Divine. If it helps, use inner words of prayer or a silent chant or melody, something that touches you deeply. By engaging your entire being, turn the whole of your attention, your heart, and your mind toward heaven, the effulgent world of Divine potential.

Not far but near, it awaits you just beyond consciousness. Neither outward nor inward, neither right nor left, neither up nor down, that realm of sacred luminosity resides outside space, time, and direction. But through you, it can enter to help this troubled world and, in the process, transform your soul.

For this week, practice turning toward the realm of the Divine potential. Draw down its blessing. Send it where it is needed.

274. Wasteful Tensions

Leaks in our spiritual vessel limit the benefit of the practices we do to increase our supply of inner energies. We waste energy in many ways, such as allowing harmful emotions to run rampant through us and indulging in physical excesses like overeating, smoking, and drinking too much alcohol. Another basic, often unrecognized waste of precious energy occurs through unintentional, unnecessary bodily tensions and fidgeting.

Habitual muscular tensions prey on us in repetitious patterns in our forehead, around our eyes, lips and mouth, shoulders, abdomen, or anywhere else in our body. Of course some tensions are required: we could not stand or walk or perform the myriad movements of life without using our muscles. But many tensions clearly serve no useful purpose and do squander our energy: hunching our shoulders, contorting our face, tightness in our belly, etc.

A second mode of energy waste through muscles is the repetitious, purposeless movement of fidgeting. Examples include playing with pocket change, drumming our fingers, playing with a pencil, moving a foot back and forth while sitting, chewing on something inedible like a pencil or the inside of our cheek, scratching when there's no itch.

If we try to contain our tensions and stop fidgeting by inner force, the energy released will find another wasteful outlet. Nonessential tensions and useless fidgeting often result from some destructive emotion looking for release. So instead of trying to bottle them up and thereby piling on yet another kind of tension, we take a different approach.

When we notice unneeded tensions or fidgeting, we

just relax into presence and let them go. In that relaxation we conserve the energy that was being wasted and allow it to enter our being and enhance our presence. The key to this method lies in not attempting to relax the tensions or stop the fidgeting directly, but rather to relax our self when we notice tensions or fidgeting. Relaxing from the inside out allows the tensions and fidgeting to subside naturally and effortlessly. We put down an inner weight and breathe a sigh of relief.

For this week, notice your own unnecessary muscular tensions and fidgeting. Relax yourself to relax the tensions and let the fidgeting calm down. Allow the energy to stay in your relaxed being.

275. The Taste of Presence

Like a fish in water or a human surrounded by air, we overlook the obvious even when it's crucial. The same situation confronts us on the path of soul development. We live in a state of non-presence and do not recognize it as such. When my thoughts ramble, when I eat without tasting, when my body moves without me being in that movement, when sounds enter my ears without me listening, when sights enter my eyes without me seeing them, when my mouth speaks without me being the speaker, when my body experiences or acts without me being the experiencer or actor — for all of this I take no notice. This is my unremarkable, ordinary, programmed and patterned mode of living, or rather half-living, my life. Such a life lives itself with little true humanity.

Nevertheless, another possibility awaits us: a deeper, more joyous, more meaningful, more productive, and more loving way of life. For that, we need to live in presence. To be aware of the sensations in our body, to be in conscious wholeness, to be the one who does whatever we do, to live kindly and mindfully, to live as attention and intention, to collect and organize our inner energies through meditation, to add to the sacred through prayer — all this and more belongs in a truer life.

The difference between the programmed life and the truer life is sometimes stark and sometimes subtle. But for this difference we need to acquire a taste. All of us live both kinds of life. Can we distinguish between them, in any given moment? Can we know which mode we are in now? And let that knowing prompt us to move from the half-life to the whole-life?

The taste of non-presence can be bitter, dull, or even sweet, but always has a layer of superficial emptiness and never truly satisfies. The taste of presence, on the other hand, adds a dimension of richness and depth to any experience or act. The practice of presence helps us acquire the taste of presence. And by contrast, the taste of presence helps develop our taste for recognizing non-presence.

These tastes consist of a nuanced inner sense of the qualities and levels of presence and non-presence. This sense enables us to recognize our inner state for what it is, especially in comparison with other possible states. Spiritual practice gives us the tools to move toward a higher state. But a finely-honed taste for presence and non-presence can help guide us through our inner landscape, help us know which tools to use and when.

The taste of non-presence can be our great ally in the spiritual path. For through it, through discomfort with our programmed-response, minimal-awareness mode of pseudo-living, we acquire the heart of longing that draws us toward the sacred, toward presence. The taste of presence, the self-evident rightness of true living, motivates our inner work in lesser states.

For this week, whenever you remember, develop your taste for presence and non-presence by noticing whether and to what degree you are present. And let that taste increase your motivation, your heart for the practice of presence.

276. Evening Presence

On most days, typically in the evening, we enter a period of relative leisure. Our duties for the day complete, we can just relax. Perhaps we read, listen to music, watch TV, engage with friends or family, or take up some other favored activity or inactivity. This is the perfect time for relaxed presence.

Whenever we can fully relax in our outer life, we take as our practice to also relax inwardly, into an easy presence. We rest simply in awareness of bodily sensation, in awareness of being here. From this easy presence, we can enjoy the company of other people or whatever we are doing. This background ease can enable us to live in presence for longer periods than otherwise possible, perhaps even for most of the evening.

Even if our evening calls for fulfilling certain responsibilities, like commuting home from work, shopping, cooking, washing dishes, or caring for our children, we have the possibility of doing it all in ease and presence. To a remarkable degree, presence adds wholeness and fulfillment to the evening, to our interactions with others, to our leisure pursuits, to performing our evening chores, to simply being in our life. All this acquires a much more satisfying dimension if done in presence.

Presence is simple and, although it has degrees, distinct from non-presence, from living in a programmed way. Presence is whole and complete; non-presence is partial and contingent.

Presence is cognizant of this moment; non-presence lets it slip by unnoticed. Presence thinks by intention; non-presence thinks by associative stream. Presence is the context; non-presence blows in the wind. Presence does; non-presence reacts. Presence is; non-presence needs.

For this week, live your evenings in presence, intentionally and knowingly being here, relaxing into awareness of your body, into awareness of the moment, into kindness, and into being the one who does what you do.

277. Swimming Upstream

The tides of our spirit ebb and flow. We relish those days when the currents carry us smoothly toward our desired destination. But the hard truth includes other days of swimming against the tide through choppy waters. Perhaps events conspire against us or our body weighs us down with inertia or pain, while inwardly we grow agitated or despondent. To maintain our inner work on those days, we reach deep into our reservoir of commitment and momentum from our previous efforts, reconnect with why we practice, remember the sacred heights that await us, and recall that help will certainly meet us if we bootstrap ourselves upward despite our difficulties.

Those times of unbridled thoughts, destructive emotions, painful sensations, and unwanted events leave us little room to maneuver. We can, however, pick a simple and familiar practice and then do our best to work at it, stay with it, and return to it again and again. The very hardships of the day can provide a source of energy, perhaps an uncomfortable energy that, nevertheless, we can use to positive result.

More subtle opportunities arise in the midst of bleak

days. We can examine our reactions, see what it is we dislike and cannot bear, and in so doing gain invaluable insight into our attachments and identifications. We can approach the crucial choice to let go of our clinging and displeasure, to let go the constraints of our self-centeredness, and to widen our horizon beyond the merely personal. Working from the specifics to the more general, we practice non-clinging on those down days of hanging onto our preferences of how life should be. This does not mean we give up trying to improve our life, inwardly and outwardly, but rather that we learn to do so without the unnecessary layers of attachment and anguish.

When the undesirable assails us, instead of seeing only at what we deem undesirable, we also look at the source of our attitude toward it and thereby loosen its grip. And we use that resulting bit of freedom to reengage our spiritual work of sensing, presence, prayer, kindness, meditation, and equanimity.

For this week, if and when necessary, practice swimming upstream.

278. Transcending Personality

At some point in our spiritual journey, we may experience the misplaced fear (or hope) of abandoning our personality. We practice with the grand but impossible idea that everything we normally take to be who we are has to go. That includes our usual drives, cares and concerns, our patterns of thinking, reacting and interacting, our desires, hopes and dreams, our pleasures and our pains. We may think that spiritual development means ridding ourselves of our entire persona. Fortunately this is not the case. It would be an insurmountable and ultimately a failed and unnecessary project.

A kernel of truth, however, does underlie this notion of banning our personality. That truth leads us toward transcending our usual self, transcending our personality, a process very different than destroying. It is a question of where our center of gravity lies, where we are, who we consider ourselves to be, and who uses or owns our personality.

Closely entwined with our personality, sits our egoism, the self-centered attitude that drives and feeds on so many of our thoughts, feelings, and actions. In the process of spiritual work, this is what diminishes. But there is nothing to fear, because our ego is just an illusion.

To loosen the grip of egoism on our personality, on us, we gradually see that the subjective "self" that ego supposedly is, the "self" that ego builds up and defends, does not in fact exist. This liberating insight in no way diminishes us. Rather, it enlarges and frees us into a greater world, where our intentions derive from a more objective reality attuned not just to our own needs, but also to the needs of our family, our society, our planet, and the Sacred.

In the spiritual path, the relocation of our center of intention goes hand in hand with an increase in the quality and quantity of our inner energies. Personality runs principally on the automatic, programmed energy and to a lesser extent on the sensitive, responsive energy. The conscious energy, the foundation of presence, opens us to a world that transcends our personality without destroying it. The personality remains in the automatic and sensitive energies, while we learn to live more in the conscious energy. We become more than just our personality.

So as our self-centered egoism weakens and is left behind, our personality stays intact, providing a ready vehicle through which our higher intentions can act and through which we can enjoy our inwardly enriched lives.

For this week, notice the automated, programmed patterns of your personality in action. See what transcending it would mean.

279. Being the Decider-Perceiver

The central fact of human life consists of our individual core, the decider and perceiver in each of us, the one who sees and acts and lives our life. This "I" occupies a pivotal position as the agent of our inner life and outer actions, as well as the agent of our relationship with the higher worlds as the one who prays, the one who opens to the sacred, and ultimately the one who surrenders in service to and union with the Divine. All these actions depend on the choices I make.

The problem is that we do not choose, we abdicate our responsibility toward ourselves and let things happen in us by habit, momentum, and the path of least resistance. Furthermore, we do not fully experience because we are not at home, we are not there to receive and participate in the experience. Our body perceives, thinks, and does things with only minimal presence of the intentional chooser and conscious perceiver in us. Conflicting desires battle it out and the stronger ones take control. We live a rather benumbed life, lost in thoughts and daydreams, half-aware.

At any given moment, however, many possible choices lie within our purview. For example, I can choose to be, to be one who experiences and lives my life right now, to be the one who perceives, inhabits, and owns my body, to be the one who thinks my thoughts or at least sees them thinking themselves.

Right now I see this page. My eyes and brain register

and interpret the perception, as would happen ordinarily. But now I am here seeing it. I am the one who sees it. I am at home at the center of my experience. I am directing my attention and focusing my powers of perception.

Certainly we see and do things all day long. But the vast majority of it goes on by itself: no one doing what we do, no chooser, no decider, no one being at home in the center of it all. The familiar patterns of our personality act as if they themselves occupy the seat of the decider and perceiver. But that is just egoism.

Living as "I," being the decider and perceiver, does not necessarily mean that we act differently than we would ordinarily. But presence, in the form of will-to-be, changes the very core of our experience and our life.

You can feel yourself being, being the one who reads these words, the one who gets their meaning. For this week, practice being the decider and perceiver, the one who inhabits your body, the one who experiences and lives your life. Work to understand what this means in practice by trying it, in a relaxed way.

280. The Arrow of Presence

In our usual mode of living, nearly all our perceptions and actions occur without us being here in ourselves to receive the perception or to participate in the action. This is like a half arrow, with a head that points toward the perception or action, but no tail, no stabilizing source behind it. The arrow points toward every perception and action, but the arrow is incomplete. By our inner work, by the work of presence, by being here at home in ourselves, by being ourselves, we can add the tail to complete the arrow.

I...see. What I see is at the head of the arrow. The seeing is the shaft. And the I that sees is the tail of the arrow of presence.

But the story does not stop there. The arrow is in truth long and deep, extending back beyond us as perceiver-decider, beyond us as individual, toward the roots of our soul in the Sacred. Ultimately there is only one Perceiver-Decider, in Whom we all share and from Whom we all derive. So when we become present as the tail of the arrow, we earn the opportunity to reconnect with the hidden reaches of will, back along the arrow shaft through our individual perceiver-decider-director of attention, toward the arrow's fundamental stability in the Source. We can approach this truest form of prayer in deep meditation, in reaching out behind and beyond ourselves to our sacred roots.

For this week, remember to be the arrow of presence. During your day's activities, work to be the stable tail, the individualized source of this arrow in your perceptions and actions. And in your quieter moments, look back behind you along the arrow's shaft toward your true identity in our shared and sacred Source.

281. The Field of Presence

Two of the primary components of presence consist of the will-arrow and the conscious field. These two complementary aspects create the foundation of our inner life, the will and the being of a whole person. Last week we studied the will-arrow of presence. This week we take up the field of presence.

Consciousness, the conscious energy, forms the

boundless being-field of presence. Abiding in the stillness of consciousness, the clear and cognizant substance of your pure awareness fills all directions. Everything falls within this vast, timeless, and spacious field of your being. Though always here and available, the ability to recognize and be in consciousness depends on an acquired taste, a perception of the subtle and usually overlooked substance of awareness itself. Once we have this taste, we grow able to enter the conscious field of presence during ordinary activities.

To acquire the taste of consciousness, however, meditation proves indispensable. Sitting quietly and patiently, letting go of our physical tensions, relaxing our emotional stress, and noticing the mesmerizing whisper of our thoughts, we enter the silence. Thoughts and images, though, continue arising, captivating us, and thus keeping us from our place in the still waters of awareness. In the stillness, any train of thought is suspect. Am I on that train or am I seeing it pass by? Again and yet again, we get off the train and return to just sitting. We allow the thoughts and images to come and go as they will, seeing them without being caught by them, without being them, without thinking them. Even as the thoughts and images continue, the stillness grows beneath them and the silence emerges. Thoughts float by on the surface of our mind, while we enter the quiet depths.

Becoming accustomed to that silence, we begin to know it as more than just a lack of thoughts and inner noise. We feel the palpable, substantive quality of the silence itself. And then it dawns on us that the silence is none other than the very substance of our awareness, our consciousness. That silent field, that stillness is consciousness, boundless and eternal. We become the silence. Thoughts, images, and sounds may pass, but we rest in and as the silence.

For this week, find times to sit quietly and relax patiently. Step off the train of thoughts, open to stillness, enter wholeness, and become the silence. Remarkable peace and joy await you here.

282. The Ground of Presence

Presence, though singular in its wholeness, has three primary and interdependent components, each one whole in itself. In recent weeks we have studied the will-arrow of presence and the conscious field of presence. Now we return to the ground of presence: sensation.

While our thoughts and emotions often take us into the past and future, our body stays here and now. Body awareness anchors us in the present moment. And the energy of sensation mediates awareness of our body.

For example, if you focus your attention in your right hand for a few minutes and then compare your experience of your right and left hands, you may notice a difference between the two. This difference signals the presence of the sensitive energy in the right hand and shows that the sensitive energy can be moved and accumulated intentionally. Through persevering in the practice of sensing parts and eventually the whole of your body, you establish yourself in the present moment.

Furthermore, the sensitive energy forms an inner platform on which the conscious energy can stand. The stronger and more complete the sensitive energy in your body, the greater your access to pure and clear awareness, to consciousness. As you sit sensing your body as a whole, the silent field of consciousness gradually emerges into your awareness and envelops you. As you become well-practiced in sensing and in entering the still field of consciousness during sitting meditation, you find yourself able to be in sensation and later even in consciousness during ordinary activities.

Consciousness may arise without whole body sensation, but with much diminished stability. Sensation gives us a substantial home in the present and consciousness naturally fills that home.

So the conscious field of presence resides on the ground of sensation. And our will acts through the conscious field. And will, in the form of attention to our body, collects the sensitive energy. Thus the three components of presence, the will-arrow, the conscious field and the ground of sensation, all depend upon and support each other. Though full presence requires all three, we start with the foundation, with working toward robust, visceral, continuing, full-body sensation. From there, the rest becomes possible and evolves organically.

For this week, increase your work with the energy of sensation. Notice how it impacts your whole presence.

283. Demands of self

Our self-centeredness, the egoism that we believe we are, expects and demands that the world adapt itself to us and our desires. A traffic jam is a personal insult. A physical illness or injury is an undeserved affront. A lack of appreciation or an insufficient salary causes an inner revolt against our employer. The least social slight rattles our self-assumed status and our superficial demanded-dignity. The world revolves around "me" and when it fails to conform to "my" desires, it throws "my" inner life into disarray.

In psychological terms, self-centeredness may paradoxically be the root of our unhappiness, because that self can never be completely satisfied. But even more seriously in spiritual terms, the whole complex of egoistic attitudes totally blocks the Sacred from reaching us. The false structure of egoism takes the Divine gift of free will, ties a knot in it, and declares the knot to be "me." That knot disrupts all possible communication and connection with the Higher, leaving us stranded in a self-created, spiritual desert.

The practice of humility is the antidote that loosens the knot of self-will and leads both to lasting happiness and to the Sacred. Where humility finds peace and contentment, self demands more. Humility begins with seeing those varied demands of self, understanding their source as egoism, and letting them go. Through prayer, humility serves and reconnects with the Sacred. The act of acknowledging a higher, more intelligent, more compassionate force inherently humbles us. Despite the disappointments and pain that come our way, humility is grateful for the gift of this miraculous life.

Of course, not all emotional upsets arise from self-centeredness. But many do. To understand ourselves means to know the difference.

For this week, notice the demands of self for what they are. Whenever you find yourself upset, notice whether the core issue concerns some demand of self. This does not require and extensive self-interrogation to investigate the source of your motives. Rather, it means an instantaneous, intuitive, conscience-based seeing of whether ego is in play in that moment. The seeing can sometimes even liberate the emotional reaction almost instantly. So form the intention to see the demands of your small self and, when the opportunities arise, be there in simple honesty to notice.

284. Shifting into Neutral: The Temple of Peace

We live in a vibrant society of action: on the go, efficiently not "wasting" time, competing, doing chores, meeting responsibilities, rushing around, and even feeling guilty when we do just relax. The results show up as an epidemic of excessive stress, as well as technological wonders and rising productivity and living standards. But what defines a high standard of living? Surely it must include time for relaxation in a life without unwanted stress.

The action-based ethic offers certain advantages to our spiritual practice. Active efforts such as focusing attention, raising the sensitive energy in our body, conscious breathing, energy breathing, speaking consciously, and intentional presence together form an essential, forward-looking side of the path.

Nevertheless, our spiritually active side needs a balancing counterweight. For that we turn to non-doing receptivity. We practice this particularly in receptive meditation, while also allowing it to enter life's activities.

In receptive meditation, we sit and do nothing, shifting our inner gear into neutral, relaxing our will into a mode of unconditional, as-is acceptance. Without falling asleep, staying alertly relaxed, we disengage from actively trying to shape or direct our inner experience. We let thoughts flow, giving them ample space to soften and fade on their own. For physical sensations, sounds, smells, images, we take the same approach, letting them be as they are, arising and fading on their own, while we sit in the peace of just being here. Early on you may find yourself drifting in a dreamy, semi-conscious fog of disjointed thoughts and images. Little by little however, the thoughts diminish, sensations and sounds dissolve into background, and the stillness of pure consciousness spontaneously emerges from the noise and distractions.

You may find it helpful to shift into neutral gradually. To begin the meditation, spend some time focusing attention, for example on following the breath. As your attention settles into the breath, relax your effort. Finally, stop making any effort whatsoever and just sit, being here. If the mental fog descends and if you have enough time, you can wait it out, doing nothing. Eventually the fog will lift, leaving you in the deep silence of your fundamental awareness.

Notably and subtly, shifting into neutral disengages our inner controller, our ego and the patterns of our personality mask. We shift into acceptance of our inner state as is and shift out of our inner critic and ego demands. Ego has no place in equanimity.

By occasionally shifting from the active will to the receptive, steeping ourselves in contentment and the peace of the conscious energy, we allow that peace to spill over into our active life. Acting from equanimity makes us more effective, even in carrying through our outward intentions.

For this week, find time to shift into neutral and let the result color your active life with peace and presence.

285. Shifting into Reverse: Tracing Back the Radiance

By shifting into neutral, we have earned the freedom to shift into reverse, to begin backing out of personality, out of our mask, and toward the sacred depths. Rather than always driving forward, always trying to control and fill our life and ourselves with more of what we want, we take time to back off, to empty ourselves. In that emptying we make room for the sacred, we invite the Higher to enter us, to become us. At least for those moments of emptying, the truest form of prayer, we offer ourselves in service to the sacred. Such worship cleanses our heart and allows the Higher to enter the world through us.

But not obvious is how to get our bearings in the vast, neutral stillness of consciousness and move from there into reverse, toward the Higher. The 12th century Korean Zen master Chinul coined a beautiful phrase that captures the process: *tracing back the radiance.* The key insight consists in recognizing that the deeper we go into ourselves the closer we come to our identity with the Divine. We ask "who am I?" and move toward the answer.

Our will, our attention, our intention, arise from our ultimate self. To shift into reverse, we open back in the direction of our self, our I, the source of our will. Finding this direction is subtle but possible, and requires persistence. The search itself purifies us.

So after shifting into neutral, meditating in the great inner temple of peace and consciousness, we use our new-found freedom to search for our deepest self. We follow the roots of our I back toward our Divine source. This search is our worship. Indeed, a brief and repeated invocation or prayer, one close and meaningful to us, can help. Each time we inwardly say the prayer, we use it to beg humbly with our entire being, to ask to enter the sacred.

For this week practice shifting into reverse by tracing back the radiance.

286. Playing Our Roles

Like actors, we adopt a wide range of roles. At work you might play supervisor, co-worker, and subordinate, service provider and client. At home you might play father, son, brother, and husband, or mother, daughter, sister, and wife. With one set of friends you might be a sports fan, artist, or music lover. With another set of friends you might be the spiritual seeker. In each of these situations we take on rather different patterns of behavior. Even with one person, we sometimes play different roles, e.g., with a child we can at times be the supportive parent, the playful friend, or the stern disciplinarian. Part of our inner work is to be aware of the role we are playing.

The best actors, rather than "acting," seem to fully inhabit their roles, believably becoming the character, with no difference between the actor and the role. Some roles come naturally and we inhabit them fully. Others don't suit us and the fit is uncomfortable. That can be due to the role being at cross purposes with our preferences and predilections, or with an image we have of who we are, or with our background, experience and habits, or with our psychological makeup. Nevertheless, some ill-suited roles may be necessary ones and may even be useful for our spiritual development. A little more inner freedom allows us to fulfill what's required of us, to do the right thing and be the right way, uncomfortable though it may be.

In the same way that God gives us our free will, we often hand over our freedom to the less-than-conscious patterns and habits of our roles. By this abdication of responsibility, we sometimes allow ourselves to act in ways unbecoming to our truer self. By giving us freedom, God takes the risk that we will abuse it. Conscience serves as our link to the source of our freedom, can guide our actions rightly, and can even lead toward allowing God to play the role of being us.

So it is with our own roles. If we can maintain a link from each role to our more essential self, we act within the role but also in accord with our deeper nature. That link is presence.

Presence has no shape and no agenda beyond being present, but carries with it a sense of who I am. Thus presence can enter any and every role we play, keeping our freedom where it belongs, with who we really are, and making the role conscious. We can be ourselves and fully inhabit our roles, without allowing the roles free reign to do the wrong thing or to live the pre-programmed life.

Notice the roles you play. Can you bring presence into your roles? For some roles, perhaps the ones we play at home, this is relatively easy: we can more readily be ourselves in those roles. For other roles, not so easy: we lose ourselves in the role. In meditation and in deep prayer we drop all roles, even the role of the meditator or supplicant.

For this week, see your roles. Be present and be yourself in them.

287. Inner Structure

Just as our body has bones to support it, our soul also needs a support structure, a framework on which everything else can depend. That support structure is our active will, in the form of directed attention, intention to practice, and the will-to-be. Imagine our body without bones: a pile of mush, unable to do what we so naturally do. So it is for our soul without the intentional will-to-be, scattered and ineffective. For examples of this we need only look at how we chase after our unintentional, kaleidoscopic, associative thoughts, how we lose ourselves in thrall to events, and how predictably our emotions react.

Now you might protest that in deep meditation and prayer we are not inwardly active, yet our soul collects itself on the outskirts of the Divine. But this also involves will, the other side of will, the receptive side that opens us to the sacred. Unless we live in a monastery in perpetual retreat, though, we do not spend the bulk of our days in deep meditation and prayer.

To enter the receptive depths takes us toward the Source of all Purpose. But the entry way depends upon and passes through a well-structured soul. No building, no door! Without some inner organization, receptiveness opens us merely to random thoughts and reactive emotions. With nowhere to stand, we are swept away by time and the depth remains hidden from view. This is not to say that we actively stand somewhere inside during deep meditation, but rather that our inwardly active work during many other moments prepares the inner place of meditation and prayer.

That inwardly active work involves attention, intention, and the will-to-be. We give attention to our body, intending to sense our body, more and more and more. This creates a foothold, a structure in the substantive world beyond our thoughts, daydreams, and reactions. It builds our soul to the point of true presence, through our intentional will-to-be. Here we are, fully aware, fully now, fully connected with ourselves and with all around us. Like a construction worker, we keep at it until the edifice of our soul is complete and ready for its intended purpose.

For this week, renew your effort to build your inner structure. Spend the inside of your days in sensing your body and willing-to-be present.

288. One Thing at a Time

In a multitasking society, simplifying is radical. Rather than do two things at once in an attempt to cram more into our limited time, we fully engage ourselves in one thing. If it's worth doing at all, then it's worth doing with the whole ourselves.

Only the unnecessary can be a true waste of time. If the action is necessary, but somehow undesirable, then doing it with full attention makes it less undesirable for several reasons. First, full attention connects the task with our inner work and helps build our presence and our soul. Second, full attention enriches any experience. And third, full attention puts more quality into what we do. The same applies to the unnecessary but desirable, like entertainments: full attention makes those even more enjoyable.

Along with full attention, we practice full intention: intending to do the action as we do it and being the one doing it. In this way we own what we do, we take responsibility for it. "I choose to do this and I am doing it." By such full intention, we avoid half-doing things and avoid the resentment that comes with doing what we must but would rather not do.

Another dimension to this issue arises when we feel overwhelmed by how much we need to do. As we do one thing, we fret about all the other things crowding our agenda. By inwardly slowing down to focus on the task at hand, we usually get it done quicker and better than when we're rushed and distracted by thoughts about other tasks. Rushing costs us our center. In rushing toward the future, we leave ourselves behind.

But even if our plate is not overfull, to actually do one thing at any given moment does require a clear intention and a focused attention. Distracting thoughts, impulses, and sensory impressions continually vie for our attention. It proves impossible to block all that out. Instead we focus on our chosen task, while letting all the irrelevant and pseudo-relevant items in our stream of awareness pass by. By relaxing into such letting go, the would-be distractions cannot hook us. We stay here in this moment, doing what we do.

So we have these two main aspects of doing one thing a time. First, we choose one thing to do. Second, we do it, while focusing on it, intending it, remaining with it, and staying free of the irregular but continuing flow of distractions. Being in contact with our body and being in presence make it possible truly to do one thing at a time. These practices offer a more stable platform in the present, a place to stand and withstand the stream of sensory impressions, a place from which to focus on our task.

For this week, practice doing just one thing at a time and staying fully engaged in it.

289. Divine Embrace

Like a loving embrace between two people, the Divine embrace is mutual: God embraces us personally and we reciprocate. And like a human embrace, the Divine embrace can be, if only briefly, not of two, but of One, as we become the other and the other becomes us. Or rather, we both become both.

But is the Divine, as it would seem, truly out of our reach? This is the crux of the matter. We go about our lives with no immediate connection to the Higher and no thought that such a directly-experienced connection might be possible for us. And because of this seeming impossibility, we make no real attempt at it. If we pray, we tend to adopt the attitude of a relatively insignificant supplicant to some remote God. That we ourselves could today actually embrace the Divine seems farfetched. Yet there it is: our promise and our hope in the Sacred.

The saints are human, just like you. The one way to discover whether you also could touch the Divine is to try it. And if at first nothing comes, then persist day after day, year after year, in a heartfelt and sincere practice, a search toward that highest possibility.

So bring yourself into your best state, through prayer or meditation. And from that place open your heart, your mind, your attention and intention, simply and directly toward the Most Sacred. Beyond all objects, beyond life, beyond thought and beyond stillness, yet right here, the Divine awaits our approach to welcome us with open arms. Not in some distant heaven, but here within ourselves, we can touch and be touched by the Most Sacred.

For this week, spend at least a few minutes each day seeking the immediate embrace of the Divine. You may need some time for preparation. But also reserve time to actually go for it, to turn toward the loving mystery, to drop your inner barriers, to direct your entire being to finding your way into that Sacred Presence. And then like a long lost child returning home, invite the Sacred to embrace you.

290. Embracing Our Life

By resisting parts of our life, we lose precious time and energy, inwardly rejecting what we do not want but nevertheless have. Some situations we can and do change. Others not. If we cannot or do not choose to change something, yet continue resisting it, we rob ourselves of that part of our life. If instead we could accept and embrace our life, warts and all, we would live more fully, create more possibilities for our inner world, and see more clearly the paths toward improving our life.

This embrace of life can only happen now, not in some abstract future. We take this moment as it is, even if distasteful. This moment is our life, our only life, and as such we honor it. We relax into acceptance, into presence, embracing our one moment. We embrace our body from within, through relaxation and full awareness of physical sensation. We embrace our emotions, even if distressed and difficult, accepting and respecting our self as is. We embrace our thoughts, even if wild or obsessive, accepting and respecting our self as is. We embrace our senses, what we see and hear and so on: this is our life now. We adopt an attitude of openness, acceptance, and respect toward the people around us. We drop our inner barriers of resistance to our experience and enter the unobstructed peace of presence, the life of here and now.

Persistent practice of meditation, presence, and prayer can establish our access to a Friend Who never disappoints, to the source of peace, joy, love, and meaning. The relationship between that higher world and our life has many layers of subtlety. One of those is the temptation to use the higher world as an escape that enables us to avoid facing, choosing, and embracing our difficulties. We have human needs, physical, emotional, intellectual, and spiritual, all of which warrant respect. Ignoring our ordinary human needs leads to trouble, though we need not overindulge our desires. Embracing our life means using judgment based on conscience in choosing how to live, in balancing conflicting needs, responsibilities, and desires. And however it is, we live it fully in each moment.

For this week, embrace your life. The more you embrace life, the more vivid life becomes, and the more there is to embrace.

291. Beyond Our Story

The core of our personality is our story, the personal story of our life, full of facts and events, plots and subplots galore. How we see ourselves, how we see the world, and what we do — all emanate from our story. Our childhood of parents, siblings, relatives, friends, home, school, home town, and all the associated events create the base story. And it goes on into adolescence and adult years: schooling, friends, jobs, relationships, religion, successes and failures, passions and dreams, difficulties and surprises.

We always carry this personal biography within us. More accurately, it is an autobiography which we selectively remember, interpret, and unconsciously rewrite to suit our current situation. It is the vast epic of who we are, or rather who we take ourselves to be. The story shapes us, perpetuating the patterns of our life. It comes complete with its own narrative voice, our ego and personality that form the central character of our story. We need only listen to our thoughts to hear our inner narrator commenting on everything and taking it all so personally. In a certain sense, we are our story, the continually unfolding tale of one, unique human life.

Our story may be rich, giving us the strength, skills, and wisdom to meet life and contribute to it. But inevitably, parts of our story become burdens and limitations that color our perceptions, our actions, and our future possibilities. This raises the question of whether we can go beyond our personal history, whether we can write our future without being limited by psychological constraints from our past.

Furthermore, because we are so utterly enmeshed in it, our story also blocks our access to the deeper realms of the spirit. The flow of events in time forms the fabric of all stories. Although the Higher also expresses Its will through time, It cannot be found there. Only in the present moment, outside of time, can we touch or be touched by the Sacred. But our interpreted story of the past and our imagined story of the future impinge so heavily on the present that we miss its depths. We stay caught in time, the surface of the present, not seeing the timeless that surrounds us.

Without past or future, though, our whole presence need not be enmeshed in the story. We can rise temporarily beyond our story by entering the eternal stillness of now. In practicing meditation and prayer we grow accustomed to the stillness, we learn to live in it, in presence, which is always and only now. And we thereby loosen the grip of our story, our personal, reactive identity, and rise toward our true individuality.

For this week, notice your story. Notice how the story you tell yourself and others about yourself shapes and creates your personality, your conditioned way of being and acting. See if there are moments when you rise beyond your story, when you cease believing and being it. Can you honor your story without being so invested in, defined by, and chained to it?

292. Within the Hour

We face a continuing challenge: how to practice more frequently. How often do we return to the inside of experience, to being aware within ourselves, to the timeless within time? Ultimately, we seek to meet this challenge with a consistent moment-to-moment awareness in the way of stabilized presence. But for those of us who have yet to attain the station of conscious stability, the demand of moment-to-moment presence throughout daily life lies well beyond our reach. There are just too many moments and they keep arriving one after another, offering endless and enticing new opportunities to lose ourselves.

We could instead back off and change the time scale from moment to day. Characterizing the frequency of our inner work by how many moments of presence we live during a day does offer a useful measure. In the evening we look back to rate our inner work for the day. Then we start the next morning with renewed intention to raise our level of practice for that very day. Depending on our ability to carry that intention and act on it, this works.

However, we have so many moments in each day that we tend to consider them expendable, from the standpoint of spiritual inner work. *I'm busy right now. I'll sense my body or work at presence later.* Using the day as our measure can dispose us to lose contact with the immediacy of each moment's opportunity for practice.

So we adopt an intermediate scale: the hour. The number of moments in an hour seems more finite than the moments in a day — and less expendable. *This is the hour. This is my hour. What can I make of it? Can I live this hour, both in time and in the eternal within?* Whenever we remember, we begin again, renewing our hour, every hour. Because the time horizon is so limited, we can readily see the inner quality of our hour, how much presence we are bringing to it. We practice now to stay here, within presence, within the hour, to deepen and enrich our hour, to make it count for our life, for our soul, for the sacred.

For this week, work within your precious hours.

293. The Sacred Dance of Emptiness

Perhaps the following will make little sense or seem out of reach, but it is in fact quite practical. It does, however, require an exploratory attitude, a drive toward the sacred, and a willingness to attempt the seemingly impossible. Through repeated exploration of the deepest realms within you, you can learn the sacred dance of emptiness. And its essential simplicity as well as the utter joy it brings may astonish you.

The sacred emptiness of our individual spirit enjoys a kinship with the Great Emptiness of the Sacred One. But what emptiness, why emptiness? We can distinguish at least three forms of emptiness: emotional, the individual spirit, and the Divine emptiness.

We fear emotional emptiness, which rejects our lack. Like loneliness and ennui, emotional emptiness stands in self-centeredness hoping to escape the abyss of not having what we want, the abyss of not being full. Emotional emptiness is paradoxically full of self. Without the self-centeredness, the emotional abyss evaporates.

Spiritual emptiness means collecting all our scattered urges and desires into the one overriding need for the sacred. We empty ourselves of ourselves, of all but our immediate need for the Divine. This true emptiness creates space for the higher to fill us.

As for the Divine emptiness, out of That the universe continuously comes into being. Only the blank slate of emptiness could allow the primordial creative acts of the One Source. Will itself, the essential nature of the Sacred Source, is empty of all substance, even empty of energy. But both our will and the Divine Will do act on and through substance. Furthermore, the

One Who chooses imparts qualities such as love in the act of choosing.

How does this matter to us? In our deepest inner work, wherein we move toward the Divine, that movement must pass through our individual emptiness. We seek, by emptying ourselves, heart and soul, to open to the Holy in Its emptiness. Through mutual attraction, our individual emptiness can touch the Great Emptiness. A kind of sacred dance of emptiness conjoins two infinities: our inner infinity and the Sacred Infinite.

How can we empty ourselves? We prepare by deep relaxation and full presence. Aware of the thoughts, emotions, and sensations continuously moving through our nervous system, we let them all be as they are. But instead of being moved along with them, we direct our entire interest and attention elsewhere, into the stillness beneath all our perceptual clutter. We shift our focus from the content of experience into the silent context of consciousness.

Now even within conscious stillness, our self-centered urges and passions remain just beneath the surface. So in those moments, we intentionally gather all our heart's desires, subsuming them into an all-encompassing passion for the Divine, for immediate connection, for completion, for true service. These acts of gathering and subsuming our desires empty our heart as we inwardly reach toward the Great Emptiness. Repeating this again and again, we move ever closer to the Sacred, tasting the confluence of our individual emptiness with the Great Sacred Emptiness, the abode of the Divine.

For this week, practice the joyous sacred dance of emptiness.

294. Our Inner Home

Just as we need a physical place to call home, a place of safety, comfort and nourishment, of familiarity and relaxation, of warmth and kindness, we also need an inner home. Through our spiritual practice we can carve a home out of the unruly and at times embattled wilderness of our inner world. By our inner work we build, furnish, improve, maintain, and occupy that inner home, which calls for as much effort and care as we put into establishing and maintaining our physical home. The general tenor of our thoughts, the patterns of our emotional responses and the character of our awareness condition and define our experience, this one and only inner space of our life that we carry with us, like a turtle in its shell. Even more than our physical home, the quality of our inner home determines the quality of our life.

Directed attention and mindful awareness of bodily sensations, thoughts, and emotions build our inner home. Prayer furnishes it with love, warmth, kindness, and joy. Meditation improves, cleans, and maintains our inner home, while always acting in accord with conscience adds a higher floor. And presence enables us to inhabit our inner home, to actually live within ourselves, within our life.

To live in true comfort, we need a home where we feel accepted and befriended. To feel comfortable within our inner home, we need to accept ourselves as we are. We work to improve, but toward our goals rather than to escape what we do not accept about ourselves.

Our physical home requires energy from external sources, for which we arrange and pay. Likewise, we need sources of inner energy. One important source comes through the air, through energy breathing. An even stronger source descends through the higher reaches of prayer and meditation.

Once our inner home reaches adequate readiness, we can invite guests. Our openness to and connection with other people gives them a welcome and honored place within our inner world.

Ultimately, we allow the walls to dissolve and our inner home to expand as it merges with the greater world of the sacred. At that point the distinction between inner and outer disappears and our life becomes a prayer lived in and as the sacred spirit. Tastes of this can flow to us even now on days when our practice surges higher.

For this week, notice the state of your inner home. How is it to live inside your life? Is it furnished and maintained well? Do you inhabit it? See what needs attention and work on the necessary repairs and improvements.

295. Rates of Inner Growth

Managing our inner work means, in part, managing our expectations of personal progress on the spiritual path. We tend to overestimate and overemphasize the value of the dramatic, short-term breakthrough into a higher state, while underestimating the long-term impact of slow but steady inner development. In the long run of a lifetime, gradual inner growth leads to revolutionary transformation.

The quick-hit spiritual high has tremendous appeal and certainly has value in giving us a taste of deeper possibilities. Occasional participation in a spiritual retreat or sessions of communal prayer or meditation can teach us important insights and put us temporarily into a higher-than-normal state. But the real power of the path lies in raising our normal state. And that takes persistence, day by day, moment by moment.

From young adulthood on, we rarely notice ourselves aging because the process is so gradual. Nevertheless, aging inexorably and irreversibly transforms our body. Yet noticing one's own progress on the spiritual path is even more difficult. Not only is it slow, but we know neither what to look for nor how to recognize our own inner development. Wonderful surprises may be in store for us as new stages of our spiritual transformation unfold, as it were, unannounced, behind our back, and without our noticing.

But transformation takes time, a great deal of time. We may only notice changes on the scale of decades. That spiritual transformation takes a long time, however, does not mean the changes are small. Like compounding interest for many years, the accumulating effects of sincere and devoted spiritual practice lead steadily toward treasure. This has even been empirically verified by physical changes in the brains of long-term meditators: the more hours on the cushion, the more significant the positive changes revealed by brain scans.

This gradual quality of the path can lead to trouble in two main ways. One, we can become frustrated with our lack of apparent progress: we always seem to be on a plateau. And that frustration, particularly in the early years, can lead to abandoning the path. One antidote for that is to recognize the immediate effects of spiritual practice. Prayer, meditation, kindness, and presence make life richer now. Morning practice enriches our whole day. A second antidote comes through recognizing that the plateau actually slopes upward toward the mountain. We recognize that true transformation requires long-term practice, so we weave inner work into the fabric of our life.

The second way to trouble comes when we slacken our

efforts because the path is long. The converse though is the real truth: the path is long because our efforts are slack. The frequency, intensity and depth of our practice determine our rate of progress. The more frequent and focused our inner work, and the more understanding, subtlety, and heart we bring to it, the more rapidly we turn the wheels of lasting transformation.

On another scale, though, we see that practice only for personal gain limits itself. We pursue the path because our inner work matters beyond ourselves. The spiritual energies we produce and the atmosphere of good will we create through our practice serves our family, our society, and the higher realms. We engage in spiritual work primarily because it's the right thing to do. Secondarily, it builds our soul and brings us joy. So we need not solely concern ourselves with the speed of our ascent, though the motivating factor of hope for personal progress does help spur us on.

For this week, reinvigorate your regular, short-term efforts in the present, in service to your long-term growth.

296. Out of Our Mind, Into Our Body

We live our life primarily in our thoughts, a world apart from reality. In moments that place little or no demand on our attention, we immediately fall into an inner reverie, passively following various associative streams of thought bouncing through our mind. We take this as normal and do not even notice that we are lost in thought. We even believe we are our thoughts. We mistakenly believe that this private inner voice of our thoughts is who we are. This tendency to identify with thoughts severely diminishes our experience of life, narrowing it down to long-held attitudes and mental patterns.

To extricate ourselves from our self-generating thoughts, we can repeatedly shift our focus to our body, to being aware of the sensations of our living body, to be in the sensitive energy of our inner body. Through practice we can train our perceptions to open to vivid body awareness. By actively attending to our body sensations, we move out of the automated flow of thinking and into contact with life.

Our thoughts, however, do not stop, nor do they relinquish their powerful attraction on us. Thoughts exert an almost irresistible pull on us. So if we practice sensing, we find ourselves at the center of a competition in which we waiver between our intention be in direct body awareness and our attraction to the familiar terrain of our thoughts.

One way out of this dilemma is to relax into awareness both of our body and of our thoughts. We reside in a broad, encompassing awareness, vigilant not to collapse into our thoughts alone. The sensitive energy of the inner body serves as a relatively stable base for awareness to expand to include noticing thoughts as thoughts. From a position of being grounded in awareness of our body, we can much more readily see each automatically-arising thought come and go, see each thought reaching to have itself labeled as "me," as what "I" think. This seeing relieves our thoughts of some of their stickiness, leaving us freer to notice thoughts as well as other sensory perceptions, freer to be, to breathe, and to live.

For this week, notice how you are in moments that place little or no demand on your attention. Notice your thoughts as just thoughts. Move out of your mind and into sensing your body.

297. Coarse and Fine

Plants grow from soil. Animals grow from plants. The human soul grows from body and psyche. Each of these processes raises the fine from the coarse, the wheat from the chaff.

When we remember to practice presence or sit down to meditate, we start from our ordinary life state: unknowingly and fitfully drifting in a jumble of sensory impressions, thoughts, and emotions, under a shattered and scattered attention, driven by self-centered motivations. This is the coarse soil from which our presence, meditation and being can grow. With patience we begin to notice our thoughts, instead of just being lost in them. We begin to notice our senses bringing bodily sensations and sounds, instead of just being lost in them. We begin to notice the emotional tenor of our state, instead of just being under it. This noticing is the first step in raising the fine from the coarse in our inner world.

Continuing, our attention begins to coalesce and gain power thereby: the fineness of collected attention from the coarseness of dispersion. Our sensory energies of body, thought, and emotion begin to settle. As they do so, their coarseness sinks revealing the fineness of pure consciousness in the upper layers of our being. From this place of consciousness we can notice our motivations. That noticing awakens our conscience, purifying our motivations by letting go of those emanating from self-centered egoism.

With (at least temporarily) pure intentions, our heart spontaneously turns toward the sacred and we may enter the finer realms of contemplative prayer, moving toward the Light of the Divine, beyond the relative coarseness of pure consciousness. In further contemplation of the Divine Itself, we open toward the finest of all.

So our inner world contains a vast hierarchy of coarse and fine, with each higher level more refined than the lower. This is the business of the spiritual path, to raise our inner life upward, to separate the wheat from the chaff.

Yet we recall that Seng T'san, the Third Patriarch of Zen, cautions against discriminating between coarse and fine, so as to maintain our freedom by not being ensnared by distinctions. So we honor and respect all the levels within us. We do not denigrate the coarseness of our human condition, just as we do not denigrate the soil from which our food grows. Indeed, we take good care of the soil if we want good food from it.

For this week raise the fine from the coarse within you, while honoring both.

298. Spiritual Heroism

Day to day, moment to moment, life presents us with the mundane and the heavenly, the trivial and the vital, the difficult and the easy, the superficial and the weighty, the pain and the joy, the problem and the solution, the ordinary and the extraordinary. In all these pairs, however, life's offering tends strongly toward the first rather than the second. So here we are, making our way in the trenches of our physical, material life while hoping for some semblance of an evolving inner life, an engagement with the sacred.

Heroes are made in these trenches. Can we rise to the challenge of fulfilling, with quality, all that our physical, familial, professional, and societal life asks of us, and still have enough inner resources left for presence, prayer, and meditation? Those inner resources derive from commitment and devotion to the path.

In the actual midst of our life, we practice. In the face of all the difficulties, demands, and distractions, we devote an on-going portion of our attention and energy to the path, to being here, to being the one living my life. The spiritual hero is the one who actually practices, who engages the methods of the path, even while living a full external life. We perform small acts of every-day inner heroism in coming back to presence even when drawn away from ourselves, in letting go the anger and the day-dream before they consume us, in praying from our heart, in sitting in the stillness of meditation, and in acts of kindness and responsibility. The more one practices, the greater the heroism.

Heroes give extraordinary service. The spiritual hero serves the sacred and thereby serves all life. Heroic personal sacrifice comes in pursuing the path in the face of distractions and obstacles, in transforming those distractions and obstacles into occasions for inner work.

Nobility of purpose drives the spiritual hero. Inner work produces the higher energies needed by our society, by the Sacred, and by our soul. Inner work guides the hero toward just, compassionate, and creative actions in accord with the will of the sacred. The further the hero advances along the path, the more refined the energies produced and the more effective and appropriate the actions undertaken.

For this week, make yourself a candidate for spiritual heroism by rising above your usual level of practice.

299. Soaking Up the Atmosphere

Without adequate physical energy from food, we cannot function well: our body lethargic and our brain responses slow.

Without adequate inner energy, our soul cannot function well: our presence weak and fleeting. In the natural process of living, we do produce some of the inner energy needed for presence. But this natural production proves inadequate to develop our soul, to proceed along the path. So we employ methods that directly, or as a byproduct, increase our supply of inner energy. Such methods include various types of meditation and contemplative prayer, which engage the higher forms of spiritual energies.

But it behooves us also to make good use of a wonderful source of one of the lower forms of inner energies, an energy that feeds the foundation level or outer layer of our soul. That source is the atmosphere, the air that surrounds us, a vast reservoir of inner energy. We can take from this source and we can give to it. Just as plant life builds up the oxygen in the air, we build up the inner energy in the air through our inner work.

The easiest way to tap the energy in the atmosphere is through breathing it: consciously and intentionally drawing the energy from the air as we inhale. Such energy breathing can be a very important part of our path, having been employed since ancient times as a spiritual practice for nourishing the human soul.

A more subtle and direct method opens to those who are well-versed in energy breathing. This is similar to the practice of casting an energy net, but does not require any association with the breath. Simply by using our attention and intention, we draw the inner energy from the air into our body. We do this by creating a "vacuum" within ourselves and allowing the energy to flow into us to fill that vacuum. As we do so, we soak up the energy into our soul by absorbing it into our sensation, into our body awareness, which acts as a sponge to retain the energy. Thereby that energy stays in us, strengthening our basis for presence through sensing this body.

For this week, try this exercise of soaking up the atmosphere. Work at it particularly during your sitting meditation practice, allowing the inner exercise to build up your body of sensation.

300. Inner Occupations

What is it that occupies your mind and heart? What plans and dreams, worries and concerns, hopes and fears take center stage and drive your inner life? Noticing what goes on in you at random moments during the day reveals some truth about your recurrent inner patterns and situation. It also shows the preoccupations that fill the mental/emotional space that you could otherwise use for your practice of presence.

Many of our cares and concerns are necessary, such those regarding our responsibilities in this life. But many others are fleeting and froth that steal our inner resources and give nothing useful in return. This is not to say that we can stop our useless thoughts. We cannot. But we can turn them to account by having them remind us of our ongoing opportunity for practice.

Let's say you frequently indulge escapist daydreams of what you would do after winning the lottery or getting that promotion. Or say you have a mild or temporary obsession with some person, with what they did or did not do. The inner resources, the time and energy that fall into such useless, though perhaps enjoyable, daydreams and obsessions serve nothing, wasting a piece of your life. If instead, you notice those daydreams and obsessive thoughts and take them as your cue to turn toward sensing your body, toward being present, that same time and energy, rather than vanishing, would feed your soul and thereby help us all.

When you notice your inner themes of fantasy or worry, you have a choice and it does matter. Will you forgo unnecessary inner occupations in favor of perfecting your eternal soul? Or not?

301. Integrity under Duress

When personal difficulties descend, our emotions sometimes pressure us toward actions we know are not right. Anger, fear, envy, and jealousy might drag us into improper and disrespectful acts such as physical aggression, dishonesty, insults, emotional abuse, negative gossip or backbiting. We need to apply the light of day (or front-page) principle: Is what I'm about to do something I will regret or feel embarrassed about later? Will my action dig me deeper into the morass?

While we may rightly take appropriate action if we have been wronged, there is a line that marks the realm of inappropriate, unethical, or rude behavior. If attacked, do I respond in kind? Between an eye for an eye and turn the other cheek, a vast gray area of situational ethics awaits our judgment. And judgment that emanates from our integrity defines who we are. Indeed, integrity and a clear conscience are our most valuable possessions: in a real sense our only permanent possessions. So even in those difficult gray areas, we exercise judgment, an exercise that bolsters our integrity.

This week we address integrity under duress: do I act on passion or do I exercise judgment in the heat of the moment? What do I do under ongoing but not acute duress, such as chronic pain, financial straits, relationship problems, failures, and traffic jams? To a great extent, our acts arise from habit. Do I typically explode, spewing verbal abuse under the influence of anger? Or withdraw into a cold shell? Maybe such responses are necessary and appropriate sometimes. Or not. If financially strapped, do I give back that extra change mistakenly tendered by the store cashier? Do I succumb to the temptation of adultery? Can I train myself to see such moments coming and conduct my life with integrity? Can I train myself to hold my integrity sacred and to act by it in all circumstances? Such training bears the fruit that fewer and fewer situations can set us wobbling on that razor's edge between right and wrong.

How we act matters, not only for the health of our relationships, but also for the health of our spiritual quest. A basic prerequisite for peace of mind is a clear conscience earned by a life of total integrity. That same clear conscience fulfills a basic prerequisite for advancing along any spiritual path. Bad behavior, even in small things, emanates from and reinforces the self-centered or group-centered egoism that prevents our rising into the spiritual realms. Judgment and integrity strengthen our will and allow us to approach the higher without the baggage of conscience-damaging acts. Furthermore, judgment and integrity entail a clarity of vision that makes us fit servants of the sacred.

For this week, notice how you act under duress. Do you follow the guide of your own integrity?

302. Listening to Sounds, Hearing the Silence

Sounds emerge from silence. By listening to sounds we can hear the silence that surrounds them — and us. Opening to that silence, we open to our being. In opening to our being, we set the stage for opening to the Spirit beyond being.

Listen to the little sounds, the undertones of life that usually go unnoticed. The creaking of the floor, the tap of the keyboard, the chopping of vegetables, the hum of the refrigerator, the murmur of air ducts, the rustle of leaves, the chirping of birds, the rumble of traffic, the clanking of silverware. By attuning your hearing to perceive such sounds, you simultaneously attune to the silence around them. Sounds hover over silence, making silence itself more noticeable by contrast.

The silence we do not hear with our ears evokes the silence we do not think with our thoughts. In both cases we perceive something more subtle than mere absence of sound: the responsive, empty canvas of consciousness.

Music can open our awareness to the silence between the notes. Great music can open us to the silence beneath the notes. Sounds do not really interfere with or disturb the silence. Although sounds may mask the silence, we can nevertheless pay attention to the silence beneath sound. Sounds can guide our attention toward the underlying silence. And we step into the vast world of silence, a world of a piece with our consciousness itself.

For this week, pay attention to the little sounds, particularly sounds with low semantic content. Conversations, TV, and talk radio draw our attention to the meaning of the words. Less semantically-laden sounds offer us more freedom to hear sound as sound, to hear the ever-present symphony, and to connect with the silence beneath all sound.

303. Karma

In the normal course of life, the consequences of our actions and of our non-actions teach us responsibility, which then entails foreseeing those consequences. However, for many actions we cannot foresee their repercussions. Those situations can tempt us into irresponsible and wrong actions. For example, another driver is rude to me on the highway. Expecting no consequences, I make an obscene gesture at him. It appears to cost me nothing. Indeed it feels good, just, and righteous, a healthy release of anger and stress. But the truth lies deeper. Every intentional act and every intentional non-action when action is called for, create karma, known in the Christian tradition as sowing what you reap and in New Age circles as "what goes around comes around."

But what is karma and is it real? This physical world we occupy is full of uncertainty. Quantum physics reveals a universe built on probabilities. Furthermore, the physics of complex systems shows that the large events of our world are influenced by the smallest of conditions, so that life-sized complex systems are inherently unpredictable, the probabilities unknowable. Through these large and small causal gaps, karma acts to shift the probabilities of our life, to change the course of our future.

All our intentional acts create karma, thereby shaping our future. Karma is our self-initiated influence on the unknowable factors that choose our future from among the infinitely-many possible events that could occur. The law of karma is Justice in the garb of Newton's Third Law of action and reaction operating in the realm of probabilistic causality. Science cannot yet prove the law of karma, nor disprove it. The clear existence of causal gaps in the fabric of our world at least makes the law of karma rationally plausible.

All that is not to say there are no accidents. There are. And not every disease is the result of karma. Yet karma exists.

So how do we know karma exists? We watch and observe our intentional actions. And we see what comes to us out of the future into our present. At times we can intuit the connection. Maybe another driver, a week later, makes an obscene gesture at me — or worse, causes me a near accident. Or maybe a stranger is unexpectedly rude to me in a public place. I am best positioned to see my karma at work, for only I can truly know my intentions. We each can see it for ourselves.

Karma covers our positive actions, as well as the negative. Selfless acts of kindness dispose our environment to deliver the same back to us. Current efforts can create a better future with more possibilities, for example by acquiring an education. The key determiner of karma is our motivation and our intention, because they emanate from and embody our will. That will sets in motion the hidden patterns of karma that shape the events of our life.

In petitionary prayer, we trust that God can stack the cards that determine what emerges out of the ongoing uncertainty and complexity of our life in the natural world. By acting in the light of karma creation, we help stack those cards ourselves.

Karma can even apply to our intentional thoughts. This does not mean that unintentional, associative, random, or reactive thoughts create our future. Thoughts are just thoughts; intentions matter. So we need not fear our thoughts per se. But the thoughts we strongly agree to, the thoughts we align with may create karma. For example, if we inwardly adopt an unsympathetic attitude when someone painfully stubs their toe, we may end up later suffering the same pain ourselves. Through our own suffering karma teaches us compassion and motivates us to clean up our inner house. We might notice those unsympathetic thoughts and ignore them rather than aligning with them, or intentionally think sympathetically instead.

Karmic events do not always relate one-to-one with our prior actions. A pattern of behavior or groups of actions may combine in unpredictable ways to influence the events of our future.

When we first begin to understand the reality of karma, the fear of certain retribution descends on us. We avoid wrong acts to avoid their consequences. We may do right acts to invite their positive consequences. In both cases our right actions and non-actions stem from mixed motives containing a dose of egoistic self-seeking. Nevertheless, by living that way, in greater awareness of our actions and motivations, we eventually come to love doing the right thing for its own sake, for the clarity of conscience, for the fulfillment of our obligations as responsible people, and for the peace of heart it affords us. Thus an experience-based understanding of the law of karma can guide us up the spiritual path of pure-heartedness.

Ultimately we may reach a spiritual station where our actions and non-actions do not arise from self-centered motives, but rather as appropriate and compassionate responses or acts of creative service. In such states of freedom, we do not create karma for ourselves, for we have transcended our self. But we may create a positive influence on the world around us.

For this week, notice the unexpected events of your life, large and small, and see if they somehow correlate with karma you previously created.

304. Self-Acceptance

All our inner shortcomings and outer imperfections lead us to obsess about them and reject certain aspects of our body and personality. That rejection wastes our precious time and energy in a self-absorbed, fruitless, and unnecessary battle among our rejected parts and our rejecting ego. Contrary to some views of spirituality, that inner battle hinders our spiritual path.

The basic and enduring resolution to the whole predicament must be founded on love for ourselves, on a radical, all-inclusive acceptance of ourselves as we are, today. If we embark on a program of self-improvement, we shall never reach its end. Neither our personality nor our body can ever be perfect enough, nor can our financial net worth ever be large enough to satisfy our ego. Not even great spiritual masters manifest complete perfection in all their actions, inner and outer. Even they fall prey to mistakes; it comes with being human. Freedom lies in transcending our personal psychology, not in totally reforming it, nor in totally indulging it.

We respect and accept that this is me, this is how I am made, this is my conditioning, this is my body, this is my mind, and these are my feelings. Some parts of myself I like, some I don't like, but it's all me, and if I am to move along the path, I must open to and accept the whole catastrophe. This sobering act of self-acceptance gradually destroys the false images we have of ourselves. We make the necessary minor reforms toward moderation and move on. Rejection of parts of our inner landscape results from the action of self-centered egoism in the cloak of the pseudo-spiritual. "I will make myself perfect. I will be better than everyone else." Or "I am terrible, weak, worthless, undeserving, and hopeless." These are but two sides of the counterfeit coin of self-centeredness, and we can easily waste years careening back and forth between them.

As our spiritual work progresses and we have more contact with the conscious energy, we sometimes see previously hidden aspects of our own makeup, of our personality and character. Often these aspects were hidden only from us and not from others. These shocking new glimpses of ourselves, these realizations that we are not exactly who we thought we were, may bring disappointment. But they arise naturally as a result of our inner work and present us with a choice. We may wallow in self-pity and self-hatred and, thereby, short-circuit the process of practice. Or we may simply accept that the good in us exists alongside the not-so-good, and practice with renewed vigor toward transformation. Not necessarily seeking to change the details of our personality, we rather seek to change our being.

One quite direct way to practice the art of self-acceptance is through mindfulness meditation. We sit and we watch what goes on in us: all the thoughts, emotions, memories, images, and sensations. We see and we allow it all to be as it is, without trying to stop the flow, without encouraging it, without allowing ourselves to be drawn into the drama or into rejection of any of it. This trains us to accept, to accept ourselves as we are. It also develops our contact with consciousness so that we can be ourselves, rather than mistakenly being our self-generating thoughts and emotions.

For this week, notice self-rejection at work in you and practice self-acceptance.

305. Inner Body for Inner Life

If truth be told, our inner life of thoughts, emotions, and sensory perceptions often seems chaotic, random, disorganized, and haphazard. In comparison, our outer, physical life seems orderly and mostly predictable. A primary reason for this difference is that while we have a well-formed physical body, we do not have a well-formed inner body. Outwardly we have a stable place, our physical body, from which we can observe our outer world, make sense of it, and participate in it appropriately and effectively. Inwardly we have no such place to stand. We are at sea and rudderless in a cacophony of inner events.

The remedy begins in concerted and consistent efforts to develop our inner body. As a starting point we put our attention into our hands, sensing the life of our hands directly. After practicing that to the point of being able to become vividly aware of our hands at will, we extend the work of sensing to our feet. Then we sense arms, legs, torso, head, and eventually our whole body. This sensing builds our inner body, which is made of sensation, the sensitive energy that enables that direct perception of our body. So that when our physical body sits, we also sit inwardly, in contact with our inner body of sensation.

That inner work of sensation leads us toward moments of more stable presence than otherwise possible. Living in our inner body, we can notice our thoughts and emotions without being at their mercy, identified with them, careening through the highs and lows, believing we are those self-generating thoughts and emotions. Our inner body enables us to see more objectively what goes on inside us, without our usual entanglement with those goings-on.

At every stage of our spiritual path, the practice of sensing, of being in our inner body, yields important benefits. For this week, work on developing and living in your inner body.

306. Recognizing Will

The many modes of will can be grouped into three overarching categories: an active type of will, an open, receptive type, and a harmonizing type. The open receives, the active affirms, and the harmonizing cooperates. We all have all three types. But we each have a unique pattern of will, our "I," that forms us as individuals. In any and every moment, our will is who we are.

Everything we intentionally do has will at its core. Every choice, every decision, every shift of attention, every attitude and intention is an action of our will. Both choosing and choosing not to choose are acts of will. Paying attention is an act of will. And so is allowing our attention to drift without direction.

Right now, for example, you are willing your eyes to take in these words, and perhaps willing your brain to consider their meaning and the ideas they represent. That will actively directs your attention toward these words. That will can receptively allow your thoughts to flow by association with these words and ideas. And so it goes with everything we intentionally do or intentionally don't do: we will it.

To perceive will is not so simple, because our will, our "I," is always the perceiver. To perceive our own will we need an inner act similar to holding up a mirror to see our face. Even then, the mirror is empty since will cannot be seen. Will is even more subtle than the stillness of consciousness. Whereas sensation and consciousness are energies, will is not an energy. Will is the user of energies.

According to the famous saying of J.G. Bennett, we are not beings who do, but rather doings who be. Human doings is a more accurate term for us than human beings. Will is primary. So instead of trying to see our will, we become our will. Hold your attention on some nearby object. Be the one in you directing your attention, the one making the continuing choice to attend to that object moment-to-moment.

We can apply that same method in any situation: we just be the one who is experiencing and doing. We be the seer and the doer. We be our own "I," our truest self. This "I" is the central feature of true presence. While perceiving will is not simple, being our own will, our own "I," is simple and direct. Just be yourself, the one doing whatever you are doing.

Besides the subtlety of will, we also encounter the difficulty presented by its fragmentation. Part of us wants something, while another part wants the opposite. An inner battle ensues and the stronger wins, or there's a compromise, or a stalemate ensues and nothing happens. The spiritual path heals these inner divisions, leading us toward unity of will as we become conscious of and embrace our disparate fragments. Simply being our will, our "I," draws the pieces together, subsuming our parts into the wholeness of who we are.

Will participates in all we intentionally do and feel, in both our antipathy and our love. This points us toward the issue of levels of will, as does the biblical "Thy will." Inanimate objects have very limited will, sufficient to maintain their shape and composition, to hold themselves together. Contrast that with the radically greater freedom of will enjoyed by plants, still greater in animals, and greatest among the higher mammals and especially humans.

Within ourselves we have the possibility of functioning with various levels of will. Habits have will behind them to the extent that we are aware of them and allow ourselves to continue engaging in the habits. Self-generated associative thoughts and reactive emotions usually have no intention behind them. But as with habits, our assent to such thoughts and emotions does involve our will. Self-indulgent, self-centered acts arise from the lower levels of will, from egoism. In the spiritual path, we seek not only to unify but also to purify our will, to raise its level beyond ego. Prayer serves as an effective means for that purification, as does letting go of identification and attachment.

Like a fish in water or a human in air, will is always with us, in us. We just do not notice it. For this week, practice recognizing will at work in you. Be your will, your I.

307. Being Seen

To see, in the spiritual sense, means to be conscious, to be in touch with that pure, cognizing stillness beneath all the content of our mind and senses, to be grounded in that pre-sensory foundation awareness. If I am conscious, I see. However that conscious energy also carries with it the feeling of being seen. Which raises the question: being seen by whom? It is not only a feeling that I am seeing myself, but also that someone is seeing me. But who is that someone? Or rather: Who is that Someone? If consciousness pervades the universe, which appears to be the case, then whose consciousness is it? Who is conscious through that all-pervasive consciousness?

Consciousness does not see itself, because energies do not use themselves. Will uses energies. That will can be our individual will, particularly for the energies under our control, such as the sensitive and the automatic. Individual will comes into play with the conscious energy also, giving us the feeling that we can see, we can cognize, and we can be fully ourselves. We perceive by means of that empty, silent background of awareness. But the conscious energy is vast, not bounded or controlled by any human individual.

So consciousness is not only in us: we can open to being in it. Our brain can serve as a perceptual organ, like the eye or ear. It generates and perceives thoughts and emotions. But it can also perceive the formless, silent consciousness beneath thought and sensation, the very substance of awareness. That self-same stillness underlies both our mind and the world around us.

The surprise comes when, upon entering that vastness, we feel seen, seen by a Will incomparably greater than ours. We see through consciousness and that great Will sees through consciousness. There we have an intuition that our will and that greater Will are of the same nature, that we could surrender to and be subsumed by that greater Will. In so doing we would take our rightful place within the Greatness, or rather allow the Greatness to take its place in us. We become not just one who sees, but part of the One Who sees all. Thus we arrive at the culmination of our spiritual path, leaving us in a position to serve well, compassionately, and wisely.

For this week, practice allowing your mind to settle into peace, so that you can open to the still waters of consciousness. Notice whether you feel seen in that vast space. And if so, look for the sacred, loving One Who sees you.

308. Walking Meditation

Walking meditation takes the work of walking presence to a deeper level. In normal walking we encounter distractions like the need to avoid obstacles and adjust our path to match our intended route, the sights and sounds along the way, and so on. In walking meditation we minimize all the distractions, to bring even more attention and energy to bear on our inner work. Here's how.

Find a quiet room with a clear lane for walking, preferably at least fifteen feet long. Stand at one end of the walking path, facing the direction you will walk. Allow your arms to hang at your sides, relaxed. Or, if you prefer, hold your hands on your belly, about navel height, with one hand in a relaxed fist and the other hand around the fist. You will maintain the same relaxed position of arms and hands throughout the walking meditation session.

Collect yourself. Become aware of your body, of the sensations in your body. Do this for a minute or two to prepare for walking. Then slowly, very slowly, walk to the other end of your walking lane, one step at a time. Let the slowness be natural, not forced, not a matter of holding back. As you enter the presence of walking meditation, you realize viscerally that you have nowhere to go, that you have already arrived, and you inwardly slow down.

To enter here, be aware of each step, each movement. Be in your foot as you raise it, move it forward and put it down. Be aware of your leg as you move it. When you reach the end of your walking lane, slowly turn around, with attention to each movement as you turn. Then slowly, very slowly, with full awareness of each step, walk back to your starting point. Again, slowly and in full awareness, turn around.

Now back at the beginning, spend a couple of minutes in standing meditation. Expand your body awareness to more, and eventually to all, of your body. Standing in stillness, enter the quiet peace of consciousness. Inhabit your body. Be the one who is standing here. Take the opportunity afforded by the stillness of standing meditation to enter the sacred as deeply as you can. Then with that depth resonating in your soul, resume the slow walking with full awareness. Continue in this fashion, walking, turning, and standing, for the time you have allotted to the session. End with standing meditation to allow the results to collect and settle into your being.

Keep attention and awareness throughout the entire session, whether walking, turning, or standing. If your attention strays into thoughts or anything else, then when you notice your mind wandering, gently bring your attention back and reenter your body.

Walking meditation can be an excellent complement to sitting meditation. We can alternate walking and sitting in longer meditation periods. If we are very tired, walking meditation can provide the energy we need to maintain our attention, to maintain our presence. While sitting meditation tends to take us deeper, walking meditation helps bridge our depth of experience into our daily life.

For this week, find time to practice walking meditation. Be the walker.

309. Grief and Mourning

In the aftermath of the death of a loved one, feelings of profound grief and sorrow, sadness and loss come naturally and at times powerfully. These normal feelings certainly bear no shame, nor are they destructive. But after a time they may tend to fall over into self-pity, which benefits no one except our ego. Add to this the helplessness we feel when confronted by the finality of death, and depression may well follow. Or perhaps it all becomes anger at, or loss of faith in, God for allowing our dear one to die. Or we may feel remorse for what we did or did not do while the person was still alive.

So in this highly-charged, emotional condition, what can our inner work be? Fortunately, we have the possibility of transforming the difficult emotions surrounding death to the benefit of our loved one.

When thoughts or feelings about the person you have lost arise in your mind and heart, turn them to love. Let those feelings be a reminder that you can do something positive for your loved one. Channel those emotions into love and send it to the one who has passed on. This may actually help them in death. All our thoughts and emotions connected with the death, though they be insistent, strong, even overwhelming, do nothing for the loved one. But love can. When we send love, we send energy that helps strengthen them, reduce their confusion, and assist them in completing their journey. It also helps us avoid the degeneration of our natural feelings of grief, while empowering us to take action useful to our loved one.

This simple method has two parts. First, picture your loved one in your mind's eye. Second, send love to the person represented by that image. You can practice this daily during a focused period of seated meditation. You can also practice this at moments during the day whenever your thoughts and feelings remind you of your loved one.

Because death takes a person beyond time into eternity, we can send love even many years after the death of our loved one, and the love we then send still benefits them. That action transcends time.

Sending love to the departed also transcends religion. Every religion has its own set of customs and practices regarding death, burial, and mourning. Engaging in the customs of our own religion certainly helps and comforts. Sending love complements and supports our religious practices, filling in the gaps.

For this week, practice sending love to one or more who have passed beyond this life.

May your loss deepen your love.

310. Personal Presence in Three Steps

The measure of our presence reveals itself in the quality, the breadth, depth and density, of our experience of this moment, of now. Because the whole of reality, both our ordinary world and the higher worlds, opens to experience only through the now, the practice of presence stands fundamental to our spiritual path. Furthermore, through the practice of presence we transform energies which serve the higher and build our soul. We can enter presence through three steps: through body, mind, and spirit.

Direct awareness of our body anchors us in the now, because our body is always now. It does not go off like thoughts into the past, future, or daydreams. This direct physical awareness is mediated by the sensitive energy. As we place and hold our attention in part of our body, say a hand or a foot, the sensitive energy begins to accumulate there, making our experience of that part more vivid, our body more alive. We are constructed, though, so that the sensitive energy also plays another role in our spiritual practice: as a key substance of the body of our soul. So by practicing presence through sensing, we enter and stay in this our only moment, and we simultaneously collect, accumulate, and organize a basic energy of our developing soul.

We begin our journey into presence by sensing parts of our body: hands or feet, arms or legs, torso or head. We refrain from attempting to sense specific inner organs so as not to interfere with their instinctive functioning. Instead, for example, we sense our torso as a whole — a breathing, active whole.

In the second step, we continue our journey into presence by sensing the entire body as a whole. This is more than a mere linear continuation of our effort in the first step. Sensing the whole body brings a qualitative difference. The quality of wholeness attracts the conscious energy, whose nature is contextual wholeness without boundary, cognizance, and spacious stillness. Whole body sensation offers a suitable platform for consciousness. Its contextual cognizance releases us from the thrall of associative thoughts, daydreams, and reactive emotions. And through its quality of spacious stillness, consciousness enables our will to relax into peace and equanimity.

The third step into presence involves responding to the question: *Who is conscious?* The Buddhist answer to this might be that no one is conscious. And what is meant by that response? We have no separate self, no ego that is conscious. Our usual sense of self is an illusion constructed of patterns of thought and emotion. A deep understanding of that truth helps free us from self-centeredness and all the ill baggage it carries.

But take the question of *who is conscious* another step and find a Self that is individual, uniquely us, but not separate in its roots, in our Source. Not an ego, but an I. An I that emanates from the Sacred. This may sound abstract, difficult, or distant from us. But it is not.

Simply be the one who is here, sensing, conscious, and present. Be the one who is. Be the one in you that can say "I am" with meaning. Inhabit your sensation. Inhabit your body. Intentionally be the one who lives in and as you, the one who sees with your eyes and tastes with your tongue, the one who is you. And stay awhile.

This is personal presence.

Now these three, sensation, consciousness, and Self, mutually support and enhance each other. Sensing the whole body provides a platform for consciousness. Consciousness provides a platform for I, for Self. And by being your Self and inhabiting your body you entrain consciousness into your body, into your sensation, further building your soul.

The path of spirituality is infinite and does not end with the personal presence described here. It continues into spiritual and even Divine presence. However, personal presence opens the way toward those higher forms. For this week, step into personal presence.

311. Intentional Attention

To become our Self, our true spirit, we need to become our will. But the term "will" carries a rather fuzzy, confusing, and contradictory set of meanings. On top of that, we cannot perceive will, because our will is the perceiver. Saying that I am my will leaves us in the same conundrum, because the notion of

I is just as fuzzy and elusive a concept as will. But if we speak of attention or intention, then we address aspects of will that are more recognizable, more tractable. We know by direct experience what it means to pay attention and also what it means to have intention.

Attention comes in several flavors. The most common is a lack of attention, like when we are lost in a daydream. Another form occurs when our attention is passively drawn to something, such as the TV, an interesting sight, or a physical pain. But for many of our life endeavors as well as for our spiritual inner work, the type of attention that matters is intentional attention: paying attention and choosing to do so.

The term "paying attention" carries the implication of effort. And indeed it takes an inner effort to direct and hold our attention on something. With practice, though, the effort becomes easier, primarily because less of it is wasted. Just as an athlete learns to be very efficient in expending energy, minimizing wasted motion, so with practice we pay attention efficiently. We come to understand attention and how to direct and hold it.

Directing our attention is an intentional act. If we say that we are after intentional attention, though, we mean more than just directing our attention. We place our attention with the whole our intention behind that act of placing. A further step and we realize that intention need not be too specific to be real and potent. For example, we can practice the will-to-be, intending simply to be here and now, fully and wholly, to be aware of our whole body, to be the one who sees and lives, to inhabit our life at this moment. This will-to-be, though general, embraces all the details and specifics of our life.

Intentional attention carries us well beyond the level of autopilot living, and even beyond the level of sensitive contact, into the realm of conscious living. When we are our self, we are conscious. And when we enter the conscious energy, we are our self. Intentional attention operates by means of the conscious energy, that vast, silent, cognizing substance. Intentional attention raises our conscious energy out of its hiding place of being submerged in and mixed with our sensitive energy.

So our work with this is to pay attention, to be the one who is paying attention, and to do it with our full intention. We feel "I am attending to this," whatever this object of attention is. In our spiritual practice the object of attention might the sensitive energy in our body, the air we are breathing, or a heartfelt prayer, to name just a few examples. But for this way of intentional attention, the object of attention could also be anything else in our life: the dishes we are washing, the food we are eating, these words we are reading, the conversation we are having, and yes, even the TV we are watching. The practice is to do what we are doing with full attention and the full intention to be here doing it.

For this week, practice intentional attention.

312. Spiritual Breathing

Our precious breath offers many powerful possibilities in support of our spiritual path. The four primary classes of spiritual breathing techniques are controlled breathing, conscious breathing, energy breathing, and soul breathing.

Controlled breathing. This refers to any intentional change to the normal physical pattern of breathing for spiritual purposes. Direct methods of breath control are found, for example, in Yoga and in Sufism. These include deep breathing, rapid shallow breathing, rhythmic breathing, alternating nostrils, and holding the breath, sometimes coupled with inwardly repeated words. More broadly, the efficacy of the spiritual chanting found in most traditions arises in part from the breath control indirectly caused by the chant.

While many people benefit enormously from the use of controlled breathing, such methods should be practiced only with the direct guidance of a teacher, so as to avoid possible negative health effects. As a personal example, for some years I practiced a spiritual technique that involves controlled breathing. During that period I first noticed that I had a mild heart arrhythmia. Eventually by experimentation, I confirmed a correlation between the arrhythmia and the controlled breathing practice. When I finally stopped that type of breathing, the arrhythmia vanished and has never returned. So I learned the lesson that even if a respected spiritual teacher personally gives you a practice, even a spiritually powerful practice, it still may not be right for you. Although our insight into the higher realms is quite limited, we should not abandon our common sense and our responsibility for the health of our body, which we need for our spiritual work.

The following methods do not entail any significant physical change to our natural patterns of breathing.

Conscious Breathing. For a leading example of conscious breathing, we turn to Buddhist mindfulness practice with its emphasis on attention to and awareness of the breath. In particular we focus on the physical sensations of breathing, at the nostrils, in the chest, and/or in the abdomen. This can be coupled with counting the exhalations, 1 to 10, and then starting again at 1. The attention should be primarily on the sensations of breathing, and secondarily on the counting which serves to help us keep focus on our breath. If we lose the count, we just start over at 1. Alternatively, we can practice conscious breathing with words, in-out or rising-falling. Again attention remains primarily with the sensations of breathing and secondarily with the words. We do not alter the natural, physical patterns and rhythms of the breathing. We only alter our attention and awareness through continuing contact with the breath. The count and the words are ancillary and can be dropped when steadiness of attention to the breath has been achieved.

Because the breath is always here, always moving and thus relatively easy to notice, it offers us an anchor in the present moment. Conscious breathing keeps us here and now. This simple and benign method holds great power.

Energy Breathing: A sea of spiritual energies surrounds us. The atmosphere carries such energies, which we continually inhale and exhale. But ordinarily we are not aware of these energies and they do not stick with us. They go in and right back out with the air. However, with sufficiently focused but relaxed attention and the appropriate inner action, we can access the energies in the air for our spiritual benefit.

As you inhale, place your full attention on the air entering your nostrils. Note the differences between conscious breathing and energy breathing. In conscious breathing the attention goes to the physical sensations associated with breathing. Here the attention goes to the air itself. In conscious breathing, we intend simply to maintain awareness of the physical sensations associated with breathing, whereas here we intend to draw the energy from the air.

Knowing, or at least accepting as a working hypothesis, that the air carries spiritual energies with it, by your attention, intention, and an inner act of will, draw the energy from the air as you inhale. While your body breathes in the physical air, you intentionally inhale the energy from the air. Thus you have the ordinary outer breath and, simultaneously, the inner breath.

We allow the energy to spread from its extraction point

in the nose throughout the body, where it blends with and increases our store of sensitive energy. So if we practice sensing our whole body at the same time as the energy breathing, we build that part of our soul whose substance is the sensitive energy.

Soul breathing: This type of breath practice is nearly the same as energy breathing, except that we draw the energy from the air semi-independently of physically breathing the air. Casting a net made of attention-intention-will to catch the energy, as we physically inhale we pull the energy into us through the entire surface of our body, not just with the air through our nose. This method can also be done completely independently of the physical breath, drawing in the energy regardless of whether we are physically inhaling or not. As with energy breathing, sensing our entire body while we practice soul breathing gives the entering energy a place to land and be absorbed into our being.

For this week, practice one or more of these methods of spiritual breathing.

313. Non-Panic

The 2008 global meltdown in the credit markets offers an example of how certain overarching stories in the news grip our inner world, riveting our attention and raising our fear and anxiety. Other recent American examples include 9/11/2001 and the subsequent run-up to the second Iraq war. The fear and anxiety with which we individually and collectively meet such situations usually exacerbate them. And while we certainly need to make judgments about the future and act accordingly, we also need to look after our inner state in the present.

For many of us who aspire to a spiritual inner life, episodic, situational anxiety drains our energies and distracts us from our work of presence. When the society around us loses itself in the burning issue of the time, can we maintain an inner equanimity while doing what we need to do externally? The answer depends on the cumulative effect of our spiritual practice. By working inwardly, with energies, presence, meditation, and prayer, we gradually change our frame of reference, widening our perspective to include both the outer, material world as well as our inner world. That inner work becomes for us an anchor in the seas of turbulent times.

By staying calm, even when actively responding to the times, we not only help ourselves personally, but we also weaken the societal forces of panic and hysteria. Rather than abdicate our decisions to a destructive pattern emerging in the society around us, we keep to our personal responsibility for our acts, our personal compass of conscience. We remain the agent who lives our life and we opt out of toxic though urgently persuasive societal patterns like those that have led to the atrocities of ethnic cleansing or the impoverishment of widespread economic depression.

So we come back to sensing our body, to the practice of presence, to meditation and prayer, to attending to the promptings of conscience, to keeping up the momentum of our inner work and establishing ourselves in peace. We let any impulses of anxiety and fear remind us to reconnect with our spiritual practice. In financial crises we invest in our spiritual present and future, an investment that will always pay dividends. We do not turn away from the difficulties, but we do face them in full presence, with the whole of our being, and we act – or not – from there.

For this week, let the gyrations of the markets, acts of terrorism, wars, natural disasters, and voices of doom remind you to reengage with your body, your breath, your presence.

314. Showering Presence

Taking a shower, or a bath, steeps us in a riot of sensory impressions, mainly touch and sound. But because our body and the motor centers of our brain are so accustomed to showering or bathing, the whole process typically goes by rote, without our inner presence. We relax and disappear into the habitual process and only later notice that we are done. This presents yet another opportunity to bring the light of presence into a semi-conscious part of our life.

We begin our work on showering/bathing presence through contact with the sensory experience. Feel the touch of the faucet as you open it. Hear the sounds of the water flowing. Feel the water on your skin. Feel the shampoo on your hands and hair, the soap on your hands and skin. Feel the movement of your hands on your soapy hair and skin. Feel and hear the water rinsing off the soap. Sense the touch of the faucet as you close it. Be aware of the texture of the towel, the sensations and movements of drying off.

Throughout all this activity and sensory awareness, be there, be the one who is showering or bathing, the one who is aware in each moment of the event. Being aware is one thing. Being the one who is aware, the one who wills your actions, directs your awareness and experiences your experience, is another and deeper movement — a movement toward our Self, toward our Source. From that one, you can truly say: "I am showering, I am bathing." For this week, practice being present while showering or bathing.

315. The Continuous Choice

So much of our life goes by habit and momentum: habits of body, habits of thought, habits of emotion. In itself, our ability to learn actions and repeat them with little cognitive effort is remarkably useful and powerful. Such autopilot-driven, habitual actions work by the automatic energy. Our will may enter, perhaps minimally, in choosing to initiate a habitual process, like deciding what to eat. But then the eating proceeds by momentum. We may choose where to walk, but the walking goes by auto-pilot. We may choose the topic of conversation, but the talking just happens.

Habits and momentum offer a necessary simplification of our life. But our presence tends to remain submerged beneath any habitual action. We are hardly aware of what we are doing in those moments. Time lives us. We lose a part of our life if we do not live it ourselves, if we are not here, aware, and present.

Sensing our inner body brings us to the threshold of presence. Full presence though, requires the moment-to-moment continuing choice to be here, to be in contact with your sensory experience, with your body, with your mind and emotions, with your awareness itself. But primarily presence means to be your self, to be the one who is here and aware, to be the one chooses what you choose, the one who does what you do, the one who lives your life.

To really live, and not to be lived by our habitual responses to the exigencies of time, we need to live in presence. The choice to be present must be made again and again, because we always fall back, abdicating ourselves to habits of body, mind, and emotion, collapsing into our personality, our preprogrammed patterns and responses to the sensory stream.

The choice to be present not only needs repeating, but also extending so that it lasts longer in time, as "I enter the here and now, and I stay here and now." And what I do, comes from me. I feel that I am doing whatever I do, saying what I say, experiencing what I experience.

The continuous choice to be present is continuous in the sense of being frequent and also in the sense of being ongoing in a given series of moments. The frequent choice is how we take the opportunity to awaken and the ongoing choice is how we turn that opportunity into a stability of presence that can survive more that a few seconds. "Here I am and here I stay." This is a dynamic continuity, not static. Our presence flows through us like a river of will into the ocean of time, and keeps flowing as long as we choose to be.

We need not stop our habits. Indeed we could hardly live without them. But we open to a deeper and parallel layer of being and action, where we enter any experience with presence, even an experience of one of our habitual or preprogrammed patterns. We enter direct contact with our experience, whatever it is at the moment. We always have a body, so we can always start by being in contact with our body through sensation. We make that continuous choice to enter and to stay here, in our body and in presence. And instead of time living us, we live in the eternal present.

316. A Place to Stand

To enter the world of presence, we need a place to stand, a body to be in. Our physical body serves so well as our place in the material world of this Earth. But this body does not directly offer us a place in the world of presence. That place is our inner body, our body of sensation. No stability of presence can be had even temporarily without being rooted in the sensitive energy in our body. Without the grounding in the present anchored by the sensitive energy, we blow away with the first distraction or random thought, falling back into the world of automatism and habitual patterns.

The difficulty lies in the fact that unlike our physical body, which is given us at birth, our sensation body is not handed to us ready-made. On the contrary, we must work indefatigably to conceive, feed, and build it. How? By focusing our attention in our body and holding it there. Gradually our attention activates the sensitive energy which gives us a vibrant, alive perception of our body. The sensitive energy is the actual substance of that perception.

So for example, if we put our attention into our hand or foot, and keep it there, our contact with the hand or foot comes alive. We feel this as the presence of an energy in the hand or foot, the energy of sensation, which is the sensitive energy in the body. We call this act sensing: attention to our body to open to and be in contact with our body through the sensitive energy. We do this with the intention of establishing our body of sensation, our inner body.

Through the persistent practice of sensing, we build up the sensitive energy in our body. Once we have developed a facility with sensing parts, like hands, feet, arms, or legs, we broaden into sensing our body as a whole. That practice of whole body perception leads to wholeness of sensation. And whole body sensation gives us a place to stand, a shelter from the winds of automatic, associative thoughts and reactive emotions. More than that, it becomes our home, with all the qualities of home: warmth, comfort, familiarity, and peace. We can strengthen our sensation body significantly through energy breathing, where we breathe in the sensitive energy from the air around us.

Notably, this inner home, our developing inner body gives us a place to pursue the deeper aspects of presence: the stillness of consciousness and the will to be. In fact presence follows in the natural progression of our inner work, once we are rooted in our sensation body. We inwardly stand in whole body sensation. With the strong and immediate intention to be, being the one who is here in this inner body, we open to the peaceful sea of consciousness that surrounds us. And thus, we are.

For this week, renew your efforts to establish your inward place to stand, your inner body.

317. Meaningful Life

An endless variety of endeavors can and do bring meaning to our life, from being with loved ones, raising children, and caring for elderly parents, to the pursuit of knowledge, creative acts, serving others through a job or profession, social activism, appreciation of the natural world, simple kindness, the enjoyment of recreation, and so on. For most of us, one or perhaps a few such areas are particularly meaningful. Our problem arises when we do not value the other areas of our life, seeing them as empty, insignificant, and meaningless, as chores to be completed as quickly and with as little personal involvement as possible. The life zones we deem meaningless, be they distasteful or just boring, rob us of opportunity, rob us of our time.

What to do? Can we eliminate those meaningless zones? Not likely. We all have tasks we dislike, but which, alas, are necessary. And by habit, we repeatedly fall into "time-wasting," unnecessary activities that offer little satisfaction or meaning. We cannot rid ourselves of all that, but we can look for a way to transform those dead time zones into living, breathing engagements with what we do and experience.

Spiritual practice, because of its high purpose of awakening to and serving the Sacred, can fill all these voids of meaning. Training yourself in inner work opens the doors of time to the entry of meaning, by connecting us to timeless values. One of the beauties of inner work consists in its adaptability to any and all situations. So whatever you are doing outwardly, you can engage in spiritual practice inwardly, engage with that ever-present dimension of substance and depth. Take any mundane chore or "time-wasting" zone and bring inner work to the scene. The timeless purpose of spiritual practice carries meaning, significance, and fulfillment into that life arena.

To take that opportunity, we stay alert to those barren zones of our life, to times devoid of meaning, often signaled by the state of our emotions, and we act to transform them through inner work, primarily through the practice of presence, and at times through the practice of prayer. Outwardly nothing may change, but inwardly a new world dawns in every such moment.

For this week, let your spiritual work bestow meaning where more is needed.

318. Total Prayer

Spiritual practice has many facets and levels. Presence, consciousness, and stillness, though necessary aspects of our path and of major, ongoing importance for us, do not tell the whole story. We seek also to go beyond these, beyond ourselves, to serve and even to enter contact with the beneficent and loving Sacred Source of all. For that we engage in and practice the essential action underlying prayer, the action of directly addressing our relationship with the Divine in this very moment.

Prayer has innumerable forms across the many religions, sects, and cultures, and across the range from simple petitionary prayer to the heights of contemplative prayer. But all the forms share this common factor of relating to the Divine. And we can work at deepening this essence of prayer directly.

Some hold the ultimate relationship to be perfect attunement and obedience to the Divine Will, while others speak of union. At their core, in practice, both views share the same basic approach: to open our own will and our whole being to the Divine.

Block off time and a quiet space for contemplation. Begin with relaxation, letting go tensions of body, heart, and mind. Letting go of tensions prepares us for the key challenge of total prayer, letting go of our self. Set aside everything: all your desires and fears, hopes and dreams, worries and concerns, wounds and angers, and especially your limiting assumptions about what is possible for you now. To set all that aside, just consider it all to be temporarily of no importance whatsoever, and let peace envelop you. When thoughts and concerns intrude on the silence and recapture your attention, simply abandon them to return to this essence of prayer. If the thoughts do not hold your attention, then they do not interfere.

Turn your self totally and utterly toward God, toward that unknown mystery for Which you yearn and you search, even now. Direct the whole of your being toward God, beyond your mind and heart, beyond your consciousness, beyond all you can know and touch, beyond space and time. In abject humility, heartfelt love, and bittersweet longing, open the deepest kernel of yourself to God. Open you, the you who decides and chooses, the you who experiences and lives your life. Don't bother thinking about how to do this. Don't doubt. Just inwardly beggar yourself while reaching up and beyond your self, beyond all, to that Most Sacred One. Give this your utmost inner effort and love. Offer your total and complete focus to this one endeavor now, utterly giving yourself over to the Sacred.

Occasionally step back and inwardly intone your favored name for God. Let that name draw you in and up, and serve as a springboard for your next foray toward the Divine. Then begin again.

At the end of the session, give up all effort and striving. Just sit quietly for a time, doing nothing, letting your work settle into your being. With no resistance or preoccupation blocking your way, God may touch you even now.

For this week, engage in total prayer.

319. Stillness: Warm, Intimate, and Cognizant

We acquire the taste of stillness through quiet contemplation, just sitting in outer and inner stillness. The outer stillness consists of a quiet space with no distractions or intrusions, as well as a relaxed body. The inner stillness just is, but to come to it is a variable process that depends on our experience, our understanding, and our current inner state. The journey into stillness is a journey from effort to non-effort.

One way is to focus at first on a very narrow aspect of experience. For example, a classic Buddhist method involves placing and holding our attention on the sensations associated with the air going in and out of our nostrils. In this, we do not intentionally change the pattern of our breathing. To help us focus, we can count the breaths 1 to 10, and then again from 1, while keeping our primary attention on the actual sensations of the breath. If we lose the count, we simply start again at 1. By the time we can stay with the breath and the counting continuously for several minutes, our thoughts are slow and sparse.

At that point we drop our exclusive focus on the breath at the nostrils, as well as the counting, and instead open our attention to include our whole body. As thoughts, impulses and sensory impressions come, we simply let them go. We do not chase them away and we do not follow them. They arise on their own and they disappear on their own.

Resting in our body, we notice the silent spaces between and behind our thoughts, the spaces of pure awareness, pure consciousness. We allow ourselves to be immersed in that stillness, letting it soak through our entire being.

That stillness of mind allows us to go yet further into the peace of stillness by opening the stillness of will. Here we no longer try to "do" anything. We do not attempt to manipulate our experience in any way. We drop all our inner burdens and reactions to them. We just sit and let things be as they are. This non-doing carries us through the last leg of our journey into stillness.

And there we find, perhaps to our surprise, that the stillness is not devoid of all qualities. First, it is cognizant. It is the very substrate of our mind and being. Stillness sees. It is awareness, consciousness itself. Further we find that this fundamental awareness is not cold, unfeeling, or foreign. On the contrary, it welcomes us into its intimate warmth, as its peace suffuses our heart. The stillness belongs to us and we belong to it, as if it were part of our body.

Once we become grounded in the ever-present ocean of stillness, outer stillness becomes less necessary. In that state, we can walk through noise and distractions, through a crowded marketplace, and remain at peace in inner stillness, even with thoughts. Thoughts do not disturb our inner stillness. We see them as thoughts and let them be, while we remain in the stillness beneath thoughts. And we can reopen our contact with the stillness at any time, at will.

But until we have that grounding, we cannot readily enter, much less sustain, contact with stillness. That is why the journey goes from effort to non-effort. The effort of focusing our attention narrowly, followed by whole body awareness, gathers our being into, and gives us a foundation in, the present. From here, we can open toward stillness without drifting off with some passing train of thoughts. If we went directly for the non-effort of stillness, we would soon fall into a pseudo-still reverie or dreamlike state. Instead we ground ourselves in our whole body and in awareness itself to enter the warm and intimate yet vast peace of stillness.

For this week, practice the journey into stillness.

320. The Challenges of Spiritual Practice

The psychologist Mihály Csíkszentmihályi researches the inner state he calls flow, similar to what Buddhists and Taoists call being at one with all things. He finds that we most readily enter flow in activities of both high challenge and high skill. The spiritual path certainly encompasses challenge and skill.

The skills we develop in spiritual practice include subtlety of perception, facility with control of attention, perception of and control of energies, purity of heart and intention in prayer, recognition of one's inner state, the ability to be, and understanding spiritual processes. These skills of the spirit translate their benefits into enhancing many life skills such as the ability to listen well, the ability to discern your true heart intuition in making choices, the ability to say what you mean and mean what you say, the ability not to do or say what you will later regret, the ability to live with regrets and get on with your life, the ability to accept yourself and your limitations, the ability to accept, relate to, and be kind to other people, and the ability to persist in pursuit of your goals.

As for challenges, the challenge of presence, the challenge of transcending our egoism, the challenge of loving, all these are high, overarching spiritual challenges indeed. The challenges of every day practice fall into several categories. Practicing presence in demanding situations, such as while in conversation, poses a challenge. In simpler situations, such as while walking or washing dishes, we have the challenge of deepening and strengthening our presence, and also of prolonging it. Another challenge lies in coming back to our self, back to presence, more frequently. And we have down days, when we feel ill, upset, lacking energy, or just off in some ill-defined way. Those days pose the challenge of pursuing our inner work regardless, though as always, adaptably.

The practice of inner work gradually alters your inner landscape, transforming your challenges into skills. What was once nearly impossible becomes easier, and then easy. So we need to ratchet up our inner challenges to keep pace with and propel the growth of our skills and abilities. Once a child masters second grade-level reading, she must go on to third grade-level reading if she is to grow. So it is with our spiritual practice. True challenges prevent stagnation and maintain our interest. True challenges teach us and develop us.

For this week, challenge yourself by practicing presence in demanding situations, and more deeply, frequently, and for longer periods in simple situations.

321. Present Through and Through

To be present, truly present, embraces several interlocking levels within our integral unity. First, we allow our automatic processes to flow as they normally would, but within the umbrella of our presence. For example, in walking, speaking, reading, or typing, our body knows quite well how to carry out those actions without our intentionally guiding every detail. Our body knows how to walk, how to form the words we speak and recognize the words we read, how to move our fingers across the keyboard to type a message, and how to tie our shoes. All such skills happen entirely by the automatic energy, once we have learned them well. The beauty of that level of action consists of its semi-independent efficacy, in not demanding our conscious involvement in each minute detail. Presence need not interfere, but we do keep our automatic actions within the purview of our intention, within our overall guidance. Without presence, we tend to be led around by our habitual patterns of behavior.

A second level of presence engages our sensory awareness, first and foremost of our body. We sense our body. That means visceral perception of our body through the sensitive energy, which enables our direct contact with our body. We also sense our thoughts, becoming aware of our thoughts as thoughts. We become able to intentionally direct them, no longer at the mercy of having our thoughts wander ceaselessly in an aimless and automatic fashion. We become aware of our emotional states and able to step back from the precipice of destructive emotions. With sensitive awareness in all three, body, mind, and heart simultaneously, we move toward wholeness, toward the next level of presence.

The third level is being the one who is present, having the sense that "I am" here, doing what I am doing, consciously experiencing what I am experiencing. Our I acts like a structural and communications column that reaches throughout our being and connects, guides, and supports the whole of us. Our I unifies us. To be present through and through means to have our intention and attention, our will, our central I extending from our innermost consciousness, our experience of being our self, through our thoughts and emotions, through our sensory and body awareness, and through our automatic functioning. Present through and through means to inhabit the whole of our being. Such presence confers true wholeness.

This third level of presence also entails being conscious, being in that energy of pure awareness, the cognizant stillness underlying all experience. By practicing the meditation style of just sitting, we acquire the taste of stillness, the taste of the crucial energy of consciousness. But that is a different matter than being in our I, being the one who is present. The will and intention that is our I is primary. By intentionally being here and now, being present, we draw the conscious energy to us. Together, I and consciousness form the core of presence.

Of course there are higher levels, where we surrender our I in moving into the Sacred Presence. But for this week, please focus on extending your presence to incorporate these first three levels.

322. Directed Receptivity

Spiritual practice gradually awakens us to new and higher perceptions, quite different from our ordinary five senses. Part of that awakening involves revising our world view to accept the possibility that higher spiritual realms actually do exist and that we personally could evolve to perceive and even enter those realms. But beyond such attitudinal adjustments, which practices enable new perceptions? Certainly the practice of presence opens us to new perceptions of our inner body, consciousness, and our own I. For here though, let us focus on what those perceptions in turn prepare us for: perceiving the higher spiritual domains.

To be receptive toward the higher seems to imply a passive state. Yet true receptivity is both awake and alert, but with an emphasis on being open toward the higher. Directed attention usually means actively focusing continuously and exclusively on a particular object of attention. But the spiritual world is not a narrow object on which we could focus. So religious and spiritual practices generally work to awaken our emotions and turn our thoughts toward the sacred by focusing on words, melodies, or concepts that represent and substitute for the higher as an object of attention. Sometimes, some people can and do make the leap from the representation to *seeing* the reality of the higher. Usually though it is a gradual opening: the veils of representation drop bit by bit.

A more direct, though more subtle, approach entails turning ourselves toward the higher without any intermediation, without the words, melodies, or concepts that represent the sacred realms. This is where new perceptions develop most immediately, because to turn toward the higher involves turning toward a direction we do not know. It is not up or down, right or left, forward or backward. It is neither inward nor outward. It is all of those at once and more. Consider the ocean of stillness that we touch in meditation or contemplative prayer. That cognizant stillness is consciousness. The sacred higher lies beyond and underneath that ocean of consciousness.

Just as we turn our head to look at our surroundings, we inwardly turn our attention and intention toward the higher in an act of directed receptivity. We are receptive, open. And we direct our receptivity toward the sacred higher. Our receptivity is not general, not passively open to whatever happens by, but turned and tuned to the spiritual reality beyond our mind. So in that moment we seek, we explore, we beg for help to find the true Direction, or at least the scent of where and how to search.

Quietly, in the stillness, we shift behind the silence and stand open to the ineffable Oneness. Who is open? I am. In our center, in our I, we give ourselves over to the sacred, we relinquish our center so that we have no center. We open a gap directed toward the higher, so that the sacred may enter our core. We surrender our Self, our I, in service to the Source. This is not just a one-time event. It is a practice. It is how we pray, again and again. It is the essential depth of prayer.

We move toward, through, and beyond the stillness. And we do so by, as, and beyond our I. This is where the work of presence matters in preparing us for true prayer. Presence teaches us about our I, trains us to be our I and to act as and from our core I. This meets the prerequisites of true prayer directly, since only I can direct my receptivity, only I can surrender, and only I can offer my very center to the Source of All.

For this week, practice directing your receptivity to the Unfathomable Source.

323. More Presence

Our inner work of presence during our daily life has a strong tendency to stay within the plateau of our level of being. We do encounter breakthrough periods where we have a significant, deeper experience, or we learn or discover some new method of inner work, or suddenly find ourselves able to practice a method we already knew about, or we become inspired by something we see or hear. But those breakthrough periods and the associated enthusiasm we feel almost inevitably wane back to our norm, back to our typical capacity for inner work. So we cannot hope for, much less depend on, unusual events to carry us to more presence.

For that we must find the fire within us and fan that flame of our spirit. Day after day we practice presence, choosing it again and again. Each day we aim for more presence, more often, more sustained, and deeper. We pay close attention to our down days, not allowing our self to fall into a zone bereft of all presence. So even on those down days of spiritual dryness, we rouse our self to practice presence, if only a little.

Our aim in this regard is stable, continuous presence. And though that may seem a distant goal, we can partially attain it now, even if our continuity only lasts 10 seconds, because 10 seconds is better than 9. And then we strive for 11. For those 11 seconds, we are more complete, living, experiencing, and engaging our life more fully in body, mind, heart, and Self.

Some say that spirituality is not a matter of striving. But to enter the deeper realms on anything more than a rare, accidental, and fleeting basis, we must strive. We strive for presence and for connection, with others through hearfelt kindness and with the higher through genuine prayer. Then we may attain a state of true spiritual effortlessness. But if we start with no effort, we merely remain in an ordinary state on the surface of life. That may be effortless, but also lacks the deeper spirit.

In presence we are our Self. In working toward more presence, we create our Self. We build the inner wholeness, our soul, that gives us access to our Self. One reason to practice presence as much as possible during our ordinary day is so that when we come to the depths of prayer, to surrender to God, we have something to surrender, namely our Self.

We can dramatically enhance our work of presence during the day by starting each day with a period of meditation. Meditation methods in general have the effect of raising the quantity and quality of the energies available for presence. And we can use part of the meditation period for direct, intensive practice of presence. That training in strong and deep presence carries over, along with the energies generated, to enliven our inner life as we go about our daily business.

But regardless of how profound or powerful the results of our morning sitting, if we just take a free-ride on those results for the rest of day, they will quickly dissipate. Instead we can take the opportunity offered by the energies generated in meditation to build on them through our intentional work on presence during our day. That way, our formal periods of meditation practice and our less structured practice of presence during our day support each other. If we are present even before we sit down to meditate, that state of presence deepens our meditation by giving it a conscious starting point. And meditation helps our work at presence, principally by the energies produced.

For this week, work to live fully, work for more presence.

324. The Way of Conscience 1: Discerning

Our truest guidance in the conduct of our life comes from our own conscience and we profit spiritually by becoming more able to notice and act on its promptings. Most people rightly consider conscience to be an innate moral sense, a sense that we need to develop further. But the same inner source, the same conscience that gives us our moral sense also applies more broadly, offering us our own personal guidance beyond questions of morality.

Life often presents us with choices, to which we react mostly by habit rather than by being in contact with our inner intuitive responses. We all face the question of how to live our life, what to do with the precious time we have. The function of conscience is not only to discern right from wrong, but also to be the voice of creative guidance within us, the voice that sees our opportunities, that knows how to respond in difficulties, that understands the subtleties of our many relationships, that distinguishes the important from the less important, the lasting values from the ephemeral.

In spiritual matters, what others may write, opine, teach or suggest to us can certainly be of great use, but only insofar as those writings, opinions, teachings or suggestions resonate with our own judgment and correspond to our particular nature and stage. Although we can be shown the way toward it by others, new understanding comes from within, not from without.

So conscience matters, not only in guiding our outer life, but in the conduct of our inner life as well. The deep reason for opening to and developing our own conscience insight, our own I, lies in the reality that our I, in turn, has the possibility of opening to the Divine Will. We could even say that conscience is ultimately the voice of God within us. Prior to that stage, conscience shapes our I. And then I become my conscience.

The big question is how. First, how can we develop our ability to notice the promptings of our own conscience? Certainly all of our inner work of presence, prayer, and meditation contributes to that capacity. But it is not only a matter of quieting our mind to hear the still, small voice of conscience. It may not even come as a voice or in words. It is more likely to be a feeling or a direct perception of the rightness or wrongness of a proposed future action, or of a past action.

One problem with learning to perceive conscience is that it can speak to us at any time. So as an exercise we can narrow the time-window by asking ourselves a question, to which our conscience, hopefully, will respond. For example, when faced with a choice that has overtones of right and wrong, ask yourself, ask your own deeper nature, whether the proposed action is right, wrong, or neutral. Is it appropriate or not? Is it bad karma? Is it wise? And then listen for the response from within you, not in words but as a feeling, as a knowing, as confidence in the action or lack thereof. Asking the question of yourself presumes that you have not prejudged the answer. If the situation is clear enough that you already have confidence in your judgment about it, then you need not ask yourself.

For this and the next two weeks, we will explore the way of conscience. This week, please practice opening to perceive the promptings of your conscience.

325. The Way of Conscience 2: Acting in Accord

When we perceive our conscience telling us what to do or what not to do, we may choose to act accordingly. Doing so encourages conscience to return to us. Not doing so, buries it deeper. When it comes as remorse about a prior misdeed, we can examine how our wrong act arose, what led us into it. We do this soberly, without beating ourselves emotionally or otherwise, but resolving not to make the same mistake again.

It may seem at first that occasions of moral dilemmas

that call forth conscience are few and far between. But on the contrary, they are frequent. Every time we face a task or chore that is necessary but somehow distasteful to us, something we would rather not do, we confront a juxtaposition of right and wrong, of need versus desire, of responsibility versus attachment, of freedom versus identification. Conscience will nearly always prompt us to freely and responsibly serve the necessary. But laziness, dislike, self-indulgence, greed, distraction and desire pull us in the other direction. So there we have a visceral choice on a fairly frequent basis: whether to strengthen and purify our will and thereby our connection to the sacred or to take the way of least resistance and go with the flow of our desires. Dilemmas that call forth conscience also arise in many other types of situations, for example regarding what we do or say when we're upset.

If we make a habit of choosing to ignore our conscience, it gradually recedes from our awareness and eventually ceases to trouble us with truth. If we choose the way of conscience despite our contrary and sometimes strong and even rebellious inclinations, we knock the rough edges off our egoism and build our I.

For all our inner promptings, including those that we believe arise from our conscience, we may need to do a rationality check. For example, we take as a baseline for all our acts obedience to the laws of the land and to the moral and ethical norms of our society. If we feel an impulse that may be from conscience, we can ask ourselves whether it meets that first test of rationality. Further, does it accord with our goals and direction in life? Will it harm anyone? The test of rationality, however, does not preclude unusual and creative acts or departures from our personality patterns. Nor does it preclude lawful acts that conform to a higher standard than societal norms.

Because the overbearing voice of our ego drowns out the voice of conscience, our perception of conscience can be murky and uncertain. Is that conscience speaking to me, or is it my ego? One clear indication that an action or omission of ours failed the test of conscience occurs when we feel remorse afterward. But we distinguish between guilt and remorse. Guilt comes from going against some learned behavioral norm and is a paralyzing, destructive emotion directed against myself. Guilt is about me, about ego. Remorse comes from our innate sense of right and wrong, from our conscience-based perception of how we acted wrongly or failed to act rightly. Remorse, though painful, is not paralyzing. Rather it spurs us to improve, to not repeat the same mistake, and, if possible, to repair or make amends for our wrong acts. Remorse teaches us how to discriminate between the voice of ego and the voice of conscience.

But recognizing the true impulse of conscience turns out to be the easier part. The more difficult is to accept and obey, to act in accord with what we know to be right. At times we are called to sacrifice our desire, to relinquish identifying with our desire in order to follow the way of conscience in what seems like an internal tug of war. But we need only let go of that rope to not be pulled by our conflicting desires and to accept the call of conscience.

For this week, notice the promptings of your conscience and notice occasions on which you inwardly rebel against it. Act in accord with your conscience nevertheless.

326. The Way of Conscience 3: Merging

"Be ye therefore perfect, even as your Father which is in heaven is perfect."[10]

When we first intentionally note the promptings of our conscience and act in accord with them, it may not fit well. Our habitual mode of living may be far from conscience and the difference jarring. We may well try to ignore it and escape, sweeping it back under the rug of our mind, pretending to our self that it was just a stray feeling, merely a passing impulse, rather than the truth that conscience offers. But if we persist in opening our perception to it, in accepting and obeying its guidance, the light of conscience gradually seeps into all the dark corners of our life, into our zones of resistance to living with integrity. And as we cooperate in narrowing the gap between what we do and what our conscience calls us to do, it reshapes us.

The way of conscience, after diligent pursuit, becomes more natural to us. By persisting along that way, we eventually arrive at the realization that we are our conscience. Then we no longer necessarily perceive it as separate from us, because one only hears the stirring of conscience when one is out of step with it. When we act from conscience, it is who we are, with no gap between us and our conscience.

Even here though, the occasional rationality check may be required to confirm its voice, like when we feel an impulse to pick up all the litter in the world after we've picked up a goodly amount, or an impulse to be generous to the point of impoverishing our self materially. Rationality defines the common sense limits to what we do.

Despite our best efforts and intentions, the conditions

10   Matthew 5:48

of life impose upon us continual tradeoffs and compromises. Say for example you have a strong sense of environmental responsibility. With our need to use electricity, with our need for transportation, with our needs for food, clothing, and shelter, the prospect of living a truly carbon-neutral, habitat-preserving, and non-polluting lifestyle is daunting if not impossible. And in many other areas of life we unavoidably confront choices where each alternative is a mix of positive and negative, right and wrong. Conscience can be our guide, our trusted guide in making our way through the thicket of inevitable tradeoffs and compromises in how we live, helping us judge what matters most.

    Abstaining from acting against our conscience, even in the little things, leads to the great and subtle power of a clear conscience. No longer inwardly at war with yourself, you evolve toward inner unity. Despite your thoughts, emotions, and impulses to the contrary, you follow your conscience and do the right thing every time, though doing the right thing does not preclude unforeseen mistakes. It means not intentionally, knowingly violating your conscience. Thus, to be a person of conscience does not make you infallible, but it does enable others to trust you implicitly, while enabling you to trust and respect yourself. To be a person of conscience keeps you on the path toward fulfilling what you uniquely were put here to do: your own creative path of inner and outer service, your own path of wisdom and love.

    For this week, for this life, be a person of conscience.

327. The Stages of Love
(Part 1 of 9 in the series: Stages of Love)

When we think of will, we think of will power, of making decisions and following through, of standing up for our principles, of determination, responsibility, and focused attention. When we think of love, we think of an emotional relationship. Will and love seem so different and unrelated. Yet these two, will and love, could not be closer. The highest form of will is love. And the truest form of love is the union of wills in the Divine Will. But from our starting point to that highest form, we may encounter the nine stages of love.

Love is not just as state of being, as in "being in love." In fact to reach the state of "being in love," we engage in a process of loving actions. We open ourselves from within. Opening to love is a series of acts of will. Each stage of love requires a particular act of will, a particular willingness. The acts of will leading toward love involve progressively moving beyond our egoism, beyond our utter self-centeredness.

Though assuredly interrelated, the stages of love need not be sequential: in one day we may live several of them, depending on who we are with, our inner state, and our intention. The following description does not represent the process of falling in love, e.g., meeting, fascination, infatuation, encountering difficulties, and so on. Rather, it describes the qualities and levels of willingness to love, the stages of the will to love.

1. **Noticing**: The first, preliminary, and rudimentary stage of love is simply to notice the other person. Often we are so preoccupied with our own issues that we do not even notice the people around us. Without noticing the person, no relation-

ship can exist. This first step of noticing, however, is a shallow one: noticing the surface, noticing their body, noticing the person as a body. But at least we notice them.

2. **Seeing the Humanity**: When we walk along a crowded sidewalk, we may notice all the many people but regard them as mere obstacles to our path. We can notice people in the same way we might notice a life-size cardboard cutout of a person: two-dimensional and devoid of life or value. But to see someone as a person, to see their living, breathing humanity brings us to the threshold of real relationship. This moves our perception of the person from outside toward inside, from surface toward depth. The person is no longer just a body.

3. **Tolerance**: We may notice someone and see them as a person, but not like what we see. The reasons for not liking him or her can span a wide gamut from ethnic, racial and religious prejudice to fear, jealousy, disgust, contempt, boredom, squeamishness or a simple difference in type. Whatever the reason may be, disliking someone puts up a barrier to love. We may not be able to drop our dislike, but we may be able to drop the barrier nevertheless. We do this by actively working within our heart-mind to tolerate the person despite our reaction to him or her. We focus on their humanity, rather than on the qualities or manifestations that we dislike. We allow ourselves to live with our dislike and rejection as a background, while letting the other's personhood rise to the foreground of our awareness.

4. **Equality**: After we can tolerate people, the next step toward love involves respecting them as our equal, in terms of innate value. If you consider yourself to be above or below, more important or less important than another person, you create an insurmountable barrier. Dropping that barrier brings us closer. But to even recognize the barrier of subjective inequality requires a fair degree of self-awareness, a quality developed

through spiritual practice, through meditation and presence. When we realize that we do not respect another person as our equal, the practice of equality calls us to be willing to drop that attitude and regard the other as our equal, in the eyes of the Sacred. This brings the possibility of friendship.

5. **Sameness**: The practice of stillness, wherein our thoughts, emotions, and intentions become relatively quiescent, ushers us into the great hall of silence, our vast and pristine consciousness itself, without boundaries. From that state we recognize that this cognizing stillness pervades all and, in particular, other people as well our self. So we come to see the stillness within the other person and perceive that their inner stillness is the same as ours, their consciousness is the very same substance as ours. Living in the stillness, we directly feel and see the sameness that we share with all people.

6. **Acceptance**: Seeing the sameness that we share with others, brings us to the point of accepting other people as they are, without reservation. We drop our inner objections and let the person be. We may still, when appropriate, try to help them grow, but we do so from a state of complete acceptance of who they are, as they are.

7. **Empathy and Compassion**: Standing in our shared sameness and accepting people as they are, carries us to the threshold of empathy and compassion, whereby we allow others' joys and sufferings to touch us directly. We willingly enter the experience of other people, celebrating their successes and suffering their setbacks. This is the place of heartfelt prayer and charitable acts for others' welfare. The walls of separation grow thin and ready to evaporate.

8. **Local Unity:** In unity we dissolve the bonds of self-centeredness to merge with another. We wish for the other what they wish for themselves. The other's joys and suffering become

our own. We become the other: separate bodies, separate experience, but one, unified, shared will. The paradigms of local unity include true marriage and the parent-child relationship. If we can love one person unselfishly, then we can learn to love others as well.

9. **Global Unity in God**: The ultimate level of love opens us to the deepest truth of unity, wherein the realization dawns that all of us human beings are children of our Common Father. The Divine Will is one, but differentiates like white light through a prism into the unique rays that form the core of our personal individuality. Trace our will back to its Source and you find the One Will from which we all arise. In that Source we have our global unity. Our individual uniqueness achieves full-flower in our participation in the Great Uniqueness, in the Great Heart of Love.

All these stages apply not only to our relationship with others, but also to our relationship with our self. To notice someone else, we also need to notice our self. To tolerate or accept another, we need to tolerate and accept our self. To enter unity with another, we need to unify our self.

Our spiritual path is a path in love, toward love. Love suffuses each stage of love. Whichever of these stages we enter with a particular relationship, it is love. Whether the first or the ninth, it is love. While we aspire to deepen our love, that aspiration is itself love.

In the coming weeks we can delve deeper into the stages of love. For this week, bear in mind the whole spectrum of love. See what points on that spectrum characterize your encounters with people.

May the Sacred Source of Love touch us all.

328. Seeing the Humanity
(Part 2 of 9 in the series: Stages of Love)

When we walk through a crowded sidewalk, marketplace, or public event, we may notice all the many people but regard them as mere obstacles to our path. Even in less crowded situations, we tend to notice people in the same way we might notice a life-size cardboard cutout of a person: two-dimensional and devoid of value. We see their body, we see it moving, and we infer that they are alive. Yet we have no contact with the fact of their aliveness, their humanity. They could just as well be animated robots.

To step beyond this superficial perception, we look at the person, with some attention to our looking, to what we see. In this looking, we intentionally see the person as a person. We open to the recognition of their living, breathing humanity. We do this without staring and making the person uncomfortable.

To see the other's humanity requires us to be in touch with our own. If I am not present in myself, I cannot have any sense of the inwardness of another.

This perception of another's humanity brings us to the threshold of real relationship. It moves our perception of the person from outside toward inside, from surface toward depth. The person is no longer just a body, but a human being like you or me.

For this week, practice seeing the living, breathing aliveness of other people. Practice recognizing their personhood, their humanity.

329. Tolerance
(Part 3 of 9 in the series: Stages of Love)

We may notice someone and see them as a person, yet not like what we see. The reasons for not liking him or her can span a wide gamut from ethnic, racial and religious prejudice to fear, jealousy, disgust, contempt, boredom, squeamishness or a simple difference in type. Whatever the reason may be, disliking someone puts up a barrier on our way to love. We may not be able to drop our dislike, but we may be able to drop the barrier of intolerance nevertheless.

To diminish this wall of dislike that separates us, we actively work within our heart-mind to tolerate the person despite our reaction to him or her. We focus on their humanity, rather than on the qualities or manifestations that we dislike. We allow ourselves to live with our dislike and rejection as a background, while letting the other's personhood rise to the foreground of our awareness. We let people be themselves without layering on our judgments, inwardly or outwardly.

The emotional wall of intolerance not only locks others out, but also locks us inside our egoism. In fact such walls directly manifest the self-centeredness of egoism. The wall can only be dismantled from within. So we begin seeing the intolerance in our own heart-mind and by learning to tolerate our self, what we deem to be our shortcomings.

Tolerance toward myself does not prevent me from trying to improve. But some things cannot be improved, for example, the basic structure and limitations of my body. As long as I reject my unchangeable aspects, I will also reject other people. Other aspects of my self may be amenable to change, but is it really worth the time and effort to change them? The answer varies. Even with those features that can and should be changed, an attitude of tolerance makes the changes more possible. Intolerance simply adds another layer to the problem, a layer that perversely serves to prevent any change in the thing I cannot tolerate in myself. For example, if I need to lose weight and have an attitude of disgust toward my overweight body, the disgust itself may drive me to eat more than necessary. If I can truly tolerate the whole of myself, I may then grow more tolerant of others.

Extending this openness outward, we practice tolerating our family and loved ones. Can we let our children be themselves and train them properly, while allowing their differences with us? Can we let our spouse be him- or herself, without pushing a program of reform onto them?

Intolerance breeds hatred and violence. Milder forms merely waste our precious energies and keep us mired in their poison. Giving up an intolerant attitude toward others is actually a great gift to our self. Intolerance toward individuals or groups, whether of another religion or race, or of someone who merely has bad manners, saps our spiritual strength.

But we cannot easily decide to be tolerant of others. We need to see intolerance whenever it rears its head in us. See it clearly. See its effects on us. See that it is just a feeling or thought passing through, a temporary, though possibly recurrent attitude. See that I am more than this ego-centered rejection, this rude visitor to my consciousness. This intolerant disliking does not define me. It does, however, claim to be me, as it says within me: "I hate ..." See how it says "I," when it is not I, but merely an intolerant attitude pretending to speak for the whole of me.

We can live with our intolerance, let it be, and defang it thereby. We can tolerate of our own intolerant impulses. We relax our attitudes toward our self, toward our own intolerant aversions, and toward others. In the spacious mind of presence, intolerance dissolves.

Why does tolerance matter to our spiritual path? Simply put, one cannot enter heaven while harboring venomous and intolerant attitudes. "Blessed are the pure in heart, for they shall see God." This describes the true structure of the higher world, where purity of heart is a necessary condition for entry. Whether from individual egoism or borrowed from a group egoism, intolerance blocks the spirit and renders love unattainable.

For this week, see your own intolerant impulses and let them go.

330. *Equality*

(Part 4 of 9 in the series: Stages of Love)

After deciding to tolerate people, the next level of love involves respecting them as our equal, in terms of innate value. This goes well beyond tolerance. It involves recognizing that, though very different outwardly in our abilities, physical traits, and personality patterns, inwardly we are all equally children of the one Creator, equally manifestations of humanness, of life on this Earth.

If you consider yourself to be above or below, more important or less important than another person, you create an insurmountable barrier of inequality. Arrogance or condescension, timidity or obsequiousness — all keep us separate behind our barrier. Dropping that barrier brings us closer.

But to even recognize that wall of subjective inequality requires a fair degree of self-awareness, a quality developed through spiritual practice, through meditation and presence. When we realize that we do not respect another person as our equal, or fail to respect ourselves as their equal, the practice of equality calls us to be willing to relinquish such attitudes and regard the other as our equal, in the eyes of the Sacred. This brings the possibility of friendship.

We can also consider our rivals and enemies to be our intrinsic equal. Notwithstanding the fact that our capitalist society, like evolution itself, thrives on competition, we regard our opponents as our inner equal, no matter who wins outwardly. We can be fierce competitors without detracting from our path toward love.

By placing ourselves neither above nor below others, we can meet them eye-to-eye and heart-to-heart, preparing the way for opening to our deeper, hidden connection.

For this week, notice how inequality enters your relationship with others. Notice any lack of respect toward others or toward yourself. Choose to let go of your attitude of inequality.

331. Sameness

(Part 5 of 9 in the series: Stages of Love)

The practice of stillness, wherein we allow our thoughts, emotions, and intentions to subside into relative quiescence, ushers us into the great hall of silence, our vast and pristine consciousness itself, without boundaries. The classic approach to stillness involves simple meditative practices: just sitting with attention on our breath or body, patiently letting the thoughts and emotions arise and pass away on their own. Gradually all these inner processes settle down, leaving us in natural awareness, in the stillness that opens the doorway to pure consciousness, the framework of our experience.

This contextual sea of consciousness is always there, but

we are distracted from it by our inner noise, by the content of experience. Stillness leads us into consciousness. Repeated stillness trains us to recognize consciousness. Repeated recognition helps establish us in consciousness, even in the midst of ordinary daily life. No longer completely distracted by our senses and actions, we live in and from consciousness. Naturally pure awareness brings naturally pure joy.

From the state of being in consciousness, we can inwardly open to recognize that this cognizing stillness pervades all and, in particular, other people as well our self. So we look to see the stillness within the other person. We perceive that their inner stillness is the same as ours, their consciousness is the very same substance as our own, and their inner experience of living is the same as ours. To be sure, the content of experience differs from person to person, but the consciousness at the foundation of experience is one and the same. Living in the stillness, we intentionally and directly feel and see the sameness that we share with all people, that mutual core of experience and being. The connection is palpable.

For this week, practice entering the inner stillness. And from that state, practice opening to that self-same stillness in others.

332. Acceptance

(Part 6 of 9 in the series: Stages of Love)

Seeing the sameness, the inner awareness of living that we share with others, brings us to the point of not merely tolerating but fully accepting people as they are, without reservation. We just drop all our inner criticisms and objections and let the person be. We may still, when appropriate, try to help them grow, but we do so from a state of complete acceptance of who they are, as they are.

Dropping, or at least putting in abeyance, our criticisms and judgments is an act of will, a spiritual practice that requires repetition and intention. Our thoughts and emotions may continue their habitual patterns of inwardly criticizing people when they do not fit our mold for them. We may not be able to stop these self-generating judgmental thoughts, but we can refuse to believe them, refuse to buy into them, and refuse to act on them. We maintain our discriminatory capacity where necessary, such as whom to trust in business dealings. But we can realize that a person is a thief and not deal with him, while nevertheless accepting him as a fellow human being. If necessary, we may lock him in jail, but we do not lock him out of our heart.

One personal benefit of practicing acceptance is the freedom it gives. Acceptance softens our egoism, whether self-centered or group-centered. It also widens our humility, a quality necessary for conscious connection with the Sacred. Acceptance relieves us of the burden of so many criticisms weighing on our heart and interfering with our relationships. Letting go of the judging mind allows us to live in natural dignity, enjoying the simple pleasure of being with other people.

For this week, practice accepting people as they are. Notice your inner criticisms and judgments of others. Notice whether you buy into these opinions. Practice letting them go. Though critical thoughts continue to arise on their own, see them now as masking the deeper truth of sameness and person-to-person connection. Do not allow such thoughts to stop you from accepting others as they are.

333. Empathy and Compassion
(Part 7 of 9 in the series: Stages of Love)

Standing in our shared sameness and accepting people as they are carries us to the threshold of empathy and compassion, wherein we allow others' joys and sufferings, as well as the basic fact of their being, to touch us directly. We willingly enter the experience of other people, celebrating their successes and suffering their setbacks. This is the place of heartfelt prayer and charitable acts for others' welfare. The walls of separation grow thin and ready to evaporate.

The path toward being able to love is a process of diminishing our self-centeredness to make room in our soul. As long as our inner world remains totally preoccupied by personal concerns, no one and nothing else can enter. Loosening the shackles of egoism creates space within our heart. Into that space we allow other people, we allow our concern for them, and we allow their joys and sufferings to touch us as our own.

And what then? Is it enough to feel someone's pain? Our conscience informs us that it is not enough. In response to suffering we can act. If we can take some outward action to alleviate the suffering, for example through charitable or other acts of kindness and responsibility, then perhaps our conscience will prompt us to do so.

Sometimes, especially with those close to us, the tone and quality of our interaction can show our concern, enabling the sufferer to feel less alone, allowing us to bear part of their pain, to share its burden with them. Sometimes, simply listening with full attention and open heart can diminish the other person's suffering.

Sometimes our presence can silently present the vast

field of presence to the other person and reduce their suffering thereby. This depends on the quality and depth of our presence and on their openness. But suffering itself can and does open people. So we can offer an effective gift of presence.

Sometimes our prayers can help. These depend on the quality of our being, the purity of our will, and our beliefs and style. We may engage in petitionary prayer. We may chant a prayer of healing.

In all of this, we approach the other's suffering with the same concern as if it were our own. In our shared sameness, it is our own. Can it be too much to feel others' pain? It can be. A typical day's news brings so many tales of sadness and suffering. To take it all in would overwhelm us, were it not for the inner strength born of regular spiritual practice, of presence, meditation, and prayer. The stronger and more refined our soul, the greater our capacity to bear suffering, both our own and others'.

But empathy and compassion are not restricted to cases of suffering. We can empathize with anyone, regardless of their state. This goes a step beyond opening to our shared sameness. Here we open to what it is to be that person, to the experience that person has of him- or herself. We enter the unique beingness of the other and stand in their shoes. This brings us to a truer understanding of and compassion for that individual. It brings us another step deeper into love.

For this week, practice empathy and compassion.

334. Local Unity
(Part 8 of 9 in the series: Stages of Love)

In local unity the shackles of self-centeredness dissolve, enabling us to merge with another, yet without losing ourselves. We wish for the other what they wish for themselves. Our loved one's joys and sufferings become our own. We become our beloved: separate bodies, separate experience, but one, unified, shared will. We also become fully ourselves: inwardly unified in our own will, yet able and willing truly to share that center point of our life with those we love.

The paradigms of local unity include true marriage and the parent-child relationship. Friendship can rise to this level. If we can love one person unselfishly, then we can learn to love others as well. The difficulties, disputes, and anger that formerly drove us apart, pale before our unity with the loved one. Those forces of separateness and egoism melt in the heart of love. "I" becomes "we." And I am no longer alone.

One perceptual indicator is seeing your loved one as yourself. When you look at your loved one, you see yourself, but not in the narcissistic way of everything revolving around you as the center of the universe. Rather, you see your loved one as an extension of your self, a larger Self that you both share.

All our inner work and all the preparatory stages of love bring us to this oneness with the other. We finally, willingly, let go of our claim to sole ownership of our inner territory and welcome our loved one into that space, previously reserved only for our self. Our inner ground becomes the hallowed ground of love.

Love is not distant and unattainable. It comes naturally and organically. Love is meant for us. It seems ordinary and it is. What is not natural is our previous life of separateness. We need only relax our heart in humility and simplicity, and love will enter.

For this week, notice the degree to which your care and concern for yourself matches your care and concern for those closest to you.

335. Global Unity in God

(Part 9 of 9 in the series: Stages of Love)

The ultimate level of love opens us to the deepest truth of unity, wherein the realization dawns that all human beings are children of our Common Father. The Divine Will is One, but differentiates like white light through a prism into the unique rays that form the free core of each individual person. Trace our will through any of us back to its Source and you find the One Will, which we all share. From that Source we have our freedom, including the freedom to love. In that Source we have our global unity. Our individual uniqueness achieves full-flower through our conscious participation in the Great Uniqueness, in the Great Heart of Love.

In the deepest of meditations, beyond thought and sensation, beyond the stillness of consciousness, beyond the Divine Light, contemplating Love, we may at times be embraced by Love Itself. We become Love. We enter the Great Heart of the World and It surrounds and suffuses us with Love, a love that we may carry into life. We may even learn to walk in Love, aware that everything around us is a manifestation of the One Will. Behind every part of this fantastically elaborate world is the Sacred One, Who loves all and Who can love through us with our participation.

Love is always one-to-one. But in global unity our love is no longer limited to a particular small subset of beings, such as our family. That one-to-one relationship of love expands into the big, inclusive tent of Love: one-to-every-one.

Entry into that big tent depends on purity of heart and openness to the Sacred One. We begin where we are, at whatever stage of love we occupy. Along the way, as we practice love, we may even enjoy rare, eternal moments of the heights of Love. But all the while, our true connection with the Sacred Source remains constant, albeit hidden behind the scenes.

Of the many mistakes we tend to make about love, three stand out:

First, we tend to confuse Love with need and attachment. Jealousy, possessiveness, anxiety, and anger follow such self-centered love like a shadow. Real Love asks for nothing in return. The privilege of Loving is itself enough. One relationship, though, can be about self-centered love at certain times and true Love at others. Indeed, the former can move us toward the latter.

Second, we assume that Love is easy and that we have it, so that no effort toward love is required of us. But the truth is that to come to Love we must leave behind its false manifestations such as jealousy, envy, possessiveness, anger, the wish to control, making demands, and setting conditions. We practice giving from our core and letting go of our desire to take and to hold on.

Third, the more deeply we see our lack of Love, the more we may doubt our ability to Love. But any normal person truly and unconditionally Loves his or her children. We have this capacity in us, though it may be hidden by the more superficial layers of our personality patterns and emotional reactions. Given that we can Love, we need only allow ourselves to Love.

At heart, our very nature is Love. To become ourselves means to become Love — uniquely, individually, joyously. Toward this, in all our dealings with living beings, we aspire to Love.

336. *The Stages of Presence*

The quality of our presence defines our humanity and shows our level of being. The stronger and deeper our presence, the more human we are and the more our unique, individual qualities enter us. The most effective spiritual paths teach engagement in the practice of presence in daily life. The practice of presence creates the essential foundation for developing our soul, for a fulfilling life, and for a loving heart.

With our yes-no minds, we think of presence as something we either have or do not have. The reality is much more interesting. Presence encompasses great stages and levels, which range from receiving the gift of momentary awakening, to making the effort to be, to effortless, robust, stable presence, to the ecstasy of opening to the Sacred.

The reasons for practicing presence likewise range from the personal ones of living a more peaceful, joyous life and fulfilling our potential, to the communal ones of being better, more effective neighbors, to the truly spiritual one of being a conduit through which the Sacred can participate in this world. The more present we are, the more real we are and the more vivid our life.

Presence is not an accident. We can practice it using a wide variety of methods. And that practice evolves with us. As we move along the spiritual path and our soul develops, our approach to presence deepens. We find our possibilities within the great stages of presence and work accordingly. While the early stages are mainly sequential, the latter stages need not be. The stages of presence are:

1. Impulse of Awakening
2. Receptivity to Awakening
3. Energies of Presence
4. Creating Partial Presence
5. Opening to Wholeness
6. I Am
7. Peace of Presence
8. Stable Presence
9. Divine Presence

In the coming weeks we will delve deeper into these stages of presence. For this week, renew your efforts to be present, to be awake, alert, relaxed, and engaged in this, our only moment.

337. The Impulse of Awakening
(Part 1 of 9 in the series: Stages of Presence)

With our very first attempts at the techniques of presence, we immediately confront the challenge of remembering to practice them. The remembering itself comes quietly as an impulse of awakening that is easily overlooked. It arises spontaneously, by plan, or by training. The inner work of presence is to notice and respond to the impulse of awakening, regardless of how it arises.

The impulse of awakening is truly a moment of grace from the depths of the Spirit, from beyond our ordinary mind and thoughts. It is an impulse of the will to awaken, our will to be. It enters us as a silent and direct knowing, as seeing and remembering the opportunity to awaken, to come back to the present, to be ourselves. It does not demand, but rather invites us to presence.

While the grace of awakening flows continuously from the Sacred, we only intermittently open to it. Some unexpected sight or sound, taste or smell, sensation, thought, emotion, or a gap in those may spontaneously open us, so that the grace of awakening can break through our veils, break through our immersion in time. Where it comes from, we cannot know. How it arises, we may not notice. The important thing is to notice the impulse itself, to recognize that opportunity to enter presence in this moment.

The impulse of awakening is not, however, always spontaneous. It can be scripted by a regular program of practice. Daily sessions of meditation and/or prayer, for example, purposely call us to drop the veils between us and the Sacred, to allow the impulse of awakening to touch us deeply.

Through repeated practice we can gradually train ourselves to open to awakening when particular triggers occur. For example, if we persist in the practice of being present while walking, the day will come when the very act of walking will prompt us to practice presence. Such training can fill our life with grace.

These three modes, the spontaneous, the planned, and the trained impulses of awakening, complement and support each other. However it arises, the opportunity created by the impulse of awakening is the starting point of all our possibilities for presence.

For this week, notice the impulse of awakening when it comes to you. Recognize it for the grace and lifeline that it is. Realize its value and significance.

338. Receptivity to Awakening
(Part 2 of 9 in the series: Stages of Presence)

When the grace of awakening offers us an opportunity to practice presence, we have a choice. Do we act on that subtle but sacred impulse by engaging in our inner work right then and there? Or not?

Just as there are many ways to practice presence, there are also many ways to choose not to. If we are too preoccupied, tired, lazy, or uninterested, we may simply ignore the impulse of awakening. This usually takes the form of sweeping the impulse under our mental carpet, an implied "not now" that lets the chance to practice slip away quietly, the same way it arose. We also can procrastinate, promising ourselves to practice later. Another escape in reaction to the realization that we have not been practicing presence in the moments or hours prior to the impulse of awakening is to feel guilty, inadequate, or frustrated, instead of taking it as a cue to practice. In short, we can always find a way out of awakening, a way to stay in our narrow channels of perception and our pre-programmed modes of living. In a vicious circle, the less we respond today to the impulse of awakening, the less likely we are to respond tomorrow. We simply cling to the habits of a semi-conscious life.

To work at this stage, we choose the other road by respecting the impulse of awakening and responding immediately to it through the inner work of presence. We can, in that moment of grace received, practice body awareness through sensation, awareness of breathing, energy breathing, or recognizing that "I am here, doing what I'm doing." We can repeat a prayer, with fullness of heart and meaning. Through any of these or similar methods, we use our inner time wisely, we grow our soul, we live our life more fully.

All such inner work leads to a virtuous circle. Our ability to respond to the impulse of awakening depends on having enough attention, enough inner space. The more we engage in the practice of presence, the wider our inner world becomes. Our ordinary thoughts and preoccupations no longer occupy the whole of our inner world. We have space for inner work, space to act on the prompts of the Spirit to come back to presence.

Our choice to respond with inner work to the impulse of awakening depends on advance preparation and commitment. We cultivate a general attitude and strong intention to awaken. We train ourselves to recognize and value the impulse. Then when the specific moment of opportunity arises, we stand ready for it.

For this week, by intention and by action, be receptive to the impulse of awakening. Honor that moment of grace, whenever it emerges, by returning to your practice of presence.

339. Energies of Presence

(Part 3 of 9 in the series: Stages of Presence)

If we are to be receptive to the impulse of awakening, we need some material to respond with. Our ability to be present depends, to a large degree, on the quality and quantity of inner energies available for it. The two energies primarily involved in presence are the sensitive and the conscious. Over the first we have some direct control. The sensitive energy enables us to be in our body, serving as the intermediary between our body and our self (our will residing in consciousness). Our intentional work with the sensitive energy will begin in the next stage of presence: Creating Partial Presence.

Over the conscious energy we have no direct control: we approach it indirectly. To do so, we create a suitable container for consciousness and open to it. Our work with the conscious energy will begin in stage 5 of presence: Opening to Wholeness. For both the sensitive and the conscious, our practices train us to perceive and recognize the energy, to conserve it, to access it, and to feed our being with it.

For this stage, we concern ourselves with not wasting energies. By staying relaxed, even as we engage in all the busyness of life, we conserve our energies. We notice how our unnecessary tensions and unconscious fidgeting drain our energies, and we allow them to drop away. We notice how our destructive habits such as overeating, smoking, and excessive talking drain our energies, and we allow those habits to decrease. We notice how our destructive emotions such as worry, anger, contempt, jealousy, envy, regret, resentment, and boredom drain our energies, and we allow them to subside. In all such cases of energy leaking from our being, we can stop the leakage by accepting and relaxing, inwardly and outwardly.

Relaxing allows the natural springs of energy from deep within the spirit to pool in our being. The first step in creating a suitable container for presence and consciousness is to stop, or at least diminish, the leaks. For this week, notice ways that you waste your inner energies and work to waste less.

340. Creating Partial Presence

(Part 4 of 9 in the series: Stages of Presence)

The sensitive energy brings our body and mind vividly alive to us. At the same time it gives us a base in the present moment and is the substance of the lower part of our soul. The importance of the sensitive energy to our inner life and spiritual path can hardly be overstated. We differentiate it from the lower energies that give us vitality and mediate our habits and patterns of responding to life situations. The sensitive puts us in contact with our life, with our senses, our body, our emotions, and our thoughts. Through it we live. Without it we fall back into programmed patterns, dull to our senses and our life.

The opportunity offered by the sensitive energy lies in its responsiveness to our will, our intention and attention, acting through the conscious energy, which we address in the next stage of presence.

We work with the sensitive energy primarily by placing and holding our attention on parts of our body. A good place to start is with hands and feet, one at a time. Gradually the energy collects there, drawn by our attention. We can notice the difference in our experience between the hand we are sensing and the one we are not, thereby training our perception of the sensitive energy. With some proficiency in sensing hands and feet, we can move on to sensing entire arms and legs. The focus of sensing an arm or a leg literally gives us something to hold onto for our place in the present. The arm or leg becomes our anchor in the stream of time. It keeps us alert and now rather than languishing half-aware and being swept away by time, thoughts, and emotions.

Another remarkable property of the sensitive energy can be found in its relationship to our emotions. Most of our stronger emotions run on the fuel of the sensitive energy. In trying to navigate the roiling waters of an emotional storm, sensing our body offers the excess emotional energy a constructive place to go. Sensing can help calm the storm of a difficult or destructive emotion by providing an outlet for some of that energy. The point lies in not being tossed around by the storm, in seeing our situation and feeling what we feel, and in channeling the excess energy to build our being. We do not use sensing to deny our feelings, to escape facing the situation squarely, or to erect an icy, unfeeling barrier to life. But sensing can save us from the ravaging storm.

For this week, practice sensing hands and feet, and, if able to do so, arms and legs. You can practice this as your sitting meditation, as well as during your daily activities.

341. Opening to Wholeness
(Part 5 of 9 in the series: Stages of Presence)

Because our body is always now, sensing gives us a base in the present, a base for presence. Keeping to this present moment through sensation, we live our real life and leave our daydreams and other inner distractions aside. By practicing persistently, we reach the point of being able to sense our entire body, able to have a relaxed, organic awareness of our whole body. We do not try to sense specific organs in our torso so as not to interfere with their functioning. Rather we establish general, overall, vibrant, all-embracing sensation throughout our body.

Full body sensation gives presence more stability in time than does sensing parts of the body. This is because in sensing parts there tends to be a split in us between our attention/intention and the part we are sensing. Then when our attention is drawn elsewhere, we lose the sensing. In whole body sensation, however, we can act and live from our sensation body, just as we do now from our physical body. Our attention and intention emanate from within our wholeness. Thus whole body sensation brings a more natural, inner unity than partial sensation.

Sensing the entire body is not just an incremental step forward from sensing parts of the body. Whole body sensation is a qualitative leap in our practice, a leap toward developing our sensation body. That wholeness, that sensation body serves as our container and stable platform for the conscious energy. This matters dearly to us because the conscious energy is the gateway to the higher and truly spiritual levels of our being.

The three primary qualities of the conscious energy are cognizance, stillness, and wholeness. In deep meditation we can open to the conscious energy through stillness, as the background of spaciousness shifts into the foreground of experience. But in the midst of life, it is whole body sensation that gives us a pathway into consciousness. The cognizing quality of consciousness then gives us presence.

For this week, practice awareness of your body as a whole, sensing the entire body at once, being in and living from your wholeness.

342. I Am

(Part 6 of 9 in the series: Stages of Presence)

At this stage of our work on presence, we need to address the question of who is present. We truly enter this life, this moment, through stillness, through the cognizing field of consciousness that underlies all. The who, the self that enters consciousness is our will: that which directs our attention, sets our intentions, makes our choices and is the doer of what we do. We cannot directly perceive will in the ordinary way, because our will is the one who perceives. But we can be that one, we can live as intention and we can act from our I Am. When we do, this special quality of will, this I Am enters our being and takes responsibility. To have a taste of this, simply mean and feel I Am as you say to yourself "I Am." That is who you are.

However, this is not our usual state. In our typical mode of living, we do not choose, we do not inhabit the center of our being. Rather, we let the habitual yet adaptive patterns of our personality make their default choices on our absent behalf. We live a pre-programmed life of habit.

Whenever we work on presence, though, we quickly come to the question of who is present. And in that very question, we begin to find and live the answer: I Am. While the question "Who am I?" may not be answerable, by taking it to heart we become the answer. In presence we become the will to be.

Presence is incomplete without someone who is present, without I Am. For this week, enter presence by being the one who is living your life.

343. The Peace of Presence

(Part 7 of 9 in the series: Stages of Presence)

Living, even temporarily, as our true self, as "I am," gives us the possibility of entering the peace of presence through an act of will. That act is letting go, not identifying with all our inner impulses, not clinging to our likes and dislikes, our desires and antipathies, our grasping and our fears. In letting go of considering any of that to be who we are, we come into our self, into "I am," into equanimity and contentment, into the peaceful confidence of knowing who we are and what we are not.

Such letting go, however, requires repeated and dedicated practice. The stickier something is, whether pleasant or painful, the less we want to let it go. Persevering, little by little, we earn our freedom through sacrificing our inner attachments, our obsessions, our false identifications.

In that relatively unburdened presence, we are less prone to unnecessary worrying about the future and unproductive rehashing of the past. In presence we can learn the lessons of the past and prepare for the future, but our wasteful relationships with past and future drop away.

That leaves us with the richness of this moment, which, fully experienced, brings deep satisfaction, natural ease, and peace of mind. "I am" just here, in this body, noticing my thoughts, emotions, and sensory perceptions pass through. Primarily "I am" just being, while doing what needs doing.

But the peace of presence goes deeper than our ordinary mind, deeper than thought and reactive emotion. The connection with the spirit that presence enables is the real source of peace and depends on the state of our conscience. In presence we tend to act responsibly and ethically. And responsible, ethical action leads to a clear conscience, a person's most valuable possession. A clear conscience leaves open the channel to the spirit, limits our regrets about the past and our fears about the future, and supports our inner peace.

Importantly, when we find peace within ourselves, we become a source of peace for those around us. With people we feel more or less at ease. The greater that ease, the less embedded we are in our personality patterns and defenses, leaving us disposed toward presence. In that spaciousness we accept rather than judge those around us. And we offer them our atmosphere of peaceful presence, our relationships enriched.

For this week, cultivate the peace of presence.

344. Stable Presence

(Part 8 of 9 in the series: Stages of Presence)

"Watch ye therefore, and pray always."[11]

When our peace is deep enough, our energies settle and our presence starts to stabilize. Then we see that presence is always available, if only we avail ourselves of it. Our continuing practice of partial presence and wholeness now pays dividends of stability. Our inner work moves into intentional steadiness in presence. We practice remaining present: "I am here, calm, alert, and fully aware of the whole of my experience, inner and outer." This is our active role: to enter presence, to be present, and to stay in the ease of presence.

We move toward continuous presence by living in our sensation body, rather than only inhabiting our physical body, random thoughts and reactive emotions. Inhabiting our sensation gives us a higher and more stable base in this moment. Our body is always in the present. Sensation is the energy of contact with our body. By keeping attention in our body, the sensitive energy collects there. Through dedicated practice of sensing our whole body, sensation gradually stabilizes, forming a sensation body within our physical body. Then we can live, not just in our physical body, but in our sensitive energy body.

That sensation body is a base that can house our consciousness. We enter stability through a shift, an opening of our awareness from sensation to consciousness, to the spacious fullness of our being. Our physical and sensation bodies reside within this awareness, but a vast new layer of spacious, cognizant stillness, of consciousness opens up. In the hall of consciousness, we come home to ourselves and enter the life intended for us.

11   Luke 21:36

For years such stability will be temporary, coming to us for limited periods ranging from minutes to days. The lengths of such periods depend on our will, on our moment-to-moment choices to remain in unbroken presence. Gradually we relax into those choices. The moments of consciousness, of presence begin to string together. We are just here, simply and directly and continuously.

To enter stable presence, however, we also need to serve receptively. The practice of presence for ourselves, for our own private benefit, proves inherently unstable, because what we deem personally beneficial is subject to the whims of our thoughts and emotions. But the intention to practice presence as a service to the sacred and to our fellow humans arises from the depths beyond egoism. Presence serves the sacred by the higher energies it produces and serves our neighbor by its atmosphere of peace. In this way, the work of presence becomes our prayer.

For this week, practice stringing together your moments of presence for a taste of stable, continuous presence.

345. Divine Presence

(Part 9 of 9 in the series: Stages of Presence)

"Be still and know that I am God."[12]

Ultimately, through devotion, surrender, and grace, we let go of our core "i am," allowing it, allowing our innermost self to be replaced by the Divine "I Am." That person, at least temporarily, enters an immeasurably larger life, a life as part of the Greatness that is All. Such people are no longer present;

---

12   Psalms 46:10

rather the Divine is present through them, as them.

Our very center, wherein we reside as "i am," opens out and transforms into the sacred ground where God may enter. Instead of attempting to penetrate the Divine, we open to allow the Divine to enter us. We do not seek to become Divine, but rather to let the Divine to become us, to fill our innermost core with Its own sacred impulses. We become a bridge between heaven and earth.

That opening is a receptive process, both actively and passively. The active and passive modes together remake our soul through a complementary dance of the sacred. In the actively receptive mode, we direct the whole of our being, heart and soul, toward the Divine. We may use sacred words, a name of God or a prayer, to focus our effort. With our attention and intention, we reach out toward the Formless One, toward the Mountain of Purpose, toward the Great Heart of the World, beyond the utter stillness of consciousness, beyond the sacred light, beyond all. And in that rarefied territory, we surrender, we empty ourselves fundamentally, we lay down our innermost self and beg God to enter. But egoism prevents us from doing this purely and adequately. So we practice it daily, again and again, with faith and with love.

In the passively receptive approach, we do nothing. We just sit in stillness, making no particular effort and no non-effort. We just allow all the thoughts, emotions, images, and sensations to come and go as they will, without grabbing onto them and without resisting them. This practice of non-doing has its own benefits for health of mind and body, which sustain us as we wait for the day of grace. On that day, while we're not looking, the Divine Will descends into our soul, unmistakably and irreversibly transforming our understanding of life, erasing the last traces of self-centeredness, and establishing the heart of love. This state inevitably passes, but leaves an indelible mark on our soul.

The process of reaching the stage of Divine presence is actually another whole cycle of entering the sacred realms of light, love, and transcendence. We will further address that cycle in the latter parts of the next inner work series: The Stages of Prayer.

For this week, practice opening to the Divine.

346. The Stages of Prayer

The starting point of all prayer consists of a kernel of faith, however vague or weak, that there is SomeOne Who receives our prayer. Throughout our life of spiritual inner work, we cultivate that seed of faith, which grows and flowers through the stages of prayer, the stages of our developing soul.

In prayer we communicate with the Divine. We find a useful analogy in modern communications theory, which highlights the importance of the communications channel. The channel of prayer is our soul and the quality of our prayer depends on the quality of our soul. Here quality relates to questions like: Is there noise interfering with the communication? Does the signal fade on its way through the channel? Is the communication one-way or two-way? Is the signal source strong enough? Can we receive and recognize the Divine response?

The source of prayer is the one who prays. That is our will, our I. The strength of that signal source derives from our will, from our need and devotion. Through our inner work, we hone and purify our will, we develop wisdom and love.

The signal itself, the content of our prayer is our intention, the why and what of prayer. Our I sets our intention, choosing the form of prayer. The many forms of religious rituals and traditional prayers each help us shape our intention, our devotion, and our heart, which constitute the true content of prayer.

The medium or channel which carries our prayer is made of spiritual energies, the substance of our soul. Through our inner work, we accumulate, refine, and organize those energies to build our soul. All effective techniques and methods of spirituality, including prayer, act on our energies and engage our will.

The channel noise that masks the signal of prayer comes primarily from random thoughts that insert themselves into our moments of prayer. More generally, preoccupations distract us from prayer, springing leaks in the channel and attenuating our prayer directly. All true paths have some notion of non-distraction in prayer, of having our attention completely engaged in the prayer. The deeper the stillness, the more focused our attention, our will, the clearer the upward-bound channel. The deeper our stillness, the more relaxed, and the more love shapes our intention, the clearer the downward-bound channel. The noisier and leakier our channel, the quicker the prayer and response signals fade before reaching their destination.

The Divine response can come to us on many different levels, independent of the level of our prayer. This depends on the acts of that great and unfathomable Intelligence. Among those acts is the grace that enables us to pray, that raises the level of our prayer, and that makes our prayer more useful to the Divine. While engaged in prayer, or in preparation for prayer, aided by grace, we work to raise our spiritual level. The higher we ascend in the spiritual worlds, the higher the energies available for prayer, the more valuable our prayer is to the

Sacred. Indeed, it may well be that the very reason we are here is because God needs our prayers.

Ultimately, with the supreme grace, prayer shifts from communication to communion, wherein the source and destination of prayer merge.

The practice of prayer serves the sacred and also serves us by developing our soul. In deep prayer high energies descend into us, blending with our sensitive energy and helping form our lower soul, our inner body. Furthermore, the unifying and purifying action on our will of deep prayer gradually forms our higher soul, the body of will.

Here is one view of the stages of prayer, from simple asking to the ultimate communion:

1. Petitionary Prayer
2. Prayer: Method and Ritual
3. I Pray
4. Commitment to Prayer
5. Faith and Doubt
6. We Serve Through Prayer
7. Contemplative Prayer
8. Ecstasy Through Prayer
9. Unification

In the coming weeks, we will delve into each of these stages. For this week, look at the role of prayer in your life. If nonexistent, consider beginning again. If you do pray, pay attention to the quality of heart and intention you bring to prayer.

347. Petitionary Prayer
(Part 1 of 9 in the series: Stages of Prayer)

Many of us as children asked God for help. And throughout our lives we may turn to God with very specific requests. All this asking, even from a child, requires some level of faith that God exists, that God hears our prayers, that God has the power to answer our prayers, that God loves us, and that God may choose to grant our requests. Thus, the exercise of petitionary prayer itself increases our faith, regardless of our assessment of God's response. We feel at heart that God can stack the deck that determines what will emerge out of the ongoing uncertainty and unpredictability of our life in the natural world. The very act of asking God for help comforts us by making us feel less alone and less vulnerable.

Petitionary prayer also presumes a kind of faith in the future: that God's Purposes affect the course of events. Yet we do not view the future as preordained, but rather as malleable and open both to our own decisions and actions as well as to Divine intervention. We feel that God can act on the future through its inherent uncertainty and through us. However, implicit in petitioning God is acceptance of the possibility that God may not grant our request. That acceptance, in the face of the Infinite, aligns our will with God's, even as we beg God to align with our petition.

Of course acceptance does not imply resignation; otherwise we would not even bother praying. The old saying, "the Lord helps those who help themselves," contains a truth. If we pray for something over which we have some control or influence, then we must do our part and not just depend on it all being done for us by God. We need to be responsible, inwardly and outwardly, thereby joining our will to God's Will in creating the brighter future. Thus petitionary prayer, in cases where there is something we can do about the object of our prayer, is a method of offering our will in service to God's Will, should God agree to support our request.

We feel that the degree of our earnestness and the depth of our need directly affect the height to which our prayer penetrates and the extent to which it is heard. Should we expect God to care more than we do?

Any practice of prayer gradually weakens our egoistic self-centeredness. Within the spectrum of petitionary prayer, we may move in the direction of selflessness, from petitioning for our personal, material benefit, to asking for forgiveness, to expressing our gratitude, to asking God to intercede on someone else's behalf, to asking God to bring us near, to asking to be allowed to serve well, to offering God our love.

For this week, renew your practice of petitionary prayer.

348. Prayer: Method and Ritual

(Part 2 of 9 in the series: Stages of Prayer)

In childhood we learn about God through the customs and rituals of our family religion. Those rituals speak to us directly and emotionally, bypassing the confused filter of our thinking brain. Communal worship rituals open the way to faith. We see and feel the faith of our fellow worshippers. Immersed in that faith ritual, it soaks into our developing soul. The community of faith and the power of its rituals lead us beyond the rational toward the ineffable.

The training we receive in religious practices opens us to the love and wisdom embodied therein. The practices and rituals of all the major religions have been honed and perfected over the centuries for maximum effect. Furthermore, the energies and will of the millions of people who have engaged in those rituals imbues them with a sacred power to draw us toward the Divine. Each time we reenact such a worship service the work of our predecessors gives us wings.

Traditional religious rituals come to us with fixed form. Some intended for community action, while others may be performed alone. We may also develop our own personal rituals, of meditation or prayer for example, that gain in power over the years. Similarly, we create family faith customs such as grace before meals. Returning to these established forms and the wisdom embodied within them, offers us tried and true methods for raising our soul toward the sacred.

When we begin practicing any religious ritual or prayer, our first challenge is to learn its form, the words and/or melody of the prayer, the gestures, the sequence, and so on. We rightly focus on these external features. However, the day may come when the practice seems empty or devoid of meaning. Then we realize that its true meaning must come from within. Thus begins our journey from form to formless, from the external ritual to its inner depth.

Within the form, we focus on adopting an appropriate prayerful attitude. For example, when we enter a religious ritual, whether in a communal house of worship or on our own, we enter a sacred space. A sober awe descends as our soul responds to the spiritual opening provided by the ritual. We feel grateful for this portal to the ocean of love. We open our heart to the Divine. We seek to draw or be drawn closer to the Sacred One. And the external form of the practice serves as the ladder with which we ascend.

The religion of our childhood can be an effective doorway to the sacred, because of our comfort with it and the connection to our family heritage. If those forms now seem empty and meaningless, we can reach toward the depth within them, within us.

For this week, renew and deepen your work with religious practices, forms or rituals.

349. I Pray

(Part 3 of 9 in the series: Stages of Prayer)

As children we pray because adults teach us to do so. After that we pray by habit, which may continue into responsible age. We may even attend a house of worship by momentum, or because we enjoy the other people socially, or because of social pressures, or because our parents always did, or because we feel guilt if we do not go. To the extent that any of these situations hold true, the prayer is not ours. Though it may touch our heart, it does not come from us. We do not choose to pray; we just go through the motions, be they inner or outer.

The whole arc of our prayer life, however, changes radically when we begin independently and freely choosing to pray, not because we should but because we ourselves actually wish to pray. At that point everything we have learned about prayer, all the external and even internal forms take on new meaning. Or rather our learned prayers lose their lack of meaning as we search for the Truth behind prayer.

Then prayer is no longer merely an external, habitual, or learned act. It originates with me. I take responsibility for my prayer. I am the one praying now. I am the anchor of my end of this communication with God. And because of all that, my prayer is always new, even when a reenactment of a traditional prayer.

We can distinguish degrees in this being the one who is praying. It starts with freely choosing to pray. That grows into being responsible for my prayer, for how and when I pray. Then we begin to see the crucial difference that presence makes in prayer. The depth and power of prayer depends on whether I am here and present as I pray, whether *I* am praying, whether I fully engage my body, heart and mind in the prayer. Allowing unrelated, intruding thoughts and images to distract me, weakens my prayer. The degree to which I can focus and hold my attention in the prayer, in its meaning and feeling, in the One to Whom I am praying, defines the quality of the prayer.

Beyond attention, we act as the source of our intention in prayer. We take responsibility for the reason for our prayer, be it a need for which we petition, the understanding that prayer is service, or the love born of faith. I am the one who, as I pray, continuously chooses to pray. I am the one making this request of God. I am the one offering my energy to God. I am the one offering my love to God. I am the one seeking to be to closer to God.

For this week, pray from yourself, from your fully engaged self. Be the one praying.

350. Commitment to Prayer

(Part 4 of 9 in the series: Stages of Prayer)

To improve at any endeavor takes practice, regular practice. To keep at something day after day, week after week, usually means that it gives some benefit, either now or in the future, either to our self or to others. Prayer offers profound benefits in all those categories. So it draws us and we respond to its gentle call. As we enter more regularly and more deeply into prayer, it becomes part of our life, part of us, like a friend that never wavers. Through that repeated choice to pray, our commitment grows. Without quite knowing how it happened, we wake up one day and realize that we are irreversibly, happily and gratefully committed to the regular practice of prayer.

That commitment, that reliable and welcome impulse to seek and to serve God through prayer, comes from and through our core, our I, from beyond consciousness. So though we may not be able to articulate just why we pray, why we seek God, we know we will persist in prayer, today and into the future. This is our choice, one that we trust ourselves to make again and again.

Commitment to prayer, however, means more than just being regular in its practice. It also means committing to quality, to the search for depth in prayer. Whenever we pray, we look to being present throughout the prayer session, to being whole-hearted and undistracted in the prayer, to being less self-centered in our motivation, to enhancing the subtlety of our perceptions, and to giving ourselves more fully to the Sacred. This is the practice of prayer that evolves as we do.

The stage of committing ourselves to the regular, deepening practice of prayer is a necessary step on the path of prayer. And though it may seem mundane, it is not. Its greatest significance lies in the depths of our will. Commitment is an action of will, of who we truly are. And our will ultimately derives from our God-given freedom, from our personal share of the Divine Will. So commitment to prayer is itself an intimate connection with the Sacred, a means by which the Higher acts in and through us. Each occasion of honoring our commitment by an act of prayer reinforces that connection, rightly evoking joy and offering solace, as we once again approach the sacred Presence.

Hand in hand with our commitment to prayer comes a commitment to the spirit and a life of integrity and service. For this week, take a step into the transformation of your inner life by recommitting yourself to the regular and deepening practice of prayer.

351. Faith and Doubt
(Part 5 of 9 in the series: Stages of Prayer)

We can expect neither certainty nor proof in matters of the spirit, because they involve worlds beyond the physical. Measurement and logic do not directly apply to the spirit. Because our ordinary life occurs entirely in this material, measurable world, which appears to be the whole of reality, doubts about the existence of God, about the reality of the higher realms arise naturally. Such doubts are inherent in and justified by our life on this material Earth. So if we demand certainty about the existence of God as a pre-condition for seeking God, we block our path before it begins.

In contrast to doubt, faith is a trans-rational intuition from beyond the realm of thought and emotion, an intuition that perceives the Sacred and receives Its blessing. Doubts occupy the mind, whereas faith engages our heart and transcends our mind.

Belief and prayer bridge the chasm between doubt and faith. The positive side of doubt, wherein we suspect that notions of the Sacred might be true, opens us to the possibility of belief. Through belief we create a mental-emotional map or representation of the Sacred realm. The more we open our mind to belief in the Sacred, the more it prods us toward the inner work of deep prayer. Prayer, in turn, opens our intuitive perceptions to the reality of the Sacred and carries us into the arena of faith. In approaching the Sacred, with doubt we suspect it's not true, with belief we think it is true, with prayer we see the Truth, and with faith we know and serve the Truth.

Even if we set aside our doubts and engage the spiritual path with vigor, doubts re-emerge from time to time. At such moments we need courage to continue in the face of doubts, the courage of our convictions, the courage to seek meaning where there is none. Courageously climbing the ladder of spiritual realms, we discover that the higher have even greater uncertainty and conversely more freedom than the physical world. Paradoxically though, our growing intuitive perception of the Sacred increases our certainty that the Divine is real, while our bodily home remains in this material world where unresolvable doubts persist.

Doubts come in all sizes and degrees, from wondering whether a particular spiritual practice or worship community is right for us, to whether God exists. The former kinds may carry some wisdom and we may need to consider them and adjust. The latter doubts, about God, we duly note and nevertheless continue with our prayer practice and other inner work. For just as we cannot have material certainty that God exists, we also cannot have material certainty that God does not exist. But as we make our way along the path, our spiritual certainty, our faith deepens.

Another realm of doubt concerns our personal inadequacies and whether they limit our spiritual potential. Such doubts may be based on real perceptions and may spur us to reform ourselves. But we cannot know the range of our potential. So this too becomes a matter of faith, of trusting that if we persist in prayer and inner work, our soul will indeed attain the station destined for us and our lives will be fulfilled thereby, as we give the full measure of spiritual service needed from us.

Faith is our perception of and response to the lifeline, or rather soul-line, cast our way by the Divine. Faith is our growing, albeit dim, awareness there is SomeOne to Whom we pray, SomeOne Who receives our prayers. Yet doubts arise unbidden. To move beyond this stage of tension between faith and doubt, we recognize that prayer is an act of service and we pray consciously. The deeper our prayer, the greater our faith becomes.

For this week, assess your own degree of faith and notice your doubts.

352. We Serve Through Prayer
(Part 6 of 9 in the series: Stages of Prayer)

Faith is contagious and communal prayer works. In churches, temples, mosques, synagogues, and other venues of worship, we band together in reverent fellowship with our neighbors to address ourselves to the Divine, to pour our heart and soul into approaching God. We each become one instrument in a sacred symphony of prayer. The power of communal worship grows exponentially with the number of worshippers, especially if everyone fully engages in the prayer service. Together in humility and devotion, the assembled carry each other on a rising tide toward the Divine.

One profound subtlety of this action is that it weakens our ego, our self-centeredness in three complementary ways. First, the mere fact of shared participation in communal prayer takes us beyond the solely personal. There we are with our fellow worshippers: unadorned, vulnerable, and equal before the Divine. The visceral and emotional evidence that we are neither more nor less special than our neighbor exposes the illusion of egoism.

Second, the closer the worship carries us to hallowed ground, the more we set aside our self-centeredness for sacred-centeredness. The strong tide of the communal worship pushes through the channel of prayer, washing away the self-centeredness that impedes the flow. Conversely, the more we set aside our self-centeredness, the more open the channel of prayer and the closer we can approach the sacred. Again, the group action supports us in letting go and transcending egoism. And our individual boundaries soften in that symphonic ritual of prayer.

Third, the devotion of our fellow worshippers and the deep wisdom of the communal prayer ritual impresses upon us that prayer is an act of service to the Divine. At times we may even "see" our collective prayer ascending to higher ground and feel our engagement in mutual support with the Divine. Then prayer, even solitary prayer, becomes more than personal, more a direct form of service to God. Simultaneously a privilege and an obligation, prayer rises as an act we participate in, rather than something that originates from us personally.

At any given moment vast numbers of people across this planet engage in prayer. Some pray alone, some in community. All serve the Divine thereby. For this week, open to the joyous privilege and sacred obligation of serving through prayer.

353. Contemplative Prayer
(Part 7 of 9 in the series: Stages of Prayer)

Contemplative prayer, in its many forms and in all religions, offers a direct approach to God. Typically such prayer begins with an effort of attention that may involve focusing or centering oneself on sacred words and/or melody, a passage from scripture, or a religious symbol. Through that effort unrelated thoughts and cares recede to background as we stay with and keep returning to the attitude and feeling appropriate to the prayer.

As the session progresses, effort turns to effortlessness and we allow ourselves more and more to be drawn, heart and soul, into the prayer. By centering first and then letting go, we enter the peace of prayer, a boundless ocean of peaceful consciousness with a heart wide enough to embrace all of life. But contrary to popular and seemingly authoritative teachings of New Age spirituality, consciousness is not God. The pure and peaceful screen of consciousness underlying all experience is not the Ultimate. For that we must go deeper still, beyond consciousness. For many though, temporarily released from all cares, this remarkable state of expansive, blissful spaciousness is more than enough.

For others, that contemplative peace is an invitation and doorway to the truly sacred. To effortlessly plunge into the depths, we give up all self-originated acts, inner and outer. We stop manipulating our experience. We let go and just be. Our lungs breathe and our heart beats, but we do nothing. Like jumping off a diving board and letting gravity take over to draw us toward the Earth, in contemplative prayer God is the great Attractor. The Earth shapes our external space to pull our body toward it, while God shapes our inner space to pull our soul toward the Divine. We simply trust our heart to flower in the dawning light of the Sacred and cross the spiritual threshold toward the One to Whom we pray. This is the deeper peace of will.

Gradually, as we open our heart, the peace and stillness of consciousness becomes porous, revealing the sacred, creative, and infinite realm of Divine light, a light that comes pouring into us in streams of energy. That level of energy feeds our soul in a direct and important way, while offering intimations of infinity and eternity that dwarf our ordinary experience. But though this realm is truly spiritual, it is still not the Ultimate, and we continue our inward, contemplative journey.

Having neared the precincts of the Divine, a more active role in surrender and submission becomes possible. We can beg from the very roots of our soul, beg to enter, beg to be entered by the sacred. Bereft in utter emptiness, we reach out toward God. For help in this perhaps we return to our earlier sacred words or melody, but now as a direct supplication addressing the Divine One. The prayer embodies our plea and carries it upward into the Holy. We offer our hope, our love, and our light to that formless and beneficent Intelligence, beyond all matter and conception, beyond space, time, and consciousness, Who nevertheless enters this world and may yet even enter us.

Through the many stages of contemplative prayer, through progress, plateaus, and setbacks, persistence serves and brings us nearer. For this week, work to take your practice of contemplative prayer a little deeper.

354. Ecstasy Through Prayer

(Part 8 of 9 in the series: Stages of Prayer)

In the upper reaches of prayer, we encounter ecstasy, a rapturous and joyful state of contact with the high spiritual energies of the world of sacred light. Methods abound for attaining such states, but quick methods alone do not offer the preparation acquired through long spiritual practice. Though that preparation is not always necessary for entering ecstasy per se, it is most helpful for enabling us to spiritually profit thereby.

The most easily accessible approach to spiritual ecstasy

goes through group prayer. Charismatic Christian prayer service, Sufi group chanting known as zikr, and Chasidic group prayer, to name but a few examples, offer rapid ways into sublime states of being. The shared energy of the group electrifies the atmosphere, empowers us to temporarily let go of being solely rooted in the physical and in our illusory selves, and connects us with the sacred essence of the world.

People with substantial experience with spiritual practices may be able to touch ecstasy through individual contemplative prayer. Having established themselves in peace, they continue their practice, not only to maintain their peace but to move deeper into the Sacred. Opening their heart and being to what is beyond consciousness, beyond inner peace, they attain the healing, nourishing, purifying, and intoxicating sweetness of Divine Light.

As wonderful as spiritual ecstasy may be, it should not be sought as an end in itself, but rather as a step along the way to a closer relationship with the Divine. A saying of the Prophet Mohammed goes: *"God's veil is light."*[13] If one seeks only ecstasy, then one may indeed find ecstasy but be trapped by it. In such cases ecstasy becomes an indulgence, effectively blocking further progress on the Way. We become enmeshed in desiring the remarkable pleasure of it, rather than allowing spiritual ecstasy to reopen our joy of living and reinvigorate our personal journey toward the Most Sacred.

Nevertheless, the nourishment and purification of the soul found in ecstasy can serve as crucial, ongoing components of our spiritual path. The soul nourishment comes from the immense reservoirs of high spiritual energies that define ecstasy. As we encounter that sea of energies, our inner world overflows.

---

13   Quoted in Chittick, William C., *Sufism: A Short Introduction* (Oxford: Oneworld, 2000), 139

"...*My cup runneth over.*"[14]

The soul purifying action is less obvious. One way this operates is by weaning us off identification with the pleasures of the material world. We need not give up enjoyment of food, sex, and movies, but spiritual ecstasy, by eclipsing the material pleasures, does loosen their grip on us. Through its impermanence spiritual ecstasy also points beyond itself: a temporary though repeatable state. We want it to last, but it does not. So we are driven deeper still.

Ecstasy, though wonderful, does not fundamentally transform us. When through repeated experience, our entry into the world of spiritual light no longer induces an intoxication with ecstasy, but rather awe and sobriety, our prayer practice can start moving beyond spiritual ecstasy toward our ultimate destiny of nearness or even union with the Divine. We come to understand that ecstasy does not confer union, being one level removed. But it does spur us on.

For this week, work to deepen your prayer practice a little more.

355. Unification

(Part 9 of 9 in the series: Stages of Prayer)

Ultimately, all true spiritual paths lead to the One God. This has little to do with what we think, believe, or imagine. The Reality is the same in Its essence for all who come to It, however they may reach It, whatever their particular creed, religion, or way. But in order to reach It, we must cross the chasm of separateness, into the realm of perfection, perfection of surrender and submission, of true and loving emptiness.

---

14   Psalms 23:5

In this the deepest of prayers, we let go of all our self-oriented cares and concerns, our posturing and opinions, our fears and desires. We let go of attending to sense perceptions, thoughts, and mental images. We stop trying to shape our inner experience. In short, we let go of dwelling in the content of our mind.

At that stage, the peace of consciousness emerges naturally. We enter the vast, comforting, and cognizant stillness that lies just beneath our thoughts and sensations. This peace touches us to the core. Finally, we can just be.

Yet the Goal lies deeper still. We become aware of consciousness itself and we may well wonder what could be deeper that this? It seems so all encompassing. But by the continuing action of egoistic self-centeredness in our inner world, we know we are not yet transformed. So we search for another direction, a perceptually difficult task. Consciousness in its essence seems utterly empty, though not empty of itself, its own substance of awareness. And it has us in it, the seer.

In seeking a way beyond, we let go of consciousness itself, the context of our mind. In so doing, our consciousness may start showing gaps, gaps through which we may contact the potent and ecstatic energy of Divine Light, as described above in *Ecstasy Through Prayer*. What a wonder!

But God is not an energy and, though we repeatedly enter the Light, transformation still eludes us. So we persist in our search, even in this rarefied realm. And we, as the seer, are still there. Then we realize that the only thing left to go beyond is our self, our I, our own inner seer and doer, in other words our will. Inwardly we reach beyond all, beyond ourselves. We may even touch the Divine. But still our central separateness persists.

So we confront the challenge of unconditional surrender

and submission to God. Through our years of physical, mental, emotional, and spiritual growth, we have wrung and wrought our own I, our own free will, from the many disparate parts of our nature. But that I has been downward- or self-facing as egoism. Now we reach the point of submission, of facing upward, of freely joining our hard-won will to the Divine Will, of allowing the Great Purpose of Life to work through us, with our conscious cooperation. Though the Ultimate Purpose cannot be reduced to, described by, or even summarized in words, It becomes our purpose.

That requires absolute purity: a clear conscience and selfless love. We stand before God and offer ourselves, root and branch, in service. We reach beyond ourselves, while giving ourselves up from the inside, inviting, begging the Divine to grace us. That inner emptiness attracts the Sacred, just as the Sacred attracts us. But egoism, our knot in the rope of will, always seeks to fill our emptiness with itself, with our own image. The purifying action of offering heartfelt submission in prayer eventually unties the knot of ego. The rope straightens and God, the Divine Will, enters such a person directly, becoming their center. That person enters God as God, not as him- or herself. In this way, the spiritual path, the work of prayer, and a human life attain fruition.

Then that person can serve God's loving purposes consciously and directly, walking with God in sacred communion, each step, each breath, each act an inspired prayer.

356. Stages of Inner Unity: I

Ordinarily, we are not ourselves. We simply have no self to be. Instead we have a personality, an agglomeration of attitudes shaped by experience. The dominant attitude changes frequently. This fact, however, is masked by the repetitious arising of certain personality patterns. Those patterns appear to tie it all together, by giving our inner experience an air of familiarity. More importantly, consciousness itself seems to tie it all together, for we always have that same background of awareness.

But the impulses that drive and define us change from moment to moment. We can hardly count on ourselves. We decide something now and later disregard that decision. Our center is effectively abandoned to transient occupants. Our center goes to whichever passing attitude happens to be on top for the moment. This is the situation of no I, so aptly presented in Buddhism. We never know who we'll be in the next moment.

Our spiritual practices strengthen our attention. Spiritual disciplines raise the efficacy of our decisions. Persistent efforts of presence bring forth our will-to-be. All that integrates our I. This is the stage of developing our I.

Gradually we become able to count on ourselves to be here. We consistently occupy our own center. We can say: I am the one who is here, I am the one who is living my life. This is the stage of having an I, of being oneself.

The tendency today in spiritual circles is to ignore the stages of developing an I, not to even recognize its possibility or its necessity. Instead we go straight for the Ultimate. But if we were to reach the Ultimate in this condition, we would have nothing to offer, nothing to give, nothing to serve with. Developing our own I, gives us the power to surrender to the Divine. Without our I, surrender can only be partial, because the part of us who surrenders cannot choose for the whole of us. Only our I can do that.

Having an I, we can hope to enter God through prayer.

We pray and we yearn and we touch the sacred. And then we see that we cannot achieve union by becoming God. Instead, we move toward union by allowing, inviting, begging God to become us. The Divine becomes our center. This does not mean that we put the Divine at the center of our life. That worthy endeavor belongs to a pre-union stage. Rather, we allow the Divine to enter our very core as us. The Divine then occupies our center in the same way that we do now. This is the stage beyond I. But our I is useful even then, as the vehicle through which we can serve.

Our I is our will and evolves in stages. Beginning in fragmentation, we pass through six stages to forge a unity in developing our personal I. In stage 7, we come to the spiritual I of the world of sacred light. And then, in 8 and 9, we open to the ultimate transformation, returning our I to its true Source, the Divine I. In the coming weeks, we will delve into these stages of inner unity, I:

1. Our Fragmented Will
2. Awareness of Fragmentation
3. Learning to Integrate Our Will
4. Partial Practice
5. Responsibility, Rebellion, and Love
6. Inner Unity: I
7. Reaching toward God, The Center of All Centers
8. Surrender
9. The One Divine Will

Your I is who you really are. For this week, assess your own stage of I.

357. Our Fragmented Will
(Part 1 of 9 in the series: Stages of Inner Unity: I)

Our personality, who we think we are, is merely a haphazard collection of attitudes and propensities shaped by experience. This personality drives our thoughts and controls our actions. Because repeating patterns of thought, attitude, and action create a veneer of continuity, we believe we are one person — me. But we are not one. This roiling mass of our mind allows external and internal events to boost the temporary status of some attitude over all the others. And for that moment, we are that attitude. Someone's rude behavior punches our anger button. Later we commit the same rudeness ourselves. We resolve to lose weight and then eat ice cream. We make promises to ourselves and others, and fail to carry through on them. We try to listen to someone, but our mind keeps thinking unrelated thoughts and our attention wanders. Today we desperately want one thing, tomorrow another.

Consciousness further exacerbates the illusion of continuity. We always have this same background of conscious awareness, from birth to death. And if we look more deeply into ourselves we may believe that we are our consciousness, our awareness. Indeed, many modern-day spiritual teachers tell us we are consciousness. But this is not true. Consciousness, like our body, is something we use. We see, cognize, and know with the aid of consciousness. The one who sees, cognizes, and knows is the one who does what we do: our will. And will is deeper than consciousness.

But our will is fragmented because our center is vacant and at the mercy of transient occupants. Our multi-headed personality forever marches into our vacant center, effectively fracturing our will into many pieces. The stage of our being has only one center, but everything in us claims that stage, claims to be me. As the changing cast of impulses occupies our center, we believe we are whichever attitude happens to be on stage at any given moment. My personality is not the many facets of one me, but rather an amorphous, unconnected set of impulses and attitudes seeking their opportunity to masquerade as me. Each pretends, in its moment at the center, to be the will of whole of me. One such temporarily dominant attitude, as me, decides something now. Later, another attitude, as me, disregards that earlier decision.

Thus, will, action, choice, and decision happen as a bottom-up, unpredictable process. We have no sense of being the agent of our actions. What rightfully belongs in our center, the will of the whole, our I, rarely enters, rarely engages, thus abdicating the field to the legion of personality. Even those people who seem to be strong-willed are usually just following strong impulses within their personality and not their own I.

This is the situation of no I. We never know who we'll be in the next moment. And this characterizes how we are as "normal" people, not some psychiatrically abnormal condition.

Yet despite this rather bleak picture, there is hope. There are ways toward inner unity, ways of defragmenting ourselves, ways we shall explore in the coming weeks.

But first we need a clear and sober assessment of our true situation. For this week, consider the foregoing description of fragmented will. Could it be true? About you?

358. Awareness of Fragmentation
(Part 2 of 9 in the series: Stages of Inner Unity: I)

The way toward inner unity begins in awareness of our fragmented state. Awareness means seeing and the willingness to see. The latter condition makes all the difference.

Our inner world effectively consists of numerous fiefdoms, independent regions of our mind, sometimes at odds with each other. Take the example of being overweight and concerned about it. One part of us wants to lose weight, but another part loves to eat large quantities of fattening foods. These two parts have no contact with each other. At meal time, the over-eater in us pushes the weight-loss wisher out of the center stage of our being. The over-eater takes control and eats. The weight-loss wisher barely knows the over-eater, and vice versa. They only "know of" each other. If the weight-loss wisher happens to awaken during an eating frenzy, it is so repulsed by what it sees that it flees the scene, leaving the over-eater in us to do what it will. We careen back and forth as control shifts between these two characters. Our other inwardly conflicted behaviors follow a similar pattern.

How can we unify such diametrically opposed desires that fear and loathe each other? A campaign of inner reform through discipline seems like the only answer, but almost always fails. The diet may work for a time, but the dieter in us eventually slips and we fall back into the inner battle. Only by befriending them can we subsume all our inner divisions into a greater whole. Toward that, we must know and accept our various parts. We practice seeing our state unflinchingly, without judgment, and with acceptance that this is how we are. The one in us that does this practice, that sees how we are, is neither the over-eater nor the weight-loss wisher. It is that in us that wishes to be inwardly free, loving, effective and unified. This, our seer, through seeing and accepting can gradually bring all the fragments of our will into its one umbrella.

So we practice seeing without judgment. Relaxed seeing carries a natural tenor of kindness. And that self-directed kindness, as it sees more and more of us, gradually attracts all our parts toward our growing wholeness. Our blinders must come off, so that we can see and befriend even the more repulsive fragments of our will. That requires the strength born of inner peace, which is where practices like meditation help. We practice seeing and noticing how we think, feel, and act, including our most banal moods and attitudes. We are not making a catalog or collecting memories of how we are. Nor are we waiting for some good or bad inner character to show its face. Rather, every act of seeing brings wholeness to its moment, drawing our will together, gradually integrating our fiefdoms of desire, whether opposed to each other or just indifferent. The more often we see, the more whole we are.

In the example of eating, we can understand why some dieting methods have us pay attention to our food, taste each bite fully rather than wolfing it down. Actually tasting our food brings awareness to the necessary and enjoyable act of eating. And it offers an umbrella for both our over-eater and weight-loss wisher, satisfying the former through enhancing the experience of taste and helping the latter through diminishing the desire to overeat by increasing the satisfaction of eating. Accepting awareness reconciles desires, not just with regard to eating, but in every domain of our fragmented inner life.

For this week, practice seeing and noticing your own thoughts, feeling, attitudes, and actions, without judgment and with kindness.

359. Learning to Integrate Our Will
(Part 3 of 9 in the series: Stages of Inner Unity: I)

Spiritual practices have the effect of integrating our fragmented will. In the practice of mindfulness meditation, we watch what goes on in our inner world, without judgment. This offers the noticed shards of desire, fear, and the rest a welcoming path toward merging into the greater whole of the accepting one in us who watches. Such watching goes beyond formal meditation into our daily life through the practice of presence. When we are present, when there is that one in us who sees what we see and does what we do, that one who is us, all those parts that show themselves can enter that one's domain, transforming from part to whole.

At times the problem of rejection arises. Some negative aspect of our character, of which we disapprove, steps forward. When this happens, a struggle may occur. If the negative succeeds in temporarily taking over the reins of our center, we, the one who sees, do not want to see and we flee the scene. We abandon ourselves to the negative, thereby aggravating and prolonging our fragmented condition. To heal, we need to let go of our self-disapproval and move toward acceptance of ourselves, of everything in us. This does not mean that we act on every base impulse, but rather that we see and acknowledge the whole catastrophe as being part of us. Then the accepting one in us who sees can continue standing in the center, even when confronted with our negative thoughts, feelings, and intentions. This non-abandonment of ourselves, especially in our less noble moments, leads us toward wholeness, integrity, conscience, and love.

In practices that require a focused attention, we bring

more and more of our intention to bear, entraining all our fragments into the single-minded effort of attention. This includes many types of meditation and prayer. As we collect ourselves in prayer or focused meditation, we enlist all our scattered parts into the one overarching endeavor. For those moments, nothing else matters. We refuse all distractions, inner and outer, everything that does not pertain to that practice. This stance of refusing distractions temporarily defragments our inner world. The wholeness achieved thereby is the fluid wholeness of will.

Spiritual practices are recipes for our will to follow. The essence of the entire range of spiritual methods and disciplines lies hidden in the acts of will that drive them. The descriptions of practices present their functional aspect, e.g., noticing our thoughts, opening emotions of longing and love, repeating a prayer with feeling and meaning, watching our bodily sensations in walking meditation. But the core of practice consists of will. We, as will, act on the inner energies of our being and on the functions of our body and mind. So the instructions and steps of any practice are only its outer clothing. We discover its true nature by acting from within, through trial and error. Gradually that actor gathers and integrates enough of our disparate impulses to reach a tipping point toward wholeness, toward inner unity. But for that we must persist in practice in a balanced way.

So in this stage of learning how to integrate our will, we learn the forms of the path we have chosen. We practice and explore those forms to discover their meaning, their purpose, and their truth. In so doing, we begin to discover our Self.

For this week renew your inner work, notice the role of your will in it, and notice its effects on your will.

360. Partial Practice
(Part 4 of 9 in the series: Stages of Inner Unity: I)

Having learned a personally suitable and effective set of spiritual practices, we put them to use as best we can. The early rush of enthusiasm gives way to our limitations. What limits us primarily is the very fragmentation of will addressed by our practices. Most of our will accords greater concern and respect to externals than to our Self, the Self of others, and the Great Self of the Sacred One. Some days we lose almost all contact with our true nature; our wish and commitment to practice wanes to near extinction. Great gaps of unaware, uncentered hours punctuate our life.

Nevertheless, in this vast desert of experience, we seek to create oases of spirituality. Gradually these oases in our day, perhaps periods of meditation or prayer, walking in presence, and the like, attract an inner coalition. Subsets of our fragmented inner world join together in the decision and commitment to practice. More of us appreciates the potential of Self and the benefits of practice. More of our inner impulses, wishes, and desires align behind the work of understanding and spiritual growth. This gathering nascent Self coalesces to become the one in us who sees, the one in us who prays, the one in us who chooses to be and is present, the one in us who seeks and wishes to serve the higher, the One Who loves.

But our sense of self remains a mixed bag, with other, many other, ones in us who have no interest in spirituality. So we, the one who does seek the path, must act accordingly. Whenever an opening presents itself, we take it. Unbidden moments come during the day when, in the midst of all our other interests and activities, we remember the sacred. The seeker in us temporarily returns to our center, temporarily awakens. This is our one opportunity, so we value it appropriately. We act.

At that moment, we return to our inner work, sensing our body, becoming present, breathing consciously, repeating a prayer, responding with kindness, or whatever our practice is. Knowing full well that some other part of us will soon take over and drop us back into uncentered unawareness, we practice now with vigor and with heart, especially heart. The heartfulness of our practice attracts and welcomes more of our desires and interests, more pieces of our will, to join the seeker in us, the one who wishes to know and to serve the higher. As more of us coalesces, our centeredness grows more stable.

Yet our current station allows only a part of us to practice and only for part of the day. But even transitory presence supports the dream and intermediate goal of continuity and wholeness, of I. For those precious moments as an awakened seeker, our heart tastes the possibilities of drinking at the sacred fountain. The quality of that taste suffuses our inner realm, setting the stage for that day when the whole of us merges into a lasting unity of intention, action, and heart.

For this week, notice that only a part of you practices, and only for part of your time. What would wholeness mean and how can you work toward that?

361. Responsibility, Rebellion, and Love
(Part 5 of 9 in the series: Stages of Inner Unity: I)

As our self begins to unify into our I, we become more responsible. But responsible to whom and for what? Ordinarily as we mature, we become more responsible outwardly: toward our body, our family, our society, and the Earth. On top of that, however, our spiritual work involves becoming more responsible inwardly as well: responsible to our higher Self and the Divine, responsible for our inner state and inner actions.

We honor and respect our Self by caring for and cultivating our inner state. This takes many forms. We make efforts not to be drawn into lower states by destructive emotions like anger, resentment, self-pity, vanity, envy and jealousy, as well as their associated thought patterns. This is a matter of true personal dignity and Self-respect. We know that such emotions not only waste the energies we need for our inner work, but also lead us to think, say and do things we later regret. On another level, we cultivate higher states and produce higher energies through presence, meditation, prayer and related practices. All this inner conscientiousness further enhances our outwardly responsible actions by making us more able to do what's necessary, more able to meet the people of our life with warmth in our heart.

But not yet being fully integrated, certain of our inner domains, desires, and impulses hide beyond the reach of our growing I. And they make trouble. They rebel against any motivation that conflicts with their own. So we find ourselves indulging in all kinds of dissipative and deleterious patterns of body, mind, and heart. These rebellious impulses interfere with our inner work, drag us into non-presence, block our feelings of devotion, and put up obstacles to meditation. Our shortsightedness in their recalcitrant grip saps our inner resources in exchange for immediate gratification, sometimes with harmful external effects.

We want to diet, but cannot. We want to quit smoking, but do not. We want to be kind, but act out of anger and selfishness. We want to be present, but lose ourselves in busyness and daydreams. We want to love, but not everyone.

And so it goes with these two sides in us: our outwardly and inwardly responsible Self and our irresponsible selves. The saving grace is that all of it is Me. This is a case where love proves much more effective than war. Force just deepens our inner divisions. But if we love our self, all of our self, including our irresponsible, rebellious selves, we gradually win them over, bringing even them under the tent of our growing I.

And there they learn that to respect our true Self ultimately benefits all parts of us. That self-respect leads our rebellious nature to impose limits on itself, limits that prevent damage to our true Self, limits that prevent interference with our inner and outer responsibilities. Love begets love, even within our own inner house. The love we give our many selves colors our inner life with its golden hues, attracting all our disparate parts to the whole that is I.

For this week notice those aspects of yourself that are responsible, outwardly and inwardly. Notice those that rebel and follow their own short-sighted impulses. We tend to think we are the former, while disavowing the latter. Notice your attitude toward your self-serving, rebellious aspects. Is it love?

362. Inner Unity: I

(Part 6 of 9 in the series: Stages of Inner Unity: I)

What can the unified person say?

Now, and in the future, I am. At this stage, with wholeness and the sense of agency, we are here and responsible for our life. Not that I cause every event that happens to and around me, but that I alone am responsible for what I do. I no longer abdicate the authorship, credit, or blame for my actions to passing but insistent impulses which I later disavow or ascribe to my brilliance, nor to any external influences.

Such a person can say more: I trust myself. When necessary, I can marshal all my inner resources to meet any situation, to do what's called for, to respond to opportunity, to create new possibilities. This rightly-based self-confidence does not mean assurance of success, nor guarantee the lack of mistakes. But though I fail or err, I am the one who chose whatever course of action I took.

Furthermore, in presence, I am the one who is present, the one whose will it is to be. This reality offers us a relatively straightforward way to understand and experience I. Though the notion of I, of inner unity manifested as one will that is I, may seem vague or difficult to grasp, in presence we experience I directly. The more will-to-be we can muster, the more I and the more presence we have in that moment.

Though the arrogantly forceful person may appear to have inner unity acting from their I, it is illusory. The ersatz unity of the arrogant is built around self, ego, not around the true I that descends from deep within. The enabling factor for that descent is humility. This is not to say that I is weak and cannot act decisively and strongly. Rather the inner condition of openness to I inevitably includes humility, even in strength and outward success.

The most obvious external manifestation of I is each person's uniqueness. One of God's names is the Unique. And as the whole of God manifests in each human being, we each are unique. And that uniqueness of will forms the core of our soul. Even through the disjointed layers that obscure our unique I, it permeates all our actions and ways of being. Further, as I is the spark of freedom we receive from God, it is not manufactured by us nor by our inner work. It is not merely a matter of unifying our disparate parts. That unification process through our inner work serves to clear the way for our I to emerge, to act without opposition.

In deep prayer, when every fiber of our being aligns in devotion to the Sacred, we become the work of our unified self, our I. In that state, I pray and I serve.

For this week, notice when your own I manifests in you. Welcome it. Become yourself.

363. Reaching Toward God, Center of All Centers
(Part 7 of 9 in the series: Stages of Inner Unity: I)

In moments of strong and extended presence, when we quite definitely and clearly know that "I am here," the higher worlds may "leak" through the veil and into our direct experience, carried by our I. This possibility exists because will reaches throughout all the worlds, from the lowest inanimate levels to the highest and most sacred.

When we become ourselves, our I, in presence, and maintain that state, we become the channel connecting the worlds. Higher energies may spontaneously descend to and through us. But we need not wait for that. We can intentionally reach upward, reach deep within our core, through our innermost self, to contact the aspect of our will that dwells in the higher world of creative, sacred light. Opening to that level, though not the Ultimate, certainly takes us a major step toward the Divine.

To reach toward God, we reach by means of, toward, and through our innermost Self, by means of, toward, and through our I, our center. And there, to quote an image from Plotinus, we "hold through our own center to the Center of all centers, just as the centers of the great circles of a sphere coincide with that of the sphere to which all belong."[15] With Plotinus, we recognize that God is the Center of all centers, including our own. By coming into and staying in our center, we approach the Center of all. Only through our own center can we come to the higher worlds, to love, and ultimately to God.

A key factor in reaching toward God is to allow for a two-way action. Even as we wholeheartedly aim and extend our Self through our center toward the Divine, we simultaneously allow God to reach toward us. We are both active and receptive. We reach upward beyond ourselves. We reach with our mind focused on the Divine and our heart full of love and longing. All the while we leave room for the sacred to flow downward to and through us. And because the higher constantly reaches toward each of us, this action of ours, this deep prayer proves both effective and repeatable at will, once we understand it experientially. The world of sacred light constantly awaits our opening to its infinite abundance and to its proximity to God.

But how do we reach upward? We turn our attention and intention inward, beyond thought and emotion, beyond the stillness of our cognizing consciousness, through our Self, and into the sacred light. Perhaps we engage one of God's names as a stepping stone to the Reality behind the name. To the rare few this entrance to a higher world comes easily. For most of us it takes decades of practice, of contemplation, prayer, and meditation, of becoming familiar with the inner landscape, of experimenting with alternative approaches, of gradually deepening understanding, longing, and love. The dedicated effort itself, however, brings meaning and expanding vistas to our life from the very beginning, even as it gradually transforms us.

Having discovered our Self, we turn to this stage of <u>directing our I</u> toward true prayer, the path of ultimate unity.

15   Plotinus, *Enneads* VI.9.8

For this week, practice being in your own center and reaching toward the Center of all centers.

364. Surrender
(Part 8 of 9 in the series: Stages of Inner Unity: I)

Having reached through our center toward the Center of all centers, we arrive at the point of surrendering to the Divine, beyond the world of sacred light. We seek to bring our entire being to the threshold of the sacred and there open our soul, focusing solely on the Divine, in love, humility, supplication, and hope for the grace of contact. We give ourselves wholly over to this one endeavor. We make God our exclusive god for those moments, setting aside all other concerns.

We do not seek a vision, for we know the Divine resides beyond inner visions. Yet we seek communion, unity. We surrender in the hope of being taken into God's tent, or rather of God entering ours, entering us, becoming us. We surrender our will, our very self, unconditionally to the Unconditioned. Nothing less will do. We beg the Greatness to embrace us, to purify us so that we may be a worthy vehicle for Its Purposes.

But how can we do this, when we do not know the way?

Take the example of a satellite dish that receives signals from the sky. The dish must be aimed properly to pick out the appropriate signal. Without the aiming, we have a passive hunk of materials. With aiming, it becomes an effective part of a receiver system. This difference between passivity and receptivity applies to our inner world as well. To be truly receptive, we aim our entire being beyond ourselves and toward the Divine.

However, we need to learn the appropriate direction. To say we aim beyond ourselves and toward the Divine is easy. To actually do it requires a subtle understanding. One excellent way toward gaining that understanding is the practice of stillness — deep, abiding, non-doing stillness. We surrender our attachment to our thoughts and emotions, to our personality that masks the stillness beneath it. In that stillness, we learn the contours of our mind and heart, we learn to recognize consciousness, the substance of cognizant stillness, and we begin to intuit the boundaries of consciousness itself. This perceptual ability matters because the Divine resides well beyond consciousness.

Another way toward discovering the direction toward the Divine is by deep prayer. In the heartfelt urgency of supplication, we can feel which inner postures and inner actions bring us closer to the sacred and which do not. Through regular and persistent prayer, with attention to discerning what works, our inner compass becomes magnetized by the Divine pole.

For example, we choose one of the great names of the Most High, and we inwardly speak that name, opening to the same awe and potency as the Sacred One speaking the universe. We speak the Divine name as if the Divine were speaking us. We speak into the infinite, beyond all conception. But what does that really mean? We learn the meaning and direction by practice and experimentation with stillness, contemplation, and prayer, by seeking the way beyond ourselves and our minds.

Fortunately, it is not all up to us. We depend for the final step on Grace from Above. But for the preparatory steps, we must do all we can, persistently bringing to bear our full intelligence, willing heart, effort and devotion. Without that preparation, without that attitude of surrender, Grace will either not come or not be recognized. Nevertheless, Grace knows no limitations. It may come in deep stillness, in heartfelt supplication, or at any time.

For this week, practice and explore surrendering to the

Divine.

365. The One Divine Will
(Part 9 of 9 in the series: Stages of Inner Unity: I)

What you are looking for is what is looking.
Attributed to St. Francis of Assisi

...I live; yet not I, but Christ liveth in me ...
Galatians 2:20

Recall God's name as given to Moses: "I AM THAT I AM." God speaks to us through Moses, not as Moses, but as God. Does the "I AM" of God have anything to do with our own "I am?" We look into ourselves. What in me could possibly be connected with God? What in me is looking, into myself and for God? Extrapolating from the famous quote from St. Francis of Assisi: that in me which looks for God is connected with God. In effect God is looking for God through me. Contemplation along that line affords an opening to the higher.

Sit quietly. Let your thoughts and emotions and body settle down. Turn your attention, your interest, your inner seeking urgently and wholeheartedly toward God. Look at what in you is doing the seeking. You may discover the difficulty here. Just as our eye cannot see itself, the seeker cannot see him- or herself, because the one who is looking is also the one who sees. So we step around that conundrum by being the seeker, being the seer, being the one who is contemplating, the one who is looking for God. So though we cannot see our Self, we can be our Self, and know our Self thereby. That Self is our will and through such contemplative prayer we can acquire the taste, the perception of will.

If God is Will and I am will, what is the connection? If God created the universe and endowed us with innate freedom, that freedom must be freedom of will, that freedom must be will. So God gives us the gift of will, which is God's own nature. Will, though it adopts many guises, is still will.

It is like water taken from the ocean into a container. It remains the same water. And it is like a hierarchical organization or company. The intention, the will, emanates from the top and flows down through the levels of the company. The more levels, the more the intention gets garbled. As people on the lower rungs acquire greater understanding of the company's goals, they can take more initiative and become more useful to those at the top. They can move up the rungs or the hierarchy can be flattened. They can have a more direct connection with the will at the top.

Similarly, as our being develops and our will grows purified of self-seeking, our connection with God's Will can deepen. We let God look through us. At certain moments we are no longer speaking, but are spoken. We are no longer acting, but action takes place through us, as taught so clearly in the Tao Te Ching. This is the difference between seeing and doing. God sees through all of us, but acts only through a few. Usually, instead of exercising our God-given freedom of will, we usurp and act in God's place by following a narrowly personal agenda. But through surrendering, we set ourselves aside and allow God to act through us.

And God does. One part of our role in this is openness to the flow from beneath our inward depths outward. It is an expansive, all-loving, all-connecting movement. We have no holding, no resistance, and no self, thus making way for the Self of all selves. This is unadulterated freedom. The initial freedom gifted us in the womb becomes perfected as we rejoin our will to God's and participate in the One Divine Will. This is not repeatable solely at our own discretion, but requires our readiness and willingness, as well as God's Will.

For God's will to be effective, we need substantial being. For this reason, any attempt to skip over the previous stages of inner work and exclusively focus one's spiritual practice on openness to God's Will, generally proves fruitless and fleeting. We end up floundering in imagined openness to the Divine and losing the direction entirely. The factors that support this search for depth include physical presence through sensation to establish us in this one moment, non-reactive equanimity in the face of desires and emotions, subtlety of perception acquired through delving into consciousness beyond thought, and deep devotion nurtured through prayer.

However, spirituality is not linear and we can profitably practice on several levels, fronts, and stages in the course of any given day. We would be wise to keep to our work on the earlier stages even as we pursue the ultimate contact with the Divine.

The movement of Divine Will passes through many levels. At the highest we may enter direct contact with the Sacred Mountain of Purpose, which is the Divine Will, and which reaches throughout every corner of the universe. But It needs us, as conscious and free beings, to transmit It with minimal distortion and maximal effectiveness into this world, several levels down from the Mountain Itself.

For this week, contemplate your own will and practice becoming your possible connection with the Divine Will.

ABOUT THE AUTHOR

The son of Holocaust survivors, **Joseph Naft** was born in a Displaced Persons' camp in northern Italy in the aftermath of World War II. Recovering from wartime devastation, the family soon immigrated to the United States. That legacy of unspeakable evil engendered Naft's abiding interest in how the seemingly intractable problem of human violence can be resolved.

While childhood experiences of the spiritual depths set the stage for Naft's lifelong pursuit of the sacred, he first learned formal meditation practice in 1970. In 1974-75, he studied Buddhist, Sufi and Christian practices during a year in residence at J. G. Bennett's school of spirituality in England. Subsequently he pursued a range of spiritual practices in Turkey under the guidance of Sufis from the Mevlevi, Helveti, Rifa'i, and Naqshbandi orders. He has also undertaken extensive training in Buddhist meditation. Finally, his Jewish roots remain close to his heart, both the traditional form of Jewish worship as well as meditation methods from Kabbalah.

Through his ongoing spiritual quest, Naft gradually came to see that the ultimate answer to the tragedy of violence must entail a radical change and evolution of the inner life of all humanity. The leading edge of that change lives in those committed to spiritual practice.

Joseph Naft has taught meditation and spiritual practices since 1976. His other books include *The Sacred Art of Soul Making: Balance and Depth in Spiritual Practice* and two novels, *Agents of Peace* and *Restoring Our Soul*.

BECOMING YOU

INDEX

A

Aberrations of Responsibility 88
Acceptance 402
Access to Wisdom 83
Active Presence 168
Act of Will 36
Adaptive Practice 220
Ad Hoc Tasks 158
Aiming Higher 287
Appreciation 111
Arrow of Presence 314
Art of Climbing 167
Asking for Help 164
Assessment and Motivation 202
Attention 81, 280, 297, 363, 364
automatic energy 52, 371, 381
Awareness of Fragmentation 446
Awareness of Posture 44
Awareness of State 52
Awareness of Talking 64
Awe 286

B

Back in the Body 98
Balance of Body, Heart, and Mind 110
Balance of Levels 135
Balancing Inner and Outer 149
Barriers to Relating 205
Being in Conversation 252
Being Seen 162, 356
Being the Decider-Perceiver 313
Being Useful 278
Being Yourself 98
Beyond Our Story 330
Beyond Paradise 283
Beyond Stillness 124

Beyond the Ordinary 158
Blue Collar Inner Work 138
Body Calm 15
Body Image 77
Body of Stillness 171
Body Presence 27
Body Scan 86
Boundaries of Awareness 108
Break with the Past 186
Breathing Energy 140
Breathing TV 194
Bridging Heaven and Earth 122
Building the Group 41
Building the Inner Body 266
Buying Presence 95

C

Care for This Moment 148
Casting an Energy Net 294
Center of All Centers 455
Challenges of Spiritual Practice 379
Character Matters 226
Chiming In 63
Choose Again 89
Choosing Your Emotions 261
Coarse and Fine 340
Color of Stillness 249
Come What May 259
Commitment to Prayer 430
Communicating Presence 268
Compassion 65, 154, 395, 404
Conscience 204, 323, 386, 388, 391
conscious energy 8, 20, 26, 28, 52, 242, 284, 312, 315, 317, 321, 352, 356, 362, 365, 382, 414, 415, 417
Consciousness and Personality 137
Conscious Walking 35
Constancy 78
Consuming 94
Contemplative Prayer 435

Content and Process 119
Continuity 71
Continuous Choice 371
Cost of Awakening 125
Counting 34
Courtesy 46
Creating Ourselves 225
Creating Partial Presence 414
Creating the Future 223
creative energy 284
Curbing a Habit 33

D

Daily Goals 104
Daily Prayer 91
Debilitating Daydreams 112
Deep Relaxation 90
Demands of self 318
destructive emotions 30, 70, 79, 133, 138, 244, 262, 284, 285, 310, 381, 414, 452
Determination and Help 187
Developing Compassion 65
Devotion 234
Dignity and Indignation 121
Directed Receptivity 382
Direct Perception 76
Distorting Perception 247
Distracting Changes 251
Divine Embrace 327
Divine light 209, 211, 436
Divine Presence 421
Divine Will 174, 219, 254, 279, 285, 290, 298, 333, 376, 387, 393, 396, 407, 422, 431, 441, 443, 459, 461
Diving into the Sacred 126
Doing the Dishes 60
Doing This 218
Doing Your Chores 263
Doors 37

Drawing Down the Blessing 304
Dressing Consciously 40
Dropping into the Body 285
Duration 66
Dynamic Presence 214

E

Earning Our Freedom 122
Eating with Presence 38
Ecstasy Through Prayer 437
Effort and Non-effort 87
Elevating Prayer 269
Embracing Our Life 328
Emerging from the Stream 130
Emerging From Thought 296
empathy 155, 237, 395, 404, 405
Empathy and Compassion 404
Emptying Yourself 160
Energies of Presence 413
energy body 11, 22, 54, 58, 67, 71, 84, 98, 140, 142, 152, 157, 171, 207, 420
Energy Breathing 21
Engagement 240
Entering Conscious Awareness 208
Entering Presence 6
Equality 400
Establishing Physical Presence 207
Eternal Values 166
Evening Presence 309
Excellence 44
Exercise Inside and Out 193
Exhaling the Negative 144
Extending Our Bodily Presence 195
Eye of the Storm 123

F

Faith and Doubt 432
Feet of Awareness 293
Fervor 231
Field of Presence 315

Filling and Fulfilling 288
Filling the Down-Time 258
Finding Time 255
Fingers of One Hand 178
First Intention 145
First Response 74
First Things First 188
Follow Through 289
Frequency 69
From Heartless to Kindness 214

G

Global Unity in God 407
Goals 104
God's View of the World 84
Grief and Mourning 360
Grounding Our Practice 157
Ground of Presence 317
Group Power 290

H

Hands and Feet 84
Hard Decisions 173
Here I Am 163
Hidden Treasure 111
Holy Day 108

I

I Am 417
I Am Not My Thoughts 49
I Am" Test 253
identification 39, 42, 49, 73, 75, 78, 90, 119, 123, 129, 130, 150, 157, 162, 192, 246, 249, 252, 258, 260, 356, 389, 439
Identity 279
Immediate Challenges 250
Impulse of Awakening 410
In Body, In Heart, and In Mind 152
In Contact 153
Increasing Our Spiritual Income 147
Ineffable 151
Inhabiting Our Life 131
Inhabiting the Body 53
Inner Body for Inner Life 353
Inner Occupations 344
Inner Responsibility 281
Inner Structure 324
Inner Unity: I 453
Inner Work in a Time of War 106
Inspiring Aspiration 156
Integrity and Wholeness 228
Integrity under Duress 345
Intentional Attention 363
Intentional Presence 213
Intentional Thought Awareness 245
Intentional Walking 67
In the Energy Body 142
In the Fog 110
In Their Shoes: Intentional Empathy 155
I Pray 429
Islands: Separation and Longing 102

J

Joy and Pleasure 113
Judging and Criticizing 115
Just Breathing 85

K

Karma 348

L

Laboratory of the Spirit 198
Labor of Love 170
Leaning Forward and Falling Back 107
Learning to Integrate Our Will 448

Let It Be 75
Lighting the Darkness 56
Lines of Time 276
Listening to Sounds, Hearing the Silence 347
Live Wire of Will 292
Local Unity 406
Long View 88
Losing Face 176

M

Making It Real 124
Managing Our Path 143
Manna from Heaven 184
Meaningful Life 374
Middle Way 162
Mirror, Mirror 41
More Body, Vivid Body 244
More Presence 384
Mourning 360
Moving With and From Sensitive Energy 106
My Universe 146

N

New Floor 191
Next Rung 102
Non-Anger 150
Non-effort 87
Non-Gossip 154
Non-Identifying 73
Non-Panic 368
Non-Suffering 78
Non-Thinking 212
Non-Waiting 229
Not Accepting the Superficial Life 185

O

One Divine Will 459
One Thing at a Time 326
One Who Sees 243
Only This Moment 120
Opening to the Divine 210
Opening to Wholeness 416
Ordinary Presence 291
Our Fragmented Will 444
Our Individual Program 238
Our Inner Home 335
Our Song 232
Out of Our Mind, Into Our Body 338
Overcoming Mediocrity 222
Owning Our Destructive Emotions 133

P

Part and Whole 62
Partial Practice 450
Participating in Purpose 139
Passivity 99
Path of Exploration 272
Peace of Being 196
Peace of Presence 418
Perfection and Imperfection 120
Persistence 100
Personal Integrity 203
Personal Presence in Three Steps 361
Person of Substance 169
Petitionary Prayer 426
Petty and the Grand 129
Place to Stand 372
Playing Our Roles 323
Political Mind 182
Posture 44
Potential 97
Prayer 91, 105, 123, 147, 216, 269, 375, 423, 426, 427, 429, 430, 432, 434, 435, 437, 439
Prayer in a Time of War 105

Prayer: Method and Ritual 427
Presence 1, 6, 11, 27, 38, 95, 116, 157, 168, 179, 195, 200, 201, 207, 213, 214, 217, 268, 275, 291, 307, 309, 314, 315, 317, 361, 370, 381, 384, 409, 413, 414, 418, 420, 421
Present Through and Through 381
Pressed Buttons 114
Procrastination 219
Pure Consciousness 141
Purpose 139, 151, 175, 203, 221, 285, 325, 422, 441, 461
Push and Pull 114
Pushing the Envelope 57

R

Rates of Inner Growth 336
Rating the Day 42
Reaching Beyond 142
Reaching Toward God, Center of All Centers 455
Reading Presence 217
Receptivity to Awakening 412
Recognizing Sensation 16
Recognizing Will 354
relaxation 2, 5, 13, 15, 16, 29, 55, 68, 90, 209, 238, 245, 307, 320, 329, 334, 335, 376
Relaxing into Now 215
Relaxing Our Body 13
Remembering 264
Renewal: Deciding to Work 93
Resistance 70
Respect 70
Responsibility 88
Responsibility, Rebellion, and Love 451
Returning 183
Review & Resolve 96
Roller-Coaster 72

Running Commentary 260

S

Sacred Chorus 265
Sacred Dance of Emptiness 333
sacred light 127, 257, 284, 422, 437, 443, 455, 457
Sameness 401
Satisfaction and Dissatisfaction 109
Scaling Up 128
Searching for Sustenance 256
Seeing the Humanity 397
Seeing Their Potential 166
Seeing with Empathy 236
self-acceptance 62, 70, 80, 81, 121, 133, 134, 227, 351, 352
Self-Acceptance 79, 351
self-centered 52, 58, 71, 122, 129, 138, 146, 155, 160, 175, 178, 206, 229, 238, 248, 284, 301, 312, 334, 340, 346, 350, 351, 356, 403, 408, 431
Self-Discipline 161
Self-Image, False Image 181
Selfing 50
Sending Good Will 300
Sensation in Movement 23
Sense of the Sacred 165
Sensing Parts 18
Sensing the Whole Body 20
sensitive energy 3, 13, 16, 18, 20, 23, 24, 26, 28, 52, 54, 63, 65, 67, 86, 106, 116, 119, 135, 140, 142, 152, 157, 159, 171, 180, 200, 207, 212, 241, 244, 258, 267, 284, 317, 320, 339, 353, 362, 365, 368, 373, 381, 413, 415, 420, 425
Shaping Your Inner Life 104
Shared Joy 96
Shifting into Neutral 320

Shifting into Reverse 321
Shift in Perspective 59
Showering Presence 370
small self and Great Self 103
Soaking Up the Atmosphere 342
Soft-Heartedness 277
Spaciousness 45
Speaking Well 235
Spiritual Breathing 365
Spiritual Friendship 298
Spiritual Heroism 341
Spiritual Momentum 282
Stabilizing Attention 81
Stabilizing Our Way 270
Stabilizing the Inner Body 25
Stable Presence 420
Stages of Body Presence 11
Stages of Inner Unity: I 441
Stages of Love 393
Stages of Prayer 423
Stages of Presence 409
Standing Presence 200
Starting Presence 275
State 52
Staying Here 241
Steady Pace 197
Stillness 377
Strong Will, Open Will 180
Subsuming the Personal 174
Success and Failure 91
Surrender 457
Sustaining Presence 179
Swimming Upstream 310

T

Talking 64
Taste of Presence 307
Telephone Presence 201
Temple of Peace 320
This Is It 303
Thought Awareness 49

Three Domains 190
Tolerance 398
Torso and Head 86
Total Prayer 375
Touching the Stillness 48
Tracing the Radiance 321
Transcending Personality 311
Transition to Stillness 274
Turning Toward the Light 209

U

Understanding Our Motivation 58
Unification 134, 439
Unseen 301

V

Valuing the Way 295

W

Waiting 47
Walking 24, 36, 67, 116, 172, 358
Walking in Stillness 172
Walking Meditation 358
Walking Presence 116
Wastefulness 38
Wasteful Tensions 306
Way of Conscience 1: Discerning 386
Way of Conscience 2: Acting in Accord 388
Way of Conscience 3: Merging 391
Wealth and Poverty: External and Eternal 118
Web of Unity 273
Well-Wishing 68
We Serve Through Prayer 434
When Is "I" Substantial? 107
Where Does My I Come From? 132
Wholeness in Prayer 216
Wider Context 84

Will 36, 67, 179, 180, 279, 284,
    290, 292, 300, 333, 354, 356,
    376, 393, 407, 422, 427, 431,
    441, 444, 448, 459
Will It Matter in a Year? 177
Wishful Thinking 94
Within the Hour 331
World View 30
Wrapped in Awareness 82

Y

You, Being You 54
Your Word 34

www.ingramcontent.com/pod-product-compliance
Lightning Source LLC
Chambersburg PA
CBHW071618170426
43195CB00038B/1340